SINGING FROM THE FLOOR

A History of British Folk Clubs

JP Bean

FABER & FABER

First published in 2014
by Faber & Faber Ltd
Bloomsbury House, 74–77 Great Russell Street
London WC1B 3DA

Typeset by Palindrome
Printed in England by CPI Group (UK) Ltd, Croydon, CRO 4YY

A CIP record for this book
is available from the British Library

FSC
www.fsc.org
MIX
Paper from
responsible sources
FSC® C101712

ISBN 978–0–571–30545–2

10 9 8 7 6 5 4 3 2 1

For Tony Capstick, Pete Civico and Malcolm Fox,
who were kind to me when I was young

Contents

Illustrations

Foreword

Rock 'n' roll was the world I grew up in. I never went to folk clubs in their heyday, I was too young – but I heard stories about them from my dad. So when my pal JP Bean showed me a book he was writing, *Singing from the Floor* – the book you, dear reader, now hold in your hands – I was fascinated and excited about it. I love the idea of singers and musicians – non-musicians, too – without managers or agents or record companies, playing in rooms above pubs, all joining together to sing old songs about good and bad times and new songs protesting about the way governments and tyrants can destroy the future . . . songs and tunes that form our heritage.

This book tells the story of a movement – a music scene that was not very well organised, to say the least; that was, it has to be said, homespun, anarchic and totally devoid of any commercial motives, for a time: four reasons, then, for newcomers to love it and totally embrace it as a way of life, which many thousands of young, and eventually old, did.

It is the story in their own words of how a few devoted folk music fans and musicians helped launch one of the biggest revolutions – musical, political and social – this country has ever seen. This is the birth of the counterculture we now take for granted. There would arguably be no punk without it. The songs those remaining dedicated men and women still sing often tell the stories of the losers in history's great battle – I hope this book will go a long way to help preserve the stories of the great battles those men and women fought themselves, so that they won't be lost to us for ever. Enjoy, and don't forget to hand it down.

Richard Hawley

Introduction

Times have changed within the British folk scene. Once, back in the heady days of the sixties and seventies, folk clubs abounded all over the country. Now, while they have not disappeared altogether, they are thin on the ground. At the peak of the folk revival, there were hundreds of clubs in and around London, seventy-two on Merseyside, a club seven nights a week in most of the big cities. Every town and many a village had a folk club. In the universities and colleges they flourished. In Edinburgh there was even one in the police social club.

Most clubs met weekly in smoky rooms above pubs, bare rooms with battered stools and beer-stained tables, where the stage was no more than a scrap of old carpet and a sound system was unknown. The organisation was amateur – there was little money around; it was all about enthusiasm.

Back then, folk club audiences were young. They didn't expect comfort. They were there to see and listen to a booked singer or group do two half-hour spots, as well as the club's resident singers or occasional performers who might drop by. Everyone joined in the choruses, humour prevailed and much drink was taken.

Now, the folk scene is different. Many of the clubs that have survived are in effect mini concert venues. Resident singers and locals who used to get up and sing 'from the floor' have been replaced by performers with no regular link to the club, booked in advance along with the main artist. At the other end of the spectrum are clubs that have become singarounds with a guest booked only a few times a year.

Today, folk enthusiasts go to arts centres and concerts rather than clubs. In their thousands they flock to festivals. In the old days their parents, when they were young and the music was fresh and before commercialism crept in, went to folk clubs.

When the folk revival began in the fifties, as many people whose voices are heard in this book will tell, the scene was driven by the Campaign for Nuclear Disarmament and by left-wing activists like Ewan MacColl, Alan Lomax, A. L. Lloyd, Bob Davenport, Karl Dallas, Peggy Seeger and John Foreman. Folk singers, with few exceptions, did not belong to the establishment. They stuck to their ideals.

When I started going to folk clubs, in Sheffield in 1966, the big night of the week was Saturday at the Barley Mow, above the Three Cranes pub. The L-shaped room held about forty people comfortably, but up to 140 crammed in – sitting, squatting, standing, wedged against the walls and perched on the piano.

The organiser and resident singer was Malcolm Fox, a genial fellow in his mid-twenties who discovered folk music through the Young Communist League and CND marches. He was full of enthusiasm and went out of his way to encourage others. He would give any floor singer an opportunity and, although his own preference was traditional song, he placed no restrictions on what anyone sang and he booked the best guests around at the time.

To a callow youth of sixteen, the Barley Mow was a marvellous place to be. The atmosphere was so cheery, boozy and upbeat that every Saturday night seemed like Christmas Eve. In the first few months alone I saw performers who made impressions that have never left me: Ewan MacColl and Peggy Seeger addressing the audience as if it were a class; Bob Davenport, whose mighty unaccompanied voice and Geordie songs captivated the room for a whole evening without any instrumental backing; the truly awesome Alex Campbell, who could hold an audience better than anyone I've ever seen; Pete Stanley and Wizz Jones – a frock-coated banjo player and a long-haired, bespectacled beatnik with an ancient guitar that was held together with sticky tape.

Other clubs followed: there were great nights at the Highcliffe Hotel, where Ralph McTell and John Martyn were regular guests and where Barbara Dickson and the Humblebums made their south-of-the border debuts. I saw the Watersons there, and the old bluesman Reverend Gary Davis, but my most vivid memories are of being rendered helpless with laughter by Tony Capstick, who I'd got to know earlier at the Barley Mow.

Capstick, when I first met him, was twenty-two and not yet a professional folk singer. He looked like a bookie's runner in his brown checked suit and old plimsolls and he played the banjo and sang a lot of Irish songs, but it was his amazing wit and inventive humour that grabbed attention. He was the funniest man I'd ever met.

The years went by and I didn't go to folk clubs so often. I was focusing on writing and had several non-fiction books published. Tony Capstick became one of the most popular performers on the national scene. One day in the late eighties I heard him on the radio in an obituary to Alex Campbell, a man who had probably played every folk club in the land.

As Tony rolled out stories of Alex and the colourful life he had lived in the folk clubs and busking on the streets of Paris, it occurred to me that there was very little written about Alex Campbell, and while many people had memories of him, they would eventually be lost.

Later, in the mid-nineties, I mentioned these thoughts to Tony. We talked about how the folk scene had been neglected in permanent print and I suggested that he should write a book about his life in the folk clubs. He had a column in a local paper and could write as articulately and humorously as he spoke. Needless to say, he never did and in 2003 he too died, taking forty years of songs, anecdotes and memories with him.

The folk scene had moved on. Some of the old stalwarts of the clubs had disappeared from the fray. Some had become famous, some had died. Others were growing old. So, deciding that action was needed before it became too late, in early 2010 I took it upon myself to seek out performers, club organisers, record producers and other relevant parties who had been involved from the earliest days of the folk clubs to the present.

I wanted to ask them questions, to hear their stories – how they had got involved in folk music, who their early influences were, why the professional singers chose the way of life, about the atmosphere in the clubs, the crazy nights and characters they had met along the way, the difficult audiences, the endless journeys and hard nights sleeping on strangers' floors. I was interested in how they had got record deals, how those who went on to bigger things achieved it. I wanted to hear about the boom years of the sixties, the declining years of the seventies and eighties and the renewed enthusiasm of the mid-nineties when a new generation began to make its mark.

I am extremely grateful to all the interviewees and others, listed elsewhere, who so willingly gave up their time to answer my questions. Their generosity is much appreciated but not surprising for, as I was reminded by many of them, 'That's what the folk scene was always about.'

It has been a privilege and a joy to be able to sit down and talk to people whose music I have admired for so many years. At times I have almost pinched myself to make sure I was where I thought I was: Billy Connolly, who I'd pursued for over eighteen months, talking about the old days as though he wished they could return; a spring afternoon in Martin Carthy's living room in Robin Hood's Bay as he talked through his long career; another afternoon with Nigel Denver and Ian Campbell, now dead,neither of whom I had seen for over forty years, in their local in King's Heath, Birmingham; Bob Davenport talking me through the early years of the London clubs in the café at the British Library; Mike Waterson telling me, 'I've got cancer, that's all there is to it; I'm here till I've gone' – just six weeks before he died; standing with Johnny Handle in the old club room at the Bridge Hotel, Newcastle, as he remembered some of the great nights he had enjoyed there with the High Level Ranters; laughing with Vin Garbutt in a Morrisons supermarket café; Harvey Andrews giving me lunch at his home in Shropshire and then lining me up to speak to Jasper Carrott; sitting in a pub in Islington with Tom Paley as he recalled playing gigs with Woody Guthrie in 1950; Peggy Seeger describing Leadbelly visiting her family's house when she was eight years old; Jon Boden in his cottage high up in the Yorkshire hills on a wild, windswept night; a voice on the phone saying, 'This is Ralph McTell, Wizz Jones has asked me to ring you but I'm not sure why'; many Friday nights at Folk at the Rock at Wentworth and later Maltby with organiser Rob Shaw, whose help with introductions to performers has been of inestimable value; days with John Tams and nights with Richard Hawley, both of whom have been unstinting in their encouragement.

From the outset, the focus of *Singing from the Floor* has been on the folk clubs and the people involved in them. Others have written about the wider aspects of the folk scene, but no one has done a book based on the clubs.

As the research went on and I interviewed more and more people from distant corners of the past sixty years, I realised that the strength of the work would lie in the interviewees' own words alone and, apart from introductions to establish context and some brief biographical details, any comment from myself would be superfluous.

All the quotations attributed to individuals have been obtained in interviews; there is nothing from printed sources apart from an occasional instance where someone, while being interviewed, read an extract from a book or newspaper that they considered pertinent. Inevitably it has been necessary to edit and compress some material.

Is *Singing from the Floor* an oral history? It might be, but in oral histories the author invariably introduces the topic that each contributor is about to address. Here, that would have intruded; instead I have arranged the material as far as possible so that each section flows like a conversation. The result is, I hope, a printed-word documentary of a social and musical movement that embraced many people – and still does today.

JP Bean

Echoes . . .

I went down to the Troubadour *and sang one Saturday and I was booked for a month later. I'd got my feet under the table. Everybody came to the Troubadour – Tom Paxton and Paul Simon . . . Bob Dylan.*

This guy, Dan Dare *– that was his real name – said, 'You want to go to the Spinners' folk club.' I didn't know what a folk club was but I went and eventually plucked up courage and played my home-made guitar. Then they asked me to join them.*

I was singing one Friday night *at the King and Queen, back of Goodge Street, and who should walk in the door but the front cover of* Sing Out! *I walked over and I said, 'You're Bob Dylan, aren't you?' He said, 'Hey.' I said, 'I saw your picture on the front of* Sing Out!*' He said, 'Oh yeah?' I said, 'Would you like to sing a couple of songs?' He said, 'Ask me later.'*

It all happened very quickly. *At this time there were far more clubs than there were artists to work them. We were created by an audience – we didn't create an audience like you have to do today. They were desperate for someone to get up with a guitar.*

Wherever you went there was a sort of repertoire *that all folk club aficionados knew. It wasn't just choruses – 'The Mingulay Boat Song', 'Whiskey in the Jar', 'Wild Mountain Thyme', 'Leaving of Liverpool', 'Last Thing on My Mind' – all those songs. It was a like a classic canon.*

Almost all the clubs were run by amateurs, *for pleasure. No one was really making a profit. No one was in control, everybody was* *piling in, as an organiser, as a floor singer, attempting to be a professional, whatever. It was a huge melting pot of talent and people who wanted to be involved.*

It was magic. *It was fantastic – very, very exciting. You were part of this huge community. It was an astonishing moment. We had this totally anarchic thing, this network of human beings who managed to co-operate with each other because they all had one thing in common – the love this music. And a love of the fact that they were discovering it for the first time.*

A Monday night at the Gaslight *in Greenwich Village you could have fifteen people, but Monday night in Bristol, it was packed. Every night, everywhere I went, it was packed because that was club night. It was like Saturday night seven nights a week. It was exciting.*

Folk clubs were like havens *for people of any age. You could go to a folk club and be perfectly safe. There was no violence, no trouble, and they were entertainment. You weren't spoken at, you were spoken to. I think the folk clubs gave everybody an idea of what responsibility was in entertainment. Comedy was more than just one-line jokes about twenty Irishmen and mothers-in-law.*

There was a guy *at Dundee University. He kept asking for 'Needle of Death', and I'm playing the banjo. Every time I finished a song, he'd shout, 'Needle of Death.' I said, 'Listen, it's not a tune for the banjo. I just don't know it. You keep asking me for a song I don't know.' I did another song and there he was again.*

So I put the banjo down. I said, 'Just stay where you are . . .' and I step into the audience. Straight up to him – and I whacked him.

Then I found out he was the treasurer. That was the end of my whacking days.

I liked the folk clubs better than concerts. The audiences listened and there was a good atmosphere. They were usually in quiet places where you could drive home without being bothered by the police.

For my generation of folk singers, to cross the 'bed barrier' was notable. It came with your fee. About 1980 I got my first hundred quid and from then on I noticed that I always got a bed instead of a settee or a floor.

I've slept in some very unpalatable places. I was doing twenty-eight gigs a month. I was never at home. It was hard work, but they were great times, a bit drink-fuelled and hazy. It was hard but it was very enjoyable.

There was a system – you went to a club and they had floor singers. That's how it worked. You could build a career from floor singing.

When Hamish Imlach first came to the Bay Horse in Doncaster, he brought John Martyn with him. John got up and we booked him straight away. That's how John Martyn got established. He travelled with Hamish, as did the Humblebums and Barbara Dickson.

It was a really kind of vibrant, underground scene. Nobody knew about it. Your parents didn't like it. It was perfect.

The clubs were and are a crucial stepping stone for young performers. I always liked the floor singer concept and for the idea to succeed the quality will vary drastically. I also liked the sometimes rather brusque equality of the clubs. As a performer you were nobody special, rather one of the crowd who happened to sing.

Folk clubs are the best place to learn your skills as a performer. You're close to the audience, something I always enjoyed. It seems to me a pity that some of the young singers have gone straight to concert performance. They've missed out on a good, *heart-warming experience. But what smoky places they were in the old days!*

A lot of the younger singers – *they're not treading the boards. They don't have to tread the boards. They're involved with record companies that have the promotion, who will tell the world that they're really good. I'd hazard a guess most of them won't last. They're brilliant performers and singers and musicians but if they haven't done the clubs they've nowhere to fall down to.*

The folk club *in its initial concept was the best political platform we've ever had, the working class. Then the middle classes came in. Now you canna go to a place that's not run by somebody that gets three months' holiday a year.*

1 In coffee bars, at singarounds, on marches

According to Ewan MacColl, the first person to foresee the British folk song revival was the American musicologist Alan Lomax in 1951. Soon afterwards Lomax introduced MacColl, hitherto an actor and writer in left-wing theatre, to a journalist who shared his political views but more importantly had a great interest in folk song: A. L. 'Bert' Lloyd.

In 1953 the BBC Home Service broadcast Ballads and Blues, *a six-part series of folk music featuring MacColl and Lloyd, who would be credited as founding fathers of the revival. That same year brought another radio series,* As I Roved Out, *which was to run for fifty-eight episodes, and a short-lived television series,* Song Hunter: Alan Lomax. *Away from the media and in the same period, the Workers' Music Association (WMA) was organising choirs like the London Youth Choir with repertoires that featured ballads and folk songs.*

The seeds of a movement were beginning to germinate and each of these events contributed to what would become known as the folk revival. Then in late 1956 Lonnie Donegan, a banjo player in Chris Barber's jazz band and a man who had no direct links with MacColl, Lloyd or anyone else on the early folk scene, took 'Rock Island Line' to the top of the British pop charts, selling three million copies.

A new musical craze – skiffle – swept the country. Teenagers raided attics and junk shops for cheap guitars and banjos. Washboards were acquired and basses improvised out of tea chests. On street corners, in back yards, youth clubs and schools, skiffle groups formed overnight.

Skiffle required little musical proficiency, but it introduced a generation to American folk and blues performers like Woody Guthrie, the Weavers and Leadbelly, the ex-convict who had first recorded 'Rock Island Line'. And when, albeit at different times, Americans Peggy Seeger and Ramblin' Jack Elliott came to London, and took up temporary residence, they were seized upon by a host of dedicated followers, among them Wizz Jones, Pete Stanley and John Foreman, who were eager to learn from their repertoires and pick up on their dazzling instrumental skills

It was a short step from looking across the Atlantic for musical inspiration to recognising that Britain had its own folk song tradition. Skiffle clubs gradually became folk clubs and in London young enthusiasts like Martin Carthy, Shirley Collins and Bob Davenport began to sing songs from their own heritage. Eric Winter published Sing, *a folk music magazine. Anti-nuclear activists sang on the Aldermaston marches. Topic Records began to issue recordings of folk music. The British folk revival was under way.*

MARTIN CARTHY *one of the most influential singers and guitarists to emerge from the folk revival. Solo, and with Dave Swarbrick, Steeleye Span, the Watersons and others, he has worked relentlessly for over fifty years*
One of the first folk clubs was the 44, at 44 Gerrard Street, run by a physics professor at London University, John Hasted. He was very much a figurehead in that whole area of music. He did a lot of English trad songs – songs that Bert Lloyd had already adapted, that they sang in the 44 in a skiffle fashion. He'd learned to play guitar and he could play the five-string banjo.

KARL DALLAS *originally Fred Dallas, singer and songwriter who was* Melody Maker *writer on folk music for many years*
John Hasted, he was music editor of *Sing* magazine and an atomic scientist. He had this laboratory in Gower Street which was full of guitars and squeeze boxes and banjos and mountain dulcimers and all sorts. I used to go there and sing my songs to him, then eventually I did it over the phone. *Sing* published all my songs in that period.

JOHN FOREMAN *known as the Broadsheet King, sang Cockney songs in folk clubs*

The 44 Club, that's the first organised club that I recall. It was a rather seedy sort of dive but it was terrific. It had Shirley Collins, Redd Sullivan, Martin Winsor . . . The 44 grew out of the Workers' Music Association. The WMA had a traditional kind of choir and John Hasted, who was ex-army, organised a younger group, pretty political, built round the international youth festivals of the communist states that went on all over Europe. It was a music club – the word 'folk' became a sort of record-seller's category.

SHIRLEY COLLINS *singer of traditional songs, president of the English Folk Dance and Song Society (EFDSS) since 2008*

Folk clubs didn't really exist as such in the early fifties, so I didn't have any preconceptions when I moved to London from Hastings. I was single-minded – all I could think about was folk songs and I knew that Cecil Sharp House in Camden Town, the headquarters of the English Folk Dance and Song Society, was the place to find them.

When I did find them, it was the utmost thrill. I'd pore through the books, and when the words of a song caught my eye and took my fancy, I'd copy down the tunes on manuscript paper and ask my sister Dolly to play them for me the next time I went home to Hastings.

The first club I went to would have been the singaround meetings at Cecil Sharp House, run by Peter Kennedy, and another at one of the London University buildings, run by John Hasted. I went to the singarounds especially, because they encouraged everyone to sing and not just to listen. How many songs we got to sing depended on how many people had to be fitted in. I sang some songs from home and certainly some from the Coppers – 'The False Bride' was my favourite. I was hunting for songs all the time and listening to the field recordings of the British Isles made by Peter Kennedy and Alan Lomax, adding to my repertoire all the time.

Early folk clubs? It's such a long time ago . . . The Troubadour is the one I spent most time at and I had a part-time job there in the coffee bar. There was always a good atmosphere downstairs in the club.

HANS FRIED *schoolboy folk enthusiast who later worked in Collett's bookshop*
A chap called Michael Bell ran a session at Cecil Sharp House on a Sunday, a singaround in the library. Everyone sat in a circle and we were expected to contribute a song. I had to sing and I remember sitting between Jean Ritchie, who I was knocked out by, and Paddy Tunney. I sang 'The Bitter Withy', which I'd learned from A. L. Lloyd. I wanted one of my best things to suit the occasion. That was in 1957. I was thirteen and incredibly serious.

KARL DALLAS
Well before that, in the early fifties, Peter Kennedy was running what he called ceilidh concerts on a Sunday afternoon. They were more like a singaround. He had traditional singers like Paddy Tunney and he had Harry Cox there. Peter Kennedy was seconded to the BBC by the EFDSS to do field recordings. He went round the country with a tape recorder and those recordings were played on the radio on a Sunday morning on *As I Roved Out*, which came on the air just after *Family Favourites*. That was the BBC Light Programme.

I remember I was in the bathroom in the house where I lived in Walton-on-Thames and I suddenly heard this voice singing. I came running down the stairs, dripping water all over the place and Harry Cox was singing 'The Foggy Dew'. That was the first time I ever heard an English traditional singer.

Apart from Cecil Sharp House, it was all in coffee bars. There was the Bread Basket in Greek Street, but the place I went to was the Gyre and Gimble, near Charing Cross station.

BOB DAVENPORT *traditional singer from Tyneside; in 1963 he was the first British singer to be invited to perform at the Newport Folk Festival. For many years resident at the Fox, Islington, and a regular guest in clubs around the country*
There was a very strong coffee-house movement where you could hear people and then it moved from the coffee bars to singarounds and then to the more formal folk club. The first folk club I went to was run by Frank Purslow at a pub in St Martin's Lane, the White Bear. That was in the late fifties.

You could sit in a coffee house in the centre of London and you could stay there all afternoon, all around Charing Cross, Northumberland Avenue, Soho. The Gyre and Gimble was just down Villiers Street at the side of Charing Cross. We used to sit there swapping songs.

MARTIN CARTHY
I lived in Hampstead, brought up there, and one of the very first coffee bars opened down Belsize Lane, called the Witches Cauldron. I remember going there on the first night, me and a couple of my mates, we were about fifteen. At that time it had a cellar and a cellar was serious stuff! Somebody talked about this guy Robin Hall, what a fantastic singer he was. He sang the Merle Travis song 'Dark as a Dungeon'. He was quite a heroic figure to this fifteen-year-old.

There was a place in Flask Walk in Hampstead, the Hideaway. I took my dad's guitar – which I smuggled out of the house – and just started singing to the sound of my knees knocking to begin with, then it was all right. I sang Lonnie Donegan songs – 'Wreck of the Old '97', 'Wabash Cannonball' and stuff like that.

I used to go to the Gyre and Gimble but I never sang there. The first time I heard a Ewan MacColl song was down there. Somebody said, 'Oh, this bloke's wrote a song called "Go Down You Murderers" about Tim Evans.' I didn't know who Tim Evans was. Then they talked about him living in the same house as Christie. I knew who Christie was – 10 Rillington Place. It's the sort of thing that burns into your mind. I went down one night and there was a bloke, completely bald. He'd tune his guitar to a chord and then just run one finger up and down. And he sang 'Go Down You Murderers'. And I just sat there, wow! That was the first Ewan MacColl song I ever heard, I still think one of his greatest songs.

I remember seeing Wizz Jones down there one time. He played 'The Molecatcher' – a very rude song, bawdy, a traditional song – 'In Manchester city by the sign of the plough/ There lived a molecatcher, I daren't tell you how/ He went a molecatching from morning till night/ And a young fellow came for to play with his wife.' I remember Wizz singing it in 1957 or '56, seeing him playing the guitar and thinking, 'Cor! he's good.'

WIZZ JONES *blues guitarist and singer, cited as an influence by Eric Clapton and Keith Richards, played folk clubs all over Britain solo and, for a spell in the sixties, with Pete Stanley*
I had my little skiffle band and I was playing round the pubs in Croydon. Then I played around Soho at the Gyre and Gimble and the Partisan. You played lunchtime at the Partisan for all the political activist people. Jimmie Macgregor used to do it and he said to me, 'I'm going away and it's a really good gig – you get a bowl of soup.'

JIMMIE MACGREGOR *best known as half of a duo with Robin Hall. They achieved national recognition through the BBC TV* Tonight *programme and performed in concerts and on television all over the world*
The Paperback in Warren Street – I first heard Tommy Steele in there. He was still in the merchant navy and he did a really corny version of 'Deck of Cards', it made me cringe. And there were a few guys singing roughly what you would call folk songs. The Paperback was quite obscure and faded away quickly. There was the Princess Louise, MacColl's club. There couldn't have been more than half a dozen clubs in London.

I was teaching in Glasgow but I used to hitch-hike to London at the weekends and I realised there were places in London at that time where you go and hear folk music and even be allowed to sing a couple of songs. There was nothing like that in Glasgow.

I just became obsessed and chucked everything, including the girl that I was engaged to, and went down to London with £60 in my pocket and an old guitar – and, as they say, a brass neck.

HYLDA SIMS *prominent on the skiffle scene, later sang in folk clubs*
I got involved with the London Youth Choir, then I got together with Russell Quaye and we started the City Ramblers skiffle group. Jimmie Macgregor joined later on. We were playing in the streets, then we rented a studio in South Kensington. It was a big space and we started a club.

Jack Elliott stayed there for a while. My first memory of seeing him was at the Roundhouse. He was amazing. He was married to his first wife, June, before he got together with Derroll Adams. The guy who owned the studio lived in a posh house behind and rather objected to all the noise and fuss.

After we couldn't continue with the studio skiffle club, that's when we found the Princess Louise in High Holborn. We were the first people to play music in the Princess Louise and that went on to be very much a folk venue when Ewan MacColl went there with Ballads and Blues, the Singers' Club.

The Skiffle Cellar in Old Compton Street was started by Russell and me in '57. It ran every night of the week. I can't remember if it closed on Sundays. There was no alcohol, just soft drinks. Halfway down the room there was a little stage. We – the City Ramblers – played down there three nights a week. Our repertoire included folk stuff. I'd come from singing ballads.

HANS FRIED
I started going to the Princess Louise about 1956 or '57, when I was still thirteen. It was still skiffle at that time. I used to sneak

into pubs under age and sit at the front in folk clubs, complete
with school uniform and a notepad on my knee, taking notes. I
don't know how I got in the places where there was drinking, but
I did. I had a bitter lemon and people said, 'Oh, he's just here for
the songs.'

Another occasion in Dougie Moncrieff's club in Rupert Street,
Ottilie Patterson, who was married to Chris Barber, was going
on a bit too long and I suggested to her that someone else should
have a turn. Dougie reminded me of this event later. He did say
that everyone agreed with me about Ottilie, although maybe not
in the way I did it.

JOHN THE FISH *aka John Langford, resident at the Count
House folk club in Cornwall, toured in duo with Brenda Wootton*
I came out of National Service in 1956 and I went to the Roundhouse in Wardour Street, Soho. Alexis Korner ran it. I was advised
by a friend to go and see Jack Elliott there. I was spellbound by
Jack – it was the first time I had seen anyone single-handedly hold
an audience for a whole evening. I followed Jack to the Skiffle
Cellar and the Princes Louise. It was the nature of folk clubs that
you had a chance to chat to the artists, as I did with Jack.

At the Roundhouse I was lucky enough to see Big Bill Broonzy
just before he died. Cyril Davies was running it at that time.
Broonzy was singing with a bloke called Brother John Sellers.

I thought I'd learn things because I'd picked up stuff from
watching Jack Elliott, but Broonzy's left hand moved so fast,
at times it was hardly touching the guitar. I remember the
organisers of the club pooled together and bought him a bottle
of whisky. He poured it into a pint glass and by the interval it
had gone. He said, 'I'll have another one of these, please', and
they scratched together enough to buy a second bottle, then he
downed that in the second half. It didn't affect his playing at all.

WIZZ JONES
Alexis Korner's club in Wardour Street . . . I used to go there.

At that time I was being very rebellious, sleeping out a lot of the time and I didn't have any money, so I'd always blag my way in. Alexis Korner's wife used to be on the door. It was half-a-crown and I'd get in without paying. I'd just smile at her and walk in with my long hair. That's where I saw Muddy Waters and Ramblin' Jack and Big Bill Broonzy – in that club, a tiny little room.

Seeing Muddy Waters – there were only about twenty or thirty people in but probably everyone in that room I knew or got to know because everybody went on from there. I remember the week before, Alexis said, 'Muddy Waters is going to play, but we can't advertise it so I'll put a code in the *Melody Maker* column and if there's this code in you'll know Muddy Waters is going to be here.' It was a great, exciting night.

MICHAEL MOORCOCK *sci-fi novelist who, as a teenager in London in the fifties, edited a folk magazine,* The Rambler
I heard a lot of good people at Alexis Korner's and met a lot of them at my friend John Brunner's. He was far more active than I was and had parties to which he invited many of the people involved in the folk scene, including visiting Americans. That's mostly where I met the blues players I became increasingly interested in – Big Bill Broonzy, Muddy Waters, Sonny Terry. I was too shy to talk to them much. My most embarrassing moment was when my cousin asked Broonzy to look at the guitar he'd bought to see if he thought it was worth the money.

I corresponded for a while with both Woody Guthrie and Pete Seeger. I was sixteen, all this was happening around the time I took over *Tarzan* magazine. There's a photocopy someone made which has a fragment of one letter on it. I've no idea what happened to the letters I had from Guthrie or Seeger.

JOHN THE fish
Peggy Seeger gave guitar lessons for five shillings an hour. The deal was you paid your money and along with another

half-dozen enthusiasts you had a master class. That was at the
Workers' Music Association in Islington and Robin Hall was one
of the pupils. I went along once a week for four or five weeks. She
was teaching clawhammer style, which I hadn't got to grips with.

PEGGY SEEGER *American banjo, guitar and autoharp player,
half-sister of Pete Seeger, came to England in 1956 and met
Ewan MacColl, with whom she sang and played until he died
in 1989*
In March of 1956 I came to Britain to act in a television play
called *Dark of the Moon*, where they need a female who sang
and played guitar. Alan Lomax brought me over from Denmark.
I was hitch-hiking round Europe. He picked me up at the station
and took one look at me – I'd been travelling for twenty-six hours
– and he took me to the house where his girlfriend proceeded to
strip me off and put me in a shower.

When I came over I was taken up by the skiffle movement here
and with the Ramblers' programme that Alan Lomax arranged
– it was his group. I was very much involved with that, and with
accompanying Bert Lloyd and Ewan MacColl. Everything was
new when you were twenty-two.

The weird thing was that the skiffle groups were singing songs
that I'd grown up with. I found it hilarious because I'd been
brought up on Southern singers whose lives were expressed in
these songs and all of a sudden I heard Cockney youths doing
English versions of them with an English accent, which to me
was very funny. They were in identity crisis when they were
singing those songs. They didn't know what they were and they
just entered into singing them with wholehearted enjoyment.

I landed in the right place at the right time, with the right
instruments, knowing these songs and singing them – not the
way they should be sung, because I was not a black sharecropper.
When I sang 'Midnight Special', I was not in a black prison in
Florida or Alabama. So I was already removed – but they were
one more removed from where I was, or two or three or four

removed – across the sea and linguistically and in terms of British experience.

I had never been part of the American scene when I came over, so I didn't have anything to compare with what was happening here. I've always been a solo flyer anyway. I don't seem to fit into jamming scenes easily. My voice is not very loud and I've never been a dominant person in groups.

All kinds of things happened in those early days. Bert and Ewan used to bring their sandwiches and eat them on the stage. I put a stop to that – the audience was sitting there and some of them hadn't even had their dinner. We also put a stop to everybody bringing a guitar and having to tune up the entire front row and then call out all the chords. But we did teach people choruses properly and we had song sheets.

SHIRLEY COLLINS
I remember one night at the Singers' Club when Alan Lomax was a guest singer and Ewan MacColl introduced him as 'the big lummox'. There was always a bit of rivalry there between the two, which was apparent however much they tried to joke about it.

WIZZ JONES
I used to go to banjo lessons with Peggy Seeger at the Workers' Music Association. It was all bohemian to us. Again, I got away without paying, stupid really. Then when she stopped doing the lessons and Ralph Rinzler took over and he looked in the books, and he said, 'Well, Peggy can't keep books, but I can – you're paying.' We were all in love with Peggy. She'd arrived and she was beautiful and Ewan was still married to his wife. That must have been the greatest love affair of all, Ewan and Peggy.

PEGGY SEEGER
Ralph Rinzler – oh gosh! Well, he was my special friend. He and Ewan didn't see eye to eye and Ralph took more to the Bert

Lloyd camp. It was kind of – whose camp are you in, Bert's or Ewan's? Bert was more relaxed with people and wasn't trying to go on a power trip.

Ralph Rinzler came over a number of times. I think we did some records together. He was my special friend. I really loved him, a lovely man. He wasn't a determined, this-will-be-my-profession-type of musician. He just enjoyed playing. He was a facilitator, an innovator.

PETE STANLEY *pioneer of the bluegrass banjo in Britain who teamed up with Wizz Jones*
When I came out of the airforce I started hanging round the Princess Louise, High Holborn – Ballads and Blues, Ewan MacColl and Peggy Seeger. One week Peggy said, 'I'll be giving guitar lessons on a Thursday night.' Everybody wanted to play 'Freight Train'. I thought, 'Great, I'm going to get guitar lessons', but I was studying for a BSc in geology – I was working for the Colonial Office – and I couldn't do it.

The next day, a Wednesday, my father said to me, 'Climb up into the loft will you. See if you can see any signs of water coming in. We've bought the house.' I said, 'There's a big black case up here, there's a banjo!' He said, 'Look at the roof!'

Peggy was giving banjo lessons the next day so I went along with my banjo. There was Barry Murphy, Dave Wiseman, Wizz – I think five or six of us in the class.

After about four or five weeks, Peggy said she had to leave the country. She'd been to Red China and her passport was running out. She was going to have to terminate the classes, so she said, 'Why don't one of you big boys take over teaching?' She said, 'I think you can do it, Pete.' I'd been playing for six weeks and now I was teaching. I was practising every night at home, four or five hours a night.

Peggy didn't like bluegrass and at that time there wasn't anybody else playing the bluegrass banjo. Lisa Turner, she played the banjo, folky stuff. Shirley Collins played it, she had had lessons from John Hasted. I met Wizz at the banjo lessons. We just hit it off. He didn't have a job, he was sleeping rough around London.

JOHN RENBOURN *one of the great acoustic guitarists, famed as a solo artist and for his work with Bert Jansch and in Pentangle* Wizz was a legend. He was really kinda famous on the beatnik scene. I first saw him when he came to the British Legion club in Guildford in the fifties, where the old guys from the trad jazz bands used to play Woody Guthrie and Leadbelly songs. Wizz showed up and he had hair down to his arse. They said, 'We don't want you.' He had a guitar on his back and he was turned away.

WIZZ JONES
In those early years you wouldn't be allowed in a folk club if you were scruffy, if you were a beatnik. I can remember going to clubs and being turned away. Stupid now, but time moves on.

MARTIN CARTHY
Coincidentally, I went to school with A. L. Lloyd's son. I didn't know who A. L. Lloyd was at the time. He was a journalist. Joe, his son, he had a skiffle group which had a fabulous repertoire. I was already playing the guitar and I asked Joe, 'Where do you get your songs from?' He said, 'I get 'em from my dad.' 'What's your dad?' He said, 'He's a singer.' He didn't say he was a journalist. He said, 'He's a singer.'

Then his mate told me about this club in High Holborn at the Princess Louise, where you could go and hear the original versions of the skiffle hits. This was Ballads and Blues – Ewan MacColl's club.

It was a folk club and I was really intrigued by all these people. Ralph Rinzler was there. He played the mandolin in those days. I'd never seen a mandolin like this before. I was about sixteen, might have been fifteen. I don't remember what people sang that night, just being excited by the moment.

From that moment on I kept my ear to the ground. Ballads

and Blues moved around a lot. It was at the Cora Hotel, near
St Pancras Church, then at a pub on the Edgware Road that's
buried under the flyover. Then I found out later on that there
were other folk clubs around.

JOHN FOREMAN
I've still got programmes from the Princess Louise . . . 'A year ago
on Sunday, 24th November 1957, the first hootenanny was held
in the Princess Louise in High Holborn . . . sixty people attended
and there was born in modest circumstances an enjoyable form
of folk music presentation which has grown steadily during the
past year. The Ballads and Blues Association, formed some time
later, has now almost 2,400 members. This first birthday will be
a quite special programme – Ewan MacColl, Fitzroy Coleman,
Rory McEwen and Ralph Rinzler . . .' He was good – he used to
play with Peggy Seeger.

'Friday Night Folk Song at the Workers Music Education,
14 February 1958 . . . Margaret Barry, Dominic Behan, Shirley
Bland, Jim Macgregor, Shirley Collins, Fred and Betty Dallas,
Michael Gorman, Robin Hall, Hamish Henderson, Stan Kelly.'
Those are the big people. I was just in the audience.

Here's another from 1958 – 'Ballads and Blues presents . . .
Princess Louise, Wednesday 29th January, 8 p.m. Ewan MacColl,
one of the most outstanding of our folk singers, will cover a
very wide range of his special programme of British material
. . . industrial ballads, some traditional Scottish ballads, children's
songs from Glasgow and Manchester . . . prison songs including
some contemporary ones, soldier songs, sailor songs . . . He will
teach you some of these and in his own style will introduce you
to his vast sources of information.' That's the kind of thing they
were doing.

BOB DAVENPORT
I was shanghaied into singing at the Bedford, Camden Town,
one Thursday evening. The Bedford wasn't a music venue. The

people were there to drink and Margaret Barry and Michael Gorman played on a little stage in a corner in the saloon bar. I was just sitting there listening and this pal of mine went up to the bar. Next thing, whiskies kept coming my way.

Then he said, 'Look, these blokes at the bar, I've told them you're a really good Irish tenor but you need a drink before you get up and sing and that's where the whiskies have been coming from . . . so you'd better sing, otherwise we won't get out of here.' There was a group of blokes wearing trilbies and crombies. It was in the Jack Spot, Billy Hill era, the gangs in Soho. So I got up. I sang 'Star of the County Down', unaccompanied. I'd heard it in the coffee bars.

You'd go to parties and hear people. By that time the skiffle movement was coming to an end and the Skiffle Cellar was putting folk on. Jimmie Macgregor was there arranging the Scots songs, some of them with the skiffle treatment, they were changing over.

My first booking was with Margaret and Michael at the Skiffle Cellar. That was my first ever folk gig. By that time I'd got confidence to sing, though I could only sing with my eyes shut. Margaret and I used to sing 'The Blarney Stone' together.

Then I went on to the Theatre Royal at Stratford East. There was an evening there, a concert with a theme – hard cases, bad lads. I sang two songs – one was the 'Trees They Do Grow High'. Ewan MacColl said the two songs were inferior Geordie versions of more superior Scottish songs.

WIZZ JONES

Ewan was quite heavy in those days. I used to go to his folk club at the Princess Louise, what later became the Singers' Club. It was all very laying down the law, but he was an amazing songwriter. It was like a school thing, very biased towards the Communist Party, the Workers Revolutionary Party – that kind of people – and him and Peggy would be teaching all those activist, political songs. I was naive. Half the time I didn't know what I was singing.

At that time I lived in Croydon where Ewan lived. I was working at a shitty job in a textile warehouse and I met Ewan one day on the train. He invited me back to his house. He said, 'I'm putting somebody up there it would be worth coming over and meeting.' It was Big Bill Broonzy. But in true Wizz Jones fashion, I didn't go. I suppose I was shy or thought, 'Is he having me on? Is he having a laugh?'

PEGGY SEEGER

I knew Big Bill Broonzy. I'd gone back to America and I was singing at the Gate of Horn in Chicago in March, April, May of 1957. Bill was on at the same time so he'd do an hour and I'd do an hour. Then everybody would rest, then he'd do an hour and I'd do an hour – from eleven o'clock to four in the morning. It was a strange mix, him and me.

During the time in between, we'd sit and eat hamburgers and he would drink straight gin and brandy or something, just right out of a bottle. He was an incredible drinker, but I never saw him drunk. Unless he was drunk all the time . . . He came over and stayed with Ewan. Ewan said that Bill Broonzy drank a bottle of brandy for breakfast. He just woke up and started on the booze.

JIMMIE MACGREGOR

At that time there were very few guitar players around. I always reckoned if you could play three chords in the late fifties you were employable – if you could play five you were a virtuoso. And if you could play any more you were a bloody show-off.

MacColl came up to Glasgow while I was at art school, with Bert Lloyd and Isla Cameron and a guy called Fitzroy Coleman, still the best guitar player I've ever heard. Lovely, easy-going guy – he suffered from perfect pitch. He used to come down to the Skiffle Cellar and he'd say, 'Jimmie, nobody's in tune.' Some of them weren't but even guys who were supposed to have a good ear – they were not by Fitzroy's standards. That's a freakish thing, perfect pitch. It was agony for him.

PETE STANLEY

I went to the American Embassy and they had a library there of books and vinyl. They had the Harry Smith Collection, three double albums. I was away! I couldn't believe it – Charlie Poole . . . the Carter Family. I got some stuff from Ralph Rinzler. He was over here, living at Bert Lloyd's place. He went to Ballads and Blues and he played occasionally with Peggy, he was a good finger-picking guitarist and quite a neat banjo player. He went back to America and formed the Greenbriar Boys.

Ralph Rinzler lent me a reel-to-reel tape of Flatt and Scruggs, live at the Rising Sun, Maryland, a bluegrass concert. I remember Scruggs played beautiful rags. I realised there's a lot more to banjo playing than I was doing. Then I ran into Rory and Alex McEwen one day and I said, 'Have you got any Flatt and Scruggs?' They said, 'Yeah, give us a tape' and they put down the first two albums and *Foggy Mountain Banjo*. That was just phenomenal.

MARTIN CARTHY

Robin Hall said, 'If you want to hear some proper folk music, go down to the Troubadour.' I don't know why I chose to go down on the particular night that I did – it was a decision I made. I just walked out of the Witches Cauldron and got on the tube, went down to Earls Court, found the Troubadour.

It always started at half past ten in the evening. I walked down the stairs and there was this music going on . . . I thought, 'Oh, that's bagpipes.' I walked in – where's the bagpipes? There was this bloke, sitting down. He wasn't blowing the bagpipes. There was the bellows. He had all the regulators and he's playing simple chords, little parts. I was absolutely thunderstruck. Then he played the whistle and then he sang. It was Seamus Ennis. I get all mystical about it and think I was drawn there – and there has to be some sort of truth in it. As far as I'm concerned I was drawn to it.

LOUIS KILLEN *the first singer of traditional songs to turn professional*

The Troubadour was a great club in those days. Shirley Collins was running a night there in '57 or '58. The weekends were run by a lass called Jenny Barton and the door was done by Anthea Joseph who was about five eleven when she wasn't wearing high heels, which she often did. Very long legs which she displayed elegantly at the door as you came in, as she took your money.

We became good friends. It was her and her family that I was living with when I came down to London in '61. Her father was a sub-editor on the *Reynolds News*, big friend of Dylan Thomas. Her mother wrote film reviews for the *Morning Star*; it was an old left-wing family.

JENNY BARTON *ran the Troubadour in Earls Court from 1958 to 1964*

In late February 1958 Shirley Collins was running a Wednesday night at the Troubadour and an American, Sandy Paton, had the Saturday night. Then Sandy went back to the States and Shirley took over Saturday.

At the end of the summer Shirley went off to America to do a collecting trip with Alan Lomax. Mike van Bloemen, who owned the lease, asked me to organise Saturday nights. He said he was getting sick of finding singers who would run the evening: how about if I found a singer and, instead of Mike paying them seven and sixpence and a plate of spaghetti, I took some money on the door and paid them. We were a small club with a small audience at this stage. Robin Hall and others dropped in now and again. I remember him bringing Martin Carthy along just before Christmas – that was a great night.

We had a thin time at first, as I hadn't enough money to get really good singers and then in the summer of 1959 Jack Elliott – Ramblin' Jack – came over and said to Mike van Bloemen that he was looking for somewhere to sing for two or three months. Mike said to me, 'How about if we have Jack here?'

Wonderful! That saved me having to look for people. We didn't have much of an audience when he started; by the time he left we were packed. He was there every Saturday night and he played all the same material every bloody time – and the audience simply loved it. His wife sat in the audience keeping a beady eye on him.

HANS FRIED

Jack Elliott came over here first in '56 and then in '57. He used to busk in the Underground at Marble Arch, I remember bottling for him there. He was that good the police would be standing round watching him and putting money in the bottle – not moving him on or arresting him as they usually did with buskers. We'd never seen anything like him. We'd never seen a flat-picker, ever. He could do what no one else did – and that voice!

I was just standing around – he called me Kid and then he called me Fritz, then he got to Hans. He said, 'Hold the tab for me. It'll go down well.' He could get £20 in a couple of hours. That was serious money back then. He didn't give me anything. He used people. He wasn't a nice person in many ways, but I adored him.

BILL LEADER *producer of many seminal folk albums at Topic, Transatlantic and later on his own labels, Trailer and Leader*

Jack Elliott was the first recording I did – at Ewan MacColl's home in West Croydon. It was an eight-inch disc, *Woody Guthrie's Blues*. Ewan said, 'There's this American in town – you should get hold of him and see if he'll do something 'cos he's got some great songs and he's wonderful.' So we did. We didn't have a studio or anything – one of the limitations on Topic's output was they had to go and use a studio and it cost money.

I used Ewan's tape recorder, that was one of the reasons for doing it. Ewan had this special model of a Ferrograph that the BBC had produced for the Coronation. It ran at a faster speed, fifteen inches a second. We used that. Ewan did the technical stuff, the production – I was still learning. That came out –

Woody Guthrie's Blues – and got incorporated into things like *Jack Takes the Floor*, which was to a great extent the recordings we did on the Isle of Wight in 1957.

JOHN RENBOURN
Jack Takes the Floor – that was my Bible. I've got my copy on the wall, a signed copy in a frame. Jack was a great flat-picker but he was also a great finger-picker and he did 'Railroad Bill' and 'Cocaine' before anybody else heard that style. It's his versions that have gone into circulation.

JOHN FOREMAN
When Jack was here I would go and watch him anywhere. He was one of the greatest influences on me, certainly on my so-called guitar style. He was in a Theatre Workshop production, *The Big Rock Candy Mountain*. He became fairly permanent with MacColl. He put on a little Scottish cap and he sang 'I Belong to Glasgow'. Jack Elliott was a marvellous performer, until his wife left him. I felt that without his wife he wasn't always doing the right thing. She was very good at stage management.

JIM MCLEAN *writer of Scottish Republican songs in the early sixties, later founder of the Nevis record label*
Round about 1960 Jack Elliott was travelling with Buffy Sainte-Marie, they were coming from America to do a gig in Glasgow. I think it was the St Andrew's Halls. Jack had broken his leg and it was in plaster. Josh McRae, who was featured on the show with him, was another who was all the time drinking, and Josh went to meet him at the airport. He couldn't find Jack or Buffy Sainte-Marie anywhere, so he went to one of the airport people and he says, 'I'm looking for a cowboy with a broken leg and a Red Indian.'

WIZZ JONES
I followed Jack Elliott and Derroll Adams around. I went to all

their gigs, all over the south of England. The Yellow Door in Waterloo was a really run-down house that somebody owned and just rented out rooms. It was called the Yellow Door because there was a crappy old yellow-painted door. Loads of people lived there – the guy who did *Oliver*, Lionel Bart. Wally Whyton and Tommy Steele lived there at one point.

One Sunday morning after we'd been to an all-nighter, we called at the Yellow Door and asked Derroll if he was coming to the pub. He went and got his banjo and we went down the pub. Jack arrived about an hour later – he had a fur, Yogi-Bear-type coat he'd put on over his pyjamas.

It was in the days when tape recorders had just happened and I'd bought an American wire recorder from a junk shop, spools of wire like fuse wire that ran seventy-eight inches per minute. The machine had a turntable for records, and you could play the records and record them on the wire. It was really heavy and I used to lug it all around places.

I was recording Jack and Derroll on this wire recorder in the pub but then the following week I followed them to the Station Hotel in Sidcup and I went to a party afterwards and got really drunk and all the wires got tangled up, so I lost the whole lot.

Then I discovered the following week that it ran on American voltage and the transformer caught fire and the whole thing collapsed. All over the country kids were going round with tape recorders. It was all underground – that's what made it so attractive, alternative. It wasn't just the music, it was like a secret society.

HYLDA SIMS

None of this folk stuff would have happened if it hadn't been for the Communist Party, thinly disguised as the Peace Movement. There was quite a lot going on and it was all really connected with the left-wing movement, the anti-nuclear movement, all of that, and the festivals inside the so-called Iron Curtain.

I went to three of the festivals with the youth choir and we were singing folk and ballads. A lot of the repertoire was political but we did sing some of Ewan's songs and John Hasted arranged quite a lot of folk tunes – 'Just as the Tide Was Flowing' is one I remember – but he also liked to present solo people like Judith Goldbloom – she was later Judith Silver – and myself.

It was on the fringes of the Communist Party's activities that Ewan MacColl and Bert Lloyd were formulating this stuff. Plus there was quite a big influence of American folk artists and magazines. The Weavers had a magazine, *Sing Out!*, and there were all those guys who, you could say, popularised folk music, like Josh White and Burl Ives.

We used to sing that sort of stuff and then Ewan MacColl and Bert Lloyd came along and said you should be singing your own songs. They were a bit puritanical about that, although I have heard Ewan do a very good rendering of 'Sixteen Tons'. The seminal work of Ewan's was *Scotland Sings*, which contained lots of ballads and some of his own songs as well.

WIZZ JONES

We were very much in awe of it all. I was a late starter. I didn't start playing till I was about seventeen. I just drifted into it. Busking was a way to travel across to Europe. That was a way to get out of your working-class background. It was a great leveller – it meant you got in on all kinds of scenes because you were playing. I just got stuck in that folk blind alley really, which I didn't really fit in. It was still quite traditional. I just drifted in. I never planned anything.

BILL LEADER

Left-wing politics played a big part because they were propagandising certain aspects of culture, but also about the same time there was the Peter Kennedy BBC radio programme *As I Roved Out*. I'd come down to London in 1955 from Bradford. The temperature was rising.

PEGGY SEEGER

I was asked if I would accompany Paul Robeson at a Trafalgar Square rally. It was for CND. He was in town and I kept saying, 'I want to rehearse with him.' They said, 'Oh, you'll know all the songs.' So I got there and his car rolled up, out he comes with all his train and I trot along behind him all dutiful with my guitar in my hand. I said, 'Mr Robeson, I'm Pete Seeger's sister and I'm here to accompany you.' He said, 'Oh, wonderful, honey', and on he strides.

As we're climbing up the plinth I said, 'What are you going to sing?' He said, 'Oh, just strum along.' It was funny, really. There's a photograph: it shows him singing here with a microphone and I'm way over there playing the guitar with no microphone – and looking like the teenage girl that I was at twenty-two or twenty-four or whatever I was. He was a mountain of man.

AUDREY WINTER *wife of the late Eric Winter, journalist and founder of* Sing *magazine*

There was a lot of the American left-wing stuff going on, union songs and protest songs. We knew about *Sing Out!* and Eric began to think that a folk magazine of his own would be a good idea. It would always be left wing, of course, because Eric couldn't do anything that wasn't left wing.

A small committee got together – Ewan MacColl was on it, a chap called Johnny Ambrose, Eric and John Hasted. It started in 1954 and it was roneoed off on our living room floor and the kids collated it, all very amateur. It always had songs in it, that was really the main thing. Eventually it got a lot of club news and articles.

Eric would publish old songs – interesting ones, not the ones that were in the school books – and also new songs. People sent in hundreds of things. He had a real hard job saying no. He had to pick and choose a bit. He would consult other people but the committee faded out and in the end it was pretty much a one-man band although he had so many contacts.

There were subscriptions and a few folk clubs starting up and

the WMA would take copies. There was a lot of CND protest
building up, a lot going on because of the Cold War, although the
first march didn't take place until later. I don't know how *Sing*
got about, really. I suppose it was a tide, gradually swelling. It
just developed as the folk clubs developed.

HANS FRIED

Collett's bookshop sold *Sing*. Collett's was originally a left-wing
bookshop in Charing Cross Road. They started to have records,
jazz and some Russian and East European imports. The big thing
in the Communist movement was the people's music at that
time, then Collett's became folk music and jazz and moved to
New Oxford Street in '56 or '57 and it became a meeting place for
folk to hang out. I helped out at first because I knew a lot about
folk music, then I started working there. I was there eleven years.

In those days a lot of the folk crowd hung out at Collett's bookshop. MacColl used to come in quite regularly. Alex Campbell
was a regular visitor, drunk or sober. Rod Stewart used to come
in. Dominic Behan. Ian Campbell and his band. Tom Paxton – he
was a nice guy, straight down the line.

JOHN FOREMAN

From 1958 the Aldermaston march was a sort of national
meeting for practically all the folk clubs and quite a lot of clubs
were formed following that. It was a singing march. The word
got around and there was a sort of network of singers.

2 All over this land

As the folk scene began to gather momentum in London, there were stirrings in other parts of the country. Out in the provinces the music was coming to the attention of the younger generation just as it had in the capital, through radio, CND, the few records that were about and, of course, skiffle.

In the vanguard of activity were the ancient universities. At Cambridge students founded the St Lawrence Folk Society as early as 1950. The Oxford University Heritage Society began in 1956 and in 1958 medical student Stuart MacGregor and folklorist Hamish Henderson started the Edinburgh University Folk Song Society. The enthusiasm of two Glasgow school-teachers who organised a lunchtime folk club for their pupils at Rutherglen Academy, Norman Buchan and Morris Blythman, resulted in the formation of Glasgow Folk Song Club in 1960.

Away from academia Ewan MacColl and A. L. Lloyd's influence was being felt in some of the industrial cities. As Archie Fisher recalls, there was already an awareness that in America Pete Seeger and Woody Guthrie had championed the songs of the Wobblies – the Industrial Workers of the World – and a desire to emulate them here.

The term 'folk club' was still unknown in 1954 when Harry and Lesley Boardman began what they called a 'folk circle' in the Wagon and Horses pub in Manchester. Harry Boardman would become a familiar figure around the clubs over the next thirty years, making many records of songs from his native Lancashire. In 1956 the folk circle he and his wife founded became Manchester's first folk club, the Wayfarers.

September 1956 saw the opening of the Topic folk club in Bradford, named after the Topic record label. It was a sign of the times that the local police soon chose to raid the Topic, suspicious that organiser Alex Eaton, a member of the Communist Party, was preaching subversion. Despite such early interruption, the Topic folk club exists to the present day, and is the oldest continuously running folk club in Britain.

In Liverpool the Spinners, who would go on to fame with concerts, records and on television, began as a skiffle group with a residency at the Cavern Club. They progressed to folk music via sea shanties and in 1958 opened their own folk club in the basement of a restaurant, a room that held barely forty people.

The same year a family group known as the Folksons started singing in a coffee bar in Hull. Like so many others they had a repertoire that in the beginning was American. After visiting Harry Boardman's Wayfarers club in Manchester, and the Spinners' club in Liverpool, they opened a folk club in a Hull dance hall, before discarding all instruments and becoming known as the Watersons.

The first folk club Louis Killen attended was the Oxford Heritage Society in the mid-fifties. Returning to his native Tyneside, he met Johnny Handle and together they organised a folk night in a Newcastle jazz club. Killen drew on earlier contacts to book such guests as Shirley Collins and Cyril Tawney. Their Folk Song and Ballad club ran for many years at the Bridge Hotel in Newcastle.

The Ian Campbell Folk Group opened a club at the Trees pub in Birmingham in 1959. Soon known as the Jug of Punch and relocated at Digbeth Town Hall, it regularly attracted audiences of up to 400 people.

In Edinburgh Dolina MacLennan, who had been present at the first night of the University Folk Song Society, started a singing night in 1959 at the Waverley Bar, a haven of folk musicians for decades to come. The following year Roy Guest, later an agent for many folk acts, opened the Howff in a small upstairs room off the Royal Mile.

Slowly, as the fifties passed into the sixties, a circuit of folk clubs was beginning to form. Its bases were scattered and many *miles apart, but the people who ran the clubs were almost all singers whose prime aim was to spread the word. And spread it they did, booking guests and encouraging other resident singers and musicians. More clubs opened, as interest developed at a brisk pace, but rather than creating animosity or competitiveness, the atmosphere was one of mutual excitement that more people were joining in to share the music.*

LESLEY BOARDMAN *wife of the late singer Harry Boardman, with whom she began one of the earliest folk gatherings outside London*

We'd been told that there was something called a guitar circle which was run at this little pub in Manchester, the Wagon and Horses, just off Deansgate. So we went along and it was from that we got the idea of starting a folk circle, about 1954. The University Socialist Society had these folk evenings and the Young Communist League had various events but folk clubs were not known at that time. We did it on a weekly basis, between twelve and twenty people would come along. They didn't all sing, some people just came to listen. Harry sang some Ewan MacColl songs and other songs that were popular at the time. He played the five-string banjo and I played the tenor banjo and mandolin. I suppose most of what we did sprang from our connection with the socialist movement.

When we started the Wayfarers club at the Thatched House in Spring Gardens, there were a few resident singers – Terry Whelan was one, and Pauline Hinchcliffe. She was a teacher from Derby and she was living in Failsworth. She and her boyfriend Jack Lewis and Harry and I formed a little group. We played some skiffle, Lonnie Donegan numbers.

That was our first real folk club, it was about 1956. We had regular visits from the Spinners, as they later became known, because Mick Groves was at teacher training college in Manchester and the others would come over.

LOUISE EATON *wife of the late Alex Eaton, schoolteacher and folk club organiser*

Alex started the folk club in the Laycock Rooms in Bradford in September 1956. With hindsight, I think it might not have been named Topic at the beginning. It was when skiffle really took off but Alex thought this has to be a folk club, singing folk.

He was inspired by John Hasted's club in London. He went down and the night he visited, the Ramblers – Alan Lomax's group – were singing there and they asked him to join in. Alex had been singing solo songs accompanying himself with simple chords on his guitar and he said he was inspired by having a backing, and how it enhanced it all.

We had Friday night as a singers' night and Wednesday was a learning evening so people would come along and Alex would be showing chords or singing songs. In the very early days we formed a committee so people were involved in knowing what was happening. When we got any profit Alex bought books that belonged to the club. And he bought records. Then he bought a record player so people could listen to them.

I think the first guest was John Hasted. His repertoire was so exhaustive. He had a notebook in which all the songs he sang were listed. He'd turn over a page and say, 'Oh, this is a good song' and there was just a title, no words. We were all awe-inspired by John Hasted's guitar playing and he played the banjo as well. Later on he brought up Shirley Collins and Nadia Cattouse. We had Redd Sullivan, Long John Baldry, Ramblin' Jack Elliott, Steve Benbow.

BILL LEADER

Alex Eaton was a teacher, a great teacher. He could enthuse people. He played the guitar, sang cowboy songs, things like that, the repertoire of the period. Alex and I had started a Bradford branch of the Workers' Music Association. He saw that kids were beginning to take an interest in music and he saw the learning advantages of pulling them together into some sort of an organisation. So he saw folk music was a good thing to have around.

WIZZ JONES

Someone said to me at a party, 'Do you ever do any gigs?' 'Cos I was just busking and playing at parties and around people's houses. They said, 'We can give you a support gig at the Topic folk club in Bradford.' They said they'd got Steve Benbow playing and I'd seen Steve Benbow on television. I'd got his record and really admired him. I thought he was a lovely singer and I'd nicked a lot of his material. They said we can only pay you the train fare. I hitch-hiked up and kept the train fare.

MARTIN CARTHY

The first time I sang really outside London was at the Topic. I travelled up from London to Bradford with Louis Killen on his scooter.

LOUISE EATON

Quite early on we were raided by the police. They thought we must have drugs and they were thinking it was a political platform, that there was a subversive element there, Alex being known as a Communist.

They came in expecting Alex to be at the front, preaching 'Down with Capitalism'. They found young people playing and listening to songs. It was teetotal. The only thing we were selling was pop.

They came in with a kind of big-mouth approach saying, 'Nobody move. Stay sitting where you are.' Nobody could leave the room. All the young people were petrified. Masses of people were in. They could see there weren't any drugs or alcohol there and they said, 'You've got far too many people in here. It's a fire hazard.'

TONY DAVIS *founder member of the Spinners*

The Spinners grew out of skiffle. There was myself and my wife, Beryl. She played guitar, better than I did. We were singing in a coffee bar in Liverpool, the Kinkajoo, and I'd be up on a stool in my open-necked shirt with the light on me, and Beryl's sat behind me in the dark, playing the guitar. Then I went to college and met Mick and we gave him a washboard to play, because he couldn't play anything.

In 1957 we had a residency at the Cavern on skiffle night and we wanted to include a broader range of folk music than the Lonnie Donegan songbook. So I looked in the telephone directory for folk music and I found the English Folk Dance and Song Society had meetings at the Friends Meeting House. Mick and I went along to one. There were these ladies and gentlemen in their overcoats and the ladies still had their hats on, all sitting round a baize table, singing sea shanties out of books.

Redd Sullian was singing blues with the Merseysippi Jazz Band at the time. He lived up here for about a year. We got to know him and he taught us quite a bit about singing as a group. He said, 'You guys shouldn't be singing these American songs. You should try singing English folk songs. You've got these wonderful sea shanties in Liverpool. You want to investigate.' We'd known a lot of them at school and we started including them. We wanted to sing somewhere regularly so we took this basement in Samson and Barlow's restaurant.

HUGHIE JONES *joined the Spinners soon after they formed and, like Tony Davis, remained in the group until they retired in 1988*
On the bus home from a Sonny Terry and Brownie McGhee concert, that's when I heard about the Spinners club, in 1958. This guy, Dan Dare, was sitting behind me. That was his real name. It was a comic strip in *The Eagle*, but Dan Dare was his real name. I was talking away to my pal, full of it, about hearing this great American music and I mentioned that I'd made a twelve-string guitar – you couldn't buy them then. And Dan Dare said, 'You want to go to the Spinners' folk club.' I didn't know what a folk club was but I went and eventually plucked up courage and played my home-made guitar. Then they asked me to join them. The club had been open about ten weeks.

It was just a bunch of people, not a band. There was Tony Davis and his wife Beryl, his half-sister Joan. Beryl played cello with a big spike. She could make a bit of a bass sound on it. And everybody joined in on the choruses. We did quite a lot of American songs, 'Worried Man Blues' – that kind of thing.

A big schism occurred in Liverpool then: whether to go electric or not. We decided we preferred the acoustic instruments. The groups, the Searchers and Gerry and all that lot – they'd been involved in skiffle. They went the electric way.

TONY DAVIS

We booked guests. Isla Cameron was acting in a play round the corner at the Shakespeare, which was then a theatre, and we asked her to come and sing at the club. She charged us some astronomical price, it seemed to me. But she was the most famous woman singer around on the folk scene. Shirley Collins hadn't really appeared at that time, Isla was the one – she was wonderful. She sang with us, taught us a lot of songs.

HUGHIE JONES

Jeannie Robertson used to come down from Aberdeen. She was an amazing singer, probably the queen of ballad singers. She had a daughter, Lizzie Higgins. She was a good singer and she came to our club, too. Jeannie Robertson got the MBE. We had Nigel Denver and Martin Carthy quite a few times. We'd swap with Ian Campbell at his club, the Jug of Punch in Digbeth. We had MacColl and Seeger up frequently. Luke Kelly we had a lot. Alex Campbell was sometimes mercurial – one night he only sang two songs but he was always entertaining. It was always fun when he was around.

In Liverpool we were fortunate because people like Dominic Behan would do the Friday night club then he'd leave for the midnight boat. That's how he came to write 'Liverpool Lou'. He was down there one night and it was raining. It was miserable. There was nobody about. And he saw this young hooker, not picking up any business, as the bells of St Nicholas's Church chimed. The ring of the bells gave him the tune to 'Liverpool Lou'. He would just drop in and do a couple of songs. He wasn't booked.

We had quite a few Americans – Hedy West, the banjo player. We had the New Lost City Ramblers. Cisco Houston, Woody Guthrie's mate, he came to our club. I was ill and he did a tape recording. 'Hugh' he said – I was Hugh then – 'I've been hearing you're not too well, this one's specially for you.' And he did 'Talking Dust Bowl Blues'. I only heard it once – Tony said he lost the tape, but I'm sure he's got it somewhere.

TONY DAVIS

In Samson and Barlow's from about 6.30 onwards on a Friday night there were queues right the way round the block. Friday night was Liverpool. We never took other bookings on Friday nights. The club was sacred. We moved the club to a Monday, eventually, because Friday was obviously a good night to go off and be doing concerts and things. We could always get back to Liverpool by Monday teatime, even if we were in Scotland or the south of England.

HUGHIE JONES

Right at the beginning we used to go down to London on a Friday. I was working in Speke, near Liverpool airport and there was a flight at five o'clock. I finished work at five so I had to sneak out and we'd get on this old Dakota and fly down to London.

We would do a club Friday night then on the Saturday morning we'd go into Cecil Sharp House, use the library, and Saturday night we would play a club and later on we would play the Troubadour in Earls Court Road. Then on the Sunday night we'd go to north London and do another club. Cliff used to take the Fridays off work and he'd drive down in the van, so we'd all come back together.

TONY DAVIS

I said we should do concerts but the others said, 'No, you're mad.'
So I booked the concert room at St George's Hall – it holds 600
people – and the first one sold out completely, with just us. Then
we booked Robin Hall and Jimmie Macgregor to be on the next
one with us, they were on the *Tonight* programme.

For three years we did concerts every month and we found out
that when we had guests it sold out eventually, but the ones we
did on our own sold out immediately. They weren't folk music
lovers. They were Spinners followers. We always tried to put in
Liverpool songs. The other people weren't singing the songs the
audience wanted to hear.

HUGHIE JONES

There were loads of songs about sailing ships between Liverpool
and New York, traditional songs. I read widely on the subject and
I heard lots of yarns. 'Champion of the Seas', that was the first
sea song I wrote. After that I did 'Marco Polo', which was about
a more famous vessel. The skipper, who was called Bully Forbes,
a Scotsman, is buried in Liverpool. It has 'Melbourne or Bust' on
his gravestone. I made up a song about the *Marco Polo*, based on
the way he used to make sure the crews didn't jump ship when
they reached Australia to go digging for gold, which was a better
job than being a sailor.

I wrote 'The Ellen Vannen Tragedy' in about 1963. I'd been to
the club and had lots of beer. I used to go with my mum and dad.
My dad was a good singer and we used to drink lots of beer, get a
taxi home and buy some chicken. We'd sit and have more beer at
home and eat the chicken. Anyhow, I stayed up one night and when
I came down in the morning there was this song that I'd written in
my drunken chickenness, and I still had the tune in my head.

We recorded it on *More Folk at the Phil*. I've got a few versions
of it by different people. I loved Richard Hawley's version – think
it's great. It's got to be my most successful song but I don't seem
to get any money for it.

LOUIS KILLEN

For me there was no beginning. Singing had always been there
in my childhood in Gateshead. My father and mother sang. My
three older brothers all sang, I sang in the house. That's what we
did in the family.

I got a scholarship to the Catholic Workers' College in Oxford.
I was there a year, September '55 to June '56, but I foolishly
walked out. I liked Oxford, I liked the whole academic thing, but
I discovered folk music. I discovered skiffle.

In the summer I was hanging around the coffee bars. One of
them had a cellar and a bunch of guys from the RAF there. Several
of them played guitars and were into the American folk music,
the Donegan skiffle-type stuff. I had a guitar and I'd learned a
few chords and I'd go down there and play. I was working on
the buildings as a carpenter. I'd served my apprenticeship as a
cabinet maker, and that was what kept me going.

The Oxford Heritage Society was the first folk club I went to.
A guest would be brought up from London. They would perform
and the students would organise singing sessions or picnics.
People who had instruments would play them. One of the guests
was Ramblin' Jack Elliott. It was Jack's first time in England, so
I went to hear him. Nadia Cattouse came one weekend. Russell
Quaye came with his group from the Skiffle Cellar. Alexis Korner
came up. I became quite friendly with Alexis and eventually
went down to London and spent a week learning how to play
blues guitar from him.

I came back to Gateshead in 1958. There was a jazz club in
Marlborough Street and Johnny Handle was playing in the interval, when the band took a break. He would do a fifteen-minute
spot, playing rhythm and blues. Then he left, so I went up to the
bandleader and said, 'Any chance of a gig? I play folk music.' About
a month later, Johnny came back. He'd got married and been off
on his honeymoon and, lo and behold, there I was, in his spot.

After about a year we started up a folk song club in the jazz
club on a Tuesday night. There was myself, Johnny Handle

and a lad called John Reavey. A friend of mine, Brian Ballinger, whom I'd met at Oxford, came up from Manchester. He'd been president of the Heritage Society when I was there.

It lasted all of about four or five weeks. The first week we charged nothing and we got eighty people in. So we said we'll charge one and six in future. The next week there was about fifty, then thirty, then twenty. Nobody wanted to pay, so we just said, 'Oh, to hell with this', and I started looking for a venue to start our own club

JOHNNY HANDLE *born John Pandrich, a key musician on Tyneside from the earliest days of the folk revival, later a member of the High Level Ranters*
Originally it was a folk and blues night, 'cos Louis knew about folk music – he'd been at Oxford. We were doing mostly American stuff. This was when it was in the jazz club. We were just expanding our repertoire to try and make it more interesting, instead of singing the same material every week. There was a few people from the floor would get up and sing, so we were the stars, like.

LOUIS KILLEN
We found a new venue in the Barras Bridge Hotel, known as 'The Sink'. It had a poor reputation, but they had this room upstairs. We ran the club there for three years, until they closed the pub and demolished it.

We booked guests but not too many. The first year we only got Brian Ballinger and then for the last night Shirley Collins, who I'd met during the previous winter when I'd been down in London and discovered the Troubadour. She was also singing at a club called Folksong Unlimited with Dominic Behan, Seamus Ennis, Stan Kelly and a few others who weren't particularly in with MacColl and his Ballads and Blues Club as it was then. That's where the Folk Song and Ballad title for our club came from.

At this time I had a whole bunch of English songs, songs of my family. My father was second-generation Irish so we had

Irish songs – we had cowboy songs, border ballads – anything that we heard on the radio or we could get on disc. I learned 'Pleasant and Delightful' from my brothers. All they knew was the chorus – they'd heard it on the radio and they began singing it. I didn't get the words until I met MacColl in '59 when we went to Birmingham to record 'Song of the Road', one of the *Radio Ballads*. So there were a lot of different songs in my repertory, but they were all rolled up together.

JOHNNY HANDLE
Louis turned professional because he fell off the ladder, window cleaning. The gypsy was in his soul. He'd get a few gigs and he'd forget about the existence of mankind and just disappear. He'd do the gigs and meet people, come back – he had no money so he would get a temporary job.

LOUIS KILLEN
Tyne Tees Television had just started up in Newcastle and an old leftie, Kurt Lewin Hack, produced a magazine programme every evening on weekdays. He was looking for talent and he came up to the club and found me and hired me on a fortnightly basis. I first did 'Blackleg Miners' on the anniversary of the founding of the Northumbrian Miners Union. He had me sitting at the bottom of a pit shaft playing banjo and singing. When we couldn't find songs, we wrote one.

JOHNNY HANDLE
One day Louis said to me, 'Why don't you start singing like a Geordie, 'cos you talk like a Geordie.' And that was the start of it. Bert Lloyd's book *Come All Ye Bold Miners* had been brought out as a paperback, which we got from the Workers' Music Shop, and looking through that I thought, 'I can sing these songs because I know what they're about.' Louis was singing quite a mixture of material and there was another feller used to come along, John Brennan, whose parents were Irish, so he could do

them. There was a couple of lads used to sing CND stuff, so we were building together a little team.

Once we'd got a regular audience, Louis knew people in other parts of the country so we started having a few guests. John Doonan, the piccolo player, brought some friends from the Irish community around Jarrow. They came to build shipyards at the turn of the century, and they brought their music, which mixed in with Geordie music. Then we moved to the Bridge Hotel in 1961 or '62.

Paddy Foley was the landlord at the Bridge, a jovial Irishman, and there was this very strong, stout Russian baritone, a big tall strapping bloke appearing at the Theatre Royal. Paddy and him had a drink one night when the club was running. So Paddy brought him upstairs and he said, 'This guy's good.' He'd never heard him sing.

He did this spot from the floor. We couldn't kind of refuse him but we were thinking, 'Oh, what's Paddy let us in for?' And he had the most fantastic voice. It was like listening to Caruso or somebody like that. They wouldn't let him off. We didn't know if he was singing Russian folk songs or opera or what. He'd say something in Russian, then 'This ees a good one', then he'd sing. One of those nights where you worried what was going to happen, but it worked.

IAN CAMPBELL *leader of the Ian Campbell Folk Group, in the forefront of the folk scene in the sixties*
I was active in the CND in Birmingham and, among my enthusiasms, I joined the Clarion Singers. They featured quite prominently in the folk song movement in those days. Clarion was a choir. It was the musical expression of the political, left-wing, co-op labour movement. This was in the late fifties.

We formed the Clarion Skiffle Group, that lasted about eighteen months. It started off with me and Lorna and Gordon McCulloch and Dave Phillips and it was very democratic. You didn't have to audition and we ended up with fourteen members.

It became unmanageable so we formed our own folk group and became the Ian Campbell Folk Group.

At the end of 1960 the Campbell group was going down to London to appear at a concert at St Pancras Town Hall. We got on the train and into a compartment and we got the instruments out and started to run through our programme. As we were strumming and singing away, the door opened and in came this little guy. 'Room for a little one?'

He came in and sat down and he'd got a fiddle case under his arm. After we'd done a couple of songs he just started to join in. He could play in any key. He just listened once through and that was it, he'd got it. For the rest of the trip we were having a ball. We said, 'Where are you going?' He said St Pancras Town Hall. 'So are we.'

DAVE SWARBRICK *the best-known fiddler in British folk music, played with the Ian Campbell Folk Group, Martin Carthy, Fairport Convention and Whippersnapper among others*
I'd met Charles Parker in Birmingham. I knew him because he socialised among the kind of people who went to folk clubs, then subsequently because he was the producer of the *Radio Ballads*. Because of my association with Charles and him knowing what I did, I got asked to do the *Radio Ballads* and I went down to London to accompany Ewan and Peggy and Bert Lloyd and I was on the same train as Ian. We met and had a play on the train. From there I played some tunes with them and then I joined them.

The first folk club I can remember was in Birmingham. I can only have been fifteen years old, it was prior to joining the Ian Campbell Folk Group. I think it was pre-Jug of Punch. The Campbell group were there but only as individuals. At that time I was an apprentice letterpress printer, an appalling one.

I used to try to fit the group in around work but music always came first. I was on the point of getting the sack many times before I packed it in. I was an apprentice and they never sacked apprentices. When I was twenty they let me out of my

indentures eight months early on the proviso that I never went
into the printing trade ever again. I was banned for life. I was
quite happy to comply with that.

MARTIN CARTHY

I did the Campbells' club, and Dave and I got on like mad. I
stayed at his house a couple of times. We both loved Bert Lloyd
– Dave used to play fiddle for Bert Lloyd. Bert loved Dave
because he could follow him anywhere he went. He sang the
most outrageous time signatures and Dave just stood behind
him and played. Dave didn't play time signatures, still doesn't.
He plays melody – if a melody goes weird, Dave plays with it.
He really is as extraordinary as he ever was. He's probably a bit
more organised now, a wonderful, wonderful player.

IAN CAMPBELL

Dave had a natural talent which was remarkable. He really
was something special. He played electric guitar and later
on electric bass guitar with Roger and Beryl Marriott. They
had been involved with the Clarion. Beryl was a pianist who
used to get traditional songs and transform them with piano
arrangements.

DAVE SWARBRICK

I'd learnt the fiddle from the village fiddler, Mr Boothman, when
I was evacuated to Yorkshire in the war. When I was eight years
old I was moved back from Yorkshire to Birmingham. I was still
playing the fiddle for couple of years but I got fed up with it, I
wasn't very good, really.

When I was about fourteen I was in a skiffle group, the Beacon
Skiffle Group. We won a contest and the prize was to meet two
famous people, which we did. It was Beryl and Roger Marriott
and, of course, we'd never heard of them. Beryl had a ceilidh
band and I went to play guitar in the ceilidh band. Then one day
I happened to mention that when I was a kid I'd played the fiddle

a bit and she persuaded me to get it out of the attic. Nobody ever came anywhere near Beryl as a musician. She was the finest player imaginable.

IAN CAMPBELL

When we got thrown out of the Trees we found the Crown in Station Street. The Crown was very convenient, right in the centre of Birmingham and we were quite happy with a crowd of 120. We often had to turn people away. We were the residents, so we would do the first half an hour, then it was floor singers and we always finished the night. It was very much an opportunity for people to meet and sing to each other, the whole idea of the folk song club. That was where we did the first ever live club record, *Ceilidh at the Crown*.

The pub hadn't been doing anything before we moved in and we were assured the room was ours for ever but towards the end of the second year we took a month off. We were going on tour to Scandinavia. We'd booked the room for when we got back and advertised when we'd be starting again – I think it was Martin Carthy we'd booked, but when we got back the room had been booked for a rock 'n' roll group.

John Dunkerley and I went all over town and we couldn't find a pub room big enough. We looked everywhere. Then we found Digbeth Civic Hall and that was when we called it the Jug of Punch. At first people didn't like it – there was no smoky atmosphere. It took us several months but we got it going and we were turning people away again and for seventeen years Digbeth Civic Hall had the biggest folk song club in Britain.

We had everybody as guests. The Weavers were the start of the folk song movement in America – they came. We did some gigs with them in the late fifties. There were only three of them came over, it was around the time the Un-American Activities thing was flourishing.

We booked Pete Seeger in '63. No folk club in the world could afford Pete Seeger. He would charge in those days £250. We didn't even have to charge the audience more than usual because we'd accumulated the money.

EWAN McVICAR *involved in the early Glasgow folk scene; his song 'Talking Army Blues' was a chart hit for another Scots singer, Josh McRae*
I heard that there was something happening in London, Ballads and Blues, and a group came up twice from London to Glasgow to a venue, the Old Iona Community. One time Ewan MacColl came and another time Peggy Seeger. MacColl was quite scathing about Scottish folk clubs. He said, 'They're all a bunch of skifflers', because we were listening to Woody Guthrie and Leadbelly and Big Bill Broonzy. MacColl was very influential. Ralph Rinzler was there one of those times.

ARCHIE FISHER *a Glaswegian from a singing family, a regular at the Edinburgh Festival, later presented* Travelling Folk *on BBC Radio Scotland*
I got guitar lessons and banjo-picking styles from Ralph Rinzler. He was the great American bluegrass and Americana instrumentalist. He was touring with Ewan and Peggy and during a break at the Iona Community Centre in Glasgow we sat down and he ran through some of the guitar and banjo licks he had used in his first set. We all had record collections of great American guitar players like Merle Travis, Chet Atkins and Big Bill Broonzy. Like many others, I'd discovered that if you slow down a 45 rpm EP to 33 rpm the octave dropped but the key remained the same, allowing you to work out the guitar or banjo piece in slomo.

EWAN McVICAR
Before the Iona Community we had a folk club at school in Glasgow, when I was fourteen. Morris Blythman, who was crucial in the folk song revival as a singer and songwriter and organiser, taught at our school, the Rutherglen Academy. It was at

a lunchtime and you could go and learn about songs. I got to meet Jeannie Robertson and Josh McRae. Hamish Henderson would bring people down from the north-east to come across to Glasgow, so Morris would have ceilidhs and musical evenings in his house. Sometimes there'd be pipers, sometimes there'd be singers.

DOLINA MACLENNAN *Gaelic singer and actress, originally from the Isle of Lewis, later appeared in many films and television plays*
The Edinburgh University folk club started in April '58 at the Old Quad at Edinburgh University. I met Hamish Henderson and Stuart MacGregor on the opening night. I was just down from the Isle of Lewis and I was at a party with my friend in the New Town. Somebody came into the kitchen and said, 'Can anybody here sing?' My friend said, 'Doli sings.' I knew lots of songs in Gaelic and English. So I started and Stuart MacGregor came in and then this great big lumbering man, Hamish Henderson, and we were friends until the day he died.

Hamish had started in the mid-fifties with Joan Littlewood, the People's Festival. He used to have concerts with Norman Buchan and Ewan MacColl. They started what was the origins of the Edinburgh Fringe. That summer, 1958, Robin Hall and myself and Jeannie Robertson and Jimmie McBeath, we sang at Gartshore Hall, at Hamish Henderson's lunchtime ceilidh.

I remember one day going round all the tables in the common room, asking which nationality they all were, and would they come and have an international night at the folk song club. A whole crowd did, from different countries. We had an amazing night with a Jamaican steel band and Jeannie Robertson and myself and a poet from Shetlands, this was in 1959. We were there before Glasgow.

Then Robin Gray, he was a dental student, and myself opened the singing at the Waverley Bar, which gave everybody their start, really. That was in '59. It wasn't a folk club but people would gather there and I would ask them to do a couple of songs.

I'd sing from seven till ten. In a night I'd sing anything up to thirty or more songs, unaccompanied, some of them Gaelic. A lot of people started learning Gaelic there, because they'd heard Gaelic folk songs. I gave the Corries their first gig there at the Waverley, paid them ten shillings each. More and more people came in. I left in 1963 but the Waverley ran for ever.

Eric Winter, who wrote for the *Melody Maker*, heard Robin and I singing at the NUJ conference in Edinburgh in 1960. He got us down to London and we sang at the Troubadour and made a record in Bill Leader's house. Eric Winter took a terrible shine to me, he was mentioning me in the *Melody Maker* non-stop. I had my tonsils out in 1962 and Archie Fisher said, 'Are you going to pickle them and send them to Eric Winter?'

JIM McLEAN

I was in this folk club and somebody recommended that I meet a chap called Morris Blythman. Morris had been working with Hamish Henderson trying to revive folk songs. He was in Springburn, Glasgow, at the time – this was 1959. I was always interested in poetry and I was always fairly Scottish Republican-minded. I'd written some stuff, anti-monarchy, humorous. We collaborated on different songs, Hamish, myself and Morris, and recorded them in Morris's house. Then Pete Seeger came to Glasgow, he met Morris and Morris played the tapes to him.

Pete Seeger took the tapes to America and they did some kind of deal and the songs came out on Folkways as an LP, *Ding Dong Dollar*. That's where it all basically started. On *Ding Dong Dollar* nobody is credited with the songs. Morris said, 'That's the cult of personality, we're not going to encourage that, so you don't put your names to it.' It was later sold on to Nat Joseph at Transatlantic.

Morris wasn't the kind of man who would do you for money. He's dead now. He started the whole of the Scottish folk scene. Hamish Henderson gets a lot of credit but Morris's house was where a lot of them started off.

I kept writing, wrote songs for anti-Polaris marches and stuff like that, and my songs were picked up by people like Nigel Denver, Alastair McDonald, a whole load of people. There was a folk club in Glasgow, down at the Trongate end, and a chap I had travelled with, Geordie McIntyre, took me there. Geordie's quite big in Scotland but in those days we just cycled together, went to folk clubs.

NIGEL DENVER *singer of traditional songs, the first British folk singer to be signed to a major label*
We got the skiffle group up from school and we were on the Glasgow Empire when I was fifteen, that was 1953 or '54, on the Carroll Levis Discoveries. The whole school turned up. That's why we won the heat. Then my schoolteacher, Morris Blythman, introduced me to Jeannie Robertson and Jimmy McBeath and all the old singers. They came to the school and Jeannie gave me a couple of songs, so I really got it from the oral tradition, I didn't get it from books. 'The Gallowa' Hills' was one of them. I can still just about sing that.

Morris Blythman brought me to traditional music, then we started getting work at little dances with the skiffle group. The guitarist's brother had made an electric bass. Nobody had ever seen anything like it in 1953 or '54.

When Lonnie Donegan was in Glasgow, he used to go to Morris Blythman's house and Morris used to invite us all. I think Lonnie got some music from him.

EWAN McVICAR
Morris Blythman used to say, 'Everybody has one good song inside them. Some people have more than one, but everybody has at least one. Away and write your good song.' I thought, 'Oh, well, I'd better go and write a song.' I had an LP of MacColl and Lloyd called something like *Barrack Room Ballads* and from that I was able to get a lot of information about joining the British Army. That was my research and I wrote 'Talking Army Blues'.

Josh McRae was known for doing talking blues, in particular for 'Talking Guitar Blues', an Ernest Tubb number, and he went down to London in 1960 to record it for Top Rank. He was looking for a song for the B-side and he remembered that I had done this 'Talking Army Blues' which had gone down very well in Glasgow folk club and he said could he get the words of it. He recorded it, but when the record came out, the reviews of 'Talking Guitar' were so-so, but they were all impressed by 'Talking Army', the B-side. So the record company turned it round and made my song the A-side.

Then Josh's agent got everybody to write in to *Two-way Family Favourites* to request it and because it was a Forces thing and it was getting played on the radio, it became a hit. I earned £200 in royalties and half that went on a wonderful party.

NIGEL DENVER
Big Bill Broonzy, he was booked in the Dixon Halls in Glasgow. He was like a magical man. He walked on with a bottle of whisky and a glass, proceeded to have a large glass and then started playing. It was flabbergasting. He went off stage for the interval and he'd drunk three-quarters of the bottle. When he came back on for the second half, he'd another bottle of whisky. He got a great ovation. He was absolutely brilliant.

The guitar playing was just out of this world. We'd all bought little EPs of him and occasionally there'd be an LP that went the rounds. Like Josh would get an LP and he'd lend it to me and I would lend him, that kinda thing. Then we went to Hamish Imlach's house and he finished off the whisky there and they put him to bed. He was a huge man, well over six feet, a big, big man.

ARCHIE FISHER
The first Glasgow folk club was held in an open-plan café called the Corner House on Argyle Street and was run by Norman and Janey Buchan and lit by fluorescent lights which created the atmosphere of a supermarket.

I had just completed a short course at agricultural college when the Weavers came to Glasgow. That turned the tide – I headed for another type of culture at the folk song club. They used to get all sorts of singers, Josh McCrae and Hamish played there, it was a healthy little scene. The byelaws in the late fifties and sixties for licensed premises in Scotland meant that it was illegal to charge at the door in pubs so there were no venues with a bar for a long time.

NIGEL DENVER
There were no pubs open on a Sunday, so you had to buy a half-bottle on the Saturday if you were going to the folk club.

EWAN McVICAR
Janey Buchan was politically active in Glasgow and an organiser in lots of ways. Her husband, Norman Buchan, was doing a newspaper column of songs every week. So in '60 or '61 Janey Buchan called a group of about half a dozen singers together and said she'd heard of this idea about a folk club and maybe we could have one. She found us a venue and the first night we put an advert in the local Sunday newspaper and hoped that some people would come. We got a full house.

We didn't have the notion of guests. It was just people who we knew would come along and sing. There was a resident singing group which was Archie Fisher, Hamish Imlach, Ray Fisher, Josh McRae. The very first time we had a guest was about six weeks in and it was Jimmy McBeath. Hamish Henderson had brought him down. I was treasurer of the club and I paid him a fee of £8. He said it was more money than he had ever got at one time from singing. He was talking to me as Mr McVicar and I was nineteen at the time.

ARCHIE FISHER
The Glasgow Art School had supplied Robin Hall and Jimmie Macgregor, along with Josh McRae. There was a very left-wing element involved at the beginning and I think an attempt to

mirror the Wobblies movement in the States.

The group I was most attached to was made up of ex-skifflers and inductees like Hamish Imlach, Ewan McVicar and later the fiddler and mandolin player Bobby Campbell. My sister Ray and I were later to form a trio with Bobby called the Wayfarers, following the wandering titling preferred by such bardic ensembles. My first non-skiffle gig was as stand-in for Josh at a corporate dance in the old North British Hotel in Edinburgh, paying a handsome £5.

Ray and I as a duo had a weekly spot on the STV evening magazine show and occasional spots on Radio Scotland's outside broadcast and studio programmes like *Come Thursday* and *For Your Entertainment*. Our Radio Scotland audition notes read: '15th June 1960 . . . Repertoire – Get along Home Cindy – Bonnie George Campbell – Mormond Braes, All My Trials Lord. Rhythmically very secure on the American Numbers. When the boy played the guitar they were like a new group and the last item attained a very high standard.'

MARTIN CARTHY

When I left school in March 1959 I worked in theatre as an assistant stage manager, until September 1960. We went all round the country with *The Merry Widow*. Only once did I see a folk club in another town and that was when we got to Glasgow. We were there for two weeks and the master carpenter, a guy called Chris Gormley, started talking about Glasgow Folk Song Club. So my ears go straight up in the air, and he took me along to meet some of his friends at this place. It wasn't a house, it was like a shack – where Hamish Imlach lived with his wife, Wilma. I walked in and there's Hamish and Archie Fisher and Ray Fisher and Bobby Campbell, all playing guitars.

The following Sunday I went along to the folk song club and sang there. The person who was in charge of the club was Norman Buchan, later an MP but at that time he was a teacher at Rutherglen Academy. It was run like Ewan MacColl's club, but a lot friendlier. Norman Buchan had a very persuasive nature and a lot of charisma, hence a lot of the very good singers in the Scots revival at that time came from that school.

STAN CROWTHER *singer and club organiser, went on to be mayor of Rotherham and later the town's MP*
We started a skiffle group and a skiffle club in Rotherham in 1956 and the folk club emerged from that. Skiffle became out of fashion and audiences were not turning up as they had. Folk was coming in. There were folk clubs starting in London and we were taking an interest, so we moved to a new pub, the Wellington Inn, and had one night of folk music every month. We called it the Black Friday Club because it opened on 13 February 1959. We booked guests – we had Johnny Handle in the early stages and Harry Boardman.

We got songs from *Sing* magazine and there were one or two records, like the ones Peter Kennedy put out. The skifflers read *Sing* and that's how we got familiar with folk songs. Like other people I was thinking skiffle's all right, but it's American, what about all the English folk music and the Scottish and the Irish? The Scottish and Irish wasn't difficult to find, but where do you find the English folk? That wasn't so easy, we had to dig it out.

MIKE WATERSON *formed the Folksons in Hull with his sisters Lal and Norma and their cousin John Harrison. They started a folk club, changed their name to the Watersons and focused on unaccompanied traditional songs*
We'd always sung together. My mam died when I was not quite five and my dad had a stroke ten days later, and we were brought up by Grandma. So we actually went back a generation and we sat round the fire and sang on a night-time, specially at the weekends. We sang musical hall songs, hymns, anything. Not folk music as such, although there was some folk songs in it.

Norma's boyfriend taught her to play guitar. She taught me, I taught Lal. Then I picked the banjo up. We went anywhere we could with the skiffle group. We would go into the pub and say, 'Can we go in the best room and sing?' All the heavy drinkers would sit in the bar and drink so the landlord would be over the moon at people drinking in his best room. There'd be half a dozen or a dozen of us and we had a night out. We weren't known by a name at that time, until we got organised we just used to go out and have a good time. None of us was old enough to drink, really.

NORMA WATERSON *like her brother Mike, introduced to folk music through skiffle. Mother of Eliza Carthy*
Big Bill Broonzy came twice in the fifties and my former husband and I were big fans. We'd got all his records. We went to Leeds to see him and met him, and then he came to the City Hall in Hull and we went backstage and met him again, and we talked about all sorts of things. He was over the moon at how many white people came to see him.

He asked if there was somewhere he could eat and we took him to this fish restaurant, the Gainsborough, in Hull. He looked up and there was everything on the menu, fish and chips, this and chips, that and chips, everything that a northern fish restaurant has. He said, 'Have they got whisky and chips?' No sorry, it's not licensed. We had a meal and he came round to our house and we just sat and talked, about prejudice, about music, about all sorts of things, and in the morning we saw him off on the train.

The last time he came was the year before he died and he was having great trouble with his throat but he was still magnificent. We were lucky in those days because in the fifties it was an absolute zenith for American musicians to come over here. Me and our Mike and Lal and my first husband saw so many people that now you can't imagine it.

MIKE WATERSON
There was five of us originally in the group when we started singing in the coffee house, the Jacaranda. The feller who ran the

coffee bar, he gave us seven and sixpence a week, for all of us, to go in and sing – and as much tea and coffee as we could drink. Most coffee houses were just a house converted and it got crowded.

One of the lads was called Pete Ogley. He played five-string banjo, looked like Pete Seeger and sang all the American stuff. Then he moved to Leeds and we lost like 99 per cent of our American music and it left us singing English music, literally.

We decided to start a folk club. It wasn't that we wanted to be famous. It was the joy of singing with your friends, so we saved all the seven and sixes and when we had £10 we packed the coffee bar in, because we were running the folk club then and we could afford a guest artist.

We'd been and looked at other folk clubs. I'd hitched down to London and went to the Singers' Club. I'd hitched across to Liverpool to the Spinners' club and we went to the Wayfarers in Manchester when Bert Lloyd was on one night. We started our first club in a dance hall, the Baker Street Dance Hall, and at the interval the woman who owned the dance hall served tea and coffee and cucumber sandwiches.

TONY DAVIS

The Spinners had a gig in Hull, at the university. It was a Sunday afternoon do. They had some sort of arts festival. It was very early days. And as we came off this girl came up to me and said, 'We've started a little folk club here, are you doing anything this evening?' I said we were going back to Liverpool. She said, 'We haven't really got any money to speak of, to pay anybody, but we'd be thrilled to bits if you'd come along and sing at our club.' So we said, 'Oh, all right', and we did. I got on well with the Watersons, really nice people.

STAN CROWTHER

One night the Watersons came over from Hull to our club in Rotherham. It's before they used their own name. They said, 'Can you fit us in?' I said, of course I could and I asked their name. They said, 'We're the Hull Folksons.' They brought about twenty people with them on a small bus. We were grateful for the extra attendance. I'd no idea they were coming. I think it was the first time they'd sung out of their own club, the Folk Union One in Hull.

MIKE WATERSON

The first guest we had at the folk club was Johnny Handle. He suggested Louis Killen, who suggested Tommy Gilfellon, and we suddenly realised everybody was ten or twelve quid, so it got to the stage where we could afford a guest artist every other week. All we wanted was to hear 'em sing, people who – we liked their singing. There was no bar on who they were, on what they sang. We had Bert Jansch . . . Sister Rosetta Tharpe . . . Felix Doran . . . Spider John Koerner . . . Clarence Ashley and Tex Isley . . . the New Lost City Ramblers. We booked who we wanted to book.

After about six weeks at the dance hall somebody suggested that perhaps we ought to find a pub that would have us, so we found the White Hart. The club became too big for there and the landlord of the Blue Bell came to us and said, 'I've got two jazz clubs in the upstairs room. Why don't you bring your folk club?' We did.

The Blue Bell was the biggest room we could get hold of. It was a long, thin room, benches along the walls two tables wide with chairs round them and an aisle right through the middle. Until the fire department stepped in we were getting 140, 150 people at the Blue Bell. Then they limited us to 120, which was a shame.

PEGGY SEEGER

The Watersons' club in Hull – I think Ewan and I sang there twice, but the room was against us. I'm used to singing with microphones now. I would not want to do a club without one, whereas in the old days there were few microphones. If you had a club full of people, especially like at Hull, where you were singing sideways on to a room that went down one way and the other and you're facing maybe six or seven rows in front of you and about fifteen rows to the left and fifteen rows to the right – even the Watersons will tell you that was a difficult club.

That's why I started singing much higher – and really strident. That's when Ewan had a lot of trouble because his tenor voice would not carry as well as mine, even though he had a street singer's voice.

MIKE WATERSON

The club being on a Sunday, we had to present ourselves every now and again to the Lord's Day Observance Society. We had to explain what we were doing and we had to have a set of books and be a non-profit-making organisation.

Later on, when we organised a concert on a Sunday for the Spinners, they said, 'We want a list of all the songs they sing.' Because we weren't allowed to make a profit, we decided to run a barn dance to lose money. By nine o'clock the bar was sold out. We made £400 on the night.

We had one or two dreadful nights, but we had some that were really good. The McPeakes, when old Francie was still alive – they were absolutely wonderful because they just stood up on the stage and played and talked among themselves but sort of brought you into them. Felix Doran was another. He was, in my mind, probably the best piper I've ever heard. He and his brother ran a scrapyard in Manchester and his brother apparently was a far better piper but he refused to play pipes in public, in folk clubs. I should have loved to have heard him because Felix was bloody wonderful.

As soon as we became professional we handed over to a committee and we did the club every other week. We weren't paid for it and then we just couldn't do it because we were having to turn weekend festivals down that paid more money.

NORMA WATERSON

Our Michael wouldn't sing what he called 'foreign songs'. He said, 'I'm gonna sing with my accent and that's it.' In those days most groups were based on the Weavers and sang with a pronounced American accent. We didn't want to do that at all. Right from the early fifties we loved traditional music so we started trying to find out more about it.

MIKE WATERSON
In the early days we'd do some Australian and American and Canadian songs, just a few, but as we became more educated, let me put it that way, we found the sources. We had a reference library in Hull that had all the Cecil Sharp stuff from the 1900s, so whenever we were looking up stuff, it was there. We obviously pinched songs from records, though there wasn't a lot of records about at that time. We didn't come across the Child Ballads for a good few years. They weren't there in Hull. Or they maybe were, but I never found them. What we found was that the English Folk Dance and Song Society had the old folk song journals from 1895 onwards, to 1930. And they were full of English songs.

JOHN CONOLLY *Humberside singer, later wrote 'Fiddler's Green' and 'Punch and Judy Man'*
Me and a mate Spud Marrows had a duo in Grimsby, the Wayfarers, consisting of me on acoustic guitar and vocals and Spud on a full drum kit. We did the standard skiffle repertoire and we toured the Women's Institutes of north Lincolnshire, to tumultuous applause.

Then we heard rumours that there were these clubs where you could listen to folk music. We found out that there was one in Hull, a place called Folk Union One, run by the Folksons, now known as the Watersons. They had guitar and banjo in the line-up in those days but even then they were pretty solid traditional in their repertoire. I can still remember the flabbergasted expression on Mike Waterson's face when we walked into their club carrying the drum kit. They were very kind. Years later, when I'd ditched the drummer, I got a booking there.

MIKE WATERSON

I remember that. John was very, very funny. The drum kit – no.

NORMA WATERSON

In the early days people would go for miles to clubs. We used to go in this old car that a friend of ours had. It always ran out of water so we had to carry water with us all the time. We would go from Hull to Manchester – and there was no M62 in those days – just to see people at the Manchester University folk club.

We saw Bert Lloyd there – loads and loads of people there. Because you wanted to know more of it and you wanted to know what made people love folk music like we loved it. You would make the effort and go, but people don't do that nowadays.

3 The big leap forward

For many people their first exposure to folk music was Robin Hall and Jimmie Macgregor on the BBC TV Tonight programme, which began in 1960. In a four-year run they sang five nights a week, bringing both themselves and folk music in general to the attention of millions. At a time when there were only two television channels – BBC and ITV – dedicated folk music programmes like Hallelujah, Hullabaloo and Hootenanny also helped spread the word in a manner that seems almost inconceivable today.

Hall and Macgregor, like Louis Killen, Ian Campbell and the Watersons, were former skifflers who had gone back to the songs of their own heritage. Not everyone took this path. Some still looked towards America, at country music and bluegrass, albeit taking a deeper interest than they had in their skiffle days, while the blues held a great attraction for others.

Alex Campbell had a foot in both camps. A larger-than-life Glaswegian who gave up his Civil Service job in London to busk in Paris before returning to Britain in 1960, he was as comfortable with 'The Mingulay Boat Song' as he was with 'Jesse James' or 'The Wabash Cannonball'. Tall, loud and imposing, clad in denim from head to toe and wielding a big Gibson guitar, year after year he kept up a relentless schedule, fuelled in no small part by alcohol. Throughout the sixties he was one of the biggest draws on the folk scene and made dozens of albums, but it was as a live performer that he was at his best.

Guitar virtuosity was rare in the early folk clubs but one musician who stood above the rest was Davy Graham. Eccentric in behaviour and eclectic in his music, he was more interested in playing and experimenting than seeking fame or fortune. He inspired a host of guitarists from Bert Jansch and Jimmy

Page to a thousand would-be players who tried but failed to master his instrumental composition 'Anji', first released on an EP 3/4 AD in 1961. His Folk, Blues & Beyond *album in 1964 was followed by a collaboration with Shirley Collins on* Folk Roots, New Routes, *a fusion of traditional folk, jazz and blues that pioneered a new genre of acoustic music.*

Like Alex Campbell, Robin Hall and Jimmie Macgregor had left Glasgow and moved to London. Another Glaswegian, Nigel Denver, did the same. Louis Killen moved down from Gateshead. His fellow Geordie, Bob Davenport, was already there, as was Bill Leader, who had arrived from Bradford.

For anyone with aspiration or ambition to make their way in folk music in the early sixties, London was the epicentre of the burgeoning scene. Bedsits were easy to find, casual work was available for those who needed it, Melody Maker *ran a folk music column each week, and on a Saturday night there was only one place to be: the Troubadour in Old Brompton Road, where the inimitable Martin Winsor and Redd Sullivan were residents.*

NIGEL DENVER

The London scene just exploded in the sixties, so many singers – Bob Davenport . . . myself . . . Martin Carthy . . . Trevor Lucas. When I came to London in 1960 there was nobody singing Scottish music so I thought, 'This is it', and turned pro.

I got to know Carthy and one or two of them. You'd go down, say, 'Any chance of a song?' and people would hear you. I went down to the Troubadour and sang one Saturday and Jenny Barton booked me for a month later. I'd got my feet under the table. Everybody came to the Troubadour – Tom Paxton and Paul Simon . . . Dylan . . . I fell out with him.

When Jeannie Robertson came to the Troubadour I had to look after her. Jenny Barton said, 'Any taxis you need, get them. The Troubadour will pay.' She was a nice old lady. I looked after her and she enjoyed herself. We went down Oxford Street. She wanted to go into Marks and Spencer. She came out and she'd bought me a pair of socks. She said, 'Wear these and you'll be famous.'

JENNY BARTON

Jack Elliott was at the Troubadour every Saturday night. When he went back to the States I got in touch with Martin Carthy and other singers started to appear – Bob Davenport, the Liverpool Spinners, Shirley Collins was back from America, Jimmie Macgregor, Seamus Ennis at least once. By 1961 I had added Enoch Kent, Alex Campbell, the Thameside Four, Louis Killen, Cyril Tawney and the Ian Campbell group.

The basement room was probably no more than sixteen foot by sixteen foot and it had an area at the back where the coffee machine was. It started at ten o'clock and if you got there by eight you might get a seat. We didn't have that many seats because they took up room. If you didn't get there at eight you sat on the floor or you sat on top of somebody else or you didn't sit at all. I'm sure it contravened every health and safety regulation going.

It ended when the singers were too tired to go on. Towards the end we were stopping by about 2 or 3 a.m. but in the early days some of us were kipping on the floor and going home at six!

By the end of the night Diz Disley would usually show up and he'd always do a bit of an instrumental if there was someone to do it with. He'd do one of his monologues and the audience knew every word of it and absolutely loved it. They'd hear the same one over and over again. He was great.

In theory we didn't have a resident, but in actual fact Martin Carthy was usually there because he'd come on from somewhere else or because he'd been booked, which was a bit more frequent than other people because he was the best singer we had by miles, and the best at handling an audience.

I was lucky to have Martin as a frequent and paid singer, often at very short notice – he helped me out of many and various holes – and as an unpaid singer when he just turned up. He acted as a magnet to other singers and musicians and his cheerfulness was infectious. He was a godsend to a club organiser.

MARTIN CARTHY
I first met Dave Swarbrick down at the Troubadour, not knowing who the hell he was. This was before I played the Campbells' club and stayed at his house. There was an American old-timey group from Harvard University called the Charles River Valley Boys. There were three of them, a guitar player, Clay Jackson, a banjo player, Bob Siggins, and a mandolin and fiddle player called Ethan Signer. They were over for their summer break and they had a hell of a lot to do with my guitar playing improving, and my understanding of music. They were fabulous. You really got a sense of how songs move around and how they change. They sang that mermaid song, 'One Sunday morn when we set sail, landlubbers lying down below'. They sang it with this chorus where the landlord lies sleeping down below.

   They were a smashing bunch and great musicians. Then the fiddle player Ethan Signer went home, so Clay Jackson and Bob Siggins were left and they wanted a fiddle player. They met Dave Swarbrick: 'You're a fiddle player, come and play with us at the Troubadour.' So my first sight of Dave Swarbrick is him standing there with a bewildered look on his face, trying to play fiddle to this old-timey music. He had no idea.

DAVE SWARBRICK
It was a night off from the Campbells. I was at the Troubadour and the Charles River Valley Boys called me up from the floor. Then they wrote me a letter asking me to go on tour with them but as it was a tour of the US Army bases I wasn't that keen. I didn't fancy it at all and I didn't do it. I wish I'd kept the letter – come and join us, we'll do the army bases and we'll make a pisspot full of money. They were the words. The pisspot full of money was tempting but that was all.

ETHAN SIGNER *Charles River Valley Boys*
In October 1962 I moved from the USA to Cambridge, England.
I lived in Cambridge for two years and during that time went
to clubs in London and elsewhere but the only one I remember
now is the Troubadour. We had a gig at the Troub but that night
it was closed by the police for some reason.

COLIN WILKIE *began in 1961 in London clubs and toured the
circuit as a duo with his wife Shirley Hart before relocating to
the Continent*
I'd put the Troubadour in the pole position of London clubs, for
its ambience, its performers, its welcomingness. The club was
down in the cellar. Upstairs the decorations were amazing –
instruments and other bits and bobs dangling from the ceiling, a
marvellous old juke box, old enamel signs, all kinds of wonderful
junk.

Downstairs, the club had a tiny stage – behind which was
a small dressing room – and an audience area which got well
crowded. There was also a garden out in the back, and when
Shirley and I held a farewell evening before returning to France
one year so many fellow performers turned up to play, and so
many punters – a whole bus load came up from Portsmouth –
that we had to throw open the doors and the overspill went out
back into the garden.

The Troub was where we all used to gather late on Saturdays,
after finishing our gigs elsewhere There were some really
incredible sessions. It was all so cool and non-pigeon-holed:
folkies and rockers and blues musos all simply having fun
together, not questioning what genre it was.

DOLLY TERFUS *folk music enthusiast*
I started to going to the Troubadour in March 1961. I heard Judith
Silver was singing there. Her voice was just something and she
had a great selection of songs. After that I went every Saturday.
Redd Sullivan was already singing there, with the Thameside

Four. The music and the atmosphere was different to anything I'd grown up with. There was no alcohol. You bought a ticket for two and six, on special nights it was five shillings, and on really special nights it was ten bob.

People had heard of the Troubadour. When Paul Simon first came over he used to sleep on Redd Sullivan's floor. He'd just come into the country and he begged room space to put his head. There was a woman called Judith Pieppe, social worker down the East End. She had a radio programme, *Five to Ten*, on the Home Service on Monday morning, and she elected that Paul would sing his song 'I Am a Rock'. I can remember him in the Troubadour, sitting on the bench, finishing off the last bits of that song. When Paul and Art came over, under their arms they had fifty pressings of *Wednesday Morning 3 A.M.*, and I've got one.

JEANNIE WINSOR *married to Martin Winsor, one-time host at the Troubadour*

Martin Winsor in his younger days performed in cabaret and working men's clubs before becoming interested in skiffle. He began to investigate the emerging folk music scene, then he went along to the few clubs and coffee bars in London where it was possible to obtain a guest spot or join in or listen.

One evening in Soho he chanced upon a huge man with red hair. It was Redd Sullivan, who happened to be on leave from the merchant navy. As Martin later described it to me, 'When I heard Redd sing, it was so exciting I couldn't wait to get on stage and join him.' They performed together in clubs, concerts and festivals, anywhere they could. In the early days they busked to make ends meet. This extremely close friendship/partnership lasted until they died two months apart in 1992.

Redd took over the running of the Troubadour with Seamus Ewens from Anthea Joseph who'd managed the club evenings and bookings for some considerable time. Redd ran the evening as host while Seamus arranged the bookings and the taking of the entrance fee. This didn't last very long and Redd then asked

Martin to join him in the running of the club. Martin arranged all the bookings as well as performing with Redd as hosts.

There were so many fantastic evenings at the Troubadour, lots of well-known American artists – Paul Simon, Tom Paxton, Buffy Sainte-Marie, Doc Watson. The nights that remain with me are the evenings with Carthy and Swarbrick when it was so packed it was hard to breathe. The audience didn't want the evening to end. Evenings with Alex Campbell were memorable too. He held an audience like no other performer did at that time, making them laugh hysterically one minute and in tears the next. There were so many other artists – the saying was if you were anyone on the folk scene then you had to have played the Troubadour.

PAUL SNOW *played the clubs in the sixties*
Martin and Redd very often would put somebody on, then nip back into a little room behind the stage. If it was somebody that Martin didn't know who'd come along and asked if they could sing, he never refused. But if he put somebody on and they were crap, he'd let them do like one verse and then he'd come out.

He was a big man, a big voice. 'Thank you so much, thank you so much, so good of you to come and sing for us . . .' pushing them off the stage. The guy's going, 'Bbbbut . . .' and Martin's saying, 'Take applause, take applause . . .' You got a lot of people who thought they were brilliant when they were actually terrible. A club like the Troubadour – they'd heard it all before and they'd heard it done better.

TONY DAVIS
We sang regularly in London at the Troubadour. I don't remember ever going to the Troubadour when Martin Carthy wasn't there. It was a great club. Whenever we went to London, whatever we did on a Saturday night, we'd finish up at the Troubadour.

There was a guy had two clubs north of London. We used to sing in London at the weekend and finish Sunday night at his club. We'd go back to his house for sandwiches and a cup of tea, then we'd all climb into the van and Cliff would drive us back to Liverpool for work on Monday morning. We were young and we were keen. Cliff used to take Monday morning off, he'd have a kip and then go to work. I went straight to school to teach. I'd be calling the register and falling asleep.

LOUIS KILLEN

In 1961 I got fired from my job and I went to London. I was staying with a friend who lived the other side of the Oval so Brixton was the nearest Labour Exchange but there wasn't any work so I was signing on. I was getting odd gigs in the London area clubs that were starting up and even some of them out of town. You got about two quid a night if you were lucky. I went to one in Reading on a Tuesday night. I couldn't get back to London to sign on as I had to on a Wednesday, so they called me. This was early 1962. They said, 'If you miss again . . .' and I said, 'Fuck you', and signed off. I was making maybe ten shillings to thirty shillings more a week singing in the clubs than I was drawing the dole.

FRANKIE ARMSTRONG *unaccompanied singer of mostly traditional songs, a resident at the Singers' Club*
I had a bedsit in Clapham and Louis Killen was singing at a folk club in south London, so I went along to hear him. I can remember sitting there, looking at this man with his very lively eyes and thinking just how wonderful his singing was, just being very struck by him.

Fairly early on we started a relationship and I would travel around to his gigs when I was free – I did floor singing. I think my voice at that point still sounded somewhat plummy. Louis said, 'Frankie – listen to some of the traditional singers and the people who base themselves on the traditional singers.' So it was particularly Jeannie Robertson, Isobel Sutherland, Ray Fisher and more of the Scots. I just started to play with my voice, to find a different way of way of producing it which had more of an edge to it. I can remember listening to the records that Louis lent me, records that I later bought, and just imitating them.

For a couple of years we sang together. We did folk clubs. We did some of the fairly classic repertoire – the Copper brothers, the Holmfirth Anthem, 'Spencer the Rover'. Louis had such a great ear for harmonies. I'm really sorry that there were never any recordings made of us because I think we did sound very good together.

As a result of travelling around and singing with him and doing solo songs myself from the floor, people started to invite me to go back as a soloist. That was how I first had this strange experience of people saying, 'And what is your fee?' My recollection is that I halved Louis's fee and said £6 or something like that. Exmouth, I think that was my first booking.

JOE BOYD *an American based in London, produced records by Shirley Collins, Incredible String Band, Fairport Convention, Nick Drake and John Martyn, among others*
My first experience of a folk club was the Roundhouse on a Monday night during the Blues and Gospel Caravan tour in April 1964. Brownie McGhee and Sonny Terry and Gary Davis came on a night off and Rod Stewart was in the audience.

After the end of the tour Redd Sullivan took me to the Black Horse in Rathbone Place, where I heard Dave Swarbrick with the Ian Campbell group. I don't haven't much recollection of the crowd, but I was stunned by Swarb's playing and the joyous sound of the group.

I met the Ian Campbell group again next time they came to London. Ian invited me to stay, so I took my motorcycle to Birmingham. We went in Ioan Allen's Bentley to a couple of gigs, one at the student union in Coventry. Ioan Allen went from managing the Ian Campbell Folk Group to running Dolby labs in the US.

I barely remember their club – I only went once, I think. I remember driving to clubs around the Midlands, wandering the

Bull Ring, and pushing Ian's sons, Robin and Ali, on the swings.

BILL LEADER
Gill Cook and I started the Broadside club at the Black Horse in about 1962. Either Bob Davenport or Enoch Kent ran the evening and held it together, and there'd be floor singers. We used to turn out a little news sheet maybe once a month. Bob Dylan came to the Black Horse at one point.

We ran several things at a place in Swiss Cottage. We had Little Walter there – they were just looking for a night for him to do something. The fee was extremely reasonable. We put him on and the place was packed out, many more times than it would ever be for any established folk act. I was busy taking tickets at the door.

COLIN WILKIE
The first night Bert Jansch sang 'Needle of Death' it was in the Black Horse folk club. Shirley and I were doing an evening with Alex Campbell. It was either the day of Buck Polly's funeral or shortly afterwards. I recall Buck being a nice lad, but as troubled as the song says. He had a photo of his baby son, who, I believe, had died, stuck to the inside of his instrument case. We weren't big mates or anything, but we did know him when we were all street singing in Paris, and then back in Blighty. Bert Jansch just named the song and played it.

JIMMIE MACGREGOR
Robin Hall came down to London about a year after me. We hardly knew each other but because we were Scottish – it threw us together. Then in 1959 we went to the Vienna Youth Festival, separately, and again we were thrown on stage together. It was rough as a bear's arse but it kinda worked. Paul Robeson was on that show and he was very encouraging to us. His line was two young guys singing the songs of their own country and all that stuff. So I said to Robin, 'Look, if somebody like Paul Robeson

gives you a pat on the back, maybe we should work on this.'

There was a guy called Malcolm Nixon, part of that left-wing coterie. I was involved with that as well, and Malcolm was setting up as an agent and he started to get Robin and me folk club gigs. Then we very quickly started picking up radio work, then later on we had the Galliard, a quartet, with Leon Rosselson. There was *Easybeat* with Brian Matthew, *Guitar Club*, there was *Saturday Skiffle Club* and there were very few people around at that time so we were picking up work.

The big leap forward was when we got the *Tonight* programme on television. Malcolm Nixon phoned them up. He said, 'Are you doing anything about Burns Night? I've got a couple of young Scots lads here who could sing you a Burns song.' In fact Robin knew bits of some Burns songs and I knew bits of others, but we didn't know one together all the way through. We just told lies, as one does. We sat in the taxi going there and I worked out the chords and harmonies and tried to remember the words to 'Rantin' Rovin' Robin'.

We went on and did it – everything was live – and they gave us a week's trial, which extended to four years, five days a week. We went through hundreds and hundreds of songs – so many we had to learn them very quickly and forget them very quickly to make way for tomorrow night.

Tonight was a colossal shop window for us. We went from singing to thirty to sixty people in a folk club to that first night we were on, when we were singing to nearly ten million people. So within weeks you were a household name. That's a corny phrase but it's true. We were in right at the very beginning and people now are acknowledging the influence of the *Tonight* programme – for the first time that kind of music was getting a general audience.

IAN McCANN *played guitar and mandolin with the Malcolm Price Trio and later Orange Blossom Sound*
There was very little recorded music and if you heard it you

couldn't always work out what was actually happening, what the fingering was. You'd get these magic kind of moments when things suddenly clicked. I remember picking up the first tune, watching Robin Hall and Jimmy Macgregor on TV. Jimmie Macgregor was a good player and they played 'Foggy Mountain Top' and I thought, 'I'll try and work that out.' Just holding a C chord and picking out the melody, and it suddenly clicked.

In 1960 I was at Goldsmiths in the School of Art. We decided to open a folk club at a pub, the New Cross House. It was probably one of the first clubs in that part of south-east London. We had a momentous night – it was that student network. These were early days, before clubs started springing up. We booked Peggy Seeger and Ewan MacColl came down. It was packed, people came from all over the place.

A real moment for me was when we had Pete Stanley, I guess in '61. That was my first experience of the bluegrass banjo, Scruggs-style picking. He had an American chap with him, Clay Jackson, the two of them were fantastic – a life-changing moment for me.

I was singing and playing at the club. I remember buying the Alan Lomax book, *American Folk Guitar* – you searched anywhere, there were so few records around and not many books either. About that time I discovered Collett's bookshop and that was a real Mecca. I used to go to the Cellar Club in Greek Street. It was a place where anybody passing through would play. A regular there was Steve Benbow – he played this old Gibson Kalamazoo. That was the first time I heard flat-picking, hearing Steve Benbow.

HYLDA SIMS

Steve Benbow was very much part of the scene and part of the crossover between American and skiffle and English folk music as well. He was a very good guitarist at a time that there weren't many about, and he had a really eclectic style. He was one of the first very good guitarists to adapt to English folk. He used to play at the Skiffle Cellar a lot. He became a taxi driver.

DAVE COUSINS *leader of the Strawberry Hill Boys, who became the Strawbs*

Tony Hooper and myself used to get together at the London Apprentice in Isleworth every Friday evening. We'd sit there and play and eventually we got a mandolin player and somebody said, 'We want to book you, what's the name of the group?' We were playing bluegrass, Flatt and Scruggs stuff in those days, and because I was interested in the Foggy Mountain Boys and the Rocky Mountain Boys I said, 'Well, we're the Strawberry Hill Boys.'

The first place we played was at Hylda Sims's house, she ran a folk club in the basement. We were doing 'Foggy Mountain Breakdown' and 'Blue Ridge Mountain Blues'. Then we met up with a couple of potential managers – Shel Talmy, who was producing the Kinks, and his partner Mike Stone. They said, 'How about doing a current pop song?' So we went away and rehearsed 'Dance on' by the Shadows and put a dance routine to it. It brought the house down in the folk clubs, went down a storm.

We applied for a BBC audition, passed it and I phoned up Jimmy Grant, who was the producer of *Saturday Club*, and he booked us. We appeared on that with the Beatles and Chris Barber's jazz band as Dave Cousins and Tony Hooper. That was our first ever radio show.

DAVE ARTHUR *singer of traditional songs with his wife, Toni*

I dropped out of school by the time I was fifteen and adopted a bohemian look of black sweater and tight jeans, duffle coat and sandals. I left home and was living in Soho with another young guy, Mik Paris, whom I'd met on the train. Mik played the guitar and we sang together in the coffee bars and clubs around London as well as under the arches below Charing Cross station.

A fellow busker and pavement artist was Clive Palmer, later a founder member of the Incredible String Band. I was fascinated by Clive's strange twenties-silent-movie-style jazzy tunes and blues on the five-string banjo. We occasionally busked together, with him playing banjo and me singing things like Donegan's 'Nobody's Child'. We had a collapsible top hat for collecting money from the crowd that could be closed and secreted under a jacket if the police came along and moved us on.

RALPH McTELL *writer of 'The Streets of London'*
I saw Wizz Jones playing on Brighton beach and I became absolutely devoted to his playing. He was the real article. He plays blues like those old black guys do. He misses bars out and he plays riffs as long as he wants to. He's almost impossible to play with, he just does his own thing.

The first floor spot I did was at Thornton Heath. There used to be a pond there at the roundabout with a pie stall and a little pub called the Wheatsheaf and I played upstairs. I played Woody Guthrie and some Elizabeth Cotten songs like 'Freight Train' and 'Oh, Babe, It Ain't No Lie'. I was seventeen.

DEREK SARJEANT *guitarist and singer, toured with his wife Hazel King and ran club at Surbiton Assembly Rooms*
In those days, in the early sixties, there weren't that many folk singers around and we used to meet together and open clubs for very little money. You'd go miles for a fiver. Diz Disley used to go for a bottle of brandy. It was a great, friendly scene. The atmosphere in clubs was completely different to what it is these days. Now you get the big festivals, but folk clubs are not supported like they used to be.

I started the club at Surbiton Assembly Rooms in 1961 with Gerry Lockran. Alex Campbell came to the opening. Sandy Denny was a member. She lived in Wimbledon, which wasn't far away. Some of these people I took for granted, I've got to say. I didn't realise Sandy Denny's potential, really. She came along and did floor spots and I reluctantly booked her a few times because Sandy Glennon, the agent, persisted. I didn't honestly recognise that she was going to be such a legend.

John Martyn used to come along, Chris Deja and Keith Relf

of the Yardbirds – I taught them the guitar. I told them, never learn clawhammer, and they went away and became famous as the Yardbirds. Eric Clapton was a member, he was studying at Kingston Art College. I never heard him play at the club but he's in the membership book, he joined in about 1962. John Renbourn was a member. I knew John when he was seventeen. He was studying classical guitar and he came along and did floor spots.

PEGGY SEEGER

When I first came to this country I didn't realise how long it would take to get from Glasgow down to Leicester. There were no motorways when we first started out. So I would book us in Glasgow one night and in Leicester the next night. It would take eight hours, nine hours. You'd arrive absolutely exhausted. I did the bookings. I did all the arrangements. Ewan didn't do any of that. But then, I'm an organisation queen, I take over!

We always refused to sing where there was a bar in the room. There was one club in the north-east where we were booked and we didn't know there was a bar. We asked if they could keep it quiet but every time we started singing an unaccompanied song they'd take out the drawer of the cash register and empty it and start counting all the cash.

The Lincolnshire clubs were often hard to sing in because the people are very quiet about their appreciation. You know, just a ripple of applause, then at the end they come up and say, 'That was great', 'That was wonderful.' In Dunstable there were no seats. There were two rows and everybody else stood.

In those days a lot of people smoked and that was very difficult. I remember singing in the Southampton club, the Foc'sle, I think it was called, and there was this guy in the front row trying desperately to light a match so that he could smoke. And Ewan said, 'What's wrong mate, not enough oxygen in here?' But Ewan smoked on stage. Oh, yes, he did until he gave it up in 1979.

JOHN RENBOURN

MacColl had a sort of stranglehold on the movement. Occasionally you'd see somebody like Gerry Lockran, who played really good blues and had a great stage presence. He was a true professional. And the fact that he knew Brownie McGhee made him practically a god. He learned first-hand from him. Gerry Lockran was just fabulous and he had all the gigs. I saw him at the British Legion in Guildford.

Gerry took me under his wing, so the first paid gig I ever had on the so-called folk club scene was at the Roundhouse in Wardour Street. I was about eighteen, so it would be around 1962. The guy who ran it then was called Curly Goss. He was a small-time hustler. Gerry Lockran got me up, gave me a big introduction, did me proud, and at the end of the night Curly Goss paid me. He gave me a note. I ran down the alleyway to buy some wine. It turned out he'd paid me a foreign note.

One of the earliest gigs I had was playing on the same bill as Jesse Fuller. That was an experience I'll never forget. He was the biggest legend of the lot in those days, in terms of 'San Francisco Bay Blues', and he was an old hobo. I was young and anticipating it all and I got to the gig. It was in this big municipal building. There wasn't a dressing room, but backstage there were all these chairs and oil paintings and big sofas – and his guitar, a twelve-string Stellar, was on the table. So I looked round to see where he was and I couldn't see him. Then I heard someone snoring under the table – he was asleep on the floor.

DEREK SARJEANT

Davy Graham was an odd character. I had him several times at my club and he never let me down, although once I was really worried. He purported to have a black belt for judo and he rang me in the afternoon. He said, 'Derek, I'm at your club tonight but I don't know what to do. I was in a bar and I bought this lady a gin and a guy came over and Bang! He knocked one of my teeth out and really hurt me. I had no chance whatsoever – you know I'm a black belt. I don't know what I'm going to do.'

I said, 'Oh dear, Davy, shall I get somebody else along?' He said, 'No, I'm going to try and make it.' He came along, there wasn't a mark on him and he didn't even mention it. And he played terrifically.

You never knew what he was going to play. People would shout 'Anji', 'Anji', but he wouldn't play it. You never knew, but they accepted whatever he did.

I went to Germany with him on a tour once and he brought his mother along. She was very domineering. The agent had put up some posters at some of the places we were playing. So Davy arrived at this place and there was a poster of him. He said, 'No, I'm not playing in a place like this, I don't like that poster.' And he didn't play. The next night, same poster in a different place. He said, 'I like that poster, that's a good one. That's the best!'

I went somewhere up north. They said, 'Davy Graham was here last week. He got here early and about an hour before he was supposed to start he sat on the stage, playing, and when it came time to go on he said, I've done my spot.'

SHIRLEY COLLINS

We made one album together, *Folk Roots, New Routes*, which I shall always be glad of and I feel privileged to have made that album with him. I remember one gig at the Lyric, Hammersmith, which I was nervous about as we were on the same bill as the London Youth Jazz Orchestra. Then there was a concert at Cecil Sharp House which I enjoyed. There were other concerts and a few folk clubs. I didn't go along with Davy's drug use – I never took drugs myself and couldn't understand why people did.

JOHN RENBOURN

Folk Roots, New Routes was the combination of those two characters: both of them had a high profile and both of them were regarded as amazing in their own way. The fact that they teamed up was an extraordinary thing but it was masterminded by Shirley's husband, Austin John Marshall, he was kinda pushing her in that direction.

It didn't last, the partnership, but when it did work they absolutely broke the door down. There's no doubt about it. That was *the* record. It changed everything. Not only was he a great player, he was a great thinker. He was the boss, old Davy. His ideas changed the whole thing. They didn't do many gigs together, Davy was spending more time in Tangiers than he was anywhere else.

I knew him, yes, but I don't know if anybody knew him very well. He was an extraordinary personality, an incredible guy but people generally shied away from him a little bit 'cos he was so kinda bizarre. There are several books in Davy Graham's life, without doubt. His mother used to go with him to gigs and in some ways she was crazier that he was.

SHIRLEY COLLINS

Davy was a wonderful, unique musician, but often difficult and moody. For instance, on a couple of occasions when we were gigging out of London, he refused to travel on the same train, and that was rather undermining, as well as inconvenient. Ultimately I felt it wasn't the way I wanted to go musically, and I wanted to work with someone I felt completely comfortable with.

Cue my sister, Dolly! I loved the sound of the early instruments that she wrote for, and her arrangements were so lovely, so sympathetic and so English. It all felt perfect and Dolly and I were always very close and had a great time gigging together.

But we couldn't really make a living at it, because we didn't own the flute-organ. We had to hire it for every booking and it was expensive. Sadly, one night at the Hampstead folk club, when I came back into the room after the interval, there was a bloke sitting in the front row with his feet up on the keyboard. That made us think twice about taking it into a club.

BOB DAVENPORT

Alex Campbell ran a fantastic club in Richmond. Cyril Davies and

I did it together once. It was like a concert, stage and everything, and it was packed every Sunday night. When I first met Alex in Long Acre, he got up and I thought, 'You've just missed out. You would have been one of the great all-time music hall performers.' He'd been singing in Paris and he was tremendous. You just felt like the ghost of Will Fyffe and all those people was up there.

With Alex it became this cycle of needing to drink to perform. And then he drank too much. But Alex – and Billy Connolly – if they hadn't moved out of Glasgow and into the folk clubs, they would have been famous in their area, working in the shipyards, working the working men's clubs. The characters who played the music halls – there was no difference.

JIMMIE MACGREGOR

Alex was an old pal. He never was a big commercial success and he wasn't a good singer or a good guitar player and when you listen to his albums they're really hand-knitted and rough, but he was a brilliant, ebullient, extrovert character. A couple of times he turned up in our audiences, as a pal, but he would always be shouting up at you. Not heckling you exactly but getting involved. At one point I stopped in the middle of a song and I said, 'Alex, for fuck's sake stop helping us, will you!'

JIM McLEAN

He could come over as a bit of a gobshite but he was very intelligent, he had great charisma. I met him first of all probably in 1960 when I moved down to London with Nigel Denver. We were in this club and Alex was guest that night. They asked for floor singers. So Nigel got up and said he was going to sing 'Maggie's Waddin', the song that I wrote about Princess Margaret's wedding. Alex said, 'You canna sing that, that's my song.' He'd heard Ewan McVicar singing it beforehand.

I was sitting in the audience, so we got chatting later on and Alex thought I was Josh McRae. He didn't really know anything about the Scottish folk scene at all. He'd just come back from

France where he'd been busking. Most of the songs that he sang were American songs.

CLIVE PALMER *banjo player, original member of the Incredible String Band*
I went to Paris to busk in 1957 and the first people I saw were Davy Graham and Alex Campbell sitting in a café. I busked there for three years. Alex was another whose downfall was the bottle.

IAN McCANN
Johnny Orange was already accompanying Alex and Alex said, 'Do you want to join me? I've got a residency at the Jolly Blacksmith at Fulwell. I'll pay you seven and six a night.' As an art student I thought that was good, a bit of money and the kudos of playing with Alex. We played Scottish folk songs, blues, whatever he felt like playing. He was living at Streatham. He had a flat with his wife Patsy and his boys. We used to go over there and have a bit of a practice. It wasn't intense rehearsal.

We played mostly around London. We didn't go far out beyond Hitchin and the Home Counties, and when I wasn't with him he was working all the time, solo. He was very supportive of young musicians – when I made the decision to give up art school and play music, he tried to persuade me not to do it. He said, 'You should finish the course.' He was very supportive of young musicians.

I made about five records with him, possibly six . . . *Way Out West . . . Folk Sessions . . . Best Loved Songs of Bonnie Scotland* . . . The first one – we went up to a studio in Swiss Cottage and it was all done in one afternoon and an evening. There was an invited audience from Addlestone Folk Club, another of the really notable clubs and a club that would book top names.

One day I ran into Alex with Bruce Dunnett and Nigel Denver at Collett's bookshop and went on a drinking spree with them. They were drinking McEwan's with Scotch chasers and we were going from club to club. We went to the Singers' Club, where

Ewan MacColl was up. There was a bit of a tension at that point with Alex, an atmosphere.

I was eighteen or nineteen and I was keeping up with these hardened drinkers until we moved on to the Troubadour. My last memory is going down the steps – Shirley Collins was on and I literally collapsed at her feet, spewing everywhere. I can remember the song she was singing – 'Come You Not from Newcastle . . .' with the banjo. There was a chap that I was at art school with, he just happened to be there and he carried me to his place in Kensington, where I recovered through the next day. I think Alex and Nigel just carried on drinking.

COLIN WILKIE

We were driving home from a gig one night in a draughty, noisy, rattly old van through one of the less salubrious areas, when two geezers reeled across the pavement clouting each other. 'Stop the van,' yelled Campbell. He leaped out and headed for the punch-up. I silently cursed him. I had no desire to get thumped, but he was my friend, so I had to help him, the daft sod. Before anyone could lay a finger on my cowardly body, it was all over. Alex put his arms round the two blokes, said, 'Come on, lads, we've got enough trouble in the world without you two fighting, now make up and be friends.' Amazingly they did just that, wrapped their arms round each other's shoulders, and staggered off down the road.

Another night, some time in 1964 or '65, we played a big concert at the Fairfield Hall in Croydon, along with Alex, Steve Benbow, John Pearse and the Strawberry Hill Boys.

We all gathered together for a grand finale and Alex said, 'We'll do "Goodnight Irene".' He stepped forward, threw back his head and started to sing the first line of the song. In that instant, two things happened: his two front teeth, which were on a dental palate, shot out of his mouth and then his hand came out like lightning, and caught his flying choppers in mid-air. He turned to Benbow and said, 'Lucky it wisnae ye wig, Steve.'

IAN CAMPBELL

I learned an enormous amount from Alex. He taught me about presentation. He could handle an audience like nobody else. He was brilliant. We were at the Troubadour, about 1960, '61. We were on the stage for about forty minutes. We sang ten songs. I'd say, 'This song is called . . .' and we'd sing it . . . 'This song is called . . .'

Alex just sat there and afterwards he said, 'How many songs did you do?' I said, 'Nine . . . ten maybe.' Alex said, 'The time you were up there, I'd have done three. But they'd have appreciated them because they would have had time to think in between . . . time to absorb the tempo and listen to the words.' He said, 'You killed your stuff. You were brilliant, tempo and everything, but they didn't have time to breathe between the songs. You've got to relax for Christ's sake.' He said, 'Imagine that you're at a family party . . . you might do four songs but you're telling us about the songs, where you got 'em from . . .'

We watched him. He did twenty minutes and I think he did three songs, and each one was introduced by a story or a joke. In one song he stopped halfway through, chatted away and changed the key then carried on. He was so relaxed. It was magic. I began to work on it and it was true enough. A year later people were saying to me, 'So who've you been studying?' Alex Campbell – he was a one-off.

BILLY CONNOLLY *original member of the Humblebums before his career as a comedian*

The first time I saw him, in his denim jacket and the cowboy boots and carrying that big Gibson guitar, I thought, 'That's what I want to be.' He had a camel-hair donkey jacket and I spent months searching for one of those.

I got to know him quite well but I didn't like a lot of the things he did, he'd become a wee bit passé. One thing I learned a great lesson from – he would turn up and there'd be hardly anyone in the club, maybe about twenty people, and he would harangue them. He harangued the ones that had turned up because he was angry at the ones that didn't. He would say to the audience, 'My name's Alex Campbell, I'm a legend.' Oh aye? I'll be the judge of that, thank you very much.

PEGGY SEEGER

Alex was a good-hearted, often very nice, singer. Ewan didn't have a whole lot of respect for his singing. Alex was an entertainer. I think both Ewan and I felt that an awful lot of serious folk songs shouldn't be used as entertainment. They should be used for people to enjoy them but Alex used to clown them. We didn't think that was kinda fair.

RALPH McTELL

I was in the shop at Watkins Music in Balham High Road when he bought that guitar, the Gibson J200. He bought it from my mate Chris Ayliffe and he didn't even have a case for it. He tied a bit of string round his neck, put it on his back and walked out the shop. That was Alex.

DEREK SARJEANT

Dominic Behan was a great performer. I'd seen him perform at the Troubadour and I wanted to have him at my club. This was 1964. Lots of clubs were making contracts over the telephone, the usual thing in those days. You didn't have an actual signed contract. The week before, the guest hadn't turned up so we were already suffering a bit from that, had to do a lot of apologising.

Then Dominic didn't turn up. I was very angry and I put an advert in the *Melody Maker*, that we deplored the fact that neither the earlier guest nor Dominic Behan had turned up. Eric Winter drew attention to it in his column: he said he supported me. So Dominic sued myself and Odhams Press, who published the *Melody Maker*, and he got the famous solicitor Ellis Lincoln on the job.

It went on for months, it seemed like years, and right at the point where we were going to go to court Dominic dropped it all. Dominic unfortunately was quite known for not turning up and I'd got support from other club organisers who he'd let down, but I was a bit worried at the time.

KARL DALLAS

The *Melody Maker* hated folk music. I wrote a few things for them and Jack Hutton, who was the editor. He said, 'Karl, I hate folk music, but there are idiots who buy the paper because we have two pages of folk in it. Fill those pages. You know what they want to read. Don't bother me and don't get me involved in any litigation.'

I'd been writing a column for the *MM* then I went off to join Billy Smart's Circus as advance publicity manager, and Eric Winter took over. Eric wanted to set the record straight on songs that Dominic Behan was claiming to have written, especially when Dominic was claiming that Bob Dylan had stolen the tune for 'With God on Our Side' from him. Dominic was very litigious and he sued the *Melody Maker*. Dominic claimed to have written songs that were common currency before he was born.

JIMMIE MACGREGOR

After a few years I said to Robin Hall we should go back into the clubs because that's where we started, and also it'll be fun. We went to our agent. He said, 'You're not going back into the folk clubs, you need to make money!' But we said, no, we are. So every summer we took a few weeks off and we did the folk clubs.

We took a lot of stick for being too commercial. Later on you realise that probably 80 per cent of it was just petty jealousy. Robin and I were really successful. We were touring the world, making a lot of money, playing the Albert Hall and the Festival Hall. You hate to think that way but a lot of the criticism comes from people who were not very good themselves.

What also I noticed was that, as the years went by, a lot of things that I was doing, the counter-melodies and canons, they're all doing that now if you listen to the folk groups that are really successful. Their arrangements are quite complicated and they don't bear any relation to the source singers like Jeannie Robertson and Sam Larner. It bears no relation and why should it? These people were the source.

4 When Dylan played the King and Queen

The week before Christmas in 1962 Bob Dylan arrived in London. He was almost unknown at the time. He had been playing coffee houses in New York City for less than two years and his first album, released the previous March, made little impact on either side of the Atlantic. He came to England at the behest of a BBC television director, Philip Saville, who had seen him perform in a New York café and cast him in a play, Madhouse on Castle Street, written by playwright Evan Jones.

Dylan proved to be a poor actor but Saville recognised where his real talent lay and had him sing four songs in the play, including the hitherto unheard 'Blowin' in the Wind', and 'Ballad of the Gliding Swan', written by Evan Jones and never released on record by Dylan. The BBC long ago discarded their recording of Madhouse on Castle Street but the night it was broadcast a young folk enthusiast, Hans Fried, sitting at home, made an audio tape recording of the two songs, to the delight of future Dylanologists.

While he was in London, Dylan took the opportunity to visit several folk clubs. At the King and Queen in Goodge Street he was invited to sing by Martin Carthy, who recognised him from the cover of Sing Out! At the Singers' Club he failed to impress. A night at the Troubadour led to an altercation with Nigel Denver. Towards the end of his stay he visited the Troubadour again with fellow Americans Richard Farina, Eric von Schmidt and Ethan Signer, after recording some tracks with them at Dobell's record shop in Charing Cross Road. The resident that night was Martin Carthy, who joined Dylan and others for what is recalled as a chaotic performance.

Dylan's short time in London was both eventful and fruitful, especially in the exposure it gave him to British folk song.

Encouraged by his brash and hard-headed manager Albert Grossman, he took in all that was going on, later acknowledging how the music he heard in the London clubs had influenced him and citing Martin Carthy and Bob Davenport in particular.

Dylan was in London only four weeks. He left in January 1963 and the next time he came was May 1964, when he headlined at the Royal Festival Hall. By now he was befriended by the Beatles and the folk clubs were in the past. His last known visit to a London folk club was in October 1987 when he turned up unexpectedly at a club run by Bob Davenport at the Empress of Russia pub in St John Street, Islington. On that occasion, he did not get up and sing.

PHILIP SAVILLE *television director*
I was working at the BBC and one of the productions I was doing was a play by Evan Jones called *Madhouse on Castle Street*. It was set in a boarding house with a group of people: there was a man who locked himself in his room – he was sick of the world as it was. One of the people in the boarding house was a young poet and a few months before I had met this young man playing the guitar with the mouth organ strapped to his mouth at Tony Pastor's club in New York, singing these amazing songs.

I said, 'I've got the perfect man for this part.' The Beeb was rather like *Alice in Wonderland* then. You gave them an idea and before you knew it you were on a plane, going ahead with the project. I told them, 'There is this young man called Bobby Dylan', and they said, 'Well, why don't you go out and see if he'll do it?'

So I went back to New York and he was still playing in Tony Pastor's. I said, 'Do you remember when I came along and introduced myself a little while ago?' He said, 'Yes.' I said, 'I've got this play.' He said, 'You'll have to talk to my manager.' I'd left him a copy of the script. I'm not sure if he actually read it or not.

He came over and we put him up at the Mayfair Hotel in London, which happened to be owned by a couple of friends

of mine, the Danziger brothers. I took him round Carnaby
Street, it was then in the full flight of London's sixties reverie.
I remember filming him trying on all these little leather hats.
He bought a couple and subsequently began to wear them in
his concerts.

I was reasonably familiar with folk music because I met Alan
Lomax when I did a production of the play *Dark of the Moon* for
ITV, a few years before. That was all about folk music. Lomax was
living in London. He was the one who, before I did *Madhouse on
Castle Street*, really tuned me in to American folk music. He told
me all about 'Hang Down Your Head Tom Dooley' and things
like that.

Bobby came to the first reading – late, in spite of us sending a
car. We had the read-through of the play and everybody's there
– sound, camera, wardrobe, make-up, the odd producer. Then it
came to his part and in the play Evan Jones had written these
very poetic speeches about the status quo in the world, a young
man beefing about inequality, et cetera.

We cued him in and he just sunk down in his chair and shot
his hands into his jeans and just muttered, 'Mm . . . mm . . .
mm . . .' things like that. I looked at Evan Jones and I called
a ten-minute break and went over to him. I said, 'What's the
problem?' He said, 'I just can't say this stuff. It's not me.' I said,
'No, of course it's not you, it's acting'

He was a complete greenhorn and we finally realised we had
a bit of a problem. A re-cast was out of the question so we got
together, Evan and I, and we came up with this idea that maybe
we could make the part two parts – one was the poet and one was
the musician who shared the room.

When we told Bobby this, his face lit up. He said, 'Hey, that's
great. I can scat some songs there.' I said, 'Yes, and you may even
say a word like "hiya" or something!' He went away a happy
person.

During the time he was staying at the Mayfair Hotel he
had a habit of falling asleep in the foyer and rolling a joint and

smoking, fumigating the place. Finally, he was asked politely to leave the hotel. I had a house then in Hampstead, so I said, 'Why don't you come and stay with us, then you can live your life as you want.'

He had his guitar with him. He liked to sing some songs. At that time I had two young au pairs from Spain and one early morning about 6.45 or seven o'clock I heard the sound of the twanging guitar. I got up, put on my dressing gown and walked along the landing and there, at the foot of the landing, were the two au pairs gazing up with their mouths open like little young birds, with Bobby, who was sitting on the staircase playing 'Blowin' in the Wind'. I'd never heard this song before. I didn't interrupt. They were rapt. Finally he got up and I asked 'Bobby, would you sing the song on the show, on the opening and closing credits? I'll build a staircase.' He said, 'Yeah, yeah, sure.'

TONY DAVIS

I met Bob Dylan in the Folk Center in New York. He was sitting there with his feet up on the table while we were talking to him. I knew about him because he'd just started sending the odd song to the New York *Broadside*, which Pete Seeger used to send to me. Bob Dylan's first songs got printed in *Broadside*. He said, 'I was thinking of coming to England, how would I go?' I said, 'Well, really nobody knows anything about you in England.'

PEGGY SEEGER

Let's put it this way – neither of us, Ewan or I, listened to a whole lot to Bob Dylan's songs. We heard some of them. Neither of us liked his singing style. We'd met him before he was Bob Dylan. We met him in Minneapolis or St Paul's, somewhere out there, in 1960. I remember very well him coming up to Ewan for an autograph and he kept trying to talk to him. This was in the middle of a lot of other people milling around.

And Nolan, our host, the next time that we were in Minneapolis, he said, 'You remember that little guy that came up with his briefcase and just kept at you and wanted your autograph – that's Bob Dylan.' Ewan said, 'Who's Bob Dylan?'

DEREK SARJEANT

Bob Dylan came to my club at Surbiton, at the end of '62, when Carolyn Hester was booked with Dick Farina, who was her husband at the time. Dylan had played harmonica on her album. He didn't play at the club. He sat there but at that particular time nobody took much notice of him. To be honest I didn't even know he was there. Somebody told me afterwards.

MARTIN CARTHY

One day in '62 I went in Collett's bookshop on New Oxford Street and they had the new copy of *Sing Out!* And on the front was a picture of this bloke, Bob Dylan. A great fuss was being made about him and they printed his song 'Blowin' in the Wind'. There was this wonderful article about him – how he's the heir to Woody Guthrie and he's spent time with Woody Guthrie and gone to visit him in hospital. Then about three weeks later I was singing with the Thameside Four one Friday night at the King and Queen, back of Goodge Street, and who should walk in the door but the front cover of *Sing Out!*

I sang a couple of songs and walked over and I said, 'You're Bob Dylan, aren't you?' He said, 'Hey.' I said, 'I saw your picture on the front of *Sing Out!*' He said, 'Oh yeah?' I said, 'Would you like to sing a couple of songs?' He said, 'Ask me later.'

I went back and Marion Grey, one of the Thameside Four, said to me, 'Is he going to sing?' I said that he'd said to ask him later, so we got up and sang a couple of songs and as I finished I looked towards him and he just gave this ever so slight nod. I said, 'Do you want to do it now?' He said, 'Yeah.' So I introduced him as the bloke on the current cover of *Sing Out!* and he came up and he sang.

He was electrifying. He was brilliant. He always sang these funny ragtimey songs. Jack Elliott's was 'San Francisco Bay

Blues' and he had one similar to that. Then he did a talking blues – 'Talking John Birch'. I can't remember what the third song was but he took the place apart.

It was an L-shaped room and we sang from the corner. There'd be a hundred there at the most, probably eighty. He was very, very good indeed. Afterwards, we talked a lot and I said, 'Are you going to come to the Troubadour tomorrow?' He said, 'What's the Troubadour?' I told him and he said, 'Oh, Albert's told me about that place, maybe I'll come.' This was his manager, Albert Grossman.

And the next night he came down to the Troubadour. He came to the King and Queen every week and the Thameside Four had a gig at the Troubadour on the Tuesday. Then I would sing at the Troubadour on Saturday. And he came to all of those and sang. Different stuff every time – he never sang the same song twice.

He sang things like 'The Death of Emmett Till' and at the Troubadour he sang that wonderful one to the tune of 'Pretty Polly' – 'Hollis Brown'. I'll never forget the night he sang 'A Hard Rain's Gonna Fall', because he started – 'Where have you been my blue-eyed son / where have you been my handsome young one' and I'm thinking, 'Oh, he's going to sing Lord Randall.' But that line was where the similarity with Lord Randall ended. He just took off on this great song, 'Hard Rain'. And in 1962 that song was revolutionary.

JIM McLEAN

When Dylan turned up in the King and Queen, Martin Carthy and Nigel Denver and the Thameside Four were doing a gig there. Alison, who's now my wife, was on the gate and I was chatting her up outside and this kid in cowboy boots came upstairs, carrying a guitar. He said, 'Is this a folk club?' I said, 'Yes. Are you gonna sing?' Because usually, if you were going to sing, you didn't pay. So I took him in and sat him in the back row and I introduced him to Martin.

Nigel was singing and at the interval Martin hadn't asked him, and Dylan came over to me. He said, 'Can I talk to you about folk music?' I said, 'Yes, down the stairs, in the loo.' In those days we couldn't afford a drink in the pub. We used to smuggle half-bottles in, half-bottles of whisky, and you went down to the loo in the interval.

We went down and he was shaking. I had to hold him by the shoulders. I don't know if it was the pot. It wasn't fear, he was just jiggling. I offered him a drink and we talked about music. I told him there's all rebel music in Scotland, even the farmers' songs. And he asked me if I was Hamish Henderson. Another question he asked me: he said, 'Does Ewan MacColl live in a slum?'

After that conversation we went back up and Martin asked him on. He did a couple of Guthrie songs. After people like Alex Campbell, who knew Guthrie's material, this young kid with a mouth organ – it was just a very kind of wishy-washy imitation. Martin asked him back that night, and at the house that he asked him back to, in Hampstead, Martin and his wife Dorothy lived in one room, Pete Stanley the banjo player lived in another room and Nigel and I had another room.

LOUIS KILLEN
At the King and Queen I was just sitting in the audience. The singers tended to go to as many clubs as were there because this was what we were devoting our lives to. Those who were professional did and I had become professional by then. A lot of my time was spent in London so I would go to all the clubs within reach.

He came to the Troubadour. Martin was living with his first wife up in Hampstead. I remember on a couple of nights us all being in there after the club, swapping songs and what have you. Bob asked me to sing again and again 'The Leaving of Liverpool'. And, of course, it was out on his next record as 'Farewell', different set of words but same tune. He didn't mention my name. Somebody wrote in the English Folk Dance and Song Society magazine that Bob Dylan got 'The Leaving of Liverpool' from Nigel Denver. Nigel didn't even sing that song, it wasn't in his repertory, not in those days.

MARTIN CARTHY

He wrote 'Farewell' . . . He took 'Scarborough Fair' and he took from 'Lord Franklin' – 'Bob Dylan's Dream' – and he did that song of Louis's and he learned songs from Bob Davenport. Nigel Denver's big party piece at the time was 'Kishmul's Galley' – he wrote an amazing song around 'Kishmul's Galley'. He'd get really excited about hearing a song and then go home and write something about it or around what he remembered. He did that all the time.

We had a flat in Belsize Park. He came back after that Saturday night at the Troubadour, the second night he was here. We laid a fire . . . settled down . . . drank lots of tea . . . just talked about music and played to each other – doing what twenty-one-, twenty-two-year-olds do.

HANS FRIED

I came into Collett's on a Thursday, late '62, and Dylan was leaning against the counter. He'd already got a name as a young singer-songwriter and his first record was just out. Collett's had ordered a couple of copies. I didn't realise that was him. I'd heard the record, listened to it and thought it was someone imitating Jack Elliott – bad of me. Then I was caught by the record and I bought a copy. I loved his version of 'The House of the Rising Sun' and I liked several other tracks a lot. I didn't like his 'Song to Woody', that was based on Woody Guthrie's '1913 Massacre'.

He was leaning against the counter, scrawling on something, and I had a book in my hand that I had borrowed from my father, *The White Goddess*, by Robert Graves. It's the history of poetic myth, poetic language. It's a very difficult book and I was trying to make sense of it. I put my book down and Dylan looked over and he said, 'You read that?' I said, 'I try, but it's a bit of a complicated book', so we started talking. And we went for a coffee – the Star in Old Compton Street.

We sat there for about three hours, talking about poetry. We talked about Dylan Thomas because my father had a reputation for translating Dylan Thomas. That went down very well. We talked about Rimbaud. He had a book of poems in America – Rimbaud, Saint John Perse and Lautréamont, *Les Chants de Maldoror*. These were English translations of French texts and Dylan loved it, this book. I had it too so we talked about that a lot.

He was very interested in anything from myth and legend – again, that was just up my street. In *The White Goddess* there's a long poem translated, *The Battle of the Trees*, which is a poem in a form called cante fable which was half sung and half spoken. It was a peculiar form; it talked about the story by talking about things around the story. It was chanted rather than sung. When you look at it you can see where he got the form of 'Hard Rain'. He got things from everywhere. When he had his muse he was a fabulous writer.

When *Madhouse on Castle Street* was on the television I knew Dylan was going to be on it. I wasn't interested in the play, only in Dylan. I put a microphone in front of the television and taped 'Blowin' in the Wind' and 'Ballad of the Gliding Swan'. He's never recorded that, not even on bootleg.

PHILIP SAVILLE

It's a long time ago, and memory is stretched, but I think in the play, as well as 'Blowin' in the Wind', Bobby sang 'The Cuckoo', 'Hang Me' and the song 'Gliding Swan', the song that Evan Jones had written.

KARL DALLAS

I saw him at the Singers' Club. He was terrible. He couldn't put over a song and the songs weren't interesting. The only person who didn't share that view was Martin Carthy. Martin must have been brilliant or something because he befriended him. There was a pub in Wardour Street, the Roundhouse. Nigel Denver ran the folk night there and when Dylan turned up Nigel wouldn't let him sing.

We regarded Bob Dylan as a very poor Woody Guthrie imitator. One of the biggest impacts on the London folk scene was Jack Elliott and he sang Woody's songs better than Bob Dylan did. That's why we didn't have a very high regard for Dylan.

PEGGY SEEGER

I remember him coming to the Singers' Club and he had almost no voice. He could hardly be heard past the front row – he was mumbling. We didn't generally allow that – when you got up on the stage or when you stood up to sing, you spoke so people could hear you. I know why it was – when you're used to singing with microphones and then all of a sudden you don't have one . . .

It's possible we treated Bob Dylan badly. I've never seen him since. I'd like to meet him. My brother Mike was a friend of his. We knew who he was by the time he came to the Singers' Club. He was fairly modest but we were kinda rude about a lot of things back then.

LOUIS KILLEN

I was at the Singers' Club when he came there and was asked to sing. It was a very strange night, I think it was a party night, because it wasn't the usual set-up. People were sitting all over the place. That's where he sang 'Nuclear Warfare Blues' or whatever it was, the basis of what it was about was that the Holocaust has come. I don't even know if any of us had heard his record. I remember his first record had been pushed around among the people who could get it, because it wasn't out here when he first came across.

BOB DAVENPORT

I met him at the Pindar of Wakefield – the Singers' Club. Bert Lloyd was the MC. Then about six months later we spoke at Newport – he introduced me to Joan Baez and him and Al Grossman came to hear me sing in New York. I did two clubs – the Gaslight and Gerde's Folk City.

After that I was due to meet him once for lunch. I couldn't make it but my partner went. Of course, at that time, when you were going to meet him for lunch you didn't think you could have lunches for the rest of your life on the fact that you'd had lunch with Bob Dylan.

JIM McLEAN

We used to see Dylan at different clubs and quite often in the Troubadour. If Nigel or somebody sang a rebel song, he would say, 'Did you write that?'

When Nigel had his kerfuffle with Dylan – this was just one night in particular. Nigel and Dylan just didn't hit it off, they never did. Nigel would do 'Pretty Peggy-O', he used to do it to take the mickey out of him.

I saw Dylan in the Troubadour. Grossman was there, Al Grossman. He had a tape recorder. They used to pay Anthea Joseph to record everything that went on in the club on a Saturday night. She set the tape recorder up in the corner, then Grossman and Dylan took the tape recorder back to the hotel to listen and you'll hear an awful lot of songs that Dylan did all based on these tapes. That's why when he used the tune of 'The Leaving of Liverpool' he sings it to the harmony – the microphone was too near the harmony singer.

NIGEL DENVER

I was compèring and singing and him and his manager Grossman and his wife and Mimi Baez and Dick Farina were there. They wouldn't stop talking. So I had to go up and say, 'Look, either shut up or fuck off.' They shut up. Then Karl Dallas asked me to write an article for *Folk Scene* magazine. I did and I pointed out all the stuff Dylan had taken from the tradition and put his own words to it and used some of the words, like 'Lord Franklin' which he got from Carthy. 'Lord Franklin' was 'Bob Dylan's Dream'. 'With God on Our Side' was Dominic Behan's 'Patriot Game', and a load of other stuff.

He was ringing up my flat in London, but I was away in Newcastle. I've heard that he learned 'The Patriot Game' from me and he could have done. I used to sing it at the Troubadour in '60, '61, '62. But I always said on stage who the writer was, so he must have known. Dominic tried to sue him but maybe he didn't have the money. And then, of course, Dominic died.

PETE STANLEY
The night Dylan got up at the Troubadour with Dick Farina, Rick von Schmidt and Ethan Signer, I had the grass. Bob and Dick Farina had been in the studio – they were recording for Doug Dobell. I knew Farina as the partner of Carolyn Hester. I'd played with them on a concert at Cecil Sharp House. The girl who was running the evening, Judith Silver, didn't want anyone to get anywhere near her stage. And, of course, eventually Bob Dylan got on the stage. It was fucking chaos, it was really funny.

ETHAN SIGNER
Von Schmidt, Richard Farina and I were all in the Cambridge, Massachusetts, scene. Von Schmidt came over to England with two objectives – one was a book he and Farina were trying to sell with integrated artwork and writing – *Been Down So Long It Looks Like Up to Me*, the other was the soundtrack to a film of his, *The Young Man Who Wouldn't Hoe Corn*, for which I did the soundtrack, recorded at Peggy Seeger's house.

I didn't really know Dylan before the recording at Dobell's, although I had met him a couple of years earlier at the short-lived Indian Neck Folk Festival in Connecticut. I ran into him once or twice while he was in London because we had a mutual friend, Janet Reynolds.

I think Martin Carthy had the gig and we all just crowded in behind him after the recording at Dobell's. What I remember is a fair amount of chaos, weed and an enthusiastic audience.

JEANNIE WINSOR

The run-in at the Troubadour was not with Dylan – it was with Albert Grossman, Dylan's then manager. Grossman arrived at the club, which Martin [Winsor] and Curly Goss were running at that time. He was accompanied by Dylan and several hangers-on and he believed that the world should know who he was. Unfortunately, I was on the door taking the entrance fee and I didn't know who he was. He became very abusive as he pushed passed me into the room, noisily making an entrance while someone was singing.

Martin came to see what was occurring. Well, Martin was known to have a short fuse, especially when dealing with those who believe they are of great importance, and a fracas developed. Grossman and party were asked to leave. Grossman was astonished to be treated in such a manner, reminding us as he left who he was.

JENNY BARTON

Dylan turned up with his manager Grossman and at the end of the evening my younger sister, who I was desperately trying to keep an eye on, disappeared on the arm of that toad Grossman. No taste that girl, absolutely none. Dylan was all right as a singer but he didn't like people talking when he sang and he talked non-stop when other people sang.

He locked himself in the loo to smoke pot and I had people dancing up and down in the corridors so, as you can imagine, he wasn't my favourite visitor. Far from it! I know some of the singers thought he was wonderful.

I spent a lot of time trying to keep drugs out of my night at the Troubadour. We didn't get raided, unlike other local clubs, mostly because we had three keen folkie policemen in the audience. The deal was that we kept drugs out and they kept their chums out.

HANS FRIED
I saw him later on in a club in Broadwick Street. He came in with bodyguards. He was then very brash, he spoke to me for a few minutes but I'd had my use. That's the man.

BILL LEADER
We were running the Black Horse in Rathbone Place when he came back the second time, to do the Festival Hall. I don't know how I communicated with him but he agreed to pop in and he said he'd do it for a bottle of wine. I had to collect him from the hotel he was staying at, which I did. They wouldn't let him into the dining room because he didn't wear a tie. They had standards in those days!

I took him down to the Black Horse and he was on the wine, took him upstairs and the feller at the door who was helping out was Nigel Denver, who greeted him firmly, then realised that he'd just written something rather scurrilous about Bob Dylan in, I think, that magazine that Karl Dallas produced.

So Nigel was convinced that Bob Dylan would haul one off and smack him in the jaw. Of course, I don't think Bob Dylan was aware that the feller in front of him had written anything about him at all. He just did a couple of songs. I can't remember the detail. I remember the landlord got uppity because we hadn't bought the bottle of wine from him, we'd brought it in. Relationships deteriorated from then on with us and the Black Horse pub.

MARTIN CARTHY
He came back for a summer concert at the Royal Festival Hall in May or June '64. He landed and the first thing he did was

phone up. I said, 'Hello, Swiss Cottage 6463 . . .' and he said, 'Are you there, Martin? Have you still got your piano?' 'Cos we'd chopped up the piano with my samurai sword to keep warm. 'No, no, the piano all got burned up.'

He said, 'Okay, are you home?' and he came straight round. The first thing he did – he picked up the guitar and he played 'Mr Tambourine Man'. He sat down at the kitchen table and played it. I was absolutely thunderstruck. I'd never heard a song like that.

He also sang it at the Festival Hall and the following year, in his room at the Savoy Hotel. Donovan was there. And Donovan – you've got to admire the man's neck – said, 'You know you sang that song "Mr Tambourine Man" – I went home and I wrote a song around it.' He wrote this song called 'Hey Golden Tangerine Eyes' – and he sang it to him. Bob was very much a person where he sang you a song and you did with it what you wanted. He wasn't offended. He just accepted it.

I saw him in '65, he'd just put out *Bringing It All Back Home*. I walked into his hotel room and he picked up a guitar and he sang, 'It's All Over Now, Baby Blue'. He just tosses an idea straight at you . . . astonishing. He always greets you with a song or a piece of music, always does it.

TOM PAXTON *American singer-songwriter*
While we were here in '65, Dylan came on his famous tour. Midge, my wife, and I were at that horrible party at the Savoy Hotel, the one they filmed in the documentary *Don't Look Back*, but we stayed way out of camera range. It was awful – people were really behaving badly, rude to the staff and stuff. I thought, 'That's not Bob. What's that all about?'

LOUIS KILLEN
The first year after I'd emigrated to America in '67 I got a gig in Woodstock. This was the period after his accident when he was reclusive. I was hardly working but I'd got this gig at the

Playhouse. It was an old wooden theatre with a proscenium arch. They put on concerts on Sunday nights and the manager had seen my publicity. I was being represented at that time by Manny Greenhill, who was Joan Baez's manager.

So I go up to the Woodstock Playhouse and I do the gig. I went with my first wife. There were maybe thirty, thirty-five, in a hall that would hold at least 300. Somebody I had known since I first went to America, a lad called Happy Traum, he came on down to the show and at the interval he came backstage and said, 'Bob Dylan's in the audience and he'd like to come back and say hello but he doesn't know if you remember him.' Odd as it sounds, it's true. So he came backstage and it was unfortunate but some young girl got back and recognised him, so he said come on up to my place afterwards.

We went back to Happy's for a meal and then Happy took us up to Bob's. By the time we got there they were all stoned out of their heads. I wasn't a doper – I've always been a drinker not a smoker. It was way past midnight by the time we got there. He and his wife put us up in their bed.

BOB DAVENPORT

When I ran the Empress of Russia in the eighties, Anthea Joseph was going to bring him but he couldn't make it. Then when Dylan came back a few years later he went round London covered in rugs and things. And he was sat in the audience. One of the things he said about me was, 'Of all the people that I met in Britain, Bob Davenport never crowded me.' So at the Empress I didn't go up to him or say anything and the MC didn't ask him to sing, but I'd re-written the words to 'I Shall Be Released' and I sang it, so he would know . . .

I'd been standing on the stairs talking to him when he came in all covered up and I said, 'Oh, wait till the song's finished and then go in.' There wasn't a single bit of him that wasn't covered and I thought it was an old woman I was talking to. I'd no idea it was him. He was wearing gloves and sat there all huddled up,

like the kind of character you'd see knocking around carrying
two carrier bags . . . 'Streets of London'. But the MC, Bernard
Puckett, he had seen the photographs in the *Melody Maker* of
Bob Dylan in this gear.

IAN CAMPBELL

I took my parents along to a club in London where they were
performing – Dave and Betty Campbell, traditional. And sitting
quietly in the back was Bob Dylan. Bob Davenport was running
the club at the time and he asked Dylan if he would like to sing
a song.

Dylan said, 'No, thank you. I've come to listen and enjoy
myself, not to work.' He was recognised – a ripple went through
the whole room – people were muttering and pointing. We told
mother, 'Bob Dylan is here.' She was in her eighties by then.
She said, 'Oh, that's nice. Who's Bob Dylan?' He sat through the
whole night but he left about fifteen minutes early. He never
spoke to us. Very strange, but it was nice that he came.

PHILIP SAVILLE

He was a young man with very few words. He sort of muttered
and mumbled, until he sang and then, of course, this astonishing
eloquence came rushing out.

Obviously he was anarchic, but he wasn't wanting to
overthrow politically. He wasn't a political animal. He wanted
you to be honest, to face up to what you truly are. He had a
natural nous about the rumbles in people. He used to say to me,
'You got too much intellect. You're too intellectual.' And I used
to say to him, 'Well, yes, but my intellectualising keeps me in
touch with what's going on.' He'd say, 'I think you should come
on the road with me.'

His success didn't come as any surprise to me at all. You just
knew. He was like any one-off person, you just knew. I suppose
being a director – it's like water-divining really. And every time
you meet someone that has this, and it's not too often, I suppose

it's a kind of genius – it's really being totally honest with yourself. Most people put on a face to meet other faces, so most people are walking masks. He led me to believe that it would be better to remove the mask, whatever was underneath.

5 A great talent, but a difficult man

James Henry Miller was born in Salford in 1915. Self-educated in the public library and active in left-wing politics from his teenage years, he was conscripted into the British Army in 1940. He deserted five months later and was on the run for the rest of the war. When he resurfaced in May 1945 he had changed his name to Ewan MacColl. In 1946 he formed Theatre Workshop with his first wife, Joan Littlewood, but by 1953, after meeting Alan Lomax, MacColl was focusing his attention on folk song, to which he had been introduced as a child by his parents. Three years later, while married to his second wife, Jean Newlove, mother of singer Kirsty MacColl, he met and fell in love with twenty-one-year-old Peggy Seeger, who had recently arrived in London.

Ewan MacColl and Peggy Seeger were one of the folk scene's most popular attractions. They appeared in concert and on radio and television, as well as making many records and undertaking tours abroad. In 1957 MacColl opened the Ballads and Blues Club at the Princess Louise, High Holborn, where residents included Dominic Behan, Seamus Ennis, A. L. Lloyd and the Trinidadian guitarist Fitzroy Coleman. MacColl started the Singers' Club in June 1961 in the Association of Cinematograph Television and Allied Technicians (ACTT) trade union building in Soho Square, the first of several bases that also included the Princess Louise, the Pindar of Wakefield, Merlin's Cave and the Union Tavern.

In 1958 MacColl and radio producer Charles Parker made 'The Ballad of John Axon', the first in a series of eight Radio Ballads *broadcast by the BBC. The programmes were musical documentaries, blending the voices of people from previously overlooked communities talking about their lives alongside newly composed songs and music, directed by Peggy Seeger.*

At his Ballads and Blues club, MacColl had introduced a policy that singers could only sing songs from their own native tradition, a policy that was enforced at the Singers' Club. He also began what became known as the Critics Group, where some members of the club were invited to meet regularly at his and Peggy Seeger's home in Beckenham.

Ewan MacColl's uncompromising and at times contradictory attitudes made him a controversial figure. Nonetheless, he was widely respected for his extensive knowledge of folk music, his pioneering spirit and for writing songs like 'The Manchester Rambler', 'Dirty Old Town', 'The Shoals of Herring', 'The Moving on Song' and 'The First Time Ever I Saw Your Face'. He died in 1989, aged seventy-four.

PEGGY SEEGER

His mother always called him Jimmy. She knew why he'd changed his name and she didn't question that. She never really questioned anything he did except that she was very distressed when he left his wife for me, but she came with us very early in the relationship.

Betsy had a very quavery voice. The best thing was hearing her sing to the children and while she was ironing or cooking. She stayed at home. She never went out with us unless we begged her. No, she never went to the Singers' Club. You know, I've never thought about that. That was very bad of us that we never even thought of it.

MIKE WATERSON

I loved Ewan's MacColl's singing, I loved his songwriting. We did a CND tour with him and we chatted in the back seat of the Citroën, and he questioned our motives and what we did – why did we do it. We said, 'Because we do.' I think he was looking for something that we weren't. I loved Ewan, I thought he was wonderful but I realised that he was a manipulator.

LOUIS KILLEN

I met MacColl in '57 or '58. I'd gone to see my friend Julian Corbluth, who was living in the south of London, and we went up to the Singers' Club together. The next time I went down I sang. By then I had learned two songs I'd collected from a shepherd, Alan Rogerson, which I sang at the Singers' Club – to MacColl's great delight. Here was a young northerner who was singing these Border songs. He was dead chuffed.

MARTIN CARTHY

I never really knew Ewan. I always stayed away. I didn't want to get involved in the politics. I was very much a sympathiser but I didn't like personality cults and I felt there was too much of a cult of personality around Ewan. I still think that. He wrote some fantastic stuff, no doubt about it. I was never crazy about the way he sang.

I sang at the Singers' Club and I always sang very badly there – because I always did what I thought was wanted instead of just … standing up and doing what you do. Only once did I do it properly – when Ewan came towards the end of his life he phoned me up a few times. He was very complimentary about my guitar playing and said he would like me very much to come along to sing at the Singers' Club. Would I come along and do a benefit, for Armenia?

I did that and then I got a phone call when he fell ill: would I be prepared to stand in for Ewan should he not be able to do this particular gig? I said, 'Yes, I'll do that.' It was a Kurdish benefit.

In between the phone call and the gig, Ewan died. So I sang there and for the first time in my life at the Singers' Club I just sang what I knew, actually did a proper gig. I was always very rebellious towards him, but always hugely intimidated. I never did a decent job when he was there.

MIKE WATERSON

I hitched down to London and went to the Singers' Club before we started our club in Hull. The Singers' Club at that time was in a school. You actually sat on the desks and all the songs with choruses were printed out on paper and everybody had to join in. The singing was wonderful, marvellous. I met Enoch Kent. He knocked me out. He was an incredible singer, and political as well. He was one of the people that I forgave for being political. We'd decided as part of the policy not to be openly political. It was like preaching to the converted.

SANDRA KERR *resident at the Singers' Club and a pupil of Ewan MacColl*
My first introduction to folk music in any conscious way was going to the Singers' Club with a couple of mates. That would be about 1961. I was eighteen. It wasn't in a pub, I think it was in the ACTT building. I can remember I was immensely moved. The song that sticks in my mind is Ewan singing Harry Cox's version of 'Van Diemen's Land' and Peggy accompanying him on guitar. It was so beautiful, I was absolutely captivated, a jaw-dropping moment for me.

It was a real introduction, not just to the idea that there were people who played and sang this music professionally to this enormously high standard, and that there was an audience for that, but that the music and the singing was truly different to what I'd been used to in skiffle. I became a regular at the Singers' Club and within a year I'd gone from singing skiffle to living with Ewan and Peggy.

ROD STRADLING *editor*, Musical Traditions
I was at college in north London in 1961 and one of my pals gave me a membership card for the Singers' Club so I went along to the Pindar of Wakefield. I can't remember who was on that first night but I ended up going pretty well every week in term time from then to 1963. I don't think that I ever had to show the membership card.

What I liked about it was the music was being taken seriously, but interestingly it wasn't all hard core traditional, they had much more popular people as well, like the Ian Campbell Folk Group. As a punter I was never aware of the policy about only singing songs from your own region – that must have come later with the Critics Group.

HANS FRIED
I can remember Bert Jansch doing a nervous 'I Once Loved a Lass' in circa 1965 at the Singers' Club, and Robin Williamson singing 'The Dowie Dens of Yarrow' a couple of years earlier. His variations on the melody changed from verse to verse, as is common among traditional performers. His unaccompanied performance was magnificent and I would have loved to have a recording of that event. Curiously, when I asked Robin about it later he couldn't recollect it.

ROY BAILEY *singer of political and traditional songs*
Ewan had a policy at the Singers' Club that you should sing the songs of the area from which you came. I remember going there one night at the Pindar of Wakefield in '61/'62 and singing 'The Derby Ram' and afterwards he came and asked, 'Where do you come from?' I replied, 'London' and he said, 'Well, why are you singing a song about Derby? You should be singing songs from London.' I was shocked. It seemed rather strange because he wasn't Scottish and he'd changed his name to Ewan MacColl.

BOB DAVENPORT
MacColl was very talented but, when it came to the Singers' Club, he laid this stuff down where you had to sing from where you came from. I knew his mother very well – she said, 'I never gave birth to anybody called MacColl.' Jimmy Miller, he was from Salford. Peggy Seeger was from a very upper-class academic family with Harvard connections. I'm not against that either – but for them to dictate was not for me. Traditional music was for entertaining, it wasn't for a further education class.

PETE STANLEY

I was playing with two American guys, Rob and Dave Mangurian, guitar and mandolin, as the Tennessee Three, and they wanted to go and see Peggy Seeger and Ewan MacColl. We all wore red double-breasted waistcoat, white shirt, shoe-string tie and a hat – a Stetson.

We went to the Pindar of Wakefield where Peggy and Ewan were performing. Rob and Dave had played there before. Ewan said, 'Does anyone else want to come and sing from the floor?' and Rob said, 'Yes, can we play?' He said, 'Yes.' 'Can we use our banjo player?' He said, 'Fine.' Then suddenly, off come our jackets, out come the hats and we go on stage. MacColl went livid!

I don't know what he expected but we did something like 'Roll in My Sweet Baby's Arms' or 'Rabbit on a Log' – and MacColl's sitting there on his backwards chair and he was exploding. As soon as we finished he went to the guy on the door and he said, 'Throw him out, throw Stanley out!' Not Rob and Dave – they were American, so it was okay for them singing American songs, but not me.

JUNE TABOR *emerged in the mid-sixties to become one of the leading female singers on the scene*

I remember being booked at the Singers' Club. You had to sit on the stage with MacColl and Seeger and the rest of the Critics Group, and occasionally you were called upon to sing. I can't remember how long I sang for but it was very restrictive on material, what you could and couldn't sing. You were aware that you were going to have to sing all English stuff.

Somebody took Pete Knight along and he asked could he play and they said, 'What do you play, young man?' He said, 'Irish tunes', and they said, 'Where are you from?' He said Borehamwood. They said, 'Go away and learn some English tunes.' It was very hard-line.

Packie Byrne told me that he went along to the Singers' Club.

He'd won the All-Ireland singing at the Fleadh. Apparently, he says, and I hope it's true, that he went up on to the stage and turned the chair round and sat astride it. Then he put his elbow on the back of the chair and his hand on his ear, just like MacColl did, and then he sang 'Lucky Old Sun', with all the showband modulations and everything.

MADDY PRIOR *in duo with Tim Hart, later Steeleye Span and Silly Sisters*
Sandy and Jeanie were Americans. They lived in Camden Town and went to Ewan MacColl and taped a lot of stuff from him. I don't know why they were over here. They stayed about a year, I think. They were interested in tradition and they had an LP out on Extra, songs like 'Eight More Miles to Louisville'. They used to go to the Singers' Club and sing there sometimes. It amused Sandy – the thing about you could only sing songs from your country. He said, 'We're from Seattle, we're about as far away from the Appalachians as you are.'

PEGGY SEEGER
We never had any doubt about the policy. It affected the size of audiences but only for a very short time. Then we started hauling out a whole stack of new songs that we had to go and find. I had the songs from when I was little. Ewan had his father's songs, but he didn't have a whole lot of other ones and he started learning songs like crazy. So did Bert – and they stopped singing American songs. Partly because I kept laughing!

MADDY PRIOR
Tim and I did the Singers' Club with Bert Lloyd – just once. It wasn't really our scene. I didn't know MacColl at all, really. He came to the club in St Albans a couple of times and I went to his house once with Sandy and Jeanie, but I didn't get to know him or Peggy then. From the outside it seemed to be very clique-ish. I always got the feeling that Peggy rather took on Ewan's

attitudes more than Ewan did. Peggy was kind of the evangeliser and it was a shame really.

Ewan had a wonderful sense of the romantic, but desperately wanted to be taken seriously. It was such a shame, because all his good songs are the romantic ones, not the political ones which are fucking awful.

SHIRLEY COLLINS

He said I shouldn't sing so many love songs. He was right, inasmuch as you need a balanced programme. And I'd had the temerity to paint my fingernails pink and he told me very waspishly that folk singers didn't wear nail varnish. But funnily enough, in 1959, Alan Lomax and I recorded a genuine mountain singer in Kentucky – eighty-year-old Ada Coombs – and she was sporting deep-red nail varnish.

PEGGY SEEGER

Sam Larner sang at the Singers' Club in 1960. He loved it – 'All those young women in them little short skirts, looking up at me!' He was the ultimate showman. And he was so pleased to be recorded – he loved being recorded. When Ewan had written 'The Shoals of Herring' and sang it, Sam Larner said, 'I've known that song all my life.' It's a wonderful feeling when somebody says that.

AUDREY WINTER

Eric helped out at the Singers' Club sometimes – so did I once or twice – although we didn't like their policy of singers having to be auditioned. We felt that anybody should be allowed to get up and sing once and if it was awful they shouldn't be asked again. The audition business was taking the spontaneity out of it all.

CAROLYN HESTER *American singer who toured British clubs in the early sixties*

The Pindar of Wakefield – I think I played there twice. The

first time I noticed that Ewan could tease Peggy mightily, he referred to her as 'Piggy' once during their set that evening. She just smiled and kept on singing. It was obvious Ewan was still smitten with his lady. That same evening I heard that Peggy had been married to someone else. There was a rumour that she had been married in name only to someone, but not in any monetary direction.

MARTIN CARTHY

Alex Campbell and Ewan – you got the impression they were at daggers drawn, but never in print did I ever see Ewan bad-mouth Alex. The reason was because he married Peggy so that she could stay in the country. I think it was a sense of honour, and it's a nice thing isn't it? I mean, there Peggy is, hugely pregnant, about to be sent back to the United States and have her passport taken away – 'cos she's a dirty commie – and Alex said, 'I'll marry you so you can stay in the country. It won't cost you anything, I'll just marry you.'

PEGGY SEEGER

We got married on 23 January 1959. There was just the three of us – Alex Campbell, Derroll Adams and me. That was it. Derroll was the best man and the person who performed the ceremony was in sneakers and surplice. Afterwards he took Alex into the vestry and proceeded to dress him down for half an hour, for getting me in such trouble. Alex came out of the room very serious and the minute we got out of the place he just howled with laughter and we went to a French drinking joint and proceeded to get stocious.

Derroll and Alex were good company. I'd palled around with them. I sang on the streets in Paris with Alex sometimes. My voice wasn't strong enough but because I was so obviously pregnant I think we brought in a little bit more money that way. It was cold, oh, so cold. The next day after the ceremony we got on the train and went to London and Ewan met us at Waterloo.

'Here's your woman,' Alex says. It was a wonderful thing to do. I never repaid him properly, I should have. I'm sorry that we didn't stay friends with him. We weren't enemies

ASHLEY HUTCHINGS *founding member of Fairport Convention, Steeleye Span and the Albion Band*
I went regularly to Ewan MacColl and Peggy Seeger's club, Merlin's Cave, King's Cross. Round about this time, in the mid-sixties, I was starting to play music with groups and we formed Fairport at the very beginning of '67. I thought MacColl was spellbinding so I went back and back to that club.

When I formed Steeleye at the end of '69, I went to see Ewan and Peggy and spoke with them. By then we'd had Fairport for a couple of years and I was confident to go up and introduce myself. They were very friendly, very kind, contrary to what you hear from many people, and I was invited to go into their house in Beckenham and spend some time there looking at their library and listening to things.

On the first Steeleye album, *Hark! The Village Wait*, were two songs which I got from staying at Ewan and Peggy's. I remember Peggy saying, and Ewan nodding, wasn't it interesting that these people were playing with electric instruments. Ewan had a whole room, a library with a sound archive and all kinds of field recordings.

JIM O'CONNOR *resident at the Singers' Club and member of the Critics Group*
In 1964, the Singers' Club was held on a Saturday night, just off King's Cross, and financed by the Co-op Society. The Critics Group, alongside Ewan and Peggy, were the residents and the first song I sang was 'The Blind Beggar of Bethnal Green'. I couldn't have known Ewan and Peggy very long at that point. There were guests as well. Bert Lloyd would often be on the platform.

People think it was all dour and serious but I remember lots of laughter, an easy, relaxed atmosphere. And people loved chorus songs. You get a hundred people in a room and most of them are really enjoying the chorus – it's a lovely feeling.

The Singers' Club moved around to three or four different places. It finally finished up in the Union Tavern, just off King's Cross. It was always very well attended. The room was packed and the air thick with cigarette smoke. Everybody smoked. I used to think, 'Bugger me, if a fire broke out now, we'd all be thundering down that one set of stairs.' I think that was typical of a lot of the folk clubs.

SANDRA KERR

Ewan and Peggy heard me when I sang at the Singers' Club and they suggested that I came and lived with them as a kind of folk apprentice/ au pair. So that's what I did. There was no question about it – that was the most amazing opportunity, because Ewan and Peggy, apart from their status in the folk world, the resources they had there, the fact that traditional music and politics was their main focus in life, apart from each other . . . it was just too good an opportunity not be involved with – and everybody said that to me.

I had one-to-one classes with both of them. I was helping with the childcare and the house while they went on tour, but I had very formal lessons with Ewan in everything. He would set me assignments, either on skills of certain traditional singers, emulating what they did, trying to copy it and so on, or he would give me essays to do on things like 'Folk hero in folk song' or the picaresque novels of Henry Fielding, or whatever. And with Peggy I had tuition on guitar but also more formalised music notation. One of the first things I did when I went there was take first notations of all the songs that were going into one of those books on Scottish songs. It was very formalised and I loved it.

People like Bert Lloyd would take singers under their wing and point them in the direction of repertoire and singers but I don't know of anybody else who formalised it as a kind of folk apprenticeship.

I lived there for a year and then Ewan initiated the Critics

Group. I always think he tried everything out on me and then continued that work in the Critics Group, which lasted for another eight years. Ewan was very stinting on praise. On one occasion Peggy gave me a huge piece of praise, not criticism, and Ewan said, 'Don't say that to her', sort of, 'It won't do her any good, she's better off being criticised rather than praised.' But I know that he felt very much that I'd learned a great deal.

As a workshop leader or as lecturer or as voice tutor, I have used a lot of the techniques that Ewan used with me, in terms of folk skills, of understanding the interpretation of traditional ballads. I'm still drawing on that experience. At the end of the day the techniques that he developed actually work.

JIM O'CONNOR

I fell under the spell of Ewan and Peggy's charisma and I was invited to join the group at their house in Stanley Avenue, Beckenham. We all caught the train down there and would gather over the space of two and a half hours, maybe three.

The others were far more experienced than me. Sometimes there would be one person who had come prepared with a programme of four or five songs and they would sing them – and would then be criticised. That's where the name came from, but at the time it wasn't called the Critics Group. It was just a group of young singers. I can remember feeling absolutely knackered having done a day's work teaching and then getting the train down to Beckenham – but coming away feeling totally elevated. He could be very inspiring.

We would do feature evenings at the Singers' Club, where we picked a theme and worked up a whole programme of songs. It might be sea songs, or crime and criminals. Some of the women would do one based around courtship and love. Round about the time we were putting the record together, we did a programme of London songs. It would incorporate some prose, Mayhew's *London*, that sort of thing. During the course of that, contemporary songs would be sung alongside traditional stuff.

We made two London records, LPs. One was *A Merry Progress to London*. I sang 'The Blind Beggar of Bethnal Green' and 'Ratcliffe Highway', both traditional songs, and 'The Ploughboy and the Cockney'. The other record was *Sweet Thames Flow Softly*, that came out of an exercise we did based on *Romeo and Juliet*.

I had the appetite for writing and I collected a lot of cuttings about the Great Train Robbery. It was in the news all the time and there was a lot of speculation about Bruce Reynolds, the supposed mastermind. On one hand he was seen as a Robin Hood character and I don't think people were particularly antagonistic. And then when they started escaping out of jail, someone posed the premise that maybe Reynolds was getting them out. After all, there was all that money out there. It all had the makings of a Jesse-James-type ballad.

So I wrote 'Have You Seen Bruce Richard Reynolds?' I wrote the song in one session and then cleaned it up the following day. I remember Peggy Seeger, when she heard it, was very impressed. I heard the recording by Nigel Denver but I think it's too fast. It doesn't need that kind of pace. I've been told about the version by the Alabama 3, Bruce Reynolds's son's band, but I've not heard it.

PEGGY SEEGER

Festival of Fools time . . . round about 1969/'70. The routine of writing *Festival of Fools* was that, during the whole year, the whole of the Critics Group would collect clippings and cuttings, interesting things from newspapers. And Ewan, in September, would end up with a pile of cuttings about four feet high and he'd go through them looking for something that interested him.

We would begin by announcing that this was January, then we'd put two or three things that happened in January, either in a skit or a song. He would write the whole thing. And in 1970, the year of Angela Davis and George Jackson, he paid a lot of attention to women in that year and he said we need a woman's song.

I wrote 'I'm Gonna Be an Engineer' in two hours. I didn't ever want to be an engineer. It was one of those magic moments when it all comes to you. It originally had a very down last verse but when I took it upstairs to play it to Ewan he liked the whole thing but he didn't like the last verse. So I went downstairs and wrote another last verse.

JIM O'CONNOR

We were together as a group, the Critics Group, for the best part of seven years. People came in and out, though the hard core of the group was there. But there came a point where Ewan withdrew for a period because he was ill.

We carried on and we quite liked the independence. We felt there were times when Ewan was kind of smothering us in a way, dominating us. We wanted more freedom and we said to Ewan at one point, 'We really would like to try and operate more independently, on our own.' It wasn't easy. Ewan didn't take kindly to this at all, and so we parted. Not on very amicable terms, I have to say.

LOUIS KILLEN

I hadn't been asked to join the Critics Group. I remember when an invitation had gone out to Enoch Kent, Nigel Denver I think, and Bobby Campbell. I had fallen out of favour with MacColl. I think it was because I had become professional. MacColl was typically paternalistic – I should have stayed working as a cabinet maker or whatever else I was working at. It's probably how MacColl thought of himself – I'm a playwright and I only sing on the side. He had a strange attitude in many ways.

FRANKIE ARMSTRONG

I met Ewan at a party at Karl Dallas's, which I went to with Louis Killen. Ewan and Louis had a somewhat spiky relationship. Ewan had formed the Critics Group the year before. Louis didn't want to join, nor did he need to, but he encouraged me to join. He said, 'It'll give you opportunities that you wouldn't get anywhere else.' It was incredibly valuable in all kinds of ways but I don't think any of us should ever have stayed in longer than two or three years.

NIGEL DENVER

The *Radio Ballads* had a big impact. MacColl had a big impact. A lot of the singers didn't like him, but I think they were jealous. We argued all the time. He wouldn't have me on the stage with him at one point, because I was a Republican and he was a Maoist.

That was at Centre 42 – Arnold Wesker got the deal with the trade unions and, of course, I was a trade union man. The McPeakes, I worked with them at Centre 42, and the Stewarts of Blairgowrie and Ian Campbell. The concerts would be Sunday. I could do the pubs and working men's clubs on a Saturday but I wasn't allowed on the concert with Ewan. I told him to stuff it. I could get well paid for doing the folk clubs.

PEGGY SEEGER

Working on the *Radio Ballads* was wonderful! The big thing was learning how to write songs out of other people's words, to write songs that sounded like them speaking. It's using the way they speak, the way they breathe, almost the way they sit, the kind of feeling you get from them.

BOB DAVENPORT

I was due to do 'Song of the Road' but I went into hospital with tuberculosis so Louis Killen replaced me. I did *The Fight Game*. That was 1963. I went to America, came back and was told, 'Oh, you got it all wrong . . . all your songs were out of key.' I was singing with guys who read notes and I was singing around the theme. I'd listened to enough jazz to sing around a theme but they said, 'Oh, we took that out and took this out.'

Then they said they want to put it out on Argo on an LP and they wanted clearance. I said, 'Yeah, you can have clearance but my name must not appear anywhere – publicity, the cover, not anywhere at all.' They agreed to that but unfortunately Tony Engle, when they put it out on CD, hadn't read that contract, so my name's on it.

When the guy who wrote the book about the *Radio Ballads* asked Peggy Seeger, 'Why didn't you use Bob Davenport more?', she said she didn't know. I think the simple reason was they didn't like my voice. Charles Parker said to me, 'We've got you in *The Fight Game*, Davenport, but you're a music hall singah.'

LOUIS KILLEN

I'd been working for British Railways catering service as a clerk for three months and I got my first rail pass. I'd gone to Doncaster for free and bought the rest of the ticket and gone off for the weekend to London, to the folk clubs. On the Saturday night I went into the Singers' Club and MacColl says, 'Oh, been trying to get hold of you, blah, blah, blah. We're doing a *Radio Ballad* . . .' It was 'Song of the Road'. I was very familiar with the first one, 'John Axon' which had come out the year before, all the folkies were. He said, 'I'd like you to be in it.' I said, 'Yes. Sure. When does it start?' He said, 'On Monday.' So I made a quick decision – bugger the job. 'Song of the Road' cost me a job.

IAN CAMPBELL

I wrote two *Radio Ballads* – 'The Jewellery' and 'Cry from the Cut'. They were centred in Birmingham. When 'The Jewellery' was broadcast, it was well received – they said, 'Considering that MacColl and Seeger were not involved, it's remarkably good although nothing like the standard of the MacColl and Seeger programmes.'

I could have wept. What they didn't know was Ewan and Peggy got six to eight months to collect the material and to work arranging, writing and so on. Then they called the singers and musicians to the studio where they had ten days to rehearse and record.

I was given three weeks' notice, with one day to rehearse and record. It was completely unfair. The people who were commenting on 'The Jewellery' didn't know. The BBC weren't going to tell them. Charles Parker wasn't going to tell them because the reason behind it all – and I never dared let it be known – was he actually came to me and quite straightforwardly asked me for a favour.

He said, 'We're in the shit with the *Radio Ballads* because they're costing far too much. A one-hour ballad is costing as much to make as a bloody one-hour television spectacular. The BBC are not happy about it. I'm under constant pressure to cut the budget. All we can do is lower the average cost by doing a programme for nothing – can you do me a programme for nothing?'

I said, 'Yes, of course. I'd be delighted. Thank you for the privilege. I'm an amateur. I'll do it for expenses.' I ended up writing all the words and a couple of tunes. A year later, he said, 'I'm really grateful for what you did, can you do us another one? I don't want a collection of musicians – use your group, with two extra musicians.' For the second one, my total fee, for writing, arranging, performing and everything else was £17. A one-hour musical documentary.

They were not brought out on the CDs of the *Radio Ballads*. I know they weren't up to standard – but they should have explained to people to get some sense of proportion.

PEGGY SEEGER
The Charles Parker Archive still call them the *Charles Parker Radio Ballads* to my knowledge. I may be wrong. We were angry about the hijacking of the *Radio Ballads*, because Theatre Workshop had already been hijacked off Ewan.

It was a basic fault on our part. We never networked, Ewan and I. We worked, we made songs, we recorded them, then didn't break our necks to try and sell them. We didn't run around to radio stations saying, 'Listen to this, we just moved on to the next thing.' We went wrong somewhere – so we were disappeared. 'This theatre is mine – these *Radio Ballads* are mine.' The fact that they talk about them so much makes people think they are.

JIM O'CONNOR

Ewan had some volatile relationships with people. I remember
he had run-ins with Bob Davenport over issues. Ewan was very
authoritarian and it would be very difficult to criticise him,
difficult for him to accept it.

BOB DAVENPORT

There was a confrontation at the John Snow pub one night. They
wanted to have a discussion on where folk music was going. I was
on the panel and there was Ewan, Bert Lloyd, Peggy, Alex Campbell
and myself. Alex did this great confession. I thought he was the
only one who was going to give me any assistance, but he stood
up and said how he was sorry for popularising the music and how
he wanted to apologise to them all and he should have been more
serious and all this. I thought, 'That's my only ally gone!'

I gave my view from the Fox club in Islington and the Elliotts'
club in Birtley. Bert got up and tried to placate things and Ewan
MacColl had the chair. The discussion ended and MacColl's
summing up as chair. So he started to give his view and this
young woman stood up and amazed me. She said, 'A point of
order, chair. You are giving your view. You're not summing up.'

MacColl was absolutely taken aback. This great fan of order
was flattened. He couldn't give his view – it was, you've heard
all the crap, now you're going to get Ewan MacColl. But she
stopped him.

Smashing glasses was one of MacColl's big gestures. I saw him
do it and threaten somebody with the glass four times. He did it in
a pub in Nottingham when I did Centre 42, when I first met Anne
Briggs. We were invited back for drinks and there were sandwiches
on. We're all sitting around, winding down, and having a chat. Joe
Heaney was there and MacColl asked Joe to sing.

We were all in a social situation and Joe was singing and
everyone round the table is muttering away and MacColl
smashes a pint glass. 'Don't you dare talk when a great singer
like this is singing these great ballads.' The landlord was across,

'Get out, the lot of you. Get out of my place, straight away!' MacColl made his big gesture and spoiled it for everybody.

If you went to his house, Betsy, his mother was there. If you went there, it was an act. You'd have the main meal and he would put the cheeses out and tell you all about them. It was very much a one-man show. He used to tap into your ego. 'Do you realise that you hold in your hand this great treasure, this culture of the north-east of England, or Glasgow, or the Highlands or wherever?' And before you knew where you were you'd be sucked into it, and some people *were* sucked in. The other thing was, he had the contacts through the BBC and the trade unions to put you on concerts and everything. It was sad because he was great as a writer and I felt that too often he took away the positive side.

JIM McLEAN

I argued with him many times. I went down to his house in Beckenham one time. There was me, Nigel Denver, my wife Alison, and Bruce Dunnett. He picked us up at the station and we went to his house and he lectured us the whole time we were there.

He sat in a chair. Peggy sat on the arm of it – she was crocheting – and all he did was argue, argue, argue. He kept jumping off his chair up to the bookshelf to make his point, then he'd lose his thread and Peggy would jag him with the crochet needle and say, 'You were talking about this . . .' Oh, yes, yes. I remember one time he pointed at me. I had a McLean tie on and he said, 'Wearing this nationalist stuff . . .' I said, 'At least my name is McLean, Mr Miller.'

I was a Republican and Scottish Nationalist and he was all for the British working man. He would record Burns songs, he would record Jacobite songs, because they were well in the past, but any modern stuff, no. And I was writing all the rebel stuff at the time.

He said, 'We need more love songs.' I think this was the time he'd written 'The First Time Ever I Saw Your Face'. I said, 'No, we need more war songs, Ewan.' I was meaning in Scotland we'd got to fight for our rights. He drove us back to the station but there was silence.

I used to go to his club at the Pindar of Wakefield but it wasn't my scene. It was far too boring. You would get a song with about ninety verses, a whodunnit, but he would tell you who done it before he started singing. And there were all the rules. I understood and agreed with what he was doing, with all the left-wing stuff. I agreed with all of that. I think MacColl was a fantastic figure. We just disagreed on the Scottish Nationalist thing.

PEGGY SEEGER

Dominic Behan would sing at the club sometimes. Dominic had a huge problem with being Brendan's brother – and with Brendan's light shining first. Dominic was very erratic. He was absolutely charming on stage, and an absolute liar off stage. He'd say he'd do something and he wouldn't do it at all – he wouldn't turn up.

He would bring the suit that he was going to wear and he would change into it before he got on stage. Of course, this was a working-class thing, whereas Ewan would come with his shirt undone. You have to take people as you find them and this was one of Ewan's problems – he wanted everybody to be predictable.

AUDREY WINTER

He was very difficult, a very difficult man. Eric and Ewan had been on very good terms – they were always on the phone to each other, singing songs down the phone, trying things out. Then Eric wrote a very mild criticism in *Sing* about something that Ewan had done. It was to do with putting American banjo riffs to our genuinely traditional folk songs.

Ewan couldn't take anything like that and he just cut Eric off, like a guillotine. Whenever they met, Ewan ignored him. He never spoke to Eric again from that day. Peggy was perfectly friendly.

JIM O'CONNOR

He was capable of being quite disparaging about Bert Lloyd, although they appeared together a number of times. Whether it was just rivalry, I don't know.

FRANKIE ARMSTRONG

Ewan and Bert tended to have their separate camps, I think I'm the only person who did concerts and recorded with both of them. I feel enormously privileged and honoured to have done that, but I didn't align myself to either of them. I was certainly fonder of Bert, because he was much easier to be fonder of.

I met Bert Lloyd at a weekend festival somewhere up north in about 1964. I was starting to open my ears to different styles of singing and harmony and just getting so excited. I travelled back on the train with Bert all the way to London and that was where I really got a chance to listen to him and to realise what an extraordinary man he was – his background on the whalers and working for *Picture Post*.

To many of us young singers Bert was a constant encouragement. He'd send me tapes, which I've still got. He'd send me manuscript paper in his beautiful writing with a song written out and dotted, saying, 'I think this would suit you, Frankie.' He really built up my repertoire.

MIKE WATERSON

Early doors, and later, I heard folk say, 'Oh, Bert Lloyd taught you all your harmonies.' But Bert Lloyd didn't teach us harmonies at all, he gave us songs, he gave us enthusiasm. Bert Lloyd was one of those people that was willing to talk to you – and it was like an injection.

SHIRLEY COLLINS

Ewan MacColl and Bert Lloyd? There was a feeling around that it would be good to gain their approval. They certainly held sway, but I didn't like either of them, and the feeling was mutual. I particularly disliked and mistrusted the pretentious and arrogant way that Ewan performed. So, the question for me might be – did they have *my* approval? And the answer was – and is – no! I always valued my independence and trusted my own judgement and instincts where folk song was concerned.

JIM IRVINE *of the Marsden Rattlers from Tyneside*
Ewan MacColl used to get up and pontificate. I remember he asked if anybody had an idea for a song and I said, 'If you look at the shipyards, Ewan, the days of the riveters are finished, it's all welding now.' And he said, 'Well, if you get to know all the nicknames, the terminology, send it down, I'll put a song together.' I thought, 'I could do that meself.' I thought he was a leech. A nice enough feller, but he made a lot of money out of people. He wrote some good stuff, but he made a lot of money.

CLIVE PALMER
When Ewan MacColl and Peggy Seeger used to come to folk clubs, they didn't allow any support – they did the whole night. MacColl was the master of the closed question. If you asked him anything he never gave you an answer. You couldn't have a conversation with him. I bumped into him a few times at Cecil Sharp House and other places. He was a genius though – he wrote some fantastic songs. I loved his records, especially the English ballads and Jacobite relics with Peggy Seeger backing him on the banjo.

HUGHIE JONES
The Spinners' club was noted as a singing club, where people would join in. Peggy once said, 'Now then, if you're going to sing the choruses, if you will sing the choruses, you may as well do it right.' And she went through the chorus, line by line. You could see our members looking at each other. She didn't judge them right. Perhaps Peggy hadn't been north of Watford at that time. I don't know.

BARBARA DICKSON *went from the Scottish folk clubs to great success in the pop charts*

They were a massive influence. One of my favourite albums when I was young was one of those Exiles albums, which I heard in Arthur Argo's house in Aberdeen. Ewan and Peggy did 'The Moving on Song' and I was captivated. I thought he was brilliant. He had a theatricality and the music, the words, were just dramatic. For many years, whenever an unaccompanied song was required, I sang, 'The First Time Ever I Saw Your Face' which I'd learned as a young woman. I reckon it's the best love song ever written. And that's Ewan MacColl, to Peggy Seeger.

PEGGY SEEGER

Ewan and I weren't getting along very well. I was in California. He was over here in England. I thought it was a very nice song but I don't remember being bowled over. When you're twenty-three, twenty-four or whatever I was, you feel the world owes you love, as a woman.

We hadn't solidified anything and I was running like hell to get away from him. I'd gone to the States. He was married, for Christ's sake. He was twenty years older than me. It wasn't my brief. Did the song help? I don't know. What helped was that when I came back I fell in love with him. After Ewan died I couldn't sing 'First Time Ever' for about four or five years, didn't even try.

Over the years we've had a number of people singing the song. We had a collection of records of people singing it – we called it the Chamber of Horrors. The ones that we thought sang it well were Peter, Paul and Mary and Bonnie Dobson. Most people drag it out. What really bothered us more than anything else was they changed the tune. Roberta Flack did, they all did.

DAVE ARTHUR

After MacColl's death, Toni and I had several meals with Peggy, at our place and hers, before she went back to the States. We had a lot of fun playing music and chatting. She seemed to be much more her own woman after Ewan's death, and came out from under his considerable shadow. I remember one evening we were all sitting around on the floor playing skiffle numbers, and I wondered at the time what MacColl would have made of it had he walked in.

DAVE BURLAND *Barnsley-based singer of traditional and contemporary songs*
I'd seen him, but I didn't know him. I was never privileged enough to sing at his club. That was considered to be a great honour. It was Tony Capstick's idea to do the record, *The Songs of Ewan MacColl*, all those old songs which nobody sang any more. Me, him and Dick Gaughan. Tony's heart was really in that sort of stuff, he could interpret those songs, and Dick was well up for it.

We did it in about three days. It's a very simple album and that's what I like about it, no pyrotechnics, just good songs. I think we did it sort of by default in a way, but I think it was the right way to do an album of MacColl songs.

I don't think we got any reaction from MacColl, but Dick sent him the record. Later on, after MacColl had died, I mentioned it once to Peggy Seeger and she said, 'Oh, you're the people trying to make money out of his death.' I said, 'No, we recorded it in 1978. Back then I thought I was going to die before Ewan.'

PEGGY SEEGER
People will pay lip service and call you a legend, but there's something in what we did. I know we put people's backs up. There's something in the way we performed that is not popular enough. It doesn't make me angry. I'm curious about what it is.

We were very kinda rude about a lot of things and dismissive of a lot of things that we didn't really know about. I will say that I followed Ewan's lead a lot and boycotted things I would not even think of boycotting. I'm trying to mend fences now because there were a lot of broken fences back then.

6 It was like a fire swept the country

The word was spreading and all over the country new folk clubs were opening. In 1961, according to Sing *magazine, there were thirty-six, a figure that rose to seventy-eight the following year. By the mid-decade several hundred had sprung up, but an accurate figure was difficult to establish as many clubs were short-lived.*

In an interview for this book Martin Carthy said, 'In the very early sixties there weren't that many clubs, but in 1970 somebody did a count-up of clubs in London and there were 400.'

Peggy Seeger conducted a wider survey which suggested there were 'about three thousand clubs in the country, just an unbelievable number. We tried to keep track, sending out forms for people to send back and we asked them to put down the names of any other clubs in their area. You'd find that half of them had closed, or some had moved to another place. There was no way of keeping track of it. There were more clubs than singers at one point.'

That was the recollection of several interviewees – a flourishing scene where performers could do a few floor spots, pick up bookings and within a short time earn their living solely from the folk clubs. Singers and musicians who ran clubs booked others who did likewise, to their mutual benefit. Students who had seen guests in their college and university clubs passed on the good word about them when they went to their home-town clubs.

The club network was now rapidly developing and out of it new performers were emerging, young men and women who would be mainstays of the folk clubs for decades to come. From Manchester came Mike Harding, from Edinburgh, the McCalmans. Future Dubliner, Sean Cannon, began in Coventry, Maddy Prior in St Albans. Robin and Barry Dransfield formed a bluegrass group in Harrogate, June Tabor sang Dylan songs, unaccompanied, in Leamington Spa.

They all began their careers the same way, by getting up in their local folk club and doing a floor spot. They received encouragement, returned in the following weeks and they were on their way. Billy Connolly attended a club in Clydebank and immediately sought out banjo lessons. Brian Golbey's father took him to one in Brighton. John Tams's discovery came about when he enrolled on a six-week course, 'How to start a folk club', at his old school in Derbyshire.

Richard Thompson, who went along to the Black Bull in north London as a schoolboy, recalls, 'There seemed to be no end of folk clubs at the time, and no end of audience and performers.'

IAN CAMPBELL

Most of the folk clubs had an audience of between sixty and eighty and a good club was a hundred. They'd charge four or five shillings admission. What some started to do – if it was a national name like say Hall and Macgregor – they might charge ten shillings. That was heavy shit. At the Jug of Punch we used to charge two shillings or one shilling if you were a student or a pensioner. We had the biggest club in the country – 400 were allowed in. This was at Digbeth Civic Hall. We paid guests every week and ran the club for seventeen years and never took a fee, except at Hogmanay.

HARVEY ANDREWS *singer and writer of topical songs*

I was teaching in Birmingham and I'd heard about the Jug of Punch and Ian Campbell so I went to the phone box over the road and started phoning up all the I. Campbells in the directory. There were four and Ian was the third one. I asked him if I could come and sing three songs I'd written, at his club. He said, 'You can come and audition.'

So I went to the Jug at Digbeth Civic Hall and Ian auditioned me and he said okay. I was sat in the audience in my jacket that still had chalk dust on and he called me up eventually. It was all a whirl. There were lights, microphones and it seemed like hundreds of people. I sang my three songs and when I finished they clapped and shouted for more. Ian said, 'Do another one.' I said, 'I haven't written any more.' He said, 'Right, sod off laddie.' He talked to me afterwards, he said, 'You come along with new songs and I'll let you up.' I was in.

After that it happened very quickly. On 2 December 1964 I did my first ever proper gig as support to the Campbells at Stratford-upon-Avon folk club. I got £2 10 shillings. By March '65 I was picking up £7 10 shillings a gig. At this time there were far more clubs than there were artists to work them. We were created by an audience – we didn't create an audience like you have to do today. They were desperate for someone to get up with a guitar.

When I look at the list of gigs I did in the first year, it was almost all local. Most of them were in Birmingham – the Communist club, the Holy Ground, training colleges, Coventry, Walsall, Cannock, Tamworth, Lichfield, Solihull, Wolverhampton. I did a concert in Exeter with Julie Felix but the first one in London was at the Troubadour, where I met Paul Simon. They paid me £10.

JOHN FOREMAN
The Campbells' club at Digbeth Civic Hall, that was terrific. There was nothing to touch it in London, the scale of it or the quality of the residents – Ian Campbell and Lorna, and Dave Swarbrick. Birmingham was packed with clubs.

Leicester was very rich in folk clubs under the aegis of Toni Savage. Often you'd go back to the organiser's house and spend all bloody night talking about what was going on. That's why I used to drive home if I could. I'd drive back to London from Hull and go to work the next morning.

SEAN CANNON *born in Galway, brought up in Coventry, joined the Dubliners in 1982*
The first folk club I ever sang in was the Cofa's Tree in Coventry.

This was 1965. It was a big room and every Sunday night the club was packed out. I saw Dominic Behan there and the first time I saw the Dubliners was there. They weren't the guests, they were on tour, and they had the night off and came along. All five of them were there – Ronnie Drew, Barney McKenna, Luke Kelly, John Sheahan and Ciaran Bourke. I never guessed that one day I'd join them.

With this friend of mine, Bill Hartnett, who'd introduced me to the folk clubs, we formed a group. We called ourselves the Gaels. We started a club ourselves at the Denbigh Arms in Monks Kirby, ten miles out of Coventry. We booked Jasper Carrott and he invited us in turn to play his place, the Boggery. Jasper had a good grounding in the folk clubs. He played the guitar and sang a lot of funnies. Harvey Andrews was a guest at our club and the Young Tradition. Christy Moore came and did a spot for £20 and so did the Fureys, they were £25. We had 2,000 members. It was a big room and it was always full.

JOHNNY HANDLE
There was a folk grapevine, people who had moved away from the north-east and started folk clubs. The first booking I got was for £6. In those days it was virtually for expenses. I didn't drive. I went on the train. If you did a good night they said, 'We'll book you next year and we'll get some more clubs, to make it worthwhile.' That was the way it went. There was less to choose from then and I was an interesting act for people from other parts of the country because I could do material articulately. I could do the Geordie slavver or not according to how the audience was taking it, with a balance of chorus songs and a few instrumentals.

MADDY PRIOR
We had Johnny Handle at the Peahen in St Albans. It was quite a big club and he came and did all his miners' stuff, we never understood a word he said. People have got used to the accent now but then we'd never heard it. He was telling stories and we

didn't know what he was on about. That would have been '63 maybe, I was still at school.

MIKE WATERSON

Louis Killen had moved down to St Albans and he was running three clubs with a bloke called Ken – St Albans, Hitchin, Watford, all round that area. Louis said, 'Come on down, I'll get you these gigs.' It was a Thursday, Friday and Sunday, I think. That was our first series of bookings out of Hull.

There was nothing on the Saturday and Louis says, 'We all go down to the Troubadour on Saturday nights, get yourselves down there.' So we went down and there was Martin Carthy on and everybody that didn't have a gig that night was there. Louis said, 'They sing' – that was us. Martin Winsor was running the night and we stood up and did three songs. That's when we met Bill Leader who made our first record.

I cringe when I think back on it, because we had no personality in the showbiz sense of the word. We believed if you talked too much in between songs, you didn't sing as many songs, and the whole object was to get as many songs over as possible, to make folk music popular. For years we just sang song after song after song without saying much at all, without introductions even.

It wasn't till I went to America for the first time in '76 that I started thinking about talking properly to the audience. We did ten days at the Bi-Centennial in Washington. We did workshops where you'd stand on the stage and they told you what to sing – sing a song about love, sing a song about war, sing a comic song.

I did a lot of comic songs. I sang and got no laughs whatsoever. One, because they couldn't understand the accent and, two, I was singing too fast. So I started slowing down, and thinking of putting the song across more. It worked and I thought, 'You silly bugger – this is what you should have been doing years ago.'

Early on we were on a CND tour with Alex Campbell. Over a week of touring in the back of a twelve-seater bus with Alex, that was amazing. The stories of his life. There were so many good people – Colin Wilkie and Shirley . . . Jackie and Bridie in Liverpool. The Campbells were lovely. The Spinners tried to help us so much with stagecraft – and it all went in one ear and out the other. At the time that wasn't what we were about.

HARVEY ANDREWS

I toured with Alex Campbell in Scotland on a CND tour in '66. I think it was in Glasgow. As I walked off I missed a step and fell, really badly sprained my ankle and had it put in plaster.

The next night we were in Edinburgh and Alex carries me out on stage, sits me down on a chair, foot up on another chair and I do my five or six songs. Alex is backstage with Bert Jansch and one or two others having a whale of a time.

I finished my set and I didn't know what to do. I was embarrassed. I didn't say anything. I just sat there. They applauded and there was silence for a bit and then they started to sort of titter, then laugh, and I was just sitting there, paralysed. It was horrible, it seemed to go on for ever.

There were a few boos and then Alex appears to this huge roar of applause and I was picked up by him and carried off. I realised then that I had to learn to communicate with an audience, to be able to talk to them and take any situation that came and deal with it. That was a quite a lesson.

STAN CROWTHER

We started the Taverners club in 1962 at the Mason's Arms in Rotherham. I'd invited Eric Winter up from London and got together all the people I could think of who were interested. I said, 'I want you to come and give me advice,' and we had a marvellous night, it didn't finish until breakfast. We had all the usual guests – Bert Jansch, Robin Williamson, Alex Campbell, Luke Kelly of the Dubliners, the McPeakes. People just turned up sometimes.

We had the Spinners. Tony Davis phoned, 'Stan, we've not had a booking at your club yet.' I said, 'Well, I was hoping to get you but I just read in Sing magazine that you've just gone

professional, full time. We shan't be able to afford you now.'
We'd just moved into the Mason's Arms, a bigger pub, and they
came for twenty-five quid.

ROBIN WILLIAMSON *founded the Incredible String Band
with Clive Palmer*
One of the first gigs I ever did outside Scotland was in
Greasbrough, near Rotherham. I hitched down and I remember
it because it took me a day and a half each way.

SHIRLEY COLLINS
I travelled all over the country and, yes, it could have been
dangerous, especially in the sixties, when I had young children
and travelled back on overnight trains to make sure I was home
for the morning. Some of those trains were grim and unnerving.
At least, some of my fellow passengers were.

But I survived. I had a hot temper and a heavy banjo case for
use in an emergency! Looking back, I wonder why I put myself
through it. But I suppose it was because I had to sing.

Fees varied from club to club, of course, depending on the size
of the audience. I think by the mid-sixties I was going out for
£15 plus train fares. I never got rich.

LOUIS KILLEN
Sometimes I struggled. Some clubs were a pain in the ass, most
of them down south in the Home Counties when folk music
became 'popular'. Round about '63 you got clubs starting up in
suburban areas, run by middle-class kids who hadn't a clue what
the songs were about really. A lot of those began to spring up,
especially in the south.

I had a terrible night in Johnstone in Scotland. I was staying
with Jim McLean at his home in Paisley, but I never saw him
because by the time I got back he was fast asleep. He had to go to
work in the morning.

Jim had one afternoon off, a Wednesday, and this was the night

I was doing the Johnstone gig so we got together at lunchtime. We met in the pub and started on the malt whiskies, knocking them back with chasers, pints of heavy. When holy hour came we stopped and found our way to Drew Moyes's place and started drinking again.

I was pissed when I went on stage. I started doing 'The Flying Cloud' and somewhere round about the third or fourth verse I found myself repeating it, but I was on the third repetition when I realised. The feller who ran the club didn't pay me, but he made me go back and do the second set.

Very rarely I had trouble getting the money. A couple of clubs over the years defaulted, they said either we don't have the money or we'll send you a cheque. When that happened you let everybody know – don't do that club, you won't get paid.

SEAN CANNON
Jean Oglesby and Jane Winder had an agency, booking people into the clubs, and they said, 'Do you want to come on our books?' I'd go away for a week and come back and there'd be a postcard from the agency with the gigs and I'd write them into my diary and off I'd go again. I had a Morris Minor and for ten years I did that. I'd go to London for a weekend and do three or four clubs.

The Morris Minor did about thirty-five to the gallon and in those days for a pound you could go a hundred miles. I was happy. it was always a revelation to me. It was educational, having an interest in the folk songs, politics, attitude to life, folklore.

JOHN FOREMAN
It was haphazard. I would turn up in Southampton and they'd say, 'Oh, hello, John, nice to see you. We weren't expecting you.' Oh dear, I should have been in Northampton.

GEF LUCENA *founder of Saydisc records in Bristol, later co-founder of Village Thing label and agency*
The first club in Bristol was at the Communist Club. I went there

in the winter of '62/'63 and it had been going for some time then. Dave Creech, who was later in the Pigsty Hill Light Orchestra, was involved. When Centre 42 came to Bristol in '62, that was a major stimulus for the folk clubs. We'd started off singing not long before and we suddenly found ourselves singing in local pubs with Cyril Tawney and Matt McGinn and the McPeakes. They had a concert at the Colston Hall which I think was sponsored by CND. It was a terrible winter, I remember helping people to get around to the Centre 42 things.

ROY BAILEY
The playwright, Arnold Wesker, had gone to the TUC annual conference and proposed that the TUC should fund cultural and artistic events as well as its industrial relations business. As I understand it, it happened to be motion number 42, so the arts project became Centre 42. One area of the project was folk song. It travelled mostly to the new council estates. The object was to show people that the UK had its own indigenous music as well as the music that came from America. We weren't opposed to the latter but we had our own culture of song and music and we should be aware of it.

When Centre 42 came to Leicester, I was invited to participate. We didn't just sing in the local folk clubs. Every night we went and sang in the pubs on the estates. I have a clear recollection of going with Ray Fisher, Cyril Tawney, Belle Stewart and her husband Alec Stewart, a pipe player, to the Rocket, a pub in Leicester. The locals were all playing cribbage or dominoes or darts.

BERNARD WRIGLEY *singer, concertina player, monologuist and actor*
If you go to a concert there's a barrier, but in a folk club it's all instant – you're there and there's no segregation. I was in the sixth form at school and I got a guitar and a friend of mine, Dave Brooks, we went to the local folk club in Bolton and it was, wow – this is good!

We used to go to the Manchester Sports Guild on a Monday, that was like a melting pot. It was run by a lad called Drony and everyone would do two or three songs. All the folk club organisers from around Manchester were there so if you did a good spot you could get six bookings out of it. It was never advertised, all word of mouth. There were so many clubs then. Bolton had one every night of the week, Liverpool had twenty or more.

When I got my first Topic album, *The Phenomenal B. Wrigley*, Bert Lloyd produced it and he did the sleeve notes. In those days you didn't really have any say. It just arrived one day – oh, my first album – and on the back it said 'Bernard Wrigley is the Bolton Bullfrog'. I thought, 'What's that?', and ignored it, but it stuck. Some people thought it was my name.

PAUL SNOW

Every club you went to there were organisers from other clubs. Everybody was so enthusiastic. When you consider that the average wage was £12 to £15 a week and you were getting £10 to £15 a night. In the sixties it was so easy. You could work every night. In those days there was a folk club in virtually every village – and not enough singers who could do an evening.

WIZZ JONES

Pete Stanley was pretty organised. He used to get the Folk Directory that the EFDSS published. He'd write to the clubs and there were so few people on the scene that, if we did a gig, they'd say, 'When can you come back?' We'd do the same club three times a year. Word of mouth, it just built up.

MIKE WATERSON

We made the mistake – once we saw somebody and enjoyed 'em – we'd book 'em again as soon as possible. It was a big mistake. It was almost like overstaying your welcome. We booked the Campbells too often, the Spinners. They were good but more or less like the Americans – at the beginning of every year they'd learn an act and if you booked 'em twice in a year you'd get the same act. There weren't enough good people to do all the clubs.

MARTIN CARTHY

Clubs were opening. I was getting gigs because I was there and it gave me a chance to learn how to be a performer, to learn the kind of songs I wanted to sing and follow my nose towards being able to sing 'A Lofty Tall Ship' like Sam Larner, playing on the guitar, which I finally did in the nineties.

ITV did a folk programme called *Hullabaloo*. It was shown everywhere except London. Rory McEwen – Nadia Cattouse was on occasionally but she was on *Hallelujah* a lot, on a Sunday. She was on that every week, so was Isla Cameron. There was the *Hootenanny* show – I was only on that at the end of the second series. The bloke would not have me on it – he had the Campbells, the Spinners and the Corrie Folk Trio with Paddy Bell.

HARVEY ANDREWS

The daftest night I ever had, I stood in for someone who couldn't make it. I think it was Martin Carthy. It was a club just outside Wolverhampton, a traditional club. I get there and the room's packed. It was about 1965, very early on in my career and the guy who ran the club didn't know anything about me so we had a quick chat.

He introduces me . . . 'The thing is – he does write his own songs. Ladies and gentlemen – Harry Andrews.' So I start this song, 'Death come easy, to a young man in his prime . . .' There's a sigh and a thud at the back of the room and there's a huge guy there, long hair, beard and duffle coat, he says, 'It's all right, it's Elsie. She's fainted again.' And he bends down and picks up this inert woman, carries her down the side of the room out the door and lays her there on this wide landing, calls down for the landlady.

He comes back in the room, looks at me and says, 'Carry on 'Arry' and goes back to his place.

'Death come easy, if you come before your time. Death come easy, to a young man in his prime. They put a gun . . .' and there's a terrific explosion of noise right in front of me – people jumping up, tables going over, glasses everywhere, a guy on the floor having an epileptic fit. Then he goes rigid.

Beard and duffle coat comes down, picks him up and carries him out, puts him on the landing next to Elsie. The poor landlady's got two of them now.

He comes back in, looks at me and says, 'Try again 'Arry.

I'm not going to give up on this song. I haven't got through the first verse yet and I'm determined to. The room had a wagon wheel with little bulbs on, hanging from a chain. So, 'Death come easy . . .'

I'm affecting the upward gaze of the serious social commentator and I notice little bits of white stuff floating down from the ceiling. I get to about the third line and there's a big bang, a flash of blue lights and the wagon wheel and chain come crashing down on this poor soul in the audience. It sort of wedges on his head. Everybody screams and he pushes himself up, he looked at me direct and he says, 'Bloody 'ell'. He levered this thing off, his eyes rolled into his head and he crashed down unconscious on the floor.

Beard and duffle coat comes along, picks him up and takes him outside. Now there's three of them.

He comes back in. There's chaos everywhere. He walks up to me, gets me by the lapels and he says, 'Listen 'Arry. If you don't change that soddin' song, there'll be none of us left 'ere soon.'

You learn to deal with it.

ROBIN DRANSFIELD *formed a duo in the late sixties with his brother Barry*
Harrogate folk club was fantastic. It was started by people who were members of the Young Communist League and the CND, which in Harrogate was remarkable. There was an art college in Harrogate and, unlike these days, back then there seemed to

be a lot of nutters and eccentric people around. My education, particularly my political education, began there, because it was the heyday of CND, the world was going to come to an end tomorrow. Then finding out about Woody Guthrie and people like that. It was an amazing time.

I started off singing Johnny Cash songs with Roger Knowles, who I'd met at a party, and we got into playing bluegrass. I was playing banjo – I got a Pete Seeger banjo tutor by post from London. Fairly soon we put the whole five-piece bluegrass band together, the Crimple Mountain Boys.

At that time, while we were doing floor spots, a lot of the other people who were singing at the Harrogate folk club were singing English stuff and gradually my eyes became opened to the tradition of my own country and the bluegrass band started to fade away, although I was still playing in it.

I was listening to people like Louis Killen, the Watersons came over from Hull and Martin Carthy from London, Shirley Collins, some really fine Scottish singers and the McPeakes. People who are legends now. This was in '62 and these people were blazing a trail.

BILLY CONNOLLY

I remember it very clearly, 1965, I was in the Parachute Regiment, the Territorials, and I liked country music and a guy called Haggerty said, 'There's some guys play down at our pub, they call it a folk club.'

I went away down. It was in Clydebank, I think it was called the Seven Seas. I paid my money and, lo and behold, these guys were playing country music. They were called the Tannahills and there was a banjo player called Ron Duff. The lead guy in the band was Danny Kyle, who became my best friend. I said to him, 'How can I learn the banjo?' He said, 'He'll show you – he'll teach you – Ron Duff.' So I went out and bought a banjo and Ron became my banjo teacher, right there and then.

I was hooked from day one. Matt McGinn was the guest.

He was a Scottish songwriter but the music all mixed very comfortably, that's what I loved about it. You could have the Incredible String Band and Diz Disley and a Scottish guy singing traditional English songs, 'Chicken on a Raft' or something. There was total acceptance – Diz doing those ridiculous poems, 'The Lion Ate Our Albert'. We even had a guy morris dancing in the Glasgow club – the bravest guy I ever saw!

There was a guy called Green and he ran a folk club on a Sunday night in the police social club in Edinburgh. It wasn't all police. They opened it to the public. There was a lot of folkies went. I got in trouble there one night. They had some guests from Ulster and I said something about the Ulster problem and they took umbrage. I said, 'Well, if you don't fuckin' like it you know what you can do . . .'

DAVE BURLAND

It was 1962 and I was twenty-one and this neighbour asked me if I'd heard about the folk club at the Alhambra in Barnsley on a Monday night, so I went down. A bloke called Tony Heald ran it. He was a very talented bloke. He seemed to know so much about this strange world of folk music. It was run on a singaround basis and just good fun, but the audiences were about ninety to a hundred people, every week. It was a real good vibe, anybody could get up and do anything they wanted.

What had a huge impact was that it wasn't a commercial type of music. To hear people singing these really strange songs, which were exploring the American tradition a bit further than the skiffle groups had, and then somebody would sing an English or Irish traditional song from the Clancys – I just thought it was great. It was something I could do as well.

The first big guest we had was Alex Campbell. He had this huge personality, I couldn't believe anybody could be like that, he was a revelation to me. It was like Elvis coming to Barnsley.

Then I got into the Barley Mow in Sheffield, that was a fantastic club. Everybody didn't just join in on the choruses, they sang the verses as well. I went back in that room at the Three Cranes recently and I couldn't believe how small it was. It was tiny yet they got so many people in. I don't think we realised at the time how amazing it was, and what a great organiser Malcolm Fox was. He had a library of books – Gavin Greig's *Folk Song of the North East*, which I bet you can't find outside Cecil Sharp House – and he lent me it for months. He really was a motivator, in a very quiet way.

What's always baffled me about these people who organised the early clubs, who were hugely influential on my life, like Tony Heald and Malcolm Fox, is, where did they get their knowledge from? How did they know all this stuff? It must have been word of mouth, but then again we tend to forget how quickly it all took off. Once it sparked, it was like a fire swept the country.

PETE WOOD *singer and concertina player, member of the Keelers*
The University Folk Song Society formed the first folk club in Sheffield in November '61. That changed my life, really. They said you've got to sing a folk song, so I went and bought a guitar and my first song was 'Dark as a Dungeon'.

When I went home on vacation, I went to the Manchester clubs. The first one was on a Sunday afternoon in the Left Wing Coffee House. There were a lot of politics around at that time. Shortly after that, when I was home, I started going to the Wayfarers, Harry Boardman's club. He was doing very fine American ballads, but he'd started to move into Lancashire stuff, which made his name. So I picked up songs there as well. That was all in the first year.

I left Sheffield in '63 and had a year in London. I had a residency at Bunjies Coffee House in Charing Cross Road. It was in a cellar, it was trendy then to have music in coffee bars. I first saw the Watersons at the Troubadour – Louis Killen had the gig and he brought these four people with him. They really looked callow and pinched.

I remember doing a first gig in Sheffield for £3. They'd had Barney McKenna the week before. He was so pissed in the bar downstairs they had to carry him up the steps. They sat him on a chair, put the banjo in his arms and he never played a wrong note all night.

JUNE TABOR

It was the summer of '63. I wasn't old enough to drink. A friend at school said there was a folk club opened in Leamington, did I want to go. I'd seen Martin Carthy on TV. He was accompanying Nadia Cattouse on a programme with Sidney Carter, *Hallelujah*, and there was something about it that attracted me. The other connection was the *Tonight* programme, with Robin Hall and Jimmie Macgregor.

So I went to the folk club, the Heart of England in Leamington Spa. The friend I went with, she'd been to folk clubs before, went straight up to the resident group and said, 'My friend sings.' So I did actually sing that first night. I sang 'Kumbaya' and 'Michael Row the Boat Ashore' and everybody joined in the choruses. I remember another time standing up and singing Dylan's 'Masters of War' unaccompanied, and 'The Gates of Eden'.

I liked it, the whole social aspect, being able to go somewhere on your own or with other girls and have some kind of social contact with people through a shared interest into which you could put as much or as little energy as possible. For somebody like me who wasn't very good at making friends outside school, it was a godsend.

I used to go to the Campbells' club in Birmingham on a Saturday night so I saw a lot of people there. I heard Anne Briggs and Shirley Collins but only on records at that time. I learned the songs off an Anne Briggs record, an EP on Topic. I just listened to it and listened to it until I knew it by heart and then I tried to imitate it, very slowly, to work out the technique. I drove my mother mad but that was how I taught myself how to sing in that style.

DAVE ARTHUR

I met Toni when I was about eighteen and was running a musical coffee bar in Wigmore Street. We started singing regularly in folk clubs around 1961 or '62 when we got married and moved to Oxford. There were a number of singers of folk songs in Oxford round that time.

One evening at Didcot folk club the guest was Karl Dallas. Toni and I were going along just to hear Karl but friends of ours had smuggled my guitar into the club and at one point in the evening they announced that Dave and Toni were going to perform two or three numbers. We were shaking with nerves as we were propelled on to the floor.

We sang with eyes shut tight, I think 'Will the Circle Be Unbroken' and a couple of other things. Karl was very kind to us and said we should do some more singing in clubs. That was the first step on the slippery slope of a career in folk music.

We moved to the Blackheath/Lewisham area into a large basement flat. Shirley Collins and her husband and kids were near neighbours in Blackheath village, as were ex-Thamesiders Marion Grey and Pete Maynard. We'd started performing professionally and we'd babysit for each other.

We did some gigs in Wandsworth Prison – they went down a storm with the prisoners. At that time we were doing a lot of chorus songs and Irish stuff, and they all joined in. Toni used to wear thigh boots and a micro skirt. She had a great pair of legs The first time we went it didn't occur to us that we were going into a prison.

When we got there all the guys were sitting there, the whole length of the gallery and below, and the stage was about six feet high at one end. So we were above them and they were looking up Toni's skirt and every time she had to bend down to pick up instruments, whistles went up. It was so embarrassing for her. Next time we went back she wore a long skirt.

RICHARD THOMPSON *original member of Fairport Convention*

I think we played in school folk clubs at first, definitely not pubs – this was when we were about fifteen. There seemed to be no end of folk clubs at the time, and no end of audience and performers. I'd go and play a song or two with a school friend for moral support. Folk music had a strong Socialist connection then and I think that brought a lot of people to it.

The songs were all American, blues or country or old-timey. I remember some Leadbelly, and Woody Guthrie, learned off records or out of books of folk song. It must have been excruciating. I'd go the Black Bull, when I lived in Whetstone – I saw the Watersons there, I think, in 1966.

When Fairport was coming together in the same year, we'd go to the Starting Gate and a couple of other clubs in the Muswell Hill area, whose names now escape me. We would also play at the local clubs occasionally, as an acoustic four-piece – myself, Simon, Ashley and Judy. With that line-up we were playing US singer-songwriter stuff – 'Strolling down the Highway', 'Pack up Your Sorrows', 'The Coming of the Roads'.

BRIAN GOLBEY *guitarist and singer of American old-timey music*

A fellow called Jim Marshall told my dad about this folk club in Brighton, Tom Paley was on. I'd been playing at home and we went down and listened and there were two of the local lads there and they were using finger picks. I thought, 'What's that about?', and on the way home I said to my dad, 'I'm never going to one of these clubs again, they're out of my league.' But I did go down again and they got me to sing from the floor. Then I'm a resident, and so on. I was singing Jimmie Rodgers songs, the Carter Family, Hank Williams. The Brighton clubs were very open, there was none of the 'you can only sing traditional songs' back then.

Jim Marshall ran a magazine that went out in tape format,

called *Folk Voice*. He managed to get me some gigs. I'd done my national service in Aldershot, that was the furthest from Brighton I'd been. The first gig was in Lincoln and the second was in Nottingham.

JOHN TAMS *of Muckram Wakes, the Albion Band and Home Service, went on to be musical director at the National Theatre* The school that I'd just left, Somercotes Secondary Modern School for Boys, put on a WEA night class, which was basically 'Build your own folk club'. Pretty progressive – this was 1965. I'd be about sixteen.

I think it was a six-week course and this little bearded guy turned up with a banjo and played songs to us, in between telling us how to bolt a club together – form a committee and that sort of thing. He actually sponsored Alfreton folk club, which was known as the Upstairs Cellar, at the Four Horseshoes. He was a Scot – I think his name was Andrew Turner. He looked like an old commie and he had a lot of songs that were either north-east or Scottish industrial songs.

I've always been attracted to industrial songs, rather than elfin knights on milk-white steeds and wack-fol-de-dols. He'd got jute mill songs and things like that, about people toiling, as you would expect from Workers' Education.

So we formed a committee and then we had to grow a resident group and we had to learn songs pretty damn quick. There weren't that many people about and it wasn't easy to get hold of the songs. Books weren't around and not too much in the way of vinyl either. It was hard accessing the songs and we were having to learn half a dozen a week to keep up with the needs of being a resident group.

All the local people who were in the Communist Party came to support it, and also became part of the committee, so it was a very democratically run organisation and on solid lines. It was a mining community then, Labour stronghold and the Communist Party was an attractive bunch of people. They were kinda creative and artistic, rather flamboyant, good fun to be around.

About six weeks later we found this pub and set about redecorating what had been a forgotten room and we turned it into a folk club. We'd got the grounding from the night classes and we were up and running. The club had old bus seats in it – we were next to the bus station and they were junking the old bus seats. They were quite comfortable once we'd nailed them to the floor. Everybody smoked at that time and we had our own little bar at the back, so there was a good atmosphere.

We had a Come All Ye in the beginning. The word got round and people would turn up and help fill a night with a kind of improvised list of turns, normally finishing with a big chorus, 'Will Ye Go Lassie, Go', that sort of thing. Annie Briggs used to come, she was living somewhere around Nottingham, and she used to bring an outfit called the Higglers – they sang unaccompanied. I think Annie was courting Johnny Moynihan at the time, so this bouzouki turned up and always a rake of lurchers. They sat on the front of the stage.

You existed on the raffle in those days. If you didn't have a raffle, you couldn't keep going. Years later I used to go the Half Moon in Putney and watch Bob Kerr's Whoopee Band. They had plants in the audience and somebody would shout, 'What about the raffle?' And Bob Kerr would say, 'Sorry, we don't do requests.' The raffle sustained us.

The first week we opened, Special Branch sent officers to keep an eye on us. They didn't quite look right – they'd got tartan shirts and neckerchiefs and their white socks always gave them away. One of them was a sergeant – he came to make sure that we weren't going to overthrow the world. He enjoyed it, so then he became a member of the committee. Whether he was trying to infiltrate us I don't know, but I thought it was funny.

JIM IRVINE
When I packed the sea in I still had itchy feet and it was my wife – she said, 'Looka, man, there's something up at the Marsden Inn,

go and see what it is.' Well, I went up in me collar and tie and me suit on and there was all these people. And the first person I saw, the guest, was Cyril Tawney. I went week after week – left me suit, put jeans on, all that sort of business.

Working in the pits, me credibility was pretty high as well and I was singing a few songs and eventually ended up on the committee to run it. We ran the Marsden club very democratically. I was the MC and I used to sing and play the fiddle with the Marsden Rattlers.

It was different to most other clubs. It started with the band playing at seven o'clock at night. The Rattlers at the time could be any five musicians from thirty-two.

We had booked guests. We had people like Seppy Broughton with his dancing dolls. He would do a quarter of an hour. He'd got entertaining patter. He was an old man, a grave digger, a seventh son. He came up and he used to have these dancing dolls on a stick. He'd sit on a board and vibrate the board by thumping it with his hand and the dolls would dance. We'd take Seppy with us to festivals, so he would be an added attraction to the Marsden Rattlers. Then he became that popular we had to leave him because he was getting more attention than us.

JOHN CONOLLY

We started the Grimsby folk club in an upstairs room above a pub, the Duke of Wellington, on 29 January 1964. You had to go up an iron fire escape at the back. It was quite bohemian. The first night there were people queuing up to get in, there weren't enough chairs. A lot of people were sitting on the floor. The atmosphere was just electric. The resident group was me and Bill Meek and Bob and Helen Blair. We were called the Meggies.

We'd been in touch with the Watersons and they'd helped us with all kind of tips on how to run a folk club – like don't bring the drum kit – and they also very kindly came across and did a guest spot. They didn't charge us. I've got the ledger and it shows all we paid was 'drinks for Folksons – 14 shillings'. They were still the

Folksons in January '64. The other expenses for that night were 'hire of room, ten shillings, drinks for landlord four shillings'.

So after the first night we asked the Watersons who we should have for our next guest, and they recommended Johnny Handle, who was a big mate of theirs. He came on 12 February for six guineas.

Within about four weeks we outgrew the room and moved to Cleethorpes, to the Queen's Hotel. We were there when Paul Simon came twice in 1965. The first time he came for £15, the second time he'd gone up to £25. There should be a blue plaque on the pub door: Paul Simon played here twice.

Bill Meek had heard him on the radio and he rang up the BBC to ask how he could get in touch with him. Paul came and he was great. We'd discovered the LP *The Paul Simon Songbook* and we were learning all the stuff off that. He stayed with me the first time. I was living with my mum in a little terraced house next door the Bird's Eye factory in Grimsby and Paul slept on our settee in the front room.

MIKE HARDING *the 'Rochdale Cowboy', later presenter of the Radio 2 Folk Awards*
I used to put loads of people up when they were on tour, whether they were doing my club or not. Tony Rose used to stay with us, Nic Jones, Bob Davenport, the Dransfields, the Yetties – they had to sleep downstairs on the floor. The McCalmans used to stay with us all the time and I went up to Scotland and did a lot of work with them.

On a Friday I'd go and buy a ham shank and I used to boil and boil it, take the fat off, chop all the meat up and get the bone and chuck that away and I used to make a huge pan of lentil and ham soup. That was notorious all over the folk scene.

SEAN CANNON
I've slept on settees and also in houses that were like five-star hotels where they gave me two hot water bottles on a cold night,

a big duvet, sheer luxury. Then there was a night when I was in a room on the settee and the owner had gerbils on treadmills in cages and they rattled away all night. I didn't sleep much but it was entertaining.

There was another night, I went to Exeter. I was hitch-hiking in those days, I did a lot of hitch-hiking when my car was broken down. This young lad approached me, saw the guitar and asked me what I was doing, so I told him. I asked him directions and he went with me to the folk club. I bought him some beer and he stayed, enjoying himself at the club.

At the end I was going back to the organiser's house and this lad said what about me? The organiser said is he with you? Well, he'd got nowhere to go, so I said yes. He took us to a nice little cottage in the country and he led me upstairs. There was just a mattress on the floor with a blanket but no pillow.

So I went with him to get a pillow and when I came back, this young lad had stripped off, got himself wrapped up in the blanket and was snoring away. He slept all night long and I was left with just the bare floor. It got cold in the night but I had an ex-RAF greatcoat, which saved me. I stayed up all night reading *Letters from a Stoic*, by Seneca, the Roman author. It was very appropriate.

GEOFF LAKEMAN *sang and played concertina from the mid-sixties with his wife Joy, later father of Sam, Sean and Seth.*
We used to put the guests up from the Herga folk club in our little flat in Wealdstone. All these people slept in our spare room or on the sofa. Folk was such a big thing at the time and we were all young, in our twenties.

We wanted to spend time with them but I very early on picked up on the fact that when they'd done the gig they'd done their job of work. They'd probably travelled all that day and the last thing in the world they wanted to do was stay up half the night. Swarb would always sit up and help you drink a bottle of Scotch, others wanted to go to bed or watch the telly to wind down.

PEGGY SEEGER
We should have said no to a lot of the places we stayed. The thing that went round then was that folk singers will sleep anywhere, they will eat anything. You can treat them any old way.

Sometimes it could be dire, but mostly they were really interesting people. You'd stay up all night talking to them and you'd hear about lives that were not your own. That was one of the wonderful things about the folk clubs.

DAVE BURLAND
I've slept in some very unpalatable places. I was doing twenty-eight gigs a month. I was never at home. It was hard work, but I'd got two young kids and my wife didn't work, so that was it. You had to bring home the bacon. But they were great times, a bit drink-fuelled and hazy. I can't remember a lot of what happened. It was hard but it was very enjoyable.

VIN GARBUTT *popular act on the British folk scene, his first album* Valley of Tees *marked him out as a notable songwriter*
I remember being on the third floor of this building. There was a cracked sewer on the bottom floor. Nobody lived on the first floor, but to go to the toilet you had to go down. I can remember the stench on the ground floor – it was terrible. And another accommodation was a derelict building with a bonfire where the chimney used to be. A rat ran over my foot as I was settling down to have a kip. To get to the room I was kipping in, there was a courtyard with a balcony that had collapsed, so you climbed up the timber that was the fallen balcony into this room where they had a fire in the middle of the floor and I slept on this manky mattress. It's going back a long time. That was a rough kip!

IAN ANDERSON *Country blues guitarist, resident at the Bristol Troubadour, later editor of the magazines* Folk Roots *and* fRoots
When I moved to live in Bristol in 1965 I went to what was then

the main Bristol folk club, the Ballads and Blues at the Bathurst Hotel. That night the main resident was Fred Wedlock and the guest was Tom Paley. At that time in Bristol there was a folk club every night of the week.

There was an enormous club at the university. This was the big *Melody Maker* folk boom year and they had all the famous visiting Americans – Buffy Sainte-Marie, Reverend Gary Davis, Tom Paxton, Phil Ochs and all the then big-draw British folk people.

They got about 500 people in every week and they got a grant from the students' union. In those days you had to spend it all to get a grant next year, so by the summer term they were putting on triple bills of really big names. It cost about sixpence to get in and they were still making a profit.

Also in Bristol but poles apart, there was a very hard-line traditional folk club, Ballads and Broadsides, which was run by Paul and Angela Carter – Paul, who was at Topic, and Angela, who would later become the famous novelist. We were told that you weren't allowed in with guitars and stuff like that, so we never went there.

JOE BOYD

The clubs in England were completely different to folk venues in America – pub assembly rooms rather than coffee houses. They were not run on a professional basis, there was no PA at all and no stages in most of the rooms. That was like Britain in general. I loved the fact that no one I knew had a fridge or a car or a stereo in 1964, while even poor folk singers and coffeehouse waiters in New York and Boston had all these things. It was probably responsible in part for the huge creativity of Britain in the early sixties. I remember in the traditional clubs there was a strong resistance to guitars and singer-songwriters in those days.

TOM PAXTON

I found the British folk clubs to be fabulous. As I explained to my colleagues at home, every night was Saturday night. A

Monday night at the Gaslight in Greenwich Village you could have fifteen people, but Monday night in Bristol, it was packed. Every night, everywhere I went, it was packed because that was club night. It was like Saturday night seven nights a week. It was exciting. And, of course, I loved the music, I loved hearing the English folk songs. In those days they actually sang English folk songs in folk song clubs.

MARTIN SIMPSON *singer and guitar virtuoso*
When I was twelve I got my first guitar, at which point Scunthorpe folk club opened, just round the corner from us in the Good Companions Hut, on a Tuesday night. It wasn't licensed premises, which meant that I could go. And that was it! It became, very rapidly, one of the best clubs in the country, one of the real landmark places, everybody went to play there. This was in 1965.

From twelve to seventeen I went virtually every week. It went from the early days of local acts to basically everybody that came through – Alex Campbell, Tony Capstick, Tim Hart and Maddy Prior, Trevor Lucas, Stefan Grossman, Nic Jones, repeatedly, Dave Burland repeatedly, Martin Carthy, Finbar and Eddie Furey.

I don't remember learning to play being very easy. I remember struggling furiously. When I first started to play was exactly the time my voice broke. I remember going to the folk club and trying to sing 'Mary Hamilton', which I'd learned from Joan Baez – 8,000 verses and an F sharp minor chord, which I couldn't play. It must have been horrendous in hindsight, but they were very kind.

MIKE HARDING
One of the first clubs I remember in Manchester was the Old Pack Horse and it was run by a fellow called Tony Clarkson-Smith who looked like a Viking in the days when nobody looked like Vikings. He had long hair, very blond and he often had it in a ponytail, and a blond beard. The next one I remember going

to was run by Harry Boardman. Harry ran a succession of folk clubs in Manchester and eventually Failsworth. He ran one at the Black Bull on Oldham Road on a Sunday lunchtime. That was more of a singaround than booked guests.

DOLINA MACLENNAN
Robin Gray and I opened the Dunfermline folk club. Falkirk was a wonderful club. Later on there was Kirkcaldy, Aberdeen – Arthur Argo's club – and St Andrews. Perth was much later. What was peculiar in those days – if you got a paying gig, you shared it. You would bring as many in of your friends, to share it.

IAN McCALMAN *co-founder of the McCalmans in Edinburgh in 1964*
We called ourselves Ian, Derek and Hamish. Then, because my parents had a phone – the other guys were in digs – we decided to get a name that was in the telephone book in case anybody wanted to book us. So we called ourselves the Ian McCalman Folk Group. I think it was based on the Ian Campbell Folk Group, to be honest. I thought they were fantastic, and the Corries and Robin and Jimmy.

We went out and got a bit merry, went along to the Waverley Bar and sang a few songs. There was always someone booked for the evening – it was a group, the Dhailla, and they let us on. John Allen, one of them, says it's the worst thing he ever did. I've got a picture of them on my kitchen wall.

The Waverley was neither a folk club nor a session. They don't really have places like that any more but then there were lots and lots of bars like that – the White Horse, the Holyrood. You went along at eight o'clock. It was ten o'clock closing. You sang with a couple of breaks until about ten past ten and you had an audience.

The most popular of the bands or singers obviously got the bigger audience. So if you got a big number in, there were always people around who'd tell other pubs – they draw a crowd.

We started doing a few clubs and getting reasonably known in a small way and then an English tour came about.

ROBIN WILLIAMSON
Anthea Joseph came up to the Edinburgh Folk Festival in 1962 and she offered me one date at the Troubadour. So me and Bert got a job picking potatoes to get the bus fare to go down to London, on the strength of that one gig. I think we did one or two gigs around London then I eventually ended up going back to Edinburgh. Then Clive Palmer came up and he and I worked the folk clubs round Scotland for a while, we were playing a mixture of old-timey and music hall.

CLIVE PALMER
I hitch-hiked up to Edinburgh and stayed at Society Buildings. This guy said there was a folk club round the corner at the Crown Bar. Archie Fisher ran it. Martin Carthy was there that night. He was doing American stuff then. I played a few banjo tunes and the people that were there liked it. Robin Williamson was one of them and we formed a duo and started getting bookings.

Club organisers would send you a postcard and say, 'Can you do this date?' You sent one back confirming it and that was it. There were no agents. When agents started getting involved, that killed the folk clubs. We were getting £40 a night, which was very good money back then, better than I get today! We did all sorts of material – old-timey songs, minstrel tunes, snatches of music hall, border ballads. I've always had a wide interest in music.

ROBIN WILLIAMSON
There was the Howff in Edinburgh. Roy Guest ran it and Archie Fisher was a resident. Archie Fisher was on Scottish TV and Robin Hall and Jimmie Macgregor were on national TV, and there was a guy called Len Partridge.

I was about eighteen. I met Bert Jansch at the Howff. We were both born in November 1943. I was singing mainly traditional songs, Scottish and some Irish. The people that dropped by was fantastic, all the big names – Jeannie Robertson . . . Davy Stewart. And about the same time as I went to the Howff, I sang a murder ballad at Camera Obscura at the Edinburgh Festival in 1961, 'The Bonnie Banks of Fordie'.

DOLINA MACLENNAN

The Howff in Edinburgh was very different from the Edinburgh Folk Song Society. I was involved with the Howff from day one. That would be 1960, after Robin Gray and I had already started the singing at the Waverley Bar. It was a tiny room, up the stairs. Before it was the Howff, the Sporran Slitters used to run it. There was no alcohol. It was based on the Troubadour in London. Roy Guest ran the Howff. He came up from London. He knew that things were moving up here in Edinburgh.

The Howff was where Bert Jansch started. He was a nuisance. He was fourteen and he got under everybody's feet, wanting to learn this and that on the guitar. There was a night when we were expecting a lot of people, I think Martha Schlamme was coming, and the toilet broke. So we sent Bert out with sixpence to the Macamba café to buy himself a cup of tea and steal the ballcock from their loo.

IAN CAMPBELL

The first four years of the Ian Campbell Folk Group, from '59 through to '63, we kept our jobs and performed in our spare time. I was a jewellery engraver, Lorna was a telephonist, Gordon McCulloch was a student at university, Dave Phillips just got by one way or the other.

One of the things it is difficult for people to understand is that we never made a lot of money. We were under constant pressure to turn pro, to take bookings – a week's tour or whatever. I'd say, 'I can't do that, I've got a job!' The fact that we were clinging to our jobs meant it limited our potential as a group.

None of the clubs had all that much money and they would say, 'We won't put you up in a hotel, you can sleep at our place.' Great! But it inevitably meant that when you left the club you went back to their place and as you walked in you'd find there were twelve mates all sitting waiting for you and there was going to be a late-night rave up. Then you were expected to play.

The weird thing was, they never regarded it as work what you were doing – you were having a ball. Like, aren't you lucky? You were knocking yourself out touring, all the travelling. You'd drive for four or five hours to work. We wouldn't stop overnight unless we had to. If we went to Liverpool we'd drive back to Birmingham. We'd drive back to Birmingham from Newcastle.

NIGEL DENVER

After the club it was always, 'Oh, would you like to come back to the house?' And then it was, 'Have a whisky, would you get your guitar out?' And they'd tape you. I don't know how many tapes there are in this country that I've done in people's houses.

LOUIS KILLEN

In those days you did a club, you went back to somebody's house, there was a bit of a party. It was enjoyable but it was gruelling. I'd go on the road for a couple of weeks and I'd come back and take a couple of weeks off, just to recuperate.

MARTIN CARTHY

Most of the time, people actually provided you with a bed. The folk club notion had built into it this idea that you would go to the club, they would pay you and they would put you up for the night. Sometimes you would get there a couple of hours early and they would feed you and put you up for the night. But usually it was do the club, put up for the night and then breakfast and off – to the next one. Sometimes you got a lift to the station, if they had a car.

IAN CAMPBELL

The big revolution for us happened in 1963. We were booked for a week at the Edinburgh Festival, to do a late-night fringe folk show in a theatre. The first night we played for an hour, started at 11.30.

Next day about six o'clock I get a call from Rory McEwen. 'Ian. I want you to bring the group, all of them, to my flat tonight. Ring the bell at nine o'clock.' We did and there was a meal laid out, a buffet. We were all standing round chatting and suddenly I hear this, 'Ian.' I turn round and it's Princess Margaret. She was president of the English Folk Dance and Song Society.

I'm a lifelong socialist. I was embarrassed that I didn't find her objectionable, but we chatted for about half an hour, all about folk music. She said, 'You appear to live in England.' I said, 'Yes, I do.' She said, 'Where?' 'Birmingham.' 'How unfortunate,' she said.

NIGEL DENVER

Princess Margaret didn't like me. I sang a song Jim McLean had written about her wedding – 'Maggie's Waddin'. A friend of Ian's said, 'Have you heard, a mate of mine sang a song about you, recorded it? She said, 'I've heard.'

IAN CAMPBELL

That week became a total sell-out. We'd become a national name and we were inundated with requests for bookings, offers of recordings, everything came flooding in. Gordon Smith said to me, 'You're supposed to be going home this Saturday aren't you? It doesn't make any sense at all. You're selling out, why don't you stay for the rest of the Festival, another fortnight?' I said, 'I can't, this is my holiday, I've got to be back at work on Monday.' He said, 'Oh, for Christ's sake . . .' So I said, 'Okay, fair enough, I'll pack in my job.' We turned professional and never looked back.

DOLINA MACLENNAN

Joe Boyd was sent to me by Bill Leader and he came up to Edinburgh to stay with us. I made a cake for his birthday. He was asking if there was anything going on the scene and George, my ex-husband, said well, there's this group called the Incredible String Band and he took him to hear them at the Crown folk club. This was just as they started and George introduced Joe Boyd to Robin and Clive.

BARBARA DICKSON

Archie Fisher ran the club at the Crown. Archie could virtually schmooze anybody to his folk club. Archie's one of these characters – it's a bit like being asked to do something for the Prince's Trust – you don't say no. He has always been my biggest influence of anybody. Nobody came close. I love his guitar playing. I love his singing. He really is masterful.

I saw the Incredible String Band at the Crown. In fact I saw Clive and Robin before Mike Heron joined them. When Mike joined them they became a jug band, they would sing 'Haul the Woodpile Down' and 'Eight More Miles to Louisville' and stuff like that.

CLIVE PALMER

I was living with a woman called Mary Stewart at Balmore. Joe Boyd knocked on the door one day. I don't know how he found me. He'd got this money to sign a number of folk acts and wanted to sign me and Robin. I said, 'Well, there's three of us now.' Mike Heron had joined. I suppose it was exciting but there was no money.

We made the record – Joe's got a good way of working: he suggests, he says why don't you try this or that, he doesn't tell you what to do. We'd got a record contract but we only got £50 advance. To put that in perspective, the standby return rail fare from Edinburgh to London was £18.

I'd been planning a trip to India and the band didn't seem to be going anywhere. I was drifting apart from them – all those songs about clouds bumping into each other wasn't what I wanted to do. I never wanted to be famous. I was quite happy how I was. I'm lazy really, but not musically. I didn't want all that having to leave all your friends behind and playing to bigger audiences. Then you find the audience has gone.

And there was always trouble, Robin and Mike falling out. I held it together – I was like the glue. I'm the sort of person that doesn't like trouble and I'll do what I can to avoid it. Of course, if you can't avoid it, you just have to deal with it. Robin likes teaming up with people but he's basically a loner.

JOE BOYD

Clive's biography confirms that he was only really interested in playing ragtime banjo, had no interest in Mike and Robin's songwriting. They were bouncing off each other as they started to write, pretty much ignoring Clive.

PETE STANLEY

First time I met Clive Palmer was at Clive's Incredible Folk Club run by Clive's Incredible String Band, who became the Incredible String Band. Me and Wizz played there. You had to get in a lift and go up to the top floor. If there had been a fire we wouldn't have stood a chance. Hamish Imlach, Archie Fisher, loads of people were there.

BILLY CONNOLLY

Clive Palmer had a massive impression on me. I wanted to be him. You know – this wild and wandering hippie, dressed like a pirate. Him and Robin – before Mike joined, they were a double act, Clive and Robin, and I loved them. Clive would be doing Appalachian stuff and Edwardian tunes, and Robin was doing the Scottish and English and Irish and it worked perfectly. He wasn't writing then, that came later.

BOB DAVENPORT

The great thing about the clubs – when you went to the Barley Mow in Sheffield, the Spinners' in Liverpool or the Elliotts' club at Birtley, or the Campbells' or the Marsden Rattlers', they set it up for you. At the Marsden Inn people were queuing to get in – it didn't matter who was on. All the performers had to do was follow it up. It was made for you. To die at the Barley Mow or any of them, you had to be bad. On the other hand at the Elliotts', if you were a chancer and one wrong word . . . the whole family were sitting there.

HARVEY ANDREWS

Almost all the clubs were run by amateurs, for pleasure. No one was really making a profit in the sixties. No one was in control, no one running anything, everybody was piling in, as an organiser, as a floor singer, attempting to be a professional, whatever. It was a huge melting pot of talent and people who wanted to be involved. Then over the years, what happens is, people start to take little bits of control. Then they amalgamate, then suddenly you find the control has gone from where it started, the revolutionary period, and it's ended up with the committee. Then, if you're not careful, from the committee to the dictator.

7 They could play better than we could

American singers and musicians who came to play in British folk clubs in the early and mid-sixties made a big impression. In the late fifties Burl Ives, Josh White, Big Bill Broonzy, Muddy Waters and Sonny Terry and Brownie McGhee had toured, but they played mostly in concert halls.

Ramblin' Jack Elliott was different. He busked on the streets, played anywhere he could and won many fans during his residency at the Troubadour. Then he was gone, although for a few years he kept popping back, sometimes with his sidekick, Derroll Adams.

Peggy Seeger, of course, was at the heart of the folk club movement and when her half-brother Pete Seeger came over in 1961, he played a series of clubs whose organisers had raised funds for him when he was targeted by the American government in the anti-Communist witch-hunts of the late fifties.

That same year, 1961, Carolyn Hester arrived on the first of several trips, accompanied by her then husband Richard (Dick) Farina. Hester had a key, if possibly now forgotten, role in Bob Dylan's career, providing him with his first opportunity to record when she invited him to play harmonica on her third Columbia album. In the studio Dylan met producer John Hammond, who signed him to the label.

For folk enthusiasts whose interest lay in old-time American music and bluegrass, there were some inspirational visitors. Ralph Rinzler of the Greenbriar Boys gave banjo and guitar lessons to Wizz Jones and Archie Fisher, among others. Eric von Schmidt and two of the Charles River Valley Boys – Clay Jackson and Ethan Signer – lived here for a while, dazzling many a club audience with their musicianship. All three were on stage at the Troubadour when Bob Dylan made his impromptu appearance in January 1962.

The New Lost City Ramblers, whose albums on Folkways did much to raise interest in old-time country music, undertook an eighteen-date tour of Britain in 1965. The group included Peggy Seeger's brother Mike. Former member Tom Paley, who had left three years earlier, was by this time living in London. Paley was a direct link with the legends of an earlier generation; as a young man he had played with Woody Guthrie and visited Leadbelly at his home.

The Cambridge Folk Festival, founded in 1965, was responsible for bringing many American performers who might not otherwise have come to Britain, and most stayed on to do club gigs. Older musicians with direct links to the roots of the American folk revival were welcomed with open arms. Clarence Ashley and Tex Isley came in 1966, quickly followed by Bill Monroe and his Bluegrass Boys and Doc Watson. Ageing bluesmen Son House, Mississippi John Hurt, Fred McDowell and Reverend Gary Davis all came over and toured to great receptions.

Stefan Grossman had taken guitar lessons from Gary Davis in New York. When he arrived in London in 1967 his clean, technically proficient playing caused an immediate stir and he was soon booked in clubs all over the country.

They were heady times. For the Americans, British folk clubs provided enthusiastic audiences and opportunities to work every night of the week. For local singers and musicians it was an opportunity to meet their heroes, to watch and learn what until then they had been able to hear only on records.

Then there were the singer-songwriters – Paul Simon, Phil Ochs and Jackson C. Frank. For a few years Frank's 'Blues Run the Game' was part of the folk club repertoire and before Tom Paxton arrived in Britain in 1965 his songs were being sung in clubs far and wide.

The traditionalists might have seen it in a different way, but long after skiffle had faded out and songs from the British tradition had become predominant in folk clubs, there was still great interest in American-influenced folk music – and its practitioners had a valid part to play in the folk revival.

BILLY CONNOLLY

The Americans had a massive impact – Tom Paley and the New Lost City Ramblers. I saw several line-ups of the Ramblers. They were great. They spent a lot of time tuning up. I used to love it.

CLIVE PALMER

When I moved up to Edinburgh, the New Lost City Ramblers used to come to the Festival – not the whole group, they came individually, Tom Paley and Mike Seeger. I'd watch what they did. You didn't get chance to sit down and ask them things, but there were a few records and I listened to them and looked in the songbooks and wrote stuff down.

DAVE BURLAND

I was a huge fan of the New Lost City Ramblers, still am. Years later I was playing in London and Tom Paley turned up. I said, 'Do you realise that you're one of my all-time heroes, as a guitarist?' He said, 'I don't play much guitar these days, I prefer to play the fiddle.' He was a great guitar player. This is why I loved the folk scene: these people were your heroes, but you were able to meet them.

TOM PALEY *as a young man played with Woody Guthrie, later banjo and guitar player with the original New Lost City Ramblers*
I met Jack Elliott out on the beach around Coney Island. He was with cowboys, doing some rodeo riding. I had a guitar, maybe a banjo. We sang a few songs and we got to be friends. And then he wanted to meet Woody Guthrie. He knew that Woody lived out on Coney Island, so we went.

I'd already gone out there before with a feller named Vic Traibush. He played guitar and he had Woody's address, 3520

Mermaid Avenue in Coney Island. Vic Traibush took me along maybe the third or fourth time he went. Then I was going back fairly often and Woody asked me if I would do some gigs with him. Of course, I was delighted. We did union meetings but the first actual public performance was the Leadbelly Memorial Concert. It wasn't so much to accompany him, but to join him. This was 1950, I was close to twenty-two.

I always found him a very pleasant guy. We got along very well, but he wasn't always completely responsible. His political views were pretty solid, but I remember showing up at one or two gigs where he didn't show up. I'd ring back to Marge, to his house, 'Where's Woody? We're supposed to be playing.' We didn't use the word gig – we had bookings. She said, 'I don't know, he went out Tuesday to get some cigarettes, he'll probably be back in a week or two.'

PEGGY SEEGER

Woody Guthrie turned up at the house we lived in, in Washington. He came with my brother, Pete. I chiefly remember him pulling his guitar along the floor and pretending it was a dog. He put a piece of string on it and pulled it. We lived in that house until I was eight and I was born in 1935. He entranced me because he was so small. Pete was six foot two and Woody was about five foot two or three. I just remember him pulling his guitar around, pretending it was a naughty dog. He didn't have a case, he slung it over his shoulder.

. . . Leadbelly came to the house. I remember standing at the front door and looking at him. Very, very black, almost blue-black. We used to run around the house with nothing on and we'd just run to the door whenever it rang and I was looking up and seeing this very, very black man. I also remember hearing him sing in a boxing ring in Washington. Pete, Leadbelly and either John or Alan Lomax was there.

TOM PALEY

I met Leadbelly, also through Vic Traibush. He used to go up to Leadbelly's house and I have a feeling that when I first went there it was with Vic and Woody. Leadbelly was regarded in our crowd as first rate. He was a better player than Woody. Woody could play, but he never bothered.

He could play fancier than he did but he wasn't a great guitarist. He played a bit of mandolin and he even played a bit of fiddle. I remember, some years later, a gal that I knew and Woody knew, said that when Woody was looking to put a group together of some sort and thinking about who to have, she suggested me. And he said, 'Well, problem with Tom is he gets too fancy on the instruments.' At that time I just played guitar and banjo.

The funny thing about Leadbelly was even at his house when it was just a gathering of other performers, he would be dressed to the nines. He would have a waistcoat on and bow-tie, everything clean and trousers knife-edged. And when he did a number he would introduce it as he did on stage. It was a whole performance, a very formal kind of thing.

I think maybe if it was just somebody like Woody coming over, he wouldn't have bothered with the formality, but generally he was, not surprisingly, kind of nervous about white people that he didn't know very, very well. I never got to know Leadbelly really well, but I was in that circle of people. Fred Hellerman, who was in the Weavers, wrote that it was every Sunday or regular, that I was always there at Leadbelly's house. I *was* there a few times but I don't remember it being a regular kind of thing.

Uncle Dave Macon was one of my heroes. I never met him but, oh, I loved his music. I was in the graduate school at Yale, mathematics, and John Cohen was in the art department. We figured one spring, when classes are over, let's go down to Nashville. See if we can find Uncle Dave Macon. He must have heard we were coming – he died.

In California I was playing at a club called the Ash Grove in Hollywood and Ry Cooder came along. He already played. He was about sixteen. He asked about blues lessons. Not that I'm a blues specialist, but I play some blues so I taught him some blues things. He also brought along Jerry Garcia at some point. I gave him banjo lessons. When I was out in California at other times in the next few years Ry sometimes came down.

John Cohen and I met in New York when I was teaching. There were various folk activities in Washington. Mike Seeger was living in Baltimore at the time but he often came down to these gatherings in the Maryland area. We'd get together and play a few numbers. I remember John saying, 'Hey, I bet Moe Asch would be interested in recording us at Folkways.' We went down to Folkways and Moe said, 'What do you guys want to call yourselves?' So we started thinking and eventually came up with New Lost City Ramblers.

After I left the Ramblers, my wife and I went to live in Sweden. This would be 1963. I'd been learning the language and we'd saved up a bit of money. We stayed three years and then we came to Britain.

I'd known Peggy Seeger in the States and I'd met Ewan one time when he was over. Once I was here I went to the Singers' Club and the Troubadour. A. L. Lloyd was around, Davy Graham, Malcolm Price . . . Alex Campbell. I got to know people fairly quickly. Ewan and Peggy got me gigs in other parts of the country, Bristol and a few places in the West Country. I always got on very well with Ewan, though I understand he could be a bit of a dictator. Of course, we weren't in competition.

I played quite a bit in Scotland. There was a club in Aberdeen that Arthur Argo used to run, a wonderful club. I loved playing there. Another guy named Drew Moyes in Glasgow ran a club there. A lot of people complained about him but I never had any problem.

ROBIN WILLIAMSON
A big influence to me was Tom Paley. I met him when I was about nineteen and we did a kind of tour of working men's clubs

round the north-east of England, along with a guy called Joe Latimer. He was a guitar player who worked with Tom. Tom was mainly playing banjo at the time. We played the New Lost City Ramblers sort of stuff, it went down well.

JENNY BARTON

Pete Seeger was in political trouble and he came over on a visit in 1961. To raise funds for him, twenty clubs booked the Albert Hall and put him on, and afterwards he worked his way round all the clubs in turn doing a thank-you appearance. We didn't sell the Albert Hall out but we did make a sizeable contribution to his campaign.

When he came to the Troubadour we crammed about 130 in. God knows how we did it. I remember feeling rather disappointed that he sounded just like he did on record, it wasn't like a live performance.

BOB DAVENPORT

Pete Seeger heard me at the Troubadour, singing unaccompanied, and I was invited to the Newport Folk Festival in 1963. To go to New York . . . I was walking along the street and this American guy said, 'Am I right for Times Square?' I said, 'Yes, you see there, you come into Times Square just walking on here.' He said, 'That's right. I saw you singing at the Roundhouse in London.'

I was appearing with singers like Mississippi John Hurt and all these people were there . . . Maybelle Carter from the Carter Family . . . Bill Monroe.

The one thing that shocked me when I went to Newport was there were workshops. The workshops I knew were like Vickers Armstrong on the Tyne. If you're having a festival, you shouldn't be having workshops – it's the typical Protestant thing, you can't go and enjoy yourself.

NIGEL DENVER

We ran a concert for Pete Seeger in Glasgow to pay for his

lawyers . . . Janey Buchan, the MEP, she organised the whole thing. She got the St Andrew's Halls. I'll never forget the guy who looked after the place, like a janitor, when Seeger threw this huge log on the stage and got an axe out and started chopping it up. The guy was shouting out – I can see his face! It was part of Seeger's act. He sang this work song while he was chopping at the log. We raised about 500 quid for him.

IAN CAMPBELL

We had an unfortunate experience with Pete Seeger the first time we met him, in '61. This was a concert organised by the Clarion Singers. It was sold out. It had been advertised as 'Pete Seeger and the Ian Campbell Folk Group'. He'd never met or heard of us before and he must have thought he'd got some local amateur group.

He was talking to me before and he asked, 'How long is the concert?' I said, 'It's two hours.' He said, 'How long do you do?' I said, 'Well, forty-five minutes, then we thought we'd have a fifteen-minute interval and then you do an hour.' 'Yes,' he said, 'but unfortunately it takes roughly two hours. I certainly can't cut it down to an hour. If you could cut yours down, as short as you can . . . could you make it fifteen minutes?' I said, 'Well, it won't be fifteen. We have a quite a big following in Birmingham.' He said, 'I understand. I'd be very grateful.' I told the group and they went, 'Oh, fucking hell!'

We went on and we did about nineteen minutes. And we finished with 'Viva la Quinta Brigada', the Spanish Civil War song. When we did it the audience would join in and stamp on the floor. So they just stood up and as we turned and started to walk off stage there's Pete going, 'No, No, get back on.' I said, 'Sorry Pete, we can't go back. We've just done our big finisher.' He said, 'I'm so sorry, I'm so sorry.' He'd expected some nonentity local group and what he found was the best group in Britain at the time.

TONY DAVIS

Woody Guthrie was a great influence on Pete Seeger and Pete Seeger was a great influence on me. We were in America and I said to Harold Leventhal, Pete and Woody's manager, could I go and see Woody. He said, 'Well, you wouldn't want to. You wouldn't like it.' He said Pete and Toshi, his wife, went to see him and were so upset they'd rather not go again. He said, 'It's a very upsetting business.' It probably was if you knew Woody in his prime, but we'd never met him and to us – me and Mick Groves – it was rather monumental to see one of the great legends of folk music.

He was in a mental hospital. It was like a big prison. You went in and there were metal doors and you had to be escorted through rooms where there were people who were obviously round the twist. There was this last room with all these jibbering people in it. They took us through there and out into a sort of conservatory and Woody was stretched out, lying on a couch or bench.

The guy who took us in said, 'This is Woody Guthrie.' He said, 'Woody, these guys have come from England to see you.' We gave him a cigarette and his hands were flailing around – he couldn't control it. His hand went across to take the cigarette out of his mouth and he sort of pulled it, tobacco flying in all directions. He could understand everything. He was lucid.

Mick said something about Lonnie Donegan and he exploded. 'That bastard,' he said. He didn't have any time for Lonnie, none whatsoever. Of course, Lonnie went on about Woody Guthrie, 'my great mentor', but Woody didn't want to know about Lonnie.

When we were leaving, Woody got up off this bench where he was lying. He was not in total control of his limbs but he came with us to see us out. The nurse took us through a room where a whole crowd of old boys were watching a flickering television. We said goodbye and went out. Every door had to be opened with a key and locked behind us. It was like a prison, it was obviously very secure.

We walked outside into this huge area with big, institutional-type buildings. We walked down the street and up in one of the rooms you could hear this woman singing the blues. My dad used to sing 'The Birth of the Blues' and there's a version with 'From a jail came the wail of a down-hearted frail/ And they made that as part of the blues.' It struck me at that moment.

KARL DALLAS

I was very friendly with Harold Leventhal, Pete Seeger's manager. He was executor or some sort of official of the Woody Guthrie Children's Foundation and Woody's son Arlo wanted to check out the folk scene in London and Harold asked me to look after him. Arlo was staying in a West End hotel, so I said to him, 'We've got a big flat in the West End. Why don't you come and stay with us? It'll save you a bit of money.' He did – and he began writing 'Alice's Restaurant' in our front room.

While he stayed with us it became very cold and I had an old topcoat I'd bought in a second-hand store in the King's Road, so I gave it to him. He wore it in the movie. I was sitting there at the press showing and he suddenly came on in my coat. I was so proud. He did quite a few folk clubs on that trip.

IAN McCANN

I was on the train going to either Brentwood or Chelmsford folk club and I kept hearing this singing and kinda yodelling and a guitar being played. So I followed where the sound was coming from, opened the door of the compartment, and there's this guy, all hair and glasses, thrashing away at a guitar and yodelling. It was Arlo Guthrie. He was booked the same night as I was, on the same bill. He was fantastic in the folk club – he had all the stories.

DEREK SARJEANT

Carolyn Hester first came over in 1961 to do a few clubs. Eric Winter rang me. I'd never heard of her but Eric said she was great, so I booked her for the club and he was right. Rory McEwen was doing a television show, *Hullabaloo*, on ITV and he booked her for that and he got her on the Edinburgh Festival.

I think she probably came six or seven times to Surbiton. Her agent rang once and I booked her with less than a week to get publicity out but the big hall – 700 people – it was packed, they were queuing up an hour before. We tried not to be like a concert. We got a very good atmosphere in the big hall.

Dick Farina played on that first tour that Carolyn Hester did. He played autoharp. He was a lovely guy, but I did think that Carolyn overshadowed him a bit. He recorded afterwards with Mimi Baez, Joan's sister, they did the song 'Pack Up Your Sorrows'.

CAROLYN HESTER

As a youngster I was aware of England so in 1961, when my then husband, Richard Farina, suggested we make a trip to the UK, I was happy to agree. He sailed and about a month later I made the trip by plane. He had discovered the Troubadour in London and he took me there immediately. What an evening! Rory and Alex McEwen were in the audience that night and asked if I would like to join them in Edinburgh for that year's Edinburgh Festival.

Another friend I made that evening was Anthea Joseph, who managed or booked the Troubadour. She became my UK booker, as well as booker/manager for many an American wayfaring stranger. She was an unforgettable character, very tall, angular, large-boned, pale, with wispy long chestnut hair and always questioning blue eyes.

We Americans could turn to Anthea about anything. A folk singer, who shall remain nameless, phoned me early on a Sunday morning stating that he was in trouble, having blessed his too-young-to-marry British girlfriend with child and what did I suggest? Yipes! All I could do was call Anthea who asked for his phone number.

I never asked either of them about it again. I assumed that

Anthea called a friend who called a friend and all was arranged. She passed away too soon, at the age fifty-seven, in 1997.

Through Rory and Alex McEwen, I met Sydney Carter, and recorded his song 'Crow on the Cradle'. I sang with Louis Killen at the folk club at his home town of Newcastle, where he and his mom put me up for the night. I met Bob Davenport, Long John Baldry, Alexis Korner, Davy Graham, Martin Carthy – a giant of talent now and, at the beginning, Swarbrick on fiddle.

I was on more TV in Britain than in the USA. And through my American record producer, Norman Petty – Buddy Holly's manager and producer – I met Peter Walsh of Starlite Artistes in London. When he saw how many people Derek Sarjeant was packing in at his folk club when I was there, Peter was having me come over three tours a year for several years. He even asked me to move to the UK.

HUGHIE JONES

Burl Ives was my introduction to folk music. They used to play him on *Children's Requests* on the radio – 'Big Rock Candy Mountain' . . . He was one of the few folk musicians you could buy records of in those days. There was very little else.

The Spinners did a mini-tour with Burl Ives. Somebody said it was an alimony tour: he'd just got rid of another wife. We did two concerts, one in Liverpool. I think they weren't too sure whether they'd fill the halls and some bright spark decided to put the Spinners on because we used to sell out Liverpool and Manchester. The consequence was the Burl Ives people stayed away because it wasn't all Burl Ives, and the Spinners people stayed away. It wasn't bad – about 80 per cent – but for the first time there were empty seats.

After the Liverpool show I went to see him, just to tell him how I'd seen him with my dad when I was fourteen. We were right up in the gods at the Empire and he came on stage and the spotlight caught his guitar and it shone in my eyes so much so that I had to blink. And I thought to myself, 'One day I'm going to have a shiny guitar like that.' I just went round to tell him this yarn but he said, 'I don't want to talk to no one.' That was a bit heartbreaking, as a fan.

Another downer was with Sonny Terry and Brownie McGhee. They were on a big bill with Muddy Waters' band. This is the first band, with Little Walter on harmonica, Otis Spann on piano. I went to get autographs and I was stood in line. I'd got a proper autograph book and Sonny went to an awful lot of trouble – he was practically blind – and he wrote his name. Then Brownie did it underneath. But when you looked – he'd got a rubber stamp.

ARCHIE FISHER
Sonny and Brownie came to a late-night party at Hamish Imlach's after a show in Glasgow, and Hamish – much to his later shame – ran a discreetly hidden slow-speed Grundig tape recorder throughout the night. For me, the combination of hearing and seeing close-up Brownie's guitar style demystified a lot of his beautifully fluid technique.

JOHN JAMES *Welsh ragtime guitarist who was popular in the clubs in the late sixties and seventies*
I was on Sonny Terry and Brownie McGhee's last British tour, 1976. They always had separate dressing rooms. Brownie's attitude to Sonny wasn't very friendly. I know they had been together a hell of a long time.

The last night of the tour at Manchester Corn Exchange was the last time they performed together in the UK. They marched off stage to the usual closing number, 'Walk On', crowd shouting for an encore, Sonny in the wings waiting to go back on.

I'm upstairs in the dressing room trying to talk Brownie into an encore. He refuses to go back on. He says, 'I ain't playin' with no sick man.' He suggests I go on or, better still, go out and get him some fried chicken.

Then Mike Harding walks in, wondering why the encore is not happening, with a full house shouting for more. I ask Mike where I can get some fried chicken around here, this time of night. He looks at me thinking I've lost it.

I asked Brownie whether a doner kebab would do. He looked at me thinking I have lost it. Sonny and Brownie didn't do an encore. They both jumped in a minibus and drove to Heathrow. I never saw them again.

RALPH McTELL

We had no one to copy. There were no videos and it wasn't till '62 or '63 that the first invasion of black musicians came over that could play that stuff. One thinks of Sonny Terry and Brownie McGhee, Reverend Gary Davis, Muddy Waters. I saw Big Joe Williams, the nine-string guitar player. He was part of a blues package that came over, then the next year Reverend Gary Davis. He remains one of my guitar heroes. I have a wonderful photograph of me and Rev. Davis, together. That's a moment I treasure.

IAN McCANN

The Starting Gate at Wood Green was a very popular club and they tended to book American-type acts. This particular night Alexis Korner was topping the bill and I was supporting him. Towards the end of the evening there was a huge commotion and Reverend Gary Davis appeared. He'd been playing somewhere and whoever was looking after him brought him along to the Starting Gate. He sat down and played. It was magical.

While I was with Malcolm Price, we did a couple of supporting gigs with Doc Watson and Ralph Rinzler at Guildford. Again, it was seeing how things were done. You're in with a better chance if you can actually see the fingering. Doc Watson was the first truly great guitar player I saw at close quarters. Just to witness his musical artistry as a flat-pick guitarist, his talent for storytelling and his ability to engage with an audience through gentle humour and the warmth of his personality was both mesmerising and inspirational. I sat spellbound in the tiny back room in a Guildford pub.

MADDY PRIOR

I drove Reverend Gary Davis about on a tour in about 1965. Just me and him for a month in a Triumph Herald. I'd never been around anybody blind before, nor black, nor anybody that smoked as much as he did. He was a chain-smoker. He was a real character and he sort of got everybody at it.

He would do anything to get a whisky – and the one thing they said to me was, 'Don't let him drink.' Of course, people are wanting to buy him drinks and I'm saying no, so everybody had a go at me. I was eighteen.

Travelling round England in 1965 with a black, blind bloke, as an eighteen-year-old was a bit of an eye-opener. But I never got any sniff of racial stuff at all. I think people were so amazed to see him. We played the Blue Bell in Hull, Redcar – ordinary folk clubs – and we played the Cambridge Folk Festival.

He used to call me Miss Maddy and when we parted at the end of the tour he said, 'Miss Maddy, you'd make a great nurse.' It was somewhere between a compliment and an insult.

DEREK SARJEANT

Reverend Gary Davis at the Assembly Rooms at Surbiton stands out as a special night. He was such a legend – the number of people who turned up! Jesse Fuller's last session was special too, about 1967 or '68. It was the last one he did in this country and Donovan turned up that night. We had Doc Watson, Sonny Terry and Brownie McGhee, Mike Seeger, Clarence Ashley and Tex Isley.

In its heyday in the sixties the Surbiton club was the biggest folk club in Britain. By the end we had about 23,000 members on the books. In those days folk club audiences were made up predominantly of students and they moved on to different places.

PEGGY SEEGER

If it hadn't happened, where would we have gone? Where would we have found examples of do-it-yourself? Tom Paxton, let's face it, is a wonderful songwriter. His songs are modest: you don't need tremendous expertise of memory or of guitar playing. They were examples of do-it-yourself. These were people who were singing unaccompanied or with just one instrument.

TOM PAXTON

The first time I came over I had no work permit. One had to be put together at the last minute. My wife and I really came over as tourists and once we got here and I played a couple of folk clubs, the offers came pouring in, so we stayed a little longer than we were going to stay.

We'd met a guy, Theo Johnson, in New York. He was over there and he came to the Gaslight and I got talking to him. He said, 'If you'd like to come over, just drop me a line and I'll set up a few folk club dates.' I had written to Matt McGinn prior to that telling him how much I liked his song 'Coorie Doon', which was in *Sing Out!* magazine, and he wrote back. He said, 'I'll get you some folk clubs in Scotland.' He got seven and Theo had about five and it went from there. I hadn't met Matt until we actually got over here.

Scotland was the first performances I did. The first one in London was at Bunjies, a folk club in Charing Cross, and I sang at some club that Eric Winter was connected with in north London. I played Jackie and Bridie's club in Liverpool and Jack Harris's at the Couriers' club in Leicester. I used to stay with him and his wife Sue. Sue introduced me to beans on toast. On that first tour I stayed in a lot of travelling people's hotels, pretty basic hotels. When I was in London I stayed at Eric Winter's house – he was the most enthusiastic man I ever met in my life.

AUDREY WINTER

Tom stayed with us on his first tour of England for about six weeks. It was on and off because he was all over the place. He was great fun but I don't think he liked being with us very much – we weren't very well off and the house was cold. We weren't up to his American standards. He stayed with us since, though.

TOM PAXTON

The album came out in '64, we were here in the spring of '65 and
the album was being imported here. I remember it was going for
forty-five and six and people said, 'That's a lot', but it had got
around the clubs. At least five or six songs from that album were
being sung a lot, so that did me no end of good. People knew the
songs, and if they knew the songs then they would take a chance
on me. That's one thing that really amazed me.

I'd written 'Last Thing on My Mind' only a few weeks before
I recorded the *Ramblin' Boy* album, so it was early 1964. The
funny thing about it was, I began to sing it at the Gaslight and
friends would come up and discreetly ask, 'Is everything all right
at home?' I'd say, 'Yes, it's just a song, how would I feel if . . . a
work of imagination.'

I write in the first person but it's very seldom Tom Paxton,
very seldom actually myself. It's anybody in the first person.
Sometimes it's as if a person was dictating the song to me, but,
of course, he doesn't exist. When he does exist then it's time to
take me away some place.

I fell in love with the music scene over here so when I'd be
home it didn't take much to get me thinking about the folk clubs.
I got a better response in England than I was getting in the States.
There was nothing to complain about the States, it was getting
better all the time, but it was in advance of that over here.

I would think about wanting to get back over to England,
so it wasn't surprising that some of my writing would reflect
that. That's when I wrote 'Leaving London' with the line about
the Troubadour. The English folk song has definitely had an
influence on my writing.

RALPH McTELL

I always liked Tom's songs. I loved the songs that promoted
that idea of 'I'm a rake and a rambler' and I liked 'Can't Help
but Wonder Where I'm Bound'. That was in my repertoire
for a while. Any of the songs that glorified the idea of travel

and freedom were all right with me and Tom did a bit of that, he wrote about it anyway, and I took that as inspiration. The conventions of good songwriting know no bounds, I love the folk narrative songs and Tom was really good at that. I never saw him in the folk clubs – it was all from record and other people playing his songs.

TOM PAXTON

Before I came I wasn't that aware of any English singers. I met Martin Carthy right away and we worked together on a tour that I did with Judy Collins. Martin and Dave Swarbrick were on that tour, '66. I met Bob Davenport, he used to do 'The Shoals of Herring' really well.

The first date I did on that six-week tour in '66 was at the Jug of Punch, so I met Ian Campbell. I was singing some of my songs and some of other people's at that time. I was mainly playing clubs when I came back in January and February of '66. That fall when I came back I played some clubs, but by then I'd started playing concerts.

ROY GULLANE *the Tannahill Weavers*

We had a gig in Fife in about 1970 – I think it was Leslie folk club – and the organiser had been at Tom Paxton's concert at the Usher Hall in Edinburgh the night before. He'd got backstage and asked him if there was any chance that he could book him for the club. Tom Paxton said, 'I don't think so, but where is your club?' The guy told him, 'It's on tomorrow night.' And he turned up! With his band and everything – he opened for the Tannahill Weavers! On his night off, he just wanted to play in a little place, and he did it.

TOM PAXTON

Paul Simon opened for me once at a folk club in north London. I tell him that was the last time he ever made less money than I did. We struck up a great friendship. We took a short-term flat in

South Kensington and many nights we would wind up playing Monopoly with him.

One night, while we were trying to decide whether to play another game or not, he said the strangest thing was going on at home. He'd made an album with his friend Artie but nothing had really happened with it but then a disc jockey down in Georgia started playing one track from it – a lot.

The distributor down there got on to Columbia, telling 'em to give 'em a single so, he said, 'They added drums and a bass to it. It's a single and it seems to be going up the charts and I'm going to have to go home pretty soon.' And, of course, it was 'Sound of Silence'.

MARTIN CARTHY

Paul Simon wrote to the organiser of Brentwood Folk Club saying, 'I'm an American folk singer. I write my own songs. I'm offering myself to you as resident singer at your club, for £5 a week. Do you agree?' And Dave, I can never remember his surname, came around among all the singers and he said, 'Have you ever heard of this bloke Paul Simon?' None of us ever had.

He said, 'He's written and asked to be resident at our club for a fiver a week. Shall I do it?' I said, 'Well, if he's an American performer, there's a really good chance that he knows what he's doing. It's the sort of thing they learn at school. He's worth a punt – and if he's rubbish you can sack him.' The feeling was that, whatever else, the bloke's not going to be rubbish. He came along and a mate of mine went to see him. He was absolutely captivated, thought he was wonderful.

IAN CAMPBELL

I owe Paul Simon a great deal. In the early sixties he came to live in Britain. He was nineteen or twenty and he bummed around the folk scene, sleeping on people's floors and singing in folk song clubs. He used to follow the Campbell group around – he loved everything we did and he has twice on television and radio credited me as a major, formative influence in his songwriting career.

He followed us around and in the end Lorna said, 'Look, we've got to book this kid. He's pestering the life out of me and he wants to do the Jug.' So we booked him and he didn't turn up on the night. The next week, we're getting everything together and he arrives. He's a week late, got it wrong in his diary. He said, 'Just let me do a spot for my expenses, to pay my fares.' I said, 'We needed you last week, now we don't. We've not got room.' 'Let me do a floor spot.' 'No.' So he sat in the bar. Lorna came to me about nine o'clock. She said, 'You've got to let that kid sing. He's weeping into his beer.' So he went on and he tore the place apart. They loved him.

He went back to America and joined up together again with Garfunkel and they made that first album. The album was songs written by Paul Simon and Art Garfunkel – except for two – one by Ewan MacColl and one by me, 'The Sun Is Burning'. I wrote it in '62. About eighteen months afterwards I got this cheque for about two grand and from then on it's trickled down. Then he released a *Best of Paul Simon,* including 'The Sun Is Burning'.

HARVEY ANDREWS
The first time I saw Paul Simon, I couldn't believe how brilliant he was. He turned up on the wrong night and Ian told him off. I was in the bar and heard him. He said, 'You'll get nowhere in this business, laddie, unless you keep your diary in order.' And Paul was saying, 'I've driven all this way, Mr Campbell. Can I just do a little floor spot?'

I sat down, a couple of rows back and this guy sat on a stool and he started. I can remember what he sang – 'A Church Is Burning', 'He Was My Brother', 'A Most Peculiar Man' and 'Sound of Silence'. And when he finished, I shot up to the ceiling with excitement. It was like nothing else existed for me. His guitar technique was like an orchestra to us. We'd not seen or heard that type of playing.

No one got to know Paul Simon well but I was the first person in the world to record a Paul Simon song – 'A Most Peculiar Man'. I've got a letter from him.

GEOFF SPEED *presenter of a folk show on BBC Radio Merseyside since 1967*
He played at the Black Diamonds club in Chester on the Friday evening and on the Sunday evening he sang at the Widnes club. He stayed with me for almost a week. I took him to Liverpool, to Birkenhead – I can't remember the rest. It was great fun, we were both the same age, twenty-three.

People still talk about his performance at Widnes. He was a beautiful guitarist and the content of the songs – to be able to write songs like 'The Sound of Silence', to have that understanding of the human condition. One night he said, 'Don't get me wrong, but if I'm not a millionaire by the time I'm thirty I shall be very disappointed.'

I taped him at the club. Paul said, 'I'd love a copy of it,' so I gave him the tape of my recording and I had a postcard from him a couple of months later. In the meantime 'The Sound of Silence' had gone to the top of the charts in the States and then in England too. I've got his card. It says, 'Dear Geoff – don't shoot! I just haven't had time to do a copy for you.'

The story goes that he sat on Farnworth station – it's now Widnes station – and wrote 'Homeward Bound'. He'd been staying with me for the best part of a week and he rang me on the Friday to say, 'I'm ready to go, Geoff.' I said, 'I'll leave the office and come and pick you up and drop you off at the station.' We got there just before the train arrived, literally seconds before, so I don't think he wrote it on the station.

During the week he was staying, my father was at home at the time and he and Paul got to talk quite a lot during the days, mostly about religion. My father was from a Methodist family and, of course, Paul is Jewish. Dad said he spent a lot of time in the lounge, writing with an Oxford pad. So I think maybe he wrote 'Homeward Bound' at 123 Coroners Lane in Widnes.

RICK NORCROSS *American singer and guitarist*
I read about the vibrant folk scene in England in *Sing Out!*
magazine in the spring of 1965, an account by Pete Seeger about
his trip to London and his visit to the Troubador with Arlo
Guthrie. I was at Florida Southern College in Lakeland, where I
opened a coffee house just off the campus called the Other Room.
Many singers from the central Florida area, including Gram
Parsons, came to the club and played because there were very few
folk music venues in Florida at the time.

Once I read about the folk clubs in England, I decided to take
some time off from college and head over to play in the clubs,
meet some other folk musicians and see the country. When I
arrived, I was amazed at the vibrancy and enthusiasm – and the
number of the folk clubs.

Most of the clubs had no sound systems so you were playing to
large audiences who had to listen closely to hear what you were
doing on stage, if there was a stage. Believe it or not, that made
for really terrific playing experiences because the audience was
totally engaged, rather than talking and noisy, that frequently
happens when a loud PA system is in place. I loved that about
playing at the folk clubs in the community rooms in pubs.

STEFAN GROSSMAN *pupil of Reverend Gary Davis, made an*
instant impression on the British folk scene
April '67, that's when I got my deferment from the draft and
when I came over to England. The only people I initially knew
personally were not in the folk scene – Eric Clapton and Ginger
Baker. I'd met them in New York when I was in a band, Chicago
Loop. The first person I went was to Ginger. He was living in
north London and he showed me a pub – to an American that
was very glamorous. Then I ended up hanging with Eric. He
went on tour and he had an apartment in Regent's Park and I
stayed there while he was away. We used to jam together.

Those were my initial contacts but a friend of mine, called Marc Silber, had been to England two years prior and he had stayed at Somali Road, where the Young Tradition were on the first floor and Bert Jansch and John Renbourn were on the second floor. Marc had given me Heather Wood's name and I went down to Cousins because the Young Tradition was playing there. I said hello to Heather. She said, 'Bring your guitar down.' I played a set and the next thing I knew I was written up in the papers.

I had no intention of staying in England at that point but then I started playing in the folk clubs and I got to be friends with the High Level Ranters – Tommy Gilfellon – and I saw it was a whole different way of performing. I was in, I guess, an interesting position because the traditional clubs would book me – usually it was, 'This is the first American we've had since Hedy West' – then the regular folk clubs and university circuits they would book me because I wasn't a blues singer per se, I was rather a blues guitar player and sort of a bridge between the people I had learned directly from. I would be performing their guitar styles and not pretending to be a blues singer.

DAVID HALLIDAY *club organiser*

We started a folk club at the Wheatsheaf in Rotherham in February '66 and I borrowed £25 off my mother to book Derroll Adams for the opening night. It was a lot of money at the time. The room was packed but he didn't stay on the stage. He walked about among the audience and had conversations with people. It wasn't what they were used to.

Afterwards I took him home to my parents' house. He'd been drinking whisky all night and he threw up all over the front garden. Then he just dived straight into bed – he didn't even take his cowboy boots off. My mother was a bit put out, particularly by the front garden. She talked about it for years afterwards.

Next morning he wanted to get a taxi to the station but we didn't go about in taxis in those days, so we went on the bus. As soon as we got upstairs he took the banjo out and he was going round the bus singing to passengers and signing autographs. Nobody knew what to make of him.

BILLY CONNOLLY

I loved Derroll Adams. I got to be friendly with him. I got to know him and I did a concert just before he died and flew him over from Belgium and put him on. He died very soon after that. He only did one song, but I said to the audience, 'I want you to see the real thing, the real deal.' He did 'Portland Town' – I asked him to. That's why I've got this tattoo of a banjo on the edge of my left hand – Derroll had it in the same place. So when I went to pick him up at the airport, I lifted my arm – 'Hi, brother' – and there it was, to greet him.

DONOVAN *achieved fame following his pop hit 'Catch the Wind' in 1965*

Derroll was the first American folk singer from the masters that I met. He played with Jack Elliott and knew Woody Guthrie and introduced me to Buffy Sainte-Marie and Joan Baez. She recorded his song 'Portland Town'. Derroll taught me how to touch the strings, and he stood up for me against the others when the press berated my arrival.

BILLY CONNOLLY

A guy I liked from then was Bill Clifton. He did old-timey stuff, good choice of songs, and a good autoharp player. People used to smirk at autoharp playing, but good playing's good playing and he was good. He had a good banjo player with him. 'Cedar Grove' was the tune I remember. I loved Clarence Ashley, too. I played 'The Cuckoo' when I did *Desert Island Discs*.

DAVE COUSINS

Mike Seeger came to stay with me for a week when he first came to England in '66. That was very interesting, just watching him play. I remember sitting at a table in the White Bear, right by my house, with him and Sandy Denny, swapping songs. Bill Clifton I got to know very well. He lived down near Sevenoaks. I saw Bill Monroe play at his house, in the garden with Peter Rowan on guitar. They were phenomenal.

IAN McCANN
Bill Monroe and the Blue Grass Boys at the Royal Albert Hall in 1966 was a hugely formative experience for me, and for so many of us who were struggling to play the music and understand its intricacies and nuances. His soaring high tenor voice and powerful mandolin style, together with the spine-tingling four-part harmonies and the outstanding musicianship of his young band, that was an unforgettable experience.

The next time I saw him was in 1974, when I played in a band supporting the Bluegrass Boys at a concert in Redcar. On that tour he had an older, more experienced band, including the legendary fiddler, Kenny Baker. Bill was often considered shy and aloof, but he was anything but on that occasion. He sat with a small group of us during the interval, chatting and answering our questions while Kenny told stories and demonstrated fiddle licks.

STEVE TILSTON *guitar maestro and songwriter from Leicester*
The first American I saw was the San Francisco Bay Blues guy, Jesse Fuller. He came and played in Leicester, I think it was '65. Then they had these blues packages that would come round every year and I saw most of those – a lot of influential blues players.

GRAHAM CAMPBELL *organiser at the Sleepy John blues club in Sheffield*
Son House played at Leeds University and at that time he was getting on in years. They just sat him down on a chair centre stage and he starts tapping his feet and slow-clapping his hands, then he starts to sing.

I've got the old chills up and down my spine just thinking about it. He played his steel National guitar and some truly great blues came out of him. It's the closest I'll ever come to knowing what it might have been like to see Robert Johnson. I was able to talk to him for some time during the break and, like the snot-nosed kid I was, I got his autograph.

IAN ANDERSON

In 1965 I went to see the Folk Blues Festival, which Mississippi Fred McDowell was on. He was still then going along with the authentic country bluesman, dungarees and acoustic guitar, and he was just mind-blowingly brilliant. I sat watching him in the Colston Hall in Bristol and I had a light-bulb moment. I'd heard people play bottleneck but I figured out that the guitar must be tuned to a chord.

I went back to my flat, listened to Fred McDowell's 'Highway 51', worked out that it was a G chord and by pure accident hit on the right tuning. Then I noticed I had a brass curtain rail so I got up there with my hacksaw and liberated two inches of my landlord's curtain rail. I stayed up all night, practised some more the next day, went up to the university folk club that night and they gave me the last floor spot in the first half. I did one other song then re-tuned the guitar and played 'Highway 51'.

It went very well. I thought I can do this open tuning and I was walking off stage when Phil Ochs was coming on to do his guest spot. And as we passed, he said, 'That was great, man.' That was it! This is what I'm going to do for a living. If a famous American star tells me I'm good then I'm going to go for this.

Later on, 1968, I'd moved to London and we formed the National Blues Federation and organised tours. We contacted Fred McDowell's agent in the States and said we would set up this tour, could he come for a month, how much would he need to be paid? A guy called Ron Watts was my flatmate and between us on the payphone in the hall at the flat we booked the Mississippi Fred McDowell tour. On about half the dates, my country blues band did the support.

That was February '69. Me and Ron and Alexis Korner went

out to Heathrow to meet him. Our last sighting of him, he'd been the guy in the dungarees – and he comes off the plane in this really sharp overcoat and hat, very shiny black patent leather shoes and carrying this thin-looking guitar case.

'What's in there, Fred?' He'd got this red electric guitar. We said, 'Okay, what's all this about?' He said, 'I did this gig with' – it was either Chuck Berry or Buddy Guy – 'and he seemed to be getting all the chicks so I decided that if got one of these . . .' We said, 'So what did you do with your acoustic?' 'Oh, I gave it to some hippie at Newport Folk Festival.'

He did the whole tour electric. A few were folk clubs and a lot were blues clubs, run on exactly the same model. He had this little amp that Alexis got him, probably about fifteen watts and some places there wasn't a microphone. This was when he came out with his catch-phrase that you hear on the live recordings – 'I do not play no rock 'n' roll' – then he launches into 'Shake 'Em on Down' on his electric guitar.

The first gig was one of these famous folk clubs – no stage and no mikes, audience all crammed in. This was the time of the blues boom. It was the fashionable music. And all these teenage girls come up to him and give him big hugs. And the very first night he kind of winced. He looked really shocked and frightened. He got used to the idea very quickly, but we suddenly realised that, where he came from, if a white girl did that and somebody saw, you could be hanging from a tree.

MARTIN SIMPSON

The Americans who came over had a massive impact. I always think about the broader sense of the folk scene and the folk club in Scunthorpe was quite catholic. This was during the period when the blues was a part of the English folk scene. Stefan Grossman was massively important in terms of the guitar in this country. He played in Scunthorpe.

The folk club would organise trips to go and see the Lippmann and Rau Blues Package, so I saw Jimmy Reed at Manchester Free

Trade Hall in '68, with T-Bone Walker and Big Joe Williams, Curtis Jones, Big Walter Horton. I was fifteen, that was one of those moments. The folk festivals were really important. I was fifteen when I went to a folk festival. I saw Tom Rush.

STEVE TILSTON

I saw Phil Ochs twice. He was part of a package with Julie Felix at the De Montfort Hall in Leicester. He was great. He stole the show. Then he came and played at the White Swan in the Market Place about a couple of months later. A load of us went from school because all of a sudden he'd got this big fan club with all the political stuff.

The briefest conversation I ever had in my life was with Phil Ochs. He had this song called 'Changes', a lovely reflective song, as was 'There but for Fortune'. He was walking by me near the stage and I said, 'Can you sing "Changes"?' He went, 'Yup', and as he said it a spittle of food came up and hit me in the eye. Not only did I have a brief conversation – I exchanged bodily fluids with him.

HARVEY ANDREWS

Phil Ochs, my hero! I went to see him at a concert in Birmingham in '65. Ioan Allen, who managed the Ian Campbell group, said, 'Can you put him up?' so I brought him back to my flat and he stayed two nights. We sat up and talked and played Buddy Holly records and we got on to Dylan.

I didn't know much about his relationship with Dylan. We were talking about the movement, the political thing. It sounds really crass now, but I can distinctly remember saying what would advance a movement more than anything was if somebody assassinated Bob Dylan, like Kennedy, then there'd be a musical martyr. Then we went to sleep.

And on the plane back he wrote the song 'Crucifixion', which is considered his greatest song. He started writing it on that tour, after he left me. In the biographies, people give a different reason for him writing it. But I'm convinced that it was that conversation that night that started him up on that song.

He wasn't very comfortable in my flat so I took him over to my mother's for lunch. Mother said, 'Oh, you can't sleep there at Harvey's – you can stay here, nice bed for you here.' She gave him a big meal and he lost his contact lens in mother's front room and we couldn't find it. We tore the bloody room to pieces. He hadn't brought a spare set with him so he only had one contact lens and he was blind as a bat. It's probably still there in 85 Kenilworth Road, Handsworth.

He sat down with my tape recorder and he recorded for me 'Flower Lady' and 'Canons of Christianity', two songs he'd performed for the first time at the concert. They went straight into my repertoire. Then off he went.

I was more interested in the Americans than the English because they were the songwriters. They could all play better than we could, they were writing story songs about topical events. No one does story songs any more. It's a shame, because that is where we are linked into the folk tradition.

COLIN WILKIE
Shirley [Hart] and I met and sang with Phil for the first time at a Cambridge gig. I think he was head and shoulders above any of the other U.S. of A. singer-songwriters of the time, both musically and with his uncompromising words.

We got friendly with him, had long discussions about politics and music, then he came to the Burg Waldeck Festival in Germany in 1968. He and his brother Mike had flown in from California. It was cold on the Waldeck and they were grateful for the fact that I, knowing what conditions could be like, had come prepared and was able to loan them some of my excess sweaters. We worked with Phil again at other concerts in Germany, Frankfurt and Karlsruhe, and a couple of others. He was a great songwriter, one of my all-time favourites. He had a distinctive voice. His death hit us hard.

STEVE TILSTON

I stayed with Jackson C. Frank one time. He made an impression in London but I don't think he ventured out too much. What did make an impression was his song 'Blues Run the Game'. I remember the first time I went to a club, somebody sang that song and I thought, 'What a wonderful song.' Then somebody would always sing 'Blues Run the Game', wherever I went. I still think it's one of the best songs and it's quite ironic that a lot of Americans don't know it still and they've never heard of Jackson Frank.

On the other hand, we had people like Bert Jansch, John Renbourn, Davy Graham and Roy Harper and I just thought our songwriters were much more interesting than the Americans, apart from Dylan, of course. And I thought the stuff they were doing guitar-wise was light years ahead of what the Americans were into.

I think even at that early age I could see a lot of their stuff, certainly the guitar work, was quite formulaic, whereas the stuff that Bert and Davy were doing was, well, somebody coined the phrase folk baroque and I think it's fairly apposite.

JOHN RENBOURN

I felt we taught them more than they taught us. I mean the guys who used to go down the Cousins were a loose bunch . . . Davy Graham, Bert Jansch – great players. So who learned more from whom?

8 There were all these prejudices and strange beliefs

Songs from the British tradition dominated the folk revival. Audiences relished joining in on the choruses of 'The Leaving of Liverpool', 'Pleasant and Delightful', 'Wild Rover' and all the rest, but they would just as readily sit and listen to a pirate ballad like 'The Flying Cloud' that took Louis Killen seven minutes to sing.

For a while all was well. What mattered was that audiences were enjoying themselves, but by the mid-sixties factions were forming with strong opinions being expressed as to which songs should be sung and how they should be sung, especially in clubs that focused exclusively on traditional music.

Some frowned upon musical instruments and decreed that only unaccompanied singing was permitted. Others considered only songs from the British Isles to be acceptable. The hard core adopted Ewan MacColl's dictum that songs should be from the singer's own heritage or region. It was an era of purists and policies. Source singers looked back to the oral and regional traditions while revival singers introduced newer elements.

But the exponents of traditional music, those who were booked in the folk clubs, did not come in homogeneous form. At one end of the spectrum were Scottish source singers Jeannie Robertson and Jimmy McBeath, along with their English counterparts Sam Larner, Fred Jordan and Walter Pardon. At the other, and extreme, end came the Young Tradition and Robin and Barry Dransfield, who brought outside musical influences and a rock 'n' roll swagger to their performance.

Somewhere in between were the singers who had emerged during the earlier years of the revival – the Watersons, Nigel Denver, Louis Killen, Johnny Handle, the Ian Campbell group, and Martin Carthy – who in 1966 would send a wave of excitement throughout the folk scene when he teamed up with fiddler Dave Swarbrick.

The source singers influenced the revival singers, who in turn influenced the next wave that came along in the mid- to late sixties. Nic Jones, who came to closely rival Martin Carthy for guitar technique, had been in a group, the Halliard, before going solo. Dick Gaughan turned professional in 1970. Tim Hart and Maddy Prior joined up to become a major attraction on the club circuit before going electric with Steeleye Span. June Tabor came forth from the Midlands, Dave Burland from Barnsley and Phil Beer from Devon.

All of them, from the source singers to the newcomers, had their own approach to traditional music. They all played the folk clubs. Whatever policies, practices or prohibitions club organisers tried to impose, within the organic nature of the tradition individuality would always prevail.

MADDY PRIOR

Traditional music never stays put. When it happens it's the sort of peak of a revival and then it kind of falls away and becomes unfashionable again, because essentially popular music goes through fashions and every so often it sweeps up traditional music and then it drops it the same way. The interesting thing is that traditional music carries on regardless because there's always some people like us that will continue, because we lived through a time when folk music was not highly regarded at all.

DAVE BURLAND

In the late sixties I was in hospital. I had a burst appendix that baffled the medical profession for a while, so I nearly snuffed it. When I came out, I didn't sing for months and I thought, 'Do I want to do this again?' I was talking to Martin Carthy and he said, 'It's an ideal opportunity for you now, to decide whether you want to do it seriously or not. If I were you I would think about singing a lot more English songs, traditional songs.'

I was very influenced by Martin in those days. He's an influential figure. He actually told me to try to stop being funny as well, which I thought was a huge mistake. I don't regard myself like, say, Tony Capstick was, as a comedian, but things do make me smile occasionally and you can't stop yourself being what you are.

When Martin Carthy brought out his first album in 1965, and before that Nigel Denver's LP, they were a huge influence. I used to do 'A Sailor's Life' in DADGAD, which I think Martin showed me. And Nigel Denver – I used to sing 'Baron o' Brackley' in a terrible Scottish accent. But in a way, there's no greater tribute you can pay than sing other people's songs, because they're songs that move you.

MIKE HARDING

I picked up the guitar and I started singing and I founded my own folk club in a pub called the Old House at Home. We went along and said to the landlord, 'Is it all right if we come in the middle of the week and play a few tunes?' He listened to us and he said, 'Why don't you come and do a Sunday night here? We never have anybody in.' You could only get about forty people in, then it was heaving.

Word got round and that first night there was Bernard Wrigley and Dave Brooks, Harry Ogden, Lee Nicholson – he went on to make a fantastic album, *Horse Music* – and Harry Boardman. There were loads there, then the club just took off and it ran for years. I had Lou Killen there, Johnny Handle, Christy Moore – it was his first or second gig, he charged me £3 and I've still got a letter from him saying I'll come for £3 again, any time you want me. I'm thinking of holding him to that.

Harry Boardman had a massive effect on me. I wandered into this pub in Manchester and there's this bloke with a five-string banjo, but playing it with a strange finger-picking style, and he's playing concertina and he's singing songs about cotton mills and the mines. And I thought, 'Bloody hell – what is this?' I sat there at his feet and thought, 'There's another kind of music that I didn't even know about, urban folk song, industrial folk song.' That really got me on a search and eventually I produced my own book of Lancashire folk songs that I'd collected. So it was a massive influence on me.

There was a feller called Frank Duffy. He was a very famous lad round Manchester. He was one of the first people I'd seen playing a banjo that style, like Harry Boardman played it, a frailing style. He did fantastic versions of songs like 'Kishmul's Galley'. I got 'Away with Rum', the song of the Salvation Army, from him. He used to do 'Manchester Rambler'. I learned a lot from Frank Duffy, a hell of a lot. As well as singing trad songs very well, he was a very entertaining singer and storyteller.

JOHN COOPER CLARKE *punk poet who did early gigs in folk clubs*
I had a bit of a downer on folk music 'cos of being at school in the post-war years where they would force us to read dialect poetry. It was enough to put me off poetry for life! When people say, 'Oh, I like the way you read poetry in your Manchester accent', it's only because I can't help it. We were forced to read this stuff written in places like Burnley and talking about weavers and shit like that. I've since come to see the value of it but the absurdity was not lost on me at ten years old.

The guy that turned me back on to folk music was Martin Carthy. He sounded like he belonged in the Napoleonic era, he looked like somebody that belonged in the Napoleonic era and there was just something about the way he phrased a song and told a story, not forgetting his music. He'd got a lovely voice, beautiful mellifluous tones, and he's a great guitar player.

I did Manchester Sports Guild and Pete Farrow, at the Black Lion in Salford, used to put me on in the early days at his club. Christy Moore was a regular there.

DAVE SWARBRICK
Martin Carthy and I got fined for turning up late at the
Manchester Sports Guild. That was after we'd been travelling in
the back of a vegetable lorry, hitching a lift. We had an accident
and by the time we got there the organiser, Jenks, fined us ten
quid for being late.

CHRISTY MOORE *was a member of Planxty and Moving
Hearts*
When I came to England I knew nothing of folk clubs whatsoever.
By chance I strayed into a room where Annie Briggs was singing,
then in Manchester I went to Mike Harding's club, then to a club
run by a singer called Frank Duffy. The Beggarmen had a club
off Piccadilly, I heard Luke Kelly in there. I was impressed by so
many singers everywhere I went.

When I first heard Martin Carthy I was amazed by his
accompaniments. The Watersons' sound still echoes in my head
from when I heard them first in the Hyde Folk Club, Cheshire,
one Thursday night in 1967. I heard Bob Davenport in Marsden
in 1968 – a wonderful session of Geordie singing with the
Marsden Rattlers. Harry Boardman was a nice man, very serious
about Lancashire songs. He was always encouraging

I started doing floor spots in late 1966. The Grehan Sisters took
me to clubs and gave me support slots. Mike Harding put me up
in his house for months in 1967. The first card I had printed cited
his address as contact. Packie Byrne took me under his wing for
a while, he was a great troubadour. He had great respect for both
his audience and for those who ran gigs. He gave me shelter too
when I was in need.

I went to folk clubs seven nights a week, sometimes I'd get a
floor spot, sometimes a gig, sometimes I'd pick up a song. It was
a very exciting time for me. The first booking I did was in May
1967 at the Wellgreen folk club in Manchester, I was paid £6. The
Wellgreen gig came about when Pete Wilmot heard me sing at
the singers' night which ran every Monday in the Manchester

Sports Guild. Then I played the Bury folk club, run by the Valley Folk from Rawtenstall. I imagine both these clubs had forty to fifty people in.

There was such a diversity of clubs. In general they were run by folk enthusiasts. The ethos of the club depended upon the taste of the organisers. Very few clubs had a PA and most of us on the circuit disliked microphones. No one had any mike technique and the gear was usually dreadful. I was terrified of mikes in 1967.

JOHN TAMS

Roger Watson, who was from Kirkby-in-Ashfield, turned up with a guy called Colin Cater. They were both teachers. Colin admired Louis Killen and got hold of some of the stuff he'd made for Topic. They took a shine to me so I started working with Roger in Muckram Wakes.

I was still working as a journalist, leading this double life, because I was editing a paper in Belper. I would edit the paper during the day, then we'd charge off and do a gig, come back and I'd carry on editing the paper. I used to sleep on the typewriter.

The first album that Muckram Wakes made was called *A Map of Derbyshire* and all the songs were from Derbyshire, so I have a lot to thank Frank Sutton for. He introduced me to Llewellyn Jewitt and *The Ballads and Songs of Derbyshire*. Then I met other local writers like Gerald Short and by and by we accumulated enough tracks to go and record with Bill Leader at Cecil Sharp House in the studio downstairs.

We made an album for Bill and it did well. It got me around, and the band. I'd been working at Sudbury Hall and met there an old singer called George Fradley. I didn't know he was a singer. I thought he was a gardener. He thought he was a gardener, until we both discovered that we liked folk music.

He didn't know what it was. It was just singing to him. He was in his seventies and he sang a ballad that he'd not sung for forty years, 'The Squire of Tamworth', and no one had ever collected it before. So to me this man was the real McCoy, at the end of an era of real McCoys – they were dying off. It was a joy, and then we started to tour with the old man. We'd turn up as Muckram Wakes with George Fradley and George would sing whatever he felt like singing.

MIKE HARDING

Folk on Wheels was something I started. The first one, we went to a pub in Holmfirth. We said to the landlady, 'Can you do pie and peas for eighty?' She said, 'Aye.' I said, 'We're thinking of coming over in a bus, it's a folk club. We'll bring some guitars and we'll have a sing.'

We hired a Manchester Corporation bus, nearly eighty people, and we all went over there. She'd applied for a late licence so we drank till about nearly midnight, had pie and peas and then came back – singing all the way there, singing all night and singing all the way back.

Another time we went to Halifax. We'd got three buses by now, the old back-loaders, and we pulled up at these traffic lights and this feller jumps on. I said, 'We're going to Manchester you know . . .' He says, 'You can't bloody fool me. I've had a bellyful of ale but I'm not bloody daft', and sat down on the back seat. We're all singing away and he's listening. I said, 'Honest mate, we're going to Manchester.' 'Nay, get singing, it's a bloody real do this,' he says.

We got to the traffic lights in Victoria Avenue in Manchester and he says, 'Where the fuckin' 'ell am I?' I said, 'You're in Manchester.' The lights were still at red. He got off. I can still see it. He says, 'The wife'll fuckin kill me!' I don't know to this day how he got home, or if he got home, or what. He probably settled down in Manchester and married again.

BILLY CONNOLLY

The Scottish clubs liked entertainers and English clubs liked educators. They seemed to like to be educated by the traditional unaccompanied songs. It was like Brussels sprouts, supposed to be good for you. I remember at some clubs it was very difficult because the crowd had been weaned on English traditional stuff and when we went, the Humblebums, they were saying, 'What the fuck's this?' They'd much rather have had the Young Tradition or something.

HEATHER WOOD *member of the Young Tradition, an a cappella trio*
The way the Young Tradition started was – on 18 April 1965 I ambled into the Scots Hoose in Cambridge Circus where Peter Bellamy and Royston Wood were singing together. I thought, 'This is fun', and, given that there were so many folk clubs in London and you could go to one every night, I ended up learning the songs and joining in from the floor. I sort of fell into singing with them.

HANS FRIED
The Young Tradition first sang together at my twenty-first birthday party. They'd met at the Scots Hoose. Peter had slept on my floor when he first came up to London. He was at Maidstone Art College. I invited them to my birthday party and I said, 'Form a group.' They said, 'We don't play anything.' Peter played concertina, sort of, and a guitar, very sort of, and a whistle. I said, 'Sing unaccompanied like the Watersons.' So they tried it and that became the Young Tradition. They had a great sort of sparring match between them, off stage and on. Shortly after my twenty-first birthday they got a flat together at 30 Somali Road.

HEATHER WOOD
Bruce Dunnett's club the Grand Tradition was supposed to have residents, the likes of Joe Heaney, and a bunch of us would show up and Joe Heaney wouldn't, so we'd get to sing, and then we got more and more organised and people started saying, 'Can we book you? We'll pay you.' Southend was our first out of London gig.

JOHN TAMS

I got completely blown away by the Young Tradition. They were a cappella rock, Bellamy with that long, blond hair and the invented voice that you either fell down laughing at or you thought was remarkable.

HEATHER WOOD

It was sort of an accident. Pete and Royston were singing Copper Family songs together and those harmonies left a lot of room for me to play around the edges. We sang what we wanted to sing and we listened to everything . . . Folkways records from all over the place, rock 'n' roll, blues. Royston was into classical music. I'd listened to the Everly Brothers. So all of that influenced what we were doing and our attitude to music.

I went to a folklore conference a few years ago and there was an incredibly serious German guy there saying he had interviewed singers from the sixties 'and they were preserving the tradition'. I said, 'Look love, I'm sorry – it was about free beer and getting laid. We were all stoned out of our gourds.'

HANS FRIED

Peter Bellamy once threatened to invite me to his home. His father was a right-hand man of Oswald Mosley. I would not have been his cup of tea, if I had been invited. He'd tell me that his mother was a good cook, but she wasn't allowed to sit at the family table. Peter had a duality about that – his politics were very confused.

BOB DAVENPORT

I gave Peter Bellamy his start at the pub the John Snow in Soho. The Singers' Club said, 'Would you and the Rakes' – Paul Gross, Reg Hall and Michael Plunkett – 'run an evening and get people up?' I was insistent on a band because if you don't know the person who's put their name down and when they get up it doesn't go well for some reason, you just nod to the band. The idea was if somebody was good they would come along to the Singers' Club itself and sing a couple of songs. It was like moving through the ranks.

One night there was a young man sitting about three rows back. He had long hair and he came up and said, 'You've got the band here, do you mind if people play an instrument, or just sing?' So he played the whistle. That was the first time Peter Bellamy played in public.

DAVE BURLAND

I met him at the station in Barnsley, and we were going back to our house for a cup of tea. It was about six o'clock, the time when all the lads were coming in from the pit villages, for their Saturday night out.

He came out of the station in this big cape and huge hat, with his long, white hair. And there's all these lads done up like pox doctors' clerks – they've got so much aftershave on you could see fumes coming off 'em, disturbing the atmosphere. They'd never seen anything like him in Barnsley, they thought it was Doctor Who. And I thought, 'Good old Pete!' In the folk clubs, he converted people with the sheer force of his personality.

HEATHER WOOD

Young Tradition came to an end in '69. It was partly economics. We tried putting our fee up and it didn't work. We were making £30 a night, occasionally with expenses if it was a long way from London.

Pete and Royston were settled by then. Royston had a kid on the way and instead of living together we were all living separately. That was like three rents instead of one, so we just decided that was it. I went off and did other things and moved to America. Peter tried to make it solo and didn't, and killed himself. The club scene changed.

JON BODEN *Bellowhead singer and fiddler*
Peter Bellamy is probably the biggest influence and certainly the
biggest impact on my repertoire. I've nicked a massive amount
of stuff from his repertoire. One of my favourite albums is Pete
Bellamy's *Live in Norwich*, which is set up to be a kind of perfect
folk club. That level of singing is something that I go out of my
way to try and experience.

JOHNNY HANDLE
Nobody really affected my singing style, but with respect for the
material – Jeannie Robertson, Norman Kennedy, meeting and
hearing Harry Cox, Cyril Tawney. For general approach to the
material . . . stage presence – Ewan.

You eyeball audiences, you work out what you need to say,
you're in charge of the audience and you haven't got to let
them down. There's a responsibility for entertainment there at
whatever level you choose, be it intellectual or light-hearted.

ROBIN DRANSFIELD
The secret of singing is phrasing and timing, and there's a few
singers I'd pick out for that. Louis Killen was one of them. Dick
Gaughan's another. Martin Carthy was a big hero who we all
fastened on to in those early days. I think in some ways it was
his best period ever, when he was on his own and before he did
anything with Swarb. It was a different style.

MARTIN CARTHY
The first time I met Dave Swarbrick was down at the Troubadour,
then later on I saw him with the Ian Campbell Folk Five. That
was the thing that made the Campbells different from any
other of the Weavers-based folk groups – the fiddle player. Oh,
boy – was he a fiddle player! Even in those days – oh, he was
good.

The Campbells' relationship with Dave was weird. Dave would
run away periodically and they would go and find him and drag

him out and put him in the car and take him to a gig. He used to drive them mad and they used to drive him mad. He just walked out on the Campbells one day.

IAN CAMPBELL

We threw him out! Musically, Dave was a genius. He stood out head and shoulders above anybody else on the folk scene. But he was unaccountable. Occasionally we'd go and pick him up and he'd say, 'Sorry can't come, got no fiddle.' He'd pawned it because he needed some money, so we'd go to the pawnshop and buy it back. We accepted it because that was what he was like.

I remember one occasion when he'd pawned the fiddle and we went to collect it. Lorna said, 'We'll look after this, Dave. It's ours now, it's not yours, and when we've finished tonight I'll take it home.' Then there was girlfriend trouble. We go off to Denmark and he falls in love with this gorgeous Danish girl, Birgitta. We were there for three days and never saw him apart from at the gig. Then when we got back he fell out with his girlfriend here and went to Denmark and his new girlfriend.

A few weeks later we were up in the north-east, a little town towards Newcastle. We'd been apologising, saying, 'When you booked us, you fully expected we had a fiddler, but we don't now. Circumstances have changed and he's working in Denmark.' There's a guy sitting in the front row; he leaned forward and said, 'He's working with Martin Carthy.'

MARTIN CARTHY

He rang me up, said, 'I've just left the Campbells, I'm going to go and live with Birgitta in Denmark. I'm not coming back, I've had enough.' 'When are you going?' He said, 'I'm going tomorrow. Can I come and stay the night?'

He came and we had a meal and Dorothy – my wife then – and I, we sat there and said, 'What a shame he's going to go.' Took him to Liverpool Street station to get to Harwich for the boat to Hook of Holland and waved him off, thinking, 'Ah, there goes a great musician! What a loss to the English folk scene, what a shame. It's awful.'

Went home. Two days later, the telephone rang. I picked it up, this voice came on. 'I could fuckin' weep. The bastards threw me out.' 'Who did, the Danish?' He said, 'No, I never got that far. I got to the Hook of Holland. They said, "Where you going?" I said, "I'm going to Denmark. I'm going to live there for the rest of my life. I've met the woman of my dreams and I'm going to get married." "Have you got a work permit?" "No." "You can't come in. You're going back to England."'

I was going away on a tour the following day. The first gig was in Sheffield. I said, 'Why don't you come with me?' He said, 'I haven't got any money.' I said, 'What we'll do – we'll go and sing at all the clubs and we'll ask them if they'll contribute to your expenses and whatever we make we'll split down the middle.' I was getting twelve quid a night.

He'd played on five tracks of my first album and on the train up to Sheffield we sat in the compartment and we worked out two ragtime pieces. He knew a thing called 'Porcupine Rag' and I knew 'Dill Pickles Rag'. I'll always remember it because we were sitting there practising and the door opened and all these Indians came in and sat down. They just giggled and clapped and nudged each other.

I think the first tour started about 6 March at Malcolm Fox's club, the Barley Mow in Sheffield. I launched into one song to start with and he knew it, 'The Black Velvet Band'. I used to sing that in those days. The great thing was, every club paid us more for expenses. And most clubs gave us a bit more on top of the fee. The last club we did they actually doubled the fee and gave us the expenses. It was absolutely phenomenal.

I'd been carrying all the money and at the end of the week I said, 'Okay, lets divi it up.' I pulled the money out of my pocket. We'd paid the fares. I divided the money out and said, 'There we are – is that okay?' And he just sat there. I put my money away and I noticed he was still sitting there. I said, 'Is that all right?' He said, 'There's seventy-five quid here, isn't there?' I said, 'Yeah.'

He said, 'I was on fifteen quid a week with the Campbells.' That was top money – he was the highest-paid person in the Ian Campbell group. He had seventy-five quid in his hand. He said, 'I've never seen this amount of money in my life.' He could have gone to Denmark with it – in fact he did, when the tour was over. I said, 'Are you coming back?' He said, 'I don't know, haven't decided yet.' I said, 'Well, if you do decide, I'm doing a tour, starting in Darlington.'

He did come back for the tour and he brought Birgitta with him. We went on the road and we stayed on the road for three and a half years. We had a fabulous time.

When we split up, when he joined Fairport, I was at a bit of a loss. I had to completely re-think my repertoire. But by the time I went out on the road I'd decided what I was going to do – I was going to ditch the guitar unless I had something to play. What that meant was that to begin with my repertoire was 75 or 80 per cent unaccompanied.

DEREK BRIMSTONE *one of the folk scene's funniest characters in the sixties and seventies*
I like old Martin Carthy. He was a dreadful performer. Once he started singing and playing he was great, but he didn't used to say a word in between songs. He'd take about three or four minutes tuning up and people would all start talking, then he'd go into three or four unaccompanied ballads, one after the other. You've got to vary your performance – fast, slow, funny and sad, don't do two songs on the same subject twice. That was Martin's one failing, he couldn't exercise his personality.

We drove from Brooklands to Durham once, about a five-hour drive, and we had a long chat all the way up. I said, 'What about you doin' a bit of chat, Martin?' He said, 'I can't, Derek, it's not my thing . . .' I said, 'But I've seen you doing a guitar workshop and you've been really funny, this bubbly personality.' He said,

'No it's not my thing, I'm not an entertainer, I'm a folk singer.' He said, 'I'm a purist', and he was smiling when he said it.

It's only a personal opinion and I'd pay to go and see him, though I've heard he does talk a lot more now in between songs. He must have listened to me.

JUNE TABOR

I'd been going to folk clubs for two to three years when I went to Oxford in '66. The Heritage Society had been going ten years by then. At one point while I was there I was treasurer and the treasurer's book had all the expenses – Paul Simon's in there, six quid. The folk club was in the upstairs room of a pub and there was a skittle alley downstairs.

There was a chap called Richard Mellish used to record what went on at the folk club. He had a recording of Anne Briggs singing in the upstairs room and you could hear underneath it the roll of the balls and the skittles falling down and people going, 'Yeah!' This is going on down below while Anne Briggs is singing upstairs.

There was no conscious effort on my part to sing professionally but I ended up being paid for the first time at a club in the winter of '68, the Fighting Cocks at Kingston. They had good residents, Pete Wood and John Kay. The standard was a lot better than me. I had to stand up and do two half-hours completely unaccompanied.

I finished my degree then worked in Oxford for a year in a library. I moved to London and got a job at Haringey Library. I was going to clubs and the number of gigs increased gradually, all by word of mouth. I lived in Muswell Hill and I used to go to Bounds Green, Enfield, the Hop Poles. It got to be ten or twelve gigs a month and I was still working in the library.

ROD STRADLING

The Fighting Cocks club in Kingston was started by an Irishman called Frank Kelly. He put out some papers asking was anybody interested in starting a folk club, to go to a meeting. So we all went along on the day. We were there – but no Frank Kelly. And nobody has ever heard or seen him again.

The people who'd turned up got together and I was asked to run it. We didn't only book traditional people at first – it was a club without any particular musical policy. Then I went to Sidmouth for the first time. This was 1964.

That first year the entire festival was in the Beach Store and when one concert was over the audience just sat there until the next concert started. I scarcely went into a pub in the whole of the week I was there. It was quite remarkable. Everyone was so enthusiastic, and I so enjoyed the traditional music and song that Arthur Knevett, who was also there, and I decided that the Fighting Cocks should book only traditional guests, which meant revivalists who only sang traditional songs and the few true traditional singers who we knew about in those days. I was involved there until 1967 when we moved to Islington and got involved with the King's Head.

We got hold of people through friends and friends of friends. We booked the Stewarts of Blair at the Fighting Cocks – a real delight to get a whole family's tradition all in one go. Somebody, I can't remember who, put me on to Jimmy McBeath so we were able to get him to come down. He was very old and uncommunicative, but when I said, 'Ladies and gentlemen, please welcome Jimmy McBeath', he leaped on to the stage and just sparkled. A great performance. It was like opening the fridge door and the light coming on. At the end of the set he resumed his seat and switched off.

The night we booked Seamus Ennis at the King's Head we must have had about two hundred people in – you couldn't move. The photos on the fronts of the Topic and Leader LPs of the time come from that gig – they attest to how crowded it was. He gave a delightful performance.

We had Phoebe Smith twice. She came with her husband and eldest son. She was our favourite English woman singer, and was stunning. When Lizzie Higgins came she sang 'London Lights', it was never recorded anywhere else. Daisy Chapman wasn't a professional by any means but she had us all in the palm of her hand by the end of the first song.

RAB NOAKES *formed Stealers Wheel with Gerry Rafferty*
Round about springtime of 1965 I went along to St Andrews folk club. The guests that night were Martin Carthy and Norman Kennedy. They were a revelation. Seeing Martin Carthy as a guitar player close-up was pretty unbelievable and Norman Kennedy was a student of the songs from the north-east of Scotland. He'd learned a lot of songs from the source singers, first-hand. The song culture of Scotland wasn't something we'd been in any way encouraged to celebrate at school.

Around the '68 period when I was getting booked to perform a wee bit more, I shared the stage with Jeannie Robertson one time and Jimmy McBeath another time. I paid a lot of attention to them. These people were highly accomplished performers. That whole thing about folkie performers – that people stumble on in their old clothes and say, 'I hope I can get to the end of this . . .' – I don't know where that came from, because it certainly didn't come from the old source singers. They'd got their craft off to a fine art. They were highly accomplished performers. They had great skill and presentation.

JIMMIE MACGREGOR
Ewan MacColl took me to task because I used to say, 'Look, you either are a traditional singer or you're not a traditional singer. You can sing like a traditional singer, you can learn to sing like a traditional singer, but you are or you are not.' Everybody wanted to be traditional.

Jeannie Robertson spent her early years living under a canvas tent and touring round the countryside, uneducated. So did Belle Stewart, all these people. Their songs came right from their basic roots. Mine didn't – I learned them. I never ever claimed to be a

Top: Ewan MacColl and Peggy Seeger

Bottom: Redd Sullivan and Martin Winsor

Top left: Harry Boardman   *Top right:* Ramblin' Jack Elliott

Bottom left: Alex Campbell

Bottom right: Diz Disley and Bob Davenport at the Troubadour

Top left: Ralph McTell   *Top right:* John Tams

Bottom left: Derek Brimstone   *Bottom right:* Barry Dransfield

Top: Pete Maynard, Martin Carthy and Pete Stanley, with Wally Whyton in the control room

Bottom: The Ian Campbell Group with Dave Swarbrick (far right)

Top left: Wizz Jones   *Top right:* Tom Paxton

Bottom: John Renbourn and Bert Jansch

Top left: Jimmy Macgregor *Top right:* Dominic Behan

Bottom: Peter Bellamy of the Young Tradition with Francis McPeake

Top left: John Martyn   *Top right:* Maddy Prior and Tim Hart

Bottom: Tony Capstick and Dave Burland

Top: The Watersons   *Bottom:* The Deighton Family

traditional singer. I said, 'I sing the songs I like, they happen to be folk songs and I sing them the way I like to sing them.'

BARBARA DICKSON
I'd met John Watt. He ran the Dunfermline folk club. I knew a little bit about folk music from the Kingston Trio and I learned songs from John Watt which were Scottish songs, beautiful songs which a woman could comfortably sing with a guitar and give meaning and a performance to. He said, 'Sing Scottish songs. There's nothing wrong with singing a Peter, Paul and Mary song, but it would be better for the tradition and for you and for the revival and for other people listening to our culture if you as a Scottish woman were to sing Scottish songs.'

DICK GAUGHAN *singer and guitarist, formerly in Boys of the Lough*
The first paid gig I ever did in an actual folk club was in 1966 at a club held in a bar called the Rendezvous Roadhouse in Bathgate in Edinburgh. I got paid £2. In those days it was all word of mouth and very informal and anarchic and clubs were generally run by dedicated and pretty fanatical amateurs.

Scotland is a bit like a large village anyway, and the folk world at that time was so small that everybody quickly got to know everybody else, and everybody listened to everything that was going on, so if you were any good the people who ran the clubs soon got to hear about you. As I got more work, I just kind of drifted into earning my living exclusively from playing, finally giving up other jobs in January 1970.

I met Aly Bain in the Forrest Hill Bar – Sandy Bell's – in Edinburgh, when he first arrived from Shetland. I think we did a couple of gigs together, but the combination of him and Mike Whellans worked better at that stage and we didn't formally play together until I asked him to play on my first album and then a few months later joined him in Boys of the Lough, after Mike left.

BILLY CONNOLLY

When Aly Bain came down from the Shetlands, he was broke. He was just this little joiner who was amazingly good at the fiddle. I went to see him in this hotel that doesn't exist any more, in Glasgow, and he did a tune called 'Maple Sugar' and I thought, 'Oh, that's great.' He wore a cape in those days, a bit like Peter Bellamy. I thought, 'I'd love to borrow that!'

I took him down to the Scotia and he was terrified – all these wild men. We got the beer out and had a little blow and I said, 'Have you got any gigs?' He said, 'No, I'll have to get some.' And I said, 'Why don't you join our band until you get better known? We'll give you equal money.' So he did. He was playing 'Sweet Georgia Brown' and all that. He was with us a couple of months, then he joined Mike Whellans

MARTIN SIMPSON

I was so into it musically that the Nic Joneses and Carthys, and Dick Gaughan when he first came down – those were the guys that really blew me away because they just transmitted the material so brilliantly and they also played the crap out of the guitar. I still remember Finbar Furey play the pipes at three feet away when I was about seventeen. It was like watching Jimi Hendrix, he was just ridiculously good. He was responsible for that quote: 'Why do you play so fast, Finbar?' ''Cos I fuckin' can.'

JOHN TAMS

Nic Jones would come up to Alfreton and play. He came first in the Halliard. He was very shadowy at the back and got on with it. There was a guy called Dave Moran at the front who'd got all the gift of the gab and the presentation skills and another guy called Nigel on mandolin, and Nic playing guitar. Mostly with a plectrum, big chords, and then, of course, he developed into one of the greatest guitarists in the business, globally I mean.

Once he'd left the Halliard, he came up and did his solo work and everybody thought this was great because we'd got

Martin Carthy as an icon and now it was like *The War of The Worlds*, Carthy and Jones, and their approaches were completely different.

Nic would come and play for not much money and he'd say, 'Come and play my club.' So we all piled into an old van and went down to Chelmsford and played there. It was great – there was like an interchange and an exchange. We went down there and played the week after Paul Simon had been at the club. Once it got going it all happened very quickly.

MAARTIN ALLCOCK *multi-instrumentalist, once of Fairport Convention*
Nic Jones was a great help to me when I was starting out because I didn't understand about different tunings for the guitar. I collared him in the interval and said, 'Can I ask you some questions?' He said, 'Yes, go on.' So he gave me lots of different tunings and drew chord diagrams. He told me what books to check out at the library – great bloke.

BOB DAVENPORT
I was brought to Leeds some years ago, a club structured the same way as the Singers' Club. It was how not to sing – 'This is a guy who is awful. Don't listen to him and don't be influenced by him.' – I was brought to the club for that reason. This guy invited me up to show his committee how not to sing. They said that traditional music was moribund and therefore it needed reviving. That was the justification for MacColl and Seeger, Bert Lloyd, all of them.

I just gave 'em two fingers and at the end I finished off with a whole range of music hall songs and the audience all joined in. For the committee, that was their life – the club and its little magazine. There was a lot of control involved.

Then about a year later, he rang me up and said would I go with the Rakes to play their club. I said, 'We haven't changed, we're still the same.' He said, 'That's what I want.'

JOHNNY HANDLE

I went down to Birtley and I saw the Elliotts' club, which was quite a revelation because, whereas we were running a stage club with residents and guests, they were running a singaround regardless of talent or material. Singers that wouldn't get up at our club would get up at Birtley. Then after getting up at Birtley a few nights, they'd come to the Bridge.

Once people began singing at Birtley and got confidence some of them started their own clubs, so a whole network of clubs started out in the early sixties and everybody would troop along to support them.

IAN CAMPBELL

A lot of the singers, the guests, were friends that we'd known a long time and they would be much happier staying with us than in a hotel. We booked the legendary singer from Aberdeen, Jeannie Robertson. We took her home and she spent three nights with Mum and Dad. To her it was like being home from home, chatting away in an Aberdeen accent.

There was one evening when she was staying with Mum and Dad and she sat until very late at night chatting, telling stories, occasionally breaking into song, then telling another story. It was all to do with ghosts. She was full of ghosts – the ghosts used to follow her around, all this sort of thing. We listened and we realised that some of them were actually well-known folk tales. Then she'd stop and start another song.

This was back in the late sixties and the old man had a tape recorder, one of those enormous, huge things. He got that out and he just left it running and she chatted and reminisced and sang. Then she went to bed and he turned the tape recorder off. 'Beautiful, we'll listen to that in the winter, we'll re-live this.' It never occurred to him that it was priceless – with editing it would have made it into something special.

About three months later, somebody was visiting and father said, 'Do you know Jeannie Robertson? I've got a lovely tape of her here.' He got the tape out, click – and what was on it? Pop music off the radio! Our little sister had thought, 'Oh, it's some old lady talking a lot of nonsense', and taped over Jeannie Robertson.

NORMA WATERSON

We had a great night when the Stewarts of Blairgowrie came to Hull. We were living in a flat then and on the way home we got fish and chips for everybody. We got home and went up to the flat – there was Alex, the dad, and Belle, the mam, and then there was Cathy and Sheila, all the kids. We got up to our flat and started singing.

The man downstairs was a horrible man and he came up and banged on the door, shouting. We just said, 'Oh, he's a miserable so-and-so, carry on singing.' It wasn't loud. And all of a sudden all the lights went out. He'd taken our fuse out of the fuse box. So we got a whole load of candles and we sat there by the light of the candles, absolutely enthralled while Alex and Belle told all these ghost stories.

JOHN TAMS

Because there were no microphones in the folk clubs in the sixties, you had to have a voice. Margaret Barry was a street singer, she'd got a voice. She could clear a room with it. Bob Davenport had. If you were blessed with a rather beautiful voice but it was quiet, you didn't get on so well. So it developed voices like Peter Bellamy, like Nic Jones, who put a slight crackle in his voice so it would edge, so it would carry, and the actual scene was developed out of acoustic singing before microphones turned up.

A lot of songs which would have been tender couldn't be, because you hadn't got the way of expressing the dynamic until microphones turned up. The folk singing style was developed out of scabby carpeted, smoky rooms, which required a muscular delivery.

So you get the likes of the great Bob Davenport, who taught me that you can join things together. He'd sometimes get up at the beginning of a night and start singing, and he never stopped. He just joined things together. It didn't matter if it was 'Delilah' and some songs from Durham, then 'Nobody Knows You When You're Down and Out', then another ballad and then he'd do a monologue. And it was great. I like to talk in between songs, but sometimes I'll put four together. There'll be a theme, but it's thanks to Bob because he blazed that trail for us.

BOB DAVENPORT

At the Fox in Islington we booked New Orleans musicians, as we did Clarence Ashley and Doc Watson. One night we booked Ravi Shankar. We were asked by his management through Rory McEwen. Ravi Shankar wanted to play somewhere else other than the Festival Hall, so we booked him at the Fox. It was a very hot evening and in town was Bill Monroe and the Bluegrass Boys, so they came along and they finished the evening off.

Another night we had six or seven African drummers as guests. They'd played at the Hyde Park free festival with the Rolling Stones. We had an Irish six-piece resident band, then the Stewarts of Blairgowrie phoned up and said, 'We're in London tomorrow night. Is there any chance of getting on at the Fox?' We had plenty of money in the kitty, so we said, 'Come along.' The second half – there was Alex Stewart playing 'Scotland the Brave' on the pipes with seven West African drummers drumming away behind him, and Cathy and Sheila Stewart doing the hula hula.

I would rather have a good singer singing country than a bad singer singing traditional ballads. It's simple to me – the audience have paid for what? Not to listen to some person who can't even remember the words.

NOEL MURPHY *one of the folk scene's great characters*
I used to go to the Fox in Islington Green where Bob Davenport

and his Rakes were resident and he sang these Geordie songs. They were wonderful, yet two of the songs I remember him mostly for – one was 'Memphis Tennessee' and the other one 'I'm The Urban Spaceman' from the Bonzo Dogs. Bob Davenport singing that was for my mind a wonderful poke in the eye for all those prudish sort of traditionalists. Oh, I loved Bob. He was in my football team at the Norwich Folk Festival.

MADDY PRIOR

I was living in St Albans and going out with a bloke who played guitar a bit, Duffy. I started doing stuff on my own, songs like 'Sinner Man' . . . 'Kumbayah'. Then I drove Sandy and Jeanie Darlington around and they said to me, 'You should stop singing these American songs. You're crap at it.'

I was rather disgruntled, but they had all these tapes and they said, 'Why don't you listen to this stuff?' So I wearily listened, but I persevered because I thought they were rather good and I didn't want to look like a clot. And gradually the tunes started to get through to me. It took a lot of work.

I did a year on my own with the banjo, hitching – down to south Wales, up to Leeds. One of the first places I sang was in Leeds. This was before I started singing with Tim. I used to go off from St Albans on my scooter to the London clubs. Bloody long way on a scooter.

JON BODEN

Maddy Prior: I grew up listening to her on Steeleye records and there's a lot in her delivery that's kind of hard-wired into the way I think about singing, though you wouldn't necessarily see any crossover. It's storytelling and also singing over a big band. She knew how to sing over a loud rock band. She was fantastic.

MIKE WATERSON

One of the most embarrassing things of my life was in St Albans. We did a concert. We did an afternoon rehearsal for it, there was loads of people on and Maddy rang her mam up and said, 'I'm bringing some friends home for tea.' We sat and had a lovely meal and were nattering away and I said, 'I've just read this wonderful book called *One Away*.' And Maddy said, 'Oh, who wrote it?' I said, 'I've forgotten the name.' She said, 'It was my dad!' Her dad's sat at the other end of the bloody table! He wrote *Z Cars* and loads of stuff for television and I'd forgotten his name.

ROBIN DRANSFIELD
In 1969 the Watersons had just packed it in for the first time. Carthy and Swarbrick had just packed it in for the first time. I'd been teaching for a year – hated it – and doing solo gigs and I said to Barry, who'd been going round the country doing a few bits and pieces with a guy called Clive Collins from Birmingham, 'There's a gap in the market here: if we're going to do this pro, this is the time to do it.'

I sent a load of flyers out to all the folk clubs and the work just poured through the door, because there wasn't anybody else much to take the place of the Watersons and Carthy and Swarbrick. I'm sure we must have picked up on work for that reason if no other, and we went off at a gallop.

It was eventually what we used to call 'country and north-eastern'. You don't need to be a rocket scientist to work out that, having started in bluegrass bands and all that New Lost City Ramblers stuff, the harmonies came from there. We did our first gig full-time pro, me and Barry, on the same day that your man walked on the moon. It was at the Herga in Wealdstone.

MIKE WATERSON
What we wanted to do was sing and enjoy ourselves, not traipse all over the country. We absolutely hated it. The joy for us was the hour on stage that we stood up and sang.

You've got to remember – there were no motorways. We had a battered old Transit van. It wasn't our scene. We weren't entertainers. It was bloody hard work. What we forgot was the agent took his 10 per cent, the van took another 10 per cent, then you'd got to stay somewhere. We'd got a mattress in the back of the van, and blankets in desperation. It was a hard way to make a living, a damned hard way. The only joy was the song. You did it – and it entitled you to nothing.

You'd go in a café on the way to London or somewhere and they'd all be Greasy Joes – lorry drivers' cafés. They really were rough. For the two girls to go in – it was not pleasant at all. But at Cromwell in Lincolnshire I wrote a poem about Moira's Nature Caff, 'cos it was wonderful, and in the middle of the night on the way back home you'd pull in and you could have a proper meal with mashed potatoes.

We'd had enough of touring. We were in Ireland at Queen's University, Belfast. They said, 'We'll come for you when we need you', and they came at one o'clock in the morning. We got there and there was a dozen singers to go on and there were people actually throwing coins – at singers we thought were wonderful. If they'd hit anybody they'd have blinded 'em. They were all pissed out of their minds.

We went on the stage and they went barmy. They loved us. We just sang and sang and sang. And we got back to the hotel and said, 'What the hell are we doing, if they liked us and didn't like the singers that we liked?' That was when we decided to stop singing.

GEOFF LAKEMAN

The Herga was an important club, very traditional. I met my wife Joy and we bought a little place out in Harrow and Wealdstone. I'd bought a concertina. Joy was already an accomplished violinist and we went along to the Herga on a Monday night, just down the road from us. John Heydon ran it for the best part of forty years.

We did one floor spot and we had a very limited repertoire but we were immediately welcomed by these people and asked to be co-residents. The guest nights were fantastic. We would have the High Level Ranters, Martin Carthy and Dave Swarbrick, Peter Bellamy, Young Tradition and also, slightly more esoteric, Jeannie Robertson and the Northumberland shepherd, Willie Scott, and Bert Lloyd.

I've got fond memories of Bert at the Herga with his squeaky little voice, singing his songs and telling his tales. Of course, he'd done it: he'd farmed sheep in Australia and he'd worked on whaling ships. He did sing songs about things he knew about. He wasn't much of a performer but we were all in awe of him, he was the first of the great musicologists and a lovely man.

AUDREY WINTER

Do you know what Bert Lloyd did for me? It was just before our son was born. We were living in Cambridge and Bert came as a guest to the Cambridge Folk Song Society. He was staying with us, and he and Eric went. I couldn't go. I didn't feel up to it. When he got back from the gig he sat in our room and sang the whole of his set to me.

ROBIN DRANSFIELD

We were young and we never bore fools gladly and I think with a lot of people we did have a reputation for being a bit mouthy. If you've got a bit of a swagger about you, and confidence, which we did have – we knew it was good stuff. I'll be honest, it was like, 'That's how we are.' We sang with a lot of power and we didn't piss about. We went for it, all the songs. A lot of thought went into doing it. We were always mavericks. We never quite fitted.

We never played the Singers' Club. We weren't traditional enough, and by the time we got into the second album in 1971, we were already writing songs and going off in a different direction. The only major festival we never did was Sidmouth. We were too arsey and in those days Sidmouth was very staid. It was run by a bloke in a cardigan and a pipe in his mouth. We did hear that they thought we were a bit too brash, not quite the right fit. We didn't give a shit. We had plenty of work anyway.

PHIL BEER *played in duo with Paul Downes, later with Phil Knightley in Show of Hands*
When Paul Downes and I heard the Dransfields, we were transfixed. They were utterly sensational, and I think Paul and I somehow tried to model ourselves slightly on them, more so than Carthy and Swarbrick. They had the swagger and the harmony work – two brothers singing together, those beautiful voices in the same range. And, of course, they were experimental.

MADDY PRIOR
Tim Hart and I knew each other from the Cock in St Albans – I suppose because we both were doing traditional music. A lot of the others were doing American, a lot of blues around. Donovan was part of our group. We sang everywhere and anywhere, people's houses, that's what you do. There was never any plan, people sometimes think you have or had a plan but as far as I'm concerned, it lurches from song to song, the plan kind of falls together afterwards.

We were very young. People used to be surprised that we were doing that kind of material, that young. We did harmonies and Tim was a nice guitar player and nice singer.

Tim and I used to do a little tour of Devon – Barnstable, Ilfracombe, Bideford, Exeter . . . You'd go and play five or six gigs. People didn't travel to the other clubs. We stayed with people, very rarely in hotels. We stayed with club organisers, whoever. You got thrown out at eight o'clock in the morning when the people went to work, then you had nothing to do all day until the gig at night. I got very good at darts and we used to go round churches and museums. You had a lot of time to fill in.

We spent a lot of time in Cecil Sharp House looking for songs. We were just around the folk clubs but you couldn't sing other people's songs. If someone else had made a song theirs, you didn't sing it. There was the odd spat that would go on when somebody sang someone else's song, it would happen sometimes.

JON BODEN

There were some very surprising attitudes that I came across when I started playing – stuff like, it was somehow naff to sing songs that had already been recorded by revival artists, that you should be searching out source material from old recordings or from books or whatever. Which for me was quite shocking.

I didn't know about that stuff. I only knew about Martin Carthy and Nic Jones. And then the whole arrangement approach, certainly in the mid-nineties, was very much about making folk music contemporary to a modern audience, which is not what the sixties and seventies was about. That was almost wilfully archaic in some of its approach. I like that.

PHIL BEER

For us, the post-folk revival thing in our area, Exeter, was very strong. There was a thriving traditional folk club at the Jolly Porter which was very much crest of the wave with the fifties revival. It was a tough place to sing and play, and with very few notable exceptions it was entirely a traditional folk club in every sense of the word. Not many people ever turned up with guitars, mostly it was unaccompanied singing.

I went there when I was fifteen, going on sixteen, in 1968 and the first time it was either Tony Rose or Pete and Chris Coe who was on. I was one of these kids who'd been playing the guitar from about nine but I was captivated by it, hearing people singing songs that we'd sung at school but without the piano accompaniment.

ROBIN DRANSFIELD

There were a lot of clubs who had a policy of only booking traditional acts, and others who didn't like traditional acts and wanted Wizz Jones or Ralph McTell.

WIZZ JONES

I did a club once and I walked in the door and a woman came

up to me and said, 'Ah, Wizz Jones, I'm the member of the committee that didn't want to book you.' That was a great start to the evening! It was quite divided in some ways in those days but it sorted itself out in the end.

DAVE SWARBRICK

A lot of the people on the folk scene back then were a bit boring. The main topic of conversation I found in those days was, 'What's going to happen when Tin Pan Alley gets hold of folk music?' It was about wanting to keep the music in the museum. It didn't make much sense to the people who were making the music. A lot of the people in the clubs in those days were left-wing. But the people who ran them always had mansions, which struck me as being a bit weird.

HARVEY ANDREWS

I'm using a broad brush here, but there are yaysayers and naysayers. The sort of clubs I was working – it was basically anything went, give it a go. So you could go in and sing a song like 'Hey Sandy', a serious song, and next you could sing a comedy song you've written about politics or something that was happening at the time. You had this broad church of artists working in them.

Then there were the naysayers – we don't touch that, we won't book that, we don't want to know that. It was like puritans and cavaliers. The traditional clubs, the ones still working on the MacColl system of 'You Are Not Allowed', they were the naysayers.

JOHNNY HANDLE

We didn't go for a policy of all British stuff for quite a long time but I think it would be in the early sixties we decided to do that – following Ewan's influence, I'm sure. We had a long discussion about it and decided that as far as the residents were concerned we do all British – except on a back-to-the-roots night once a year when we'd sing what we liked. What we were trying to do with the British-only policy was push the boundaries of material out.

LOUIS KILLEN

Despite being something of a purist, certainly as far as my performance of the songs was concerned, I was very heavily influenced by MacColl and Lloyd, the way they presented the songs, especially by Bert.

At my peak I'd already cut out all the American songs. So what I had was a list which regularly got lost, and every time it got lost some of the songs would get lost because that was my memory, the list of titles. I'd have between 250 and 300 songs. Every four or five years I'd lose it and have to rebuild it again, and not all the songs would come back.

MIKE WATERSON

There were all these prejudices and strange beliefs going on all over the place. I remember walking into a club in Leeds one night, and John [Harrison] was carrying his guitar which we used as a tuning fork. And the woman on the door said, 'These won't be any good – they've got a fuckin' guitar!' I mean, would you tell Martin Carthy to put the guitar down ? You bloody wouldn't. It was ridiculous the ideas some people had, like biting the hand that feeds you.

PHIL BEER

For a lot of people the tradition is an end in itself, for me the tradition is a place to start from, it's the foundation of everything but it's not the be-all and end-all.

JOHN TAMS

The Nottingham Traditional Music Club was a special one. The committee sat on a windowsill behind you while you were singing. It had a kind of Nuremberg War Trials feel to it. They'd be burning into the back of your head. Then your customers out front, who you were trying to make contact with, were looking over at these people behind you. Even when great, celebrated, traditional musicians came, the back wall was still sat on the windowsill.

It was a traditional club. You were hard-pressed to get away with something that was hand-made, even though MacColl would have been one of the club's generators. Roy Harris, the organiser, was one of the great folk club organisers, but it was quite a tense space to be in when you'd got this back wall of luminaries sitting on the windowsill.

HEATHER WOOD

We were getting the 'It's Not Traditional' snarl from the folk Nazis and Bert Lloyd said, 'Do whatever you like with a song, as long as you feel that you're adding to it.' That to us was important. They tried to set up a rivalry between the Young Tradition and the Watersons.

Frankly, we loved them, they loved us and some of the most fun we ever had was when we managed to get on stage together and sing seven-part harmony if we were booked for the same festival or the same concert. Mike Waterson said it best: 'We're diggin' in t' same field, we're just diggin' different holes.'

9 Maybe there was something in the air

As the folk scene became divided between traditionalists and enthusiasts who leaned towards American roots or contemporary music, a new wave of singer-songwriters emerged. In the forefront was Bert Jansch, a precocious guitarist who, in the early years of the sixties, had hung around the Howff in his native Edinburgh before taking to the road and winding up in London. Alongside him was John Renbourn, a student of classical guitar who, like Jansch, was influenced by Davy Graham and Wizz Jones. When Jansch and Renbourn moved into a flat together in Somali Road, Camden, they formed a formidable duo, and the basis of what would become the band Pentangle.

Wizz Jones, at this point, had drifted temporarily away from the blues to play old-time country music and bluegrass with banjo wizard Pete Stanley. They headed to Cornwall and a residency at the Folk Cottage, a tumbledown building in a hamlet near Newquay. When, in 1966, Pete Stanley couldn't make the trip, Wizz took Ralph McTell along, giving him his first break as a performer.

Cornwall was the summer retreat for many acoustic blues and folk followers, but the hotbed of the new contemporary scene was a shabby basement coffee house in Greek Street, Soho. Les Cousins opened in 1965 and quickly became the place to play, especially on the Saturday all-nighters. Jansch and Renbourn made Les Cousins their second home, while Al Stewart, Sandy Denny, Roy Harper and the Incredible String Band were regulars, as was Paul Simon during his time in London.

That same year the Bristol Troubadour opened, booking many of the Cousins regulars. In 1967 schoolteacher Win White opened a folk and blues club in Sheffield at the Highcliffe Hotel, bringing in the cream of contemporary performers and giving *the Humblebums and Barbara Dickson their first bookings in England.*

Contemporary musicians brought new ideas and original songs to the folk scene. Their subject matter was diverse but a few, like Ralph McTell's 'Streets of London', Harvey Andrews' 'Hey Sandy', 'Needle of Death' by Bert Jansch and 'Fiddler's Green' by John Conolly would be taken up by floor singers everywhere. As Steve Tilston, who moved from Leicester to London to be able to play regularly at Les Cousins, says, it was 'a golden age' for guitarists and singer-songwriters.

JOHN RENBOURN

There were a lot of good ideas knocking around on the music scene. It was pretty vibrant and things were just kinda kicking off. It was new, but I don't think anyone thought that much about it. We were just carried away with the fact that it was so great. Looking back now, maybe there was something in the air or the water. I don't know what was going on but it certainly did kick off in the early and mid-sixties.

It's difficult to lump folk clubs together. There were clubs where characters like myself used to go and play. They weren't really organised clubs and they weren't part of the English Folk Dance and Song Society. They were kind of alternative to it. There was an old boat in Kingston where they used to have music. Derek Sarjeant's club was great. He used to book all kinds of people. He played nice guitar. Everybody was pretty open-minded. Gerry Lockran used to play there. The other ones, the purist clubs, were just sheer hell. They still are.

RALPH McTELL

I still think that Bert Jansch is the most important thing that happened to the British acoustic guitar scene, much more important than many of the others that have got bigger reputations. He truly fused the British tradition of song with his wonderful guitar playing.

JOHN RENBOURN

I met Bert at the Scots Hoose when he was falling off his arse. We wound up sharing a whole lot of different places together and we played most of the time because we'd be sitting around not doing very much. We had a flat in Somali Road. Bert, me and Les Bridger were upstairs and the Young Tradition were downstairs – Royston and Peter and Heather. They were working at their harmonies, so round about six o'clock in the morning they used to get up and sing 'Hal An Tow' as the sun was rising. It was agony.

HEATHER WOOD

I'm an early riser. 'Hal An Tow' does have a stamp in it. Mark you, they were upstairs and Bert was a foot-stamper and so occasionally we'd amble up there and stuff a cushion under his foot.

NIC JONES *singer of traditional songs and innovative guitarist*

Bert Jansch, he was God to me. He used to come along to the Chelmsford club, and John Renbourn too. It was the style of playing, the way they played. It's how you feel, how you play. I didn't like guitarists who played too many notes. What I thought is – the best thing is space. Emptiness, that's the best thing to listen to. You fill it in yourself. A flash guitarist plays millions of notes but too many notes.

RAB NOAKES

I was doing a floor spot at the Scots Hoose. Bruce Dunnett used to run it and Bert was there. I did a couple of songs, one of them was 'The Merchant's Son'. It's from the north-east of Scotland, and when I'd finished this figure came slightly wobbling before me with a pint in his hand and he gave it to me. It was Bert Jansch and he had bought me a pint for singing that song. I was so delighted I was quite taken aback,

STEVE TILSTON

The first folk club I went to was at the Victoria pub in Leicester.

I started going regularly and saw some great acts and about the third or fourth time it was absolutely rammed, people round the corner queuing for this guy called Bert Jansch.

I'd never heard of him but he stood out because everybody else was in jeans and he was in a grey suit that looked like it had come from an Age Concern shop, and plimsolls. And he hadn't got his own guitar. He borrowed Mark Newman's, but when he played, it was just absolutely fantastic.

He played 'Needle of Death'. I'd heard Mark Newman sing that and I'd fallen in love with it. I thought it was a traditional folk song. I was only fifteen. Then I found out that he'd written these songs, that most of the songs he was singing were his own.

I'd started to write songs and all of a sudden a musical blueprint was laid out before me. A friend's older brother who was at university – he'd got this Charlie Byrd album, *Blues Sonata*, and I'd taped that and I was getting into a finger-style by then. I was really drawn to finger-style guitar and Charlie Byrd, really playing jazz but with a finger-style, so when I saw Bert I was kind of primed for it.

DEREK SARJEANT

I played at Leeds University, 1962, and I had a Martin guitar, which I still use. The guy that was running the club came up to me and said, 'There's a guy in the audience – he's a bloody good player, he'd like to borrow your guitar.' I said, 'I don't really want to lend it.' He said, 'He'll be very careful with it. I've heard him play.' It was Bert Jansch and he played 'John Henry'. I don't know what he was doing there.

PETE WOOD

We booked Robin Williamson at Sheffield University and he turned up accompanied by Bert Jansch. Nobody had heard of him. He didn't have a guitar, so he borrowed one. He was a knockout, completely unique. The next night we had a club swap with Leeds University club. So we took a coach up to Leeds – a massive folk club, hundreds of people in this big pub – and we took Bert Jansch with us. We said to the organiser, 'You've got to put this guy on.'

There's hundreds of people, all yakking away. It's the interval and he borrows a guitar and he starts tuning up. The place went silent – when he was just tuning up. He was phenomenal, nobody had heard a sound like it. That was about '62.

STEVE TILSTON

It all happened very quickly. My first performance in a club was at the age of fifteen in Leicester. The feller who ran the club was called Toni Savage. He'd been an opera singer. He apparently had burst a lung on stage. What a way to go . . . He used to tell it with great relish.

He kind of took me under his wing and I did a floor spot. I did an instrumental, then I started to learn all the Bert Jansch stuff and lots of Bob Dylan songs. My first gig – I was just turned sixteen – was in Northampton, thirty miles south, opening for Malcolm Price. I was expected not just to sing a few songs, but to run the whole show. At sixteen years old! I made thirty bob and spent it all on a roast chicken from a chip shop. There was no turning back after that.

I started writing my own songs and at the age of seventeen I went over to Loughborough, and there was this Dave Evans who was running a club there. He was a great guitar player and we really hit it off. I left home at eighteen and moved into a flat with Dave and we played quite a few gigs as a duo, one of them was at the Nottingham Playhouse. That's where a guy came up and said, 'I really like what you're doing.' It was Wizz Jones and he said, 'You want to come down to London and come to Cousins.'

DAVE DEIGHTON *guitarist and melodeon player, of the Deighton Family*

I'd been playing in Shadows-type bands and I got fed up with it. Then Graham Campbell started the Sleepy John folk club in the

Wicker in Sheffield, and I got interested after seeing people like Davy Graham. He turned up in a sky-blue suit and no guitar. He borrowed Graham's guitar and did an incredible gig, so I thought there was a bit more to this folk scene than I'd realised. I saw Spider John Koerner with his big long legs and cowboy boots, Joanne Kelly, Pete Stanley and Wizz Jones . . . It was a fantastic little club in a grotty little boozer.

ROBIN DRANSFIELD

The folk club in Glasgow on Saturday night started after the pubs shut. They booked two guests: you'd have a headliner and a second on the bill. This night Alex Campbell was the headliner and I was second on the bill. I'd got halfway through introducing a song in my first set and some bloke at the back, pissed, started having a go, the anti-English bit, 'You fuckin' bastard, we'll fuckin' get you next time, fuckin' Bannockburn, we willnae forget . . .' It was quite frightening. Alex went straight to the back of the room and got this bloke thrown out. And he came up to me in the interval and said, 'Och, dinna worry aboot him.'

Then in the interval John Martyn buttonholed me 'cos I'd sung 'Spencer the Rover', which he forced me to teach him. I think it was the only traditional song John Martyn ever sang. Me and him went back to Alex's place, where I was staying and I went through 'Spencer the Rover' with him a couple of times, gave him the words and, of course, he then altered it in the way that only John Martyn could, in the usual folk process. I still can't believe how good his version of it was.

JOHN JAMES

John Martyn was represented by the Sandy Glennon Agency but he wanted off to join Witchseason, which was tied up with Joe Boyd and Island Records. Johnnyboy said to Sandy Glennon, 'The man you need to replace me is John James.' Sandy did what he was told and soon I was off to Brighton, Rugby, Liverpool and Alnwick on the trot, and Sandy Glennon never heard me play.

He just phoned the gigs the day after and got the thumbs up.

I'd moved to London in May 1967. The first floor spot I did was at the Half Moon in Putney. I went without a guitar, borrowed a guitar from another floor singer, Gordon Giltrap.

But just before Sandy Glennon rang, I had a phone call from some bloke called Win White in Sheffield saying, 'John Renbourn has pulled out and Wizz or John Martyn tell me you're the man to fill his shoes.' So the first gig I did up north was the Highcliffe Hotel, Sheffield.

RALPH McTELL
John Renbourn had introduced me to the Highcliffe. It was the best club of its type in the north in my view, because Win White, who probably wasn't part of the social revolution, was actually in it to make a few quid. And that meant he ran a very tight ship.

Win booked me, John Renbourn, John Martyn, Wizz Jones and a few of the others, and rotated us. I used to drive up to Sheffield, do the gig for £8 then drive back again. Then one day I went and he said, 'Oh it's great you could come, Ralph', and all that, so I said, 'Win, don't get me wrong – I love playing here but I can't keep coming up for eight quid.' He went 'I'll double it, sixteen.' I said, 'Oh, I didn't mean . . .' He said, 'All right, twenty', and I was trying to say I'm not trying to haggle. Anyway, I got twenty quid. It was my biggest payday till then and I remember taking the twenty quid home and in the proverbial manner throwing it on the bed. I don't think my wife understood what was going on.

IAN ANDERSON
In Bristol the Troubadour was the peaking of the era. The guy who opened it, Ray Willmott, had picked up the wisdom that folk music was big business and that maybe he could open up a coffee house on the American model. It was tiny. It had two floors, and the ground floor held about sixty and this other floor was downstairs, so when it was full they could get 120 people in.

For the first year there was no fire escape. You went in one door, down this rickety staircase. The way out was the way in. There were two performances going on at the same time – they switched over. At its peak it was open six nights a week. No alcohol, just a poorly equipped coffee bar.

Because it didn't have a licence, they had quite a young audience – people under eighteen could go. The only real equivalent at the time, and the two clubs became a sort of axis, was Les Cousins, non-licensed, open several nights a week and booked similar performers. Quite often people who'd done a gig at the Bristol Troubadour would then jump in their car or on the train to London and do the all-nighter at the Cousins.

The Troubadour definitely made a difference. If you were a musician and you went off and did a gig, you'd end up back there. It was open late, open most nights, and you could meet all your mates and sit around till three o'clock in the morning. You couldn't do that in pubs.

If I remember correctly the first big guest that came was John Renbourn. He did several nights and there were queues round the block. Various regulars, like myself, would go up to London and we'd see people like Sandy Denny, and we'd come back and say to the manager, 'Hey, book this person or that person.'

Al Stewart used to come down regularly, whether he was booked or not. Keith Christmas was at college in Bristol, Sally Oldfield was at the university. You also had the Old Vic Theatre School – Norman Beaton, the actor, would come up and sing calypso. That sort of college input brought people in, because there was this scene connected with the club.

Ralph McTell recommended Steve Tilston, so Steve moved to Bristol, and he'd invited Dave Evans to play on his record. Dave Evans took one look at the place, and him and his girlfriend moved up. Shelagh McDonald moved there. Because it was such a great scene it kind of had this sort of snowball effect. If you hadn't had the Troubadour, I doubt very much whether that side of things would have happened.

Other than the Cousins, there can't have been any other club in the country where you could say that a dozen people who were club regulars actually had albums out and you'd read about them in the *Melody Maker*.

JOHN THE FISH

The Troubadour in Bristol – that was weird, it was on two floors. The deal was, you did your first half downstairs and then you went and did your first half upstairs. Then you'd come downstairs and do it all again. You didn't get any extra money for it, and they used to say, 'Would you please make sure you sing all the same songs upstairs as you did downstairs.' We'd forget what we'd just sung.

IAN ANDERSON

There was a night at the Bristol Troubadour in '71 when John Martyn threw a big wobbler. He was very drunk or stoned and effing and blinding at the top of his voice. The whole audience could hear it and the manager said, 'This won't do. Tell him we don't need him to play. We'll give him his money, we'll get him a taxi to the station. He's not playing.'

I drew the short straw 'cos I was standing there. I wasn't happy, but I did it. I then got up on stage and said to the audience, 'Well, we have a little local problem as you may have noticed . . . John Martyn is unable to play tonight. However, in the audience we have Keith Christmas, Shelagh McDonald, Dave Evans, Steve Tilston, Fred Wedlock, all of whom will get up and do a couple of songs. If any of you want your money back, ask now. It's not a problem.' Not a single person asked – because every one of those people had an album out on a national label.

I poured him into his cab and sent him off. Somebody told me the next day that he'd gone up to Cousins and he'd got up on stage, still effing and blinding and he said, 'Fucking Bristol – that Ian Anderson, I knocked him out and I left him lying in the street.'

JOHN JAMES

John Martyn was best man at my wedding. The venue was
Lambeth Registry Office, January 1970. I'd already been to John
and Bev's wedding at Hampstead Town Hall. He wore his tweed
suit that day. He didn't wear it to mine.

Nick Drake turned up at John's wedding, though not for
long because Joe Boyd took him off to do some recording in the
evening, after a bit of a scare when a girl standing next to Nick
stuck a match back in the box after lighting a fag and the whole
box went up with a bang. Poor Nick looked quite shaken. Who
wouldn't?

This was before John thought it a good idea that I should do
some gigs with Nick – like look after him, see him okay. We, me
and Nick, only did a couple, down at Les Cousins as far as I can
remember.

Anyway on the day of my wedding nothing spectacular
happened, except for John M. accidentally smashing a bottle of
champagne over the registrar's antique desk.

PHIL BEER

I did a show in Woolwich with Tim Hardin. He was so off his
head that he was incoherent in the dressing room. You thought,
'How's this gig going to take place?' He had this bloke with
him who tuned his guitar, hung it round his neck and propelled
him to the microphone. Then something amazing appeared to
happen. He was so completely unco-ordinated and incoherent in
the dressing room. He certainly couldn't talk to anyone, but he
delivered an hour's set which was just astounding.

JOHN RENBOURN

Wizz was down in Cornwall in the early sixties, and that started
a lot of people going down to join up with the beatniks that were
down there. A lot never quite got there – I only got as far as
Brixham – that's where I met Mac MacLeod.

It was the same sort of thing – if you were trying to play

a bit of blues and finger-picking, you just weren't part of the folk scene. Mac used to sit in a pub called the Rising Sun, down on the quayside in Brixham and occasionally we played for the fishermen.

Amazingly, they knew more about Big Bill Broonzy than you would imagine. Broonzy was pretty famous across all of England and I remember those guys sitting me up on the bar as a joke and me playing 'Hey Hey' and the guys saying, 'That kid can really play. He's got the thumb.' It shows you how much Big Bill was appreciated.

WIZZ JONES

Me and Pete Stanley used to busk together in the streets in London. I'd heard a lot of bluegrass on the radio – *Johnny Duncan's Tennessee Songbag.* I liked the excitement of it and Pete could do all the Scruggs stuff – he was a fanatic for all that old-timey music. We used to do 'Leaving Home' and 'Bald Headed End of a Broom'. When we arrived down in Cornwall in '65, we shook 'em up. Bang, bang! We broke new ground because all the pubs had organ players or the odd jazz duo.

The Folk Cottage was an old barn. It had two floors. You went up these rickety steps. Everyone took their own booze. It probably held about sixty people. The folk club was actually very traddy. A local schoolteacher, John Sleep, was a folk music enthusiast and he knew this young farmer guy who had a farm right out in the woods, miles from anywhere off the main road, and he arranged to have a folk club there in a barn, every Friday night.

It was a very straight folk club with all the schoolteachers coming down in their Morris Travellers. We were doing the Mermaid and the Porth pub gigs and we found out about it and went there. We said, 'Can we do some other nights – Monday, Wednesday and on Friday, when the folk club ends, we'll do an all-nighter.' He said, 'You can't do that!'

Anyway, we did and the place was jumping. It was amazing

because you'd get all the traditional people driving up the lane after the folk club on a Friday night – and all the rough nutters from Newquay coming the other way. It was pandemonium, but a legendary place.

The following year Pete couldn't do it. He had some work playing in Italy. Ralph McTell had come round to see me. He'd just come back from Paris. He was down in the dumps. He didn't know what to do. He said, 'I think I'll get a job on the dustbins. It's good money.' I said, 'No, I'll bring you down to Cornwall – this pub I do the summer season in, three nights a week.' So I took him down to Cornwall. That's how it all happened. The Folk Cottage was still going then and Brenda Wootton had her club down Penzance way, so Ralph used to hang around down there. That's where Ralph really started.

RALPH McTELL
I'd been hitch-hiking round Europe and playing in Paris for the last six months and Wizz said, 'Look, I've got some gigs in Cornwall, do you want to come down and play with me?' I nearly died. I can't remember when I was more excited – Wizz Jones had given me a chance to play alongside him! I'd learnt to play a bit in Paris and John Renbourn heard me playing some ragtime guitar and it was him that put the word in for me with Wizz.

We did fantastic – we actually got sacked because too many people were coming to the pub, the Mermaid in Porth. Then, of course, Pete Stanley came back. He'd been in Italy, and by this time Wizz and I had found our way into the Folk Cottage.

At that time Wizz was very entrepreneurial. He was very go-ahead. He printed posters up, stuck 'em on lamp posts and we had the place packed. By the second year when we went back, the place was running seven nights a week. No fire escape, no drink, no PA and, wherever I have been in the world, without fail I have met someone who's begun their chat with me by saying, 'You'll never guess where I first saw you . . .'

DAVE DEIGHTON

Pete and Wizz were doing a summer season at the Folk Cottage in Mitchell. I was playing somebody's guitar and I met Ralph McTell. He said, 'You should do a floor spot', so I sent home for my guitar. My mother sent it in a big cardboard box through the post and I had to pick it up in Truro or Bodmin.

I started doing floor spots at the Folk Cottage and playing in this little band they had there, a jug band, then I started hanging about with Wizz and doing floor spots at his gigs. That winter I went to London and got invited to play on Wizz's first solo album. A lot of the time I was staying with him and went with him to his gigs, folk clubs all over London. He introduced me to a lot of people, Wizz.

GEOFF LAKEMAN

My first connection with folk clubs was this now famous club the Count House at Botallack. This was 1964, I was only sixteen. I couldn't drive. I used to have to get lifts out to Botallack.

It was an old counting house, part of these very spectacular mine workings on the edge of the cliff. People used to be rammed in there and if I wasn't already aware of folk music, that's what turned me on. People like Ralph McTell used to turn up, and Wizz Jones. I remember seeing Brenda Wootton, who went to school with my mum, accompanied by John the Fish.

JOHN THE FISH

Botallack is just a few houses and a pub. It's right on the cliff, really out of the way. I remember Cyril Tawney having a booking there and he couldn't find it. When he managed to find it, he turned up a week late. People used to come from miles around. It was the first folk club in Cornwall.

We ran every night of the week, two sessions on a Saturday night, an all-night session. Singers would come down and spend the whole week there. They did every night without having to travel around.

The Count House played such a big part in my life. People were there on holiday and they were there to enjoy themselves so you'd won the battle already. They would get up and sing where they wouldn't do that at home. You could get about seventy-five people in, but it seems so tiny now, when I've been back.

This is where Brenda Wootton came in – her young daughter Sue wanted to go to the club and Brenda thought she ought to give it the once-over. She loved it that much that she came every week. Up on stage I suddenly became aware of this ethereal harmony coming from the audience, and it took a while to establish where it was coming from. Eventually it was pinned down to Brenda, so I lured her up on to the stage and her folk-singing career began.

DAVE DEIGHTON

When I was in Cornwall, George Kaye the fiddler came to stay in the cottage that I was living in. He stayed for about a week and we played – old-timey stuff like Charlie Poole, New Lost City Ramblers. Then he said, 'I'm going to Ireland. Come with me.' He usually played with his brother Thaddeus but he'd cut his fingers in a wood machine accident so he couldn't play for a few months.

The two of us hitch-hiked to the ferry terminal in Liverpool. George had an address in Dublin, a pub called O'Donoghue's. We went straight there with no sleep, and people kept buying us drinks so we kept playing. Food didn't come into it. We got invited to some gig and we took it by storm, and within two weeks me and George were working every night of the week in Dublin.

These were pubs, not folk clubs like back in England. In the afternoons we used to go in O'Donoghue's to practise, and they'd never heard of old-timey fiddle. There was country and western which they didn't allow in there – it was all Irish music. They allowed George to play because they thought the old-timey was fairly close to Irish music. Then a kid called Clive Collins from

Birmingham started playing banjo with us and the three of us went out as the Mitchell County Ramblers – it was the Mitchell in Cornwall connotation, where the Folk Cottage was.

It was great, loose, like a holiday, but we were getting paid for it. Then we met this guy who became our agent, Leo Mooney, and he had us work every night of the week, three times on a Sunday. We were dashing about everywhere in taxis.

One Sunday night we were playing in this theatre. There were about 300 people. We went into the first number and Leo Mooney's shouting from the side of the stage, 'Get off.' We thought, 'No, we're here now', so we carried on playing. We finished the first number and nobody clapped. He's still at the side of the stage. He said, 'I've told you – get off.' So we walked off in single file. 'What's wrong, Leo?' He said, 'It's the wrong gig. They're waiting for the conjuror. They're all deaf and dumb.'

WIZZ JONES

Pete Stanley and me got on all right for a while. It was a love–hate type relationship, then we went our separate ways after four years. We split up in '67. I had already been doing solo gigs and I just carried on. I've never made enough to live reasonably well. It's always been a struggle. I'd be doing temp driving jobs, bits and pieces.

Ralph McTell's brother, Bruce, tried to manage me, but I'm unmanageable. The first thing Bruce did was, he tripled my fee – and I didn't get any gigs. I didn't have the name. Bruce had Bert Jansch, John Martyn, Ralph and me. He sent me on tour with John Martyn, that was great. John had Paul Kossoff in the band and John Stevens on drums. They were nutters, they were flying. I loved that tour, but I took a back seat. I kept out of the way. I saw John Martyn at his peak.

I am where I belong. Keith Richards says nice things in his book and he must have been there. Eric Clapton has done. I never knew them personally. Eric Clapton was inspired by all our crowd. He went on to do it really well. Rod Stewart did it really well in the early years. He did what we were all kind of trying to do, in a way. Rod was a bit younger and our paths crossed a few times. I'm honoured and happy that a lot of musicians that I admire like what I do.

PETE STANLEY

A lot of the folk clubs didn't like Wizz and me because we were playing American stuff. A lot really loved it. Then we were doing Newquay and Wizz said, 'I've decided to go solo. There's more money in it.' That was the problem.

I'd seen Brian Golbey at Folk Voice, which Jim Marshall and Mike Storey ran at Cecil Sharp House. I remembered at one of their things a friend of mine said, 'You've got to come and see this guy. He's amazing. He's doing all this Jimmy Rodgers stuff.' And Golbey *was* amazing – he could yodel, he could sing in tune and he had a nice presence. So I got in touch with Brian. He'd just given up his day job and started out solo and I had a reputation, so we got together and we worked together for three or four years.

BRIAN GOLBEY

Pete wrote me a letter saying would I be interested. He was a big name at the time in the clubs. I didn't give it too much thought – I said yes. We evolved this act and it was very unique. We did nothing but folk clubs all over the country. We did tours of Scotland, starting in Glasgow and up the coast, Arbroath, Montrose, then over to Fort William and finally back to Glasgow. We went everywhere on the train.

NOEL MURPHY

One night I was in the Scots Hoose in Cambridge Circus with Derroll Adams, who was my lodger from time to time. Derroll was a legend, a philosopher. I owe an awful lot to him. We were in there and a young public-school gentleman called Phil Phillips approached us and said, 'Mr Adams, I'm opening a new all-night folk club in a basement that was a French club called Les Cousins, under a Greek restaurant. I was wondering if you'd like to compère the first all-night session?' And Derroll said, 'You don't want me for that. They'd never stay awake and I wouldn't either. You want young Murphy here.'

So I did the very first night at Cousins and he gave me three quid. It was from eleven o'clock at night until about eight in the morning, and within a few weeks the place was world-renowned because all my folkie friends from around London – John Renbourn, Les Bridger, Bert Jansch, Jackson Frank and others – used to come along and sit there, have a coffee and they would all get up.

It was about the size of the inside of a single-decker bus. Its reputation is so big but the place itself was small. You went down some narrow stairs. It was run by an Anglo-Greek called Andy Matthews. One guy who came – I think he had four different names. We first knew him as Steve Adams. His parents had a café round the corner but then he went on to be Cat Stevens. He used to come down to do a floor spot. He was very shy. 'Matthew and Son', that was written about Andy Matthews.

JOHN RENBOURN

People seem to remember that place as being somehow magical – it was a basement in Greek Street, that's all it was. It wasn't really a folk club or a music club – it was just a sort of dosshouse. Once a gig is a gig and word gets out, everyone wants a gig, so people used to come down and it really took off.

One reason was that it had no musical policy whatsoever. It wasn't aligned to any folk scene. It just happened to be a joint in Soho. They had those all-nighters, so you could play there or sleep. Alexis Korner used to come down and play all night, it was fabulous hearing him, man.

Les Bridger was responsible for opening the Cousins. Me and Bert stayed at his place. Les had a Martin guitar he'd bought on the never-never and never paid for it, so Bert used to play it the whole time. Les would go out at night and nobody knew what he was doing. He told us that he was doing very important gigs, which was impossible because he was a terrible player.

The reality was he was acting in the pirate scene in *Peter Pan*, down in Soho. He was pissed one night, he fell down an alleyway and knocked himself against a door, and it turned out this place was called Les Cousins. It was a girls' club for the girls who were up in the home for foreign students. When Les opened his eyes, so he said, he played the guitar for them and got in there. Eventually, me and Bert found out, but when we went down they'd taken all the girls away and they kept it going as a club. Last time I saw old Les, he was busking in Copenhagen.

As well as Bert, one of the people I used to play at the Cousins with was Gina Glazer, who was an artist potter at Kingston Art School. Gina was a friend of Dave Van Ronk's from Greenwich Village. Her dad had been a left-wing character and they'd known Woody Guthrie and all this. Gina played old-time music. She was a huge influence on Sandy Denny. Sandy modelled herself on Gina.

I met Jacqui McShee because I used to have a mate in Kingston when I was supposed to be going to the art school but wasn't. Chris Ayliffe was a pavement artist in Paris and he used to go busking with Jacqui.

DAVE DEIGHTON
I played at Les Cousins – all-nighters for three quid. I wouldn't do it now. You'd arrive at ten o'clock and leave at seven in the morning. People would come in late on. They'd missed the last bus home and were willing to play because they'd got nothing better to do. When I think back, it wasn't very nice to play. At five o'clock in the morning everybody just wanted to go home.

STEVE TILSTON
I was working as a graphic artist in Leicester and I'd got sick of doing it, so I went down and knocked on Wizz's door. He was very

gracious. He and Sandy took me up to Cousins and I met Andy Matthews, who was running it, and I got a spot on an all-nighter.

There was a whole kind of coterie of guitar players and singer-songwriters. When I think about it, it was a real golden age for the standard of playing. After the spot on the all-nighter I got a bit better known and for three or so years it was a regular gig. There wasn't much money, but Cousins had that cachet. I remember the first time my name was in the *Melody Maker*. I opened it at the page and it said Ian Tilston. I was crestfallen.

This was 1968 and by that time I'd already met John Martyn. He was not long professional, and he played the folk club in Loughborough and came and stayed with us. He had these wonderful elephant cord trousers on and we went to a Chinese restaurant. Wizz was a mentor. He took me round a few places. It was a great entrée, having somebody like Wizz.

WIZZ JONES

John Renbourn rang me up and said, 'This guy Phil is gonna start a folk club. Would you like to come along?' So really it was John and Bert that got that off the ground. I don't know what happened to Phil. He went, and the people who owned the Greek restaurant upstairs, the son, Andy, took over running Cousins. He booked me quite a lot but often it would be those late-night graveyard shifts, all through the night. People would be sleeping on the floor, but it was a good place.

I remember Roy Harper arriving at one of my gigs. He said, 'Can I do a spot?' 'Yeah, okay, do a couple of songs.' He did 'Sophisticated Beggar', over twenty minutes and I thought, 'This bloke's never gonna go anywhere.' Just shows how wrong you can be 'cos he turned out to do some pretty good stuff.

DONOVAN

Cousins was always packed when I was there. We sat on the floor if there were no seats. I had no experience playing in the folk clubs. They didn't like my stuff. I played on the beaches of St Ives and around people's pads. I was never allowed to play in the clubs. I was considered too American in my tastes at the time, it seemed.

RICK NORCROSS

So many of us lived in London and went out on the train, played the gig and then came back to town afterwards on the weekends. We all came together at Les Cousins for the all-nighters that lasted until 7 a.m. Sunday morning. Once you got there, you stayed there as the tube lines and buses stopped. You were basically stuck, so you had plenty of time to listen to what others were writing and playing and had time to talk and make friends.

The reason I never came back to England after 1974 was that I had a major setback when someone stole my Martin D-45 guitar from me following a show at the Troubadour. I was invited to a party at a nearby flat and like a fool I left the guitar in the car. This was a very special guitar so it was a real blow.

Even after all these years, it still must be out there some place and someone who knows great guitars must have seen it. So if anybody knows anything about a Martin D-45 guitar, number 236645, hey – get in touch!

STEFAN GROSSMAN

When I came to England in '67 I was very impressed at that point with the people who had been influenced by the same people I had been influenced by – Big Bill Broonzy . . . Gary Davis. They had used that as a starting point, but then people like Bert and John Renbourn and Martin Carthy had tried to use the guitar in a different way than boom-chick, boom-chick, to play against English traditional music.

I thought that was so unique, so fascinating, plus discovering the Celtic music, the music of the Scots. I didn't realise there was this incredible treasure chest in the British Isles, full of music and full of living musicians. So I just thought, 'Well, I'd like to stay here.'

The scene I liked best was centred around Cousins. We all

had the same interests but were taking it in our own personal direction.

DAVE COUSINS

We opened a club at the White Bear in Hounslow about 1965. It was one of the better folk clubs, I think. I ran it with a guy called Chas Upton. Sometimes he'd start the night off, sometimes I would. We had all the regular guests but it began to develop into something more than that when the BBC came down and filmed us playing there, doing 'The Man Who Called Himself Jesus' for a programme, *Colour Me Pop*.

Suddenly the White Bear became a real hang-out for people. Lonnie Donegan turned up and did an astonishing set for us, one of the most exciting nights I've ever had. I became very friendly with him, went round to his house in Chiswick a lot. Mary Hopkin came down.

I carried on until about 1972, even though we were everywhere by that time. By then the band was playing there with Rick Wakeman and John Ford and co., so it became far more than a folk club. I started another club alongside it, a fortnightly club, the Hounslow Arts Lab. David Bowie came along with his band called Hype, who were actually the Spiders from Mars, with Tony Visconti on bass. We had the Edgar Broughton Band. We had Pete Brown, who wrote the Cream hits, reading poetry. We had a mime artist, then we did *Colour Me Pop* and David Bowie came and mimed on the show to 'Poor Jimmy Wilson', one of my songs. Unfortunately the BBC have wiped it. I bet he's glad they have!

BILLY CONNOLLY

The Humblebums started when I met Tam Harvey in a pub. They had a folk club in the pub and he'd been in rock bands and country bands. Just as I come off stage he said, 'I like your playing.' I said, 'Do you play yourself?' He said, 'Yeah, I'm a plectrum guitarist.' He'd been into all that index-finger playing

– he could do all that and I said, 'Well, actually I don't like that shit, as soon as a jazz chord comes in I lose the will to live.'

I said, 'I fancy a bit of playing but don't go beyond the fifth fret 'cos I need a Sherpa to go up there. There could be fuckin' tree bark. I live down there at the bottom of the neck.' And we went to his house and practised a bit. He liked the songs I had, 'Crow Black Chicken' and all that. After that we started to write . . . 'Won't You Come Back to Dunoon' and that stuff.

We showed up at clubs and somebody said, 'There's a folk club on a Sunday at the Windmill Hotel in Arbroath.' So we went up and they gave us a floor spot and they said, 'God, you're fuckin' amazing. If you come next Sunday you can be the guests.' We didn't go home. We stayed in the town for a week. We just pulled women and slept in their places, and women who worked in hotels gave us food. It was lovely. I thought that was the idea – I wanted to be Luke the Drifter, on the road and all that. It was a new world. It was the sixties.

We came to England with Hamish Imlach. This would be about '68. I was going somewhere else and he had a gig at the Highcliffe in Sheffield and he said, 'You should go on here.' We had some great nights at the Highcliffe. We used to have a competition with Ralph McTell – Win White would squeeze another one person in and say, 'McTell broke the record again.' We'd go back and he squeezed another person in.

RALPH McTELL

I don't know where I wrote 'Streets of London'. I know that I started the tune in Paris and the second chord of the chorus is an F to an E minor which I think I got from Tom Paxton, 'Can't Help But Wonder Where I'm Bound'. The tune is from 'In the Good Old Colony Days'.

I started the song in '66 or '65 and the words were all about people in Paris. Then I remembered this old man who used to kick through the rubbish after the street market in Croydon, when I was a little boy, then one image led to the other. They were mostly images of people I'd seen in and around Croydon and London so I switched from writing about Paris to writing about London.

I had offered it to John the Fish, which would date it to about '67 at the Folk Cottage. He said, 'Oh yeah, bit sad though, innit mate?' I thought, 'He's missed the point', so I sat on the song for a long time. I played it for Derek Brimstone, three verses, and next time I saw him he said he'd been playing it and it went an absolute storm, so I looked at the song again and it needed a fourth verse. I probably wrote the fourth verse some considerable time after, based on a working men's hostel at the end of the street where I grew up, called Factory Lane.

I can remember the first time I sang 'Streets of London' in a club, but not where. I have a feeling that it was in Cornwall. All I can remember is the reaction. I finished the song to absolute silence, the longest silence. And then, like thunder . . . I could not believe the reaction. It was staggering.

The first time I played it on the radio was on *Country Meets Folk*. I never knew this until about fifteen or twenty years later, but Broadcasting House switchboard got jammed. It had an instant reaction and, two days after that, the album was released and Nat Joseph rang me up to tell me we'd got our first cover version, by Danny Doyle, then a week later someone was doing it in Australia and the song went round the world. It was hard to believe.

I did Cambridge in 1969 and introduced it as one of my songs. I started playing it and the whole tent, five or six thousand people, started singing the chorus. I nearly cried. I think I was confirmed in my original belief that music was about changing things, that if you had purity of intent you would change the world.

HARVEY ANDREWS

'Hey Sandy' on *Writer of Songs* was written in response to the shootings at Kent State University in 1970. At the time we felt very much that we were part of what was going on over there, because of the Vietnam War and so forth. The day after

I'd written it I went over and sang it to a friend of mine, Geoff Bodman, on to his tape recorder.

I decided I didn't really like it all that much, so I forgot about it, but Colin Scott had been doing Geoff's club in Wolverhampton and he'd stayed with Geoff, and Geoff played it to him. He learnt it and started singing it round the clubs and it really took off.

I went to the Cambridge Folk Festival. I wasn't booked. I was sitting in the audience, and Scotty got to the end of his set and he said, 'What do you want to hear?' And all these voices shouted, 'Hey Sandy'. I thought, 'Blimey, that's my song!' I remember the hair literally rising on the back of my neck and Scotty went into it and all these people started singing the chorus and I'm sitting there thinking, 'What is this?' And when he'd finished, bless him, he said, 'And here's the feller that wrote it – stand up Harvey Andrews.'

STEVE TILSTON

I wrote 'Slip Jigs and Reels' after I'd read a novel about the gangs of New York and they had slip jigs and reels there first of all. The songwriter Stephen Foster was interwoven into the plot. I've lost count of the different versions.

Fairport did a version and I was at the Whitby Festival one year, watching the telly. Keith Donnelly was in the room. We were having some fish and chips, and up comes this guy who's answering questions on Fairport Convention. And he's asked which singer-songwriter wrote 'Slip Jigs and Reels' and 'The Naked Highwayman'. I subsequently got to know the guy – his name's Steve and he lives over in Cheshire. He got the right answer.

WIZZ JONES

Bruce Springsteen did 'When I Leave Berlin' at a concert in Berlin in 2012. It came out of the blue. I had an email from a friend in Germany who'd been at the concert, then a lot more emails when it appeared on YouTube. I wrote the song in 1972 when I played a couple of nights in Berlin. That weekend the border was opened for the first time in many years and people were allowed to visit friends and relations in the GDR. I put it on my 1973 album, *When I Leave Berlin*. Bruce did it pretty well, he only left out a minor chord here and there.

JOHN CONOLLY

I wrote 'Fiddler's Green' about 1966-ish. I can never remember exactly. Somebody had written a letter to the Old Codgers column in the *Daily Mirror* saying that they'd heard this story that sailors had their own special version of paradise, full of all the things that sailors like and had anybody got any further information. The tune, like most of my tunes, is bits of traditional tunes.

Tim Hart and Maddy Prior were the first people to record it. They were guests at our club not long after I'd written it and the group, the Meggies, sang it, and Tim and Maddy brought it out on their first album. I never really had a publisher until years later when I signed with Jim Lloyd's publishing company Maypole Music. It wasn't until then that I got any royalties at all.

The Dubliners recorded it, the Yetties, the McCalmans. George Hamilton IV did the schmaltziest version I've ever heard and Max Boyce did one of my favourite versions of it. He had all the best folk musicians, like the Dransfields and Finbar Furey.

It's listed as traditional on some records – that's partly a compliment and also annoying, because you lose out on royalties if nobody credits it properly. It's come to my notice that there are two movies that feature 'Fiddler's Green'. One is quite an old one, *The Green Journey* with Angela Lansbury, the other is more recent featuring Donald Sutherland. There's a scene in that where somebody plays 'Fiddler's Green' all the way through on a concertina.

TOM PAXTON

Something I try to tell young songwriters is, 'Don't bet the whole wad on your own songs.' When you go out on that stage you're not a songwriter any more, you're a performer and you want the strongest material you can possibly have. I had been performing professionally for like nine years before my shows consisted only of my own songs.

Up until then I sang Woody Guthrie songs, Pete Seeger songs, Weavers songs, whatever I thought was really strong. I sang 'Roll on Columbia', 'Pastures of Plenty', 'Where Have All the Flowers Gone', really strong songs that were there to sing. Finally I had enough of my own songs of a quality that I could do just them. There's a lot of great songs out there that'll pull you through, while you are developing.

RAB NOAKES

I used to meet Tam Harvey and Billy Connolly at the Folk Centre in Montrose Street in Glasgow around 1967/'68 and was subsequently invited to play as a guest on the first major Humblebums concert in Glasgow City Halls in '69.

Billy was organising the concert and he said, 'Oh, you'll have to come along and be part of it. Speak to Arthur Argo.' So I called up Arthur Argo and Arthur said, 'Well, I don't know if there'll be room.' I was determined I was going to be part of it so I kept on badgering him and eventually I was on.

There was a wee sort of gathering at Billy's in the afternoon, where we rehearsed, that was where I met Gerry Rafferty for the first time. We were the same age and recognised something in each other from the start. He wasn't part of the Humblebums yet. Tam Harvey and Billy were the Humblebums and Gerry was a guitar-playing songwriting guest. He performed solo on the concert, soon after that he became part of the Humblebums and it was a trio for a little while.

BILLY CONNOLLY

I told Mike Harding on his radio show, 'I've slept on so many carpets I can tell the difference between Wilton and Axminster.

By taste!' Your contract always said so much money plus accommodation. That was to cover a multitude of sins – a lot of couches and chairs.

Tam Harvey and I were backing Matt McGinn, who had a terrible fear of homosexuality. I think he'd been in a corrective institution when he was a boy and he'd been a bit touched up or something. There were two chairs in the room and a huge bed. So Matt was in the bed and Tam Harvey and I, we had the chairs. We slept on a series of chairs and floors in some unbelievable smelly places – but it was a good education.

I look back on those times with great love and affection – I had a banjo and a guitar and a bag and sometimes I was on my own, running for trains and stuff. I was young and keen but I must have had the strength of ten.

JOHN LEONARD *singer and later producer of BBC Radio 2 Folk Show*
The best people I ever saw in a folk club were the Humblebums. The first time was at the Troubadour in London. They came in and did a guest spot. It was that power that Connolly had. He was with Tam Harvey – it was before Gerry Rafferty. Then I saw them in Doncaster at a club. There were only about ten people in. I recorded them. I lost the cassette but I'd listened to it for years. I used to take the tape recorder to learn songs. I learned two of Gerry Rafferty's songs from that night – 'Patrick' and 'Her Father Didn't Like Me Anyway'.

RALPH McTELL
I was starting to get all kind of invites all over the place but then I managed to blag a place at teacher training college, not because I had qualifications, but because I'd been round the block a bit. I went there, but by the end of the second term I was working every night and trying to get into college the next day. I found a date sheet recently and I can't believe what kind of travelling I did. I had an ex-GPO minivan with a sleeping bag in the back

and I used to drive to the gig, do the gig, drive back and go to college the next day.

There was no structure to it until my brother, who had become a lecturer, said, 'You need to be more organised.' Then he plunged in as manager at the age of about twenty-two or -three and that was the period where I began to leave the folk clubs and go into the universities.

I played a lot of clubs I can't remember. I have been to towns and said, 'This is my first time. I've never been here before', and somebody will say, 'You have. You played the Frog and Bucket down the road in 1967 or '68.'

JOHN RENBOURN

Pentangle used to play down in the Cousins and when that closed we had to have somewhere to play so we got the Horseshoe. Me and Bert said we were going to start a band. Nat Joseph just said, 'No thanks, I don't want it. I've got you both as solo artists, that's all there is to it.' Me and Bert were for the sake of music. It wasn't a career move – I've never had a career move. It was just something we liked playing. It caused a few problems with the contracts to that company but later on it got straightened out.

I knew Jo Lustig because I used to play guitar for Julie Felix and Jo was handling her. He used to be the publicist for the Beat writers. He was a hustler. He represented Kerouac and Burroughs and Ginsberg. So when Pentangle got together, Jo was interested.

ROBIN WILLIAMSON

Me and Mike Heron were still playing folk clubs. We were working as a duo and playing small venues. I suppose we were sort of managed by Joe Boyd. Getting out of the folk clubs into the rock venues wasn't ever intentional, but it was lucky.

It was an accident really, largely because of the gig we did with Tom Paxton and Judy Collins. We were opening for them in larger venues. A number of things we struck lucky with and we ended up having a large following on the west coast of America because what we were doing coincided with the 'Back to the Country' movement.

We played at Woodstock and Fillmore East and West, but since then I've kind of come full circle. I not only like playing small gigs, when I work as a duo with my wife Bina we often play gigs that don't even have a PA. We prefer to work small rooms acoustically, if at all possible, just like it was at the beginning. I love it, I never liked that big-time stuff.

10 We got ripped off rotten

In 1955 HMV Records issued a ten-inch LP, Folksong Today, *featuring among other singers, Harry Cox, the Copper Family and twenty-year-old Shirley Collins, whose one track, 'Dabbling in the Dew', marked her recording debut.*

At the time folk music on record was a rare commodity. Topic had released a 78 rpm single by Ewan MacColl, 'The Asphalter's Song', in 1950 and brought out more singles by MacColl, Isla Cameron and A. L. Lloyd over the next few years, but for purchase-tax reasons each release was limited to ninety-nine copies.

Argo, founded as an independent label but acquired by Decca in 1957, showed some interest in folk, later releasing Ewan MacColl and Charles Parker's Radio Ballads *in LP form, while Collector brought out 'Football Crazy', a single that became very popular on the radio, by Robin Hall and Jimmie Macgregor, and EPs by Jeannie Robertson, Bob Davenport, Dominic Behan and Ramblin' Jack Elliott.*

By 1964, as Bob Dylan, Joan Baez and other folk-based American artists were beginning to achieve commercial success in Britain, Nigel Denver became the first British folk singer on a major label when his album Nigel Denver *was released by Decca. The following year Martin Carthy followed suit with Fontana.*

Transatlantic, who before 1963 had released mostly language and sex-education records, recruited the Ian Campbell Folk Group and the Dubliners a year later. Soon many leading folk artists, both traditional and contemporary, were signed to Transatlantic by founder Nat Joseph.

Topic advanced more steadily, its reputation earned largely through the creative talents of Bill Leader, who recorded many classic folk albums in his Camden flat, notably the Watersons'

Frost and Fire *and the Dransfields'* The Rout of the Blues. *Leader is a seminal figure in British folk music: besides his work at Topic, he also freelanced for Transatlantic before starting his own labels, Leader and Trailer. He launched the recording careers of many artists who would move on to achieve fame and fortune elsewhere, but commercial constraints eventually led to both his labels folding.*

In Bristol in 1969 John Turner of the Pigsty Hill Light Orchestra, together with blues aficionado Ian Anderson, and Gef Lucena, who had founded Saydisc in 1965, began Village Thing. Despite Fred Wedlock's 'The Folker' selling very well and critically acclaimed albums by Wizz Jones, Derroll Adams, Steve Tilston and others, the label lasted only four years, meeting a similar fate to Trailer and Leader.

In these early years of British folk music on record, the major companies controlled the industry. Their interest proved to be short-lived, with the exception of Philips, who from 1963 enjoyed continuing success with the Spinners. The small labels could find the artists, produce the music and manufacture the records, but they were beholden to the majors when it came to distributing them. That, in the end, proved to be their undoing.

BILL LEADER

The WMA – Workers' Music Association – in London started Topic Records in 1939, delicate shellac things which fractured in the post. The first few were songs from Unity Theatre, that had started in the same year as WMA. It was leftish, but not very focused.

I went to the WMA as a voluntary worker, licking envelopes. Then records began to look like a good thing because LPs had started happening, so they decided to have somebody who could look after the record side. As I was the only one around who didn't have a proper job, let alone a career, I got the job. I'd dabbled, I'd messed about and I got a lot of help from Dick Swettenham, who went on to be heavily involved in setting up Olympic Studios.

After Ramblin' Jack Elliott – the first recording I made – the next one was Bert Lloyd and Alf Edwards, a drinking songs LP. That was done at Bert's place in Greenwich.

I lived in Camden Town, and Michael Gorman and Margaret Barry were performing at the Bedford Arms. It became a place where lots of people were beginning to get an interest in Irish music. I came across Reg Hall there, so we dragged them all down to what was the top floor of WMA headquarters in Bishop's Bridge Road, opposite a fairly noisy bit of the railway into Paddington station. We'd got a tape recorder of our own by now and some microphones. We got them into a little room – Paddy Breen, Patsy Goulding, Michael Gorman and Margaret Barry – and made a record.

There was no commercial distribution. We were pressing ninety-nine copies. If you went beyond that, you had to pay purchase tax on the next hundred – and the first hundred. So the second hundred carried double tax and it wasn't till you got further along that you could start making reasonable money.

Distribution was very limited. Topic never managed to get national distribution in those days – EMI and Decca had it all sewn up. For years and years we had a little place in Birmingham called Taylors, which used to do the sort of mop-up for people who couldn't find anywhere else.

I did many of the recordings in my flat – a two-room, kitchen and bathroom on the first floor of an Edwardian house. The back room was lined with books and tapes – that's a great acoustic treatment. We'd be monitoring and recording in the front room, and the room that they were recording in was the bedroom. We did the Watersons' *Frost And Fire* there.

NORMA WATERSON

We were still called the Folksons and Louis Killen asked, 'Why do you call yourself the Folksons? Why don't you just use your names?' He was living in London, he'd moved down from Gateshead.

We did two gigs on the Friday and Sunday, but the Saturday night we had off and everybody said, 'You should go down to the Troubadour. That's the place where everything happens.' So we went down, and Martin Carthy was running the night and he asked us if we wanted to do two or three, so we did. We got a good reception and in the interval this man came up to us and said, 'Do you want to make a record?'

We were as green as grass, really. He organised for us to go round the next day to meet Gerry Sharp, who was then the head of Topic Records. When we got there, they'd already made out the contract. We had a cup of tea and they said, 'Sign here. This is for three records.' We signed, and what we didn't know was that they had the option then for us to make some more. We made *Frost and Fire*, *Yorkshire Garland* and *The Watersons* and then there was a big long gap.

MIKE WATERSON

We made *Frost and Fire* in Bill Leader's flat in Camden. Bill's a wonderful sound man and a great bloke. He's a gent. We worked with Bert Lloyd on *Frost and Fire*, and that was an achievement because we were very interested in what we called 'calendar custom' songs and we were singing quite a lot of them, but not enough for a choice. I think it was Bert Lloyd that had the idea. We said, 'Yes, but we don't do enough songs.'

He said, 'I'll give you some songs.' And he just sent us reams of calendar custom songs. Then we met up with him and we said, more or less, 'What do you think?' He was a guru to us. We sang one and he said, 'Mm, we shan't use that one. It's too subservient.' It was a harvest home song, where they're praising the farmer all the time.

Then we sang another one and he said, 'Sing it again . . . sing it again . . . sing it again.' We sat there in this back room, singing it again and again, and Norma said, 'What's the matter with it?' He said, 'Nothing, my dear, just self-indulgence.' That was 'Greenland Whale Fishery'.

JOE BOYD

I heard the Watersons for the first time at Cecil Sharp House. Like everyone else I was impressed by their great voices, the harmonies and their authentic presence. Recording them in Bill Leader's flat – it was thrilling hearing them up close. There may have been a few more sessions at his house when I was staying there. Bill had a quiet affection for the music and the artists and it made a strong impression on me. He led the sessions with subtlety rather than heavy-handedness and that was a very important lesson.

BILL LEADER

Everybody was slinging their hammock. Joe Boyd – I don't know where I first met him. I think he was sleeping on people's floors and the floor got taken away or something. He moved in and I think at that time I was doing the Fisher family for Topic, so I went up to Ray Fisher's place and settled in for a day or two and recorded the whole family.

Joe had been involved with recording before, but he'd never seen this sort of al fresco way that I did all the time. He was fairly startled at what you get out of not having a fish-tank glass wall between the performer and the engineer. I think that was the only time we really worked on something specific together but he was around quite a few weeks. A bright lad, Joe.

After that I didn't see very much of him. We used the same studio, Sound Techniques in Chelsea – that's where he did his Fairport Convention things, that's where I did Gerry Rafferty and the American guitarist, Stefan Grossman. We pass in the night now, but we didn't see each other for decades.

BOB DAVENPORT

In 1959 I won a competition at Collett's record shop to do an EP with Collector and then a trip to the Youth Festival in Vienna. Paul Carter was one of the guys who ran Collector. We went to record in the basement of the shop. I was so nervous, I'd never recorded before and I'd no idea.

Then I was in hospital for six months with tuberculosis and I couldn't go to Vienna. I was contracted to sing with Paul Robeson at the Festival Hall and I couldn't do that. I'd been singing his songs since I was three years old. I was fortunate because penicillin had come in and I came out of the sanatorium in 1961. Do you know what I got for my Christmas present while I was there? Fifty cigarettes.

One of the songs I recorded on the EP was written by my great-great-uncle, George Ridley. He wrote 'Cushie Butterfield'. He also wrote 'Blaydon Races'. He was a miner and a music hall performer like Joe Wilson, who wrote 'Keep Your Feet Still, Geordie Hinnie'. There was a very strong music hall influence in the north-east. When I got a copy of the record I was still in the sanatorium with tuberculosis. The first time I heard it, it was played over the hospital intercom.

JIMMIE MACGREGOR

Seamus Ennis had this song 'Football Crazy' as a Dublin song, and he sat and dictated the words and I scribbled them down. I re-wrote it as a Glasgow song and we recorded it for Collector. To me it was just another of these throwaway songs. The way we recorded it was that Robin Hall sang the tune, I sang the harmony and played the guitar, then I double-tracked the mandolin on it. That was all there was to it, but somebody in Decca heard it and they bought it from Collector and it became a very successful song.

It was played on the radio all the time and in all the football grounds. A lot of money was made out of that song – and almost none of it came our way. In our day the publishing companies and the record companies got the money and we got the dregs. Where we made our money was in the live performances. We got ripped off rotten.

BILL LEADER

We didn't do a lot of recording in folk clubs but we did the Spinners at their club in Liverpool and the Campbells at the

Crown in Birmingham. It was mono so you had nothing to set up. We did have a speaker, so you just plugged the one mike you'd got into the speaker and drove it into the tape machine and tried to be fairly clever as to where you put that one mike to hear the balance. An acoustic group you can record on one microphone, no problem at all.

TONY DAVIS

Bill Leader came up to our club with a microphone and a Ferrograph tape recorder, plonked it down and recorded the night. It came out as an EP on Topic, *The Spinners – Songs Spun in Liverpool*. It was the best-selling EP Topic ever brought out.

SHIRLEY COLLINS

I was thrilled to have been asked to record two albums – *Sweet England* in 1959 for Argo Records and *False True Lovers* for Folkways in America. I was pleased with some of the recordings, but felt that some of the songs were far too insignificant.

Still, they were what we sang at home, so it's representative of the time and place, and I think that's why Alan Lomax and Peter Kennedy selected them for those albums. It makes me cringe a bit when I listen to them nowadays. Some forty songs were recorded over just two days. I was aware that it was an honour to be recorded by two such great field recordists.

NIGEL DENVER

Bruce Dunnett got me the first LP with Decca. He ran the Scots Hoose and he went to see Hugh Mendel and he said, 'Come into the studio', so I brought the music that was with me, that I knew. Gordon McCulloch was on it and Alf Edwards, who played with MacColl. He played the concertina. He was very square Alf, on the beat, but he could play anything. The night before we went in the studio I had to go to his house and we went over it and he wrote it all down.

I'd done *Ding Dong Dollar* in 1961. Folkways sent us a

thousand copies and we sold them on the Aldermaston march. Funnily enough, MacColl was a director of Folkways. That was before we fell out

I was the first on a major label in this country – Decca, 1964. They listened to the pilot and they said, 'We'll bring it out as a record.' It was just called *Nigel Denver*. Then I did *Moving on* and then *Rebellion* with Martin Carthy and Dave Swarbrick, and *Scottish Republican Songs*, which got me barred from the BBC. I made six records with Decca, two with Major Minor.

BILL LEADER

I was still working for the WMA, or Topic Records as it became, and Topic was in a really bad way, so I went out and got a job at Collett's record shop, which had not been open very long. People were looking for a shop that carried folk music. I was there about three years, then Gill Cook took over.

One day while I was at Collett's, Nat Joseph walked in. He was trying to sell me language records. A very clever lad – he'd got the importation rights on the language records, but no one was interested. He brought out a series, *Living with Love*, all about the birds and the bees. Then he got interested in this thing that was starting up called folk music. That was looking more like a runner, so he built a studio but he didn't know how to deal with it.

He discovered that I had been involved in producing records, so he got me involved in Transatlantic. We went across and signed the Dubliners. I knew Luke Kelly. I'd come across him in Camden. We met up in a famous pub in Dublin and we drank Guinness and signed them up.

I was freelancing for Transatlantic, doing things like the Humblebums. There was one period when they hired me to do the Humblebums during the day and a group called Storyteller during the night. Billy Connolly you knew would become successful. The first time I met him I was with Archie Fisher in a pub in Glasgow, and just standing next to you chatting, you could tell he was an exceptional person.

BILLY CONNOLLY

It was a great feeling when *Merry Melodies* came out. I felt like Elvis. I'd got an LP, because in those days when you got a record contract you were in the newspapers. Today, buskers have got CDs.

Bill Leader produced it. I used to live at his house when he lived in Camden. He put us up, Tam Harvey and myself. He was very kind to us. We made the record in Edinburgh on a four-track with a red button. If you wanted to edit, you pressed the button and a pair of scissors came out and cut the tape. We had the songs all pretty much ready from doing them in the clubs.

When I played with Gerry I started to hate the studio, because he was really good at it and his goodness made me feel crap. When we made *The New Humblebums*, we first saw the record in Ramsbottom in Lancashire. We were on the road and it was delivered, that was first time we saw it. What a beautiful sleeve it had.

HEATHER WOOD

Pete Bellamy was working for Transatlantic down in the basement, unpacking shipments and stocking the shelves and we would go down there and join him and sing. Nat Joseph said, 'Oh, you guys sing. You want to make a record?' The first contract he offered us – he would give us nine hours of studio time, he would pay us £27, he would own everything including publishing. We said, 'No, thanks very much', and then he made it a better offer so that's when we did the first record, *The Young Tradition*. It came out in 1966. The songs were ones we'd been doing in the clubs.

CHRISTY MOORE

Transatlantic turned me down. They gave no reason but I can reveal it was because Nat Joseph was a prick. It was a lucky escape in retrospect because I met Dominic Behan at a Northern Ireland Civil Rights Concert in London in 1968. I stayed with him and his family for a short time and he brought me to Mercury Records, who recorded my first album in 1969.

DAVE SWARBRICK

Nat Joseph fined me for playing on Martin Carthy's first LP. I was making another record for him, *Rags, Reels and Airs* with Martin and Diz Disley, and he deducted part of the fee. It was no big deal. I was only getting twelve quid. That's record people for you, mean-spirited goes with the job. Would you please print that?

DAVE ARTHUR

Toni and I had got to know Bill Leader and he was scouting for performers for Nat Joseph's Transatlantic record label. One evening he took us up to Nat's Hampstead house and got us to sing for him. Nat agreed to record us. He'd just recorded the first Young Tradition LP, and we recorded the album *Morning Stands on Tiptoe* in Bill's bedroom.

It was a very ad hoc affair but perfectly in keeping with the non-commercial attitude of many of us young singers. Toni and I had turned down a contract with one of the top London variety agents who wanted to turn us into the English Sonny and Cher. We didn't want to be part of the showbiz world. We preferred the folk clubs and recording in Bill's bedroom.

BILL LEADER

I recorded Bert Jansch in the flat in Camden but that wasn't for Transatlantic – we did it on spec. Transatlantic eventually bought it, for nothing, virtually. I realised with Bert that he wouldn't become successful unless people actually went all the way to find out his merits. He didn't sell himself. I did Davy Graham in my mother's flat. She'd moved into the basement. So 'Needle of Death' and 'Anji' were recorded two floors apart.

JOHN RENBOURN

The first record – I didn't know it was going to be a record. We were all a bit pissed and we went down to a place in Denmark Street, in one of those publisher places. Someone had the keys and started messing around making tracks. Somebody sold that to Transatlantic, who were keen to buy a cheap record anyway, and it came out. The second album was recorded in Bill Leader's flat in Camden.

RALPH McTELL

I was discovered, if you like, down in Cornwall. An ex-music publisher came up and asked me if I'd written one of the songs I played. I had and he said to go and see this publisher he'd worked for in London, Essex Music. They signed me as a house writer and they eventually introduced me to Transatlantic, who were unsure, but they made me sign a contract to say that I wouldn't sign a contract with anybody else for six months, while they made up their mind. I was so excited that I signed it, bigger fool me, but Nat Joseph bless him gave me my opportunity and I made my first record with Gus Dudgeon, who went on to do rather well himself.

HARVEY ANDREWS

I was recorded way too early by Transatlantic. I did five songs, my first five songs. It was pretty dreadful really, like a choirboy singing with his guitar. Listening to them now, you couldn't understand why people thought I had anything. I couldn't anyway.

Ioan Allen got me the deal. He represented the Campbells and, of course, they were on Transatlantic, who wanted to sign everybody up. They were looking for the next Dylan. Anybody who wrote got signed up. There were stacks of us.

I signed with Cube Records and brought out *Writer of Songs*. That was a big seller in Britain and Europe. Then I teamed up with Graham Cooper and the record company got us a new agent, a fellow called Tony McArthur, who managed Charles Aznavour. That moved me and Graham into a different world and we almost left the folk world behind. The next thing I knew we were opening for Focus, the Dutch prog rock band, and those tours were incredibly successful for us. It worked. Then we opened for the Kinks. Then Graham and I split up amicably after about three and a half years because we couldn't break through this glass ceiling.

MADDY PRIOR

The first LP with Tim Hart in 1968 – oh, it was a very big deal to us. It definitely moved us up the ladder in the sort of pecking order. It established us because not too many people had records out then. We recorded it all in one go on a Revox. I suppose it must have put our fee up but Tim did all that. He was really good at all that, at the business.

I remember once he got a letter from a club organiser offering us a gig at not very much, and Tim was looking at this letter and he could see the imprint of the letter that the guy had written before. And whoever it was, they were getting more money than us. So Tim wrote back and said what he'd offered was not enough: we wanted however much these other people were getting – and he got it. He was very quick-witted and funny and clever.

WIZZ JONES

Chas McDevitt was kinda famous 'cos he'd had a hit record, 'Freight Train', a good while before. He saw Pete Stanley and me play in a folk club and said, 'Would you like to record?' We had no management or infrastructure or anything to push it on. You couldn't get on the box. We got on in Scotland a couple of times but down south it was very limited. It was all very much a compromise. We bashed it out in two days in a demo studio. All those extra tracks we put on the CD later are from that session. I was annoyed that we didn't have any real control.

PETE STANLEY

Apparently in the rare records book, if you can find *Sixteen Tons of Bluegrass* – mint – it's worth about 200 quid. Columbia didn't take us up. They pressed 1,500 copies, which accounts for why it's so valuable now. Columbia sent me about half a dozen copies, so we sold them around the clubs. Got back home and called up Columbia, said, 'We want some more records.' They said, 'What you doing, selling them? You can't sell them. You've got to get in touch with the local music store and they'll sell the records for you.' That was the end of *Sixteen Tons of Bluegrass*.

WIZZ JONES

Pierre Tubbs said to Roy Harper he wanted to record some more people and Roy said, 'Forget about original songs. Record some original people.' It wasn't a good step, really, because original songs was where it was at. If you could give 'em twelve, thirteen songs, you were in.

He recorded Clive Palmer and recorded me. There was no control over it at all. It was in the days where session musicians were booked, arrangements written, you sang the vocals over the backing track and it was all a terrible mess. It was going to be called *A Common or Garden Mystery*.

Alan Tunbridge was enthusiastic because some of his songs were on there and he designed a beautiful cover, multicoloured, a caterpillar like in a Van Gogh painting with a green leaf. They said, 'Nah, nah, we don't like that. We're going to call it *Wizz Jones*'. Pierre persuaded me to go on Clapham Junction – stand on a diesel train – and they took a stupid fish-eye lens photograph. When I think back, I was always very obstinate and dug my heels in, but I obviously didn't dig my heels in enough. After that I just went to the smaller people.

I wanted to get a hit single, because that's where you survived. I did 'Teapot Blues' and I recorded it in the studio with a background tape that Ron Geesin did for me. I asked him to make me a party tape, so there was 'Teapot Blues' over the top of this uproarious party and drinks spilling over. I thought it was great but they weren't interested, so that never came out. Anyway, Clive Palmer took it and did it differently with the Incredibles. Then another time with Ralph, later on, we did that 'Easy Rider'

single, 'cos I knew that the film was gonna be big. But the film
hadn't come out.

BILL LEADER

At the time I started the Leader and Trailer labels, I was working
on a freelance basis for Transatlantic and Topic. There was all
this stuff I was aware was going on and it was too commercial
for Topic, not commercial enough for Transatlantic. Transatlantic
tended to go for the guitar records, things like that.

I'd met up with Helen, who became my second wife, and we
sat down and figured it all out. The idea was that, if we sold direct
by post and didn't have to pay a wholesaler or even a retailer a
mark-up, then we didn't have to sell very many to break even.
The folk clubs were growing and contact was becoming easier.

We thought that if we're going to sell by mail then people need
to know what it is they're buying, which is why it was Leader and
Trailer. We wanted to do traditional material – roots material as
they say these days – and we also wanted to do more entertainment
stuff. Leader was the roots label and Trailer the entertainment.

We didn't have any finance. We owned a tape recorder. I had a
couple of microphones. So we set that up. We did *Jack Elliott of
Birtley* from tapes that were sent to us, a tribute thing. We did
Archie Fisher and Barbara Dickson – *Fate o' Charlie* – which I
went up to Scotland to record. They were our two first releases,
one from each label.

When Transatlantic heard this was happening, the sales
manager said, 'I want to sell these.' So – dilemma! Here we had
up-and-coming artists who wanted and deserved exposure. Do
we say, 'No, we're not going to give you national distribution
'cos it's not going to work out.' Or do we grit our teeth and go
along with it – and only get pence per copy?

It was very flattering that you hadn't released a record yet
and here were people knocking on your door. They offered
manufacture and distribution from EMI. We couldn't turn that
down. We'd been dogged by people who made small-run records,

pressing factories in the back streets, absolutely appalling technically.

The distribution meant that what would normally have sold about fifty if we were lucky – 5,000 had gone out and were in somebody's warehouse. In the case of EMI, that's where they stayed. They flogged them off into the remainder shops. The Dransfields' *Rout of the Blues* was by far and away our best seller. I can't remember how many, but it was many thousands.

ROBIN DRANSFIELD

I went to Bill and said, 'Look, we fancy trying to make a record, what would you advise me to do.' And Bill said, 'I'm just setting up my new label.' I think he'd put two or three out. He said, 'Why don't you come and do it with me.'

We recorded *Rout of the Blues* in the legendary flat in Camden Town where you used to have to stop recording when an aeroplane went over. He was doing it on a two-track Revox. We were living in north London, and we'd go in and do a track then go off and do a gig in Southend or somewhere.

Halfway through one session we had to stop because there was a phone call. It was Nat Joseph from Transatlantic was on the line, wanting to speak to me. He tried to talk me out of recording for Bill, he said, 'Why don't you just do it with Bill, but for Transatlantic?' I said, 'No, we're going to stick with Bill.'

Nat was quite annoyed about it, but we recorded it with Bill and then did some overdubs at Livingston Studios in Barnet with Nick Kinsey. He was the only genius I ever worked with. He never saw daylight for about twenty years. He was recording all the time. Died very young, just keeled over one day.

DICK GAUGHAN

Robin Dransfield took me round to Bill Leader's house and demanded that Bill listen to a few songs. We arranged for me to record at Bill's in June 1971 and *No More Forever* was the result. It was recorded on a two-track Revox in Bill's front room in Camden and I simply sang a bunch of songs I knew and Bill recorded them. It was *Melody Maker's* Folk Album of the Year in 1972.

DAVE BURLAND

Bill Leader had recorded Robin and Barry Dransfield with *The Rout of the Blues,* a corking album, still is. I think he'd done Nic Jones and one or two of the more traddy people. He had two bits of his label – the revival singers on one and the contemporary people like Richard Digance on the other. I might have been the fourth or fifth person to record with him.

He rang me up and said, in his very quiet voice, 'I would like to record you.' I said, 'Well you haven't heard me.' He said, 'I've heard of you.' I stayed at Bill's house and recorded *Dalesman's Litany* – apart from one track – in an hour and a half.

GEF LUCENA

Saydisc started in May '65. The first thing we ever recorded was a Fred Wedlock EP at the Bristol Poetry and Folk Club. We started on a very small scale, with limited edition – ninety-nine – records. The first three or four that we did, like Fred's, had all sold out before we produced them, and they were all paid up front, so I had no outlay. It escalated very slowly.

IAN ANDERSON

Gef Lucena, John Turner from the Pigsty Hill Light Orchestra and myself started Village Thing in '69 as a real reaction against experiences some of us had with major labels. I didn't want to record for majors any more and the Pigstys were about to make their first record, and John Turner decided we'd do a record label and an agency as well and just look after our own destiny.

Bill Leader was doing most of the traditional thing and we did the so-called contemporary thing. We were both distributed by Transatlantic, so we were kind of bookends. With most of the albums, we pressed 2,000. The big seller was Fred Wedlock. He sold 20,000. He did his 'Talking Folk Club Blues'. There was a line in it about Prince Philip being the Queen's slave and the ladies of the EMI pressing department refused to press the record.

That was the best publicity you could get. It was in the *Daily Mail*. It's interesting – you could have somebody that's nationally known for selling two or three thousand albums and then somebody like Fred Wedlock who's only locally known for selling 20,000 albums.

What we expected when that album came out was that Paul Simon's publishers would jump on us but they never did. 'The Folker' is 'The Boxer' with the words changed. Loads of people did that song, it became a folk club standard.

STEVE TILSTON

I'd got enough songs for an album so I was looking to record and Ralph McTell was very supportive of me. He said, 'There's a small label in Bristol, Village Thing', and he rang up Ian Anderson. I went down and they'd organised a gig at the Troubadour in Bristol, a wonderful club, and they offered me a recording contract.

The album was done live on a Revox and it's still the case that I'm constantly aware of every mistake, and the mistakes are magnified. I remember, when it came out, feeling really disappointed, then all of a sudden it started getting great reviews and record companies were trying to poach me.

We got quite a lot of coverage on the radio, so it sold quite well. One was sent to a guy, Mike Cable, who was the music writer for the *Daily Mail*. He was really taken with the album and it was the time when Rod Stewart had 'Maggie May', so he was like the biggest thing. He was interviewing Rod Stewart and he knew Rod was an old folkie, and he said, 'Oh, you might like this', and played him a bit, and apparently Rod loved it and his management rang up and ordered a boxful, which were then given out to various key people

I did an interview with *Zig Zag* magazine and John Lennon sent them a telegram but nobody told me. I found out from an

American source via the Internet, asking 'Are you the Steve Tilston that John Lennon wrote to?' I said, 'I'm sorry, what's this about?' Then they clammed up. Basically, the telegram that had been sent to me at *Zig Zag* had been sold for a small fortune and it ended up with some collector in America. John Lennon wrote the letter in 1971. He'd read the interview in *ZigZag* magazine but I didn't know about the telegram until 2005.

I said to the people in America, 'Look, I'll relinquish all rights, but I want to see it.' This is a handwritten telegram. It wasn't so much that Lennon liked my record: he was alluding to something I said in an interview about wealthy musicians losing their mojo.

It was very frustrating, nothing to do with any financial value, because if I'd received the telegram I would never have sold it. When I got a copy from the guy who bought it, I saw it was handwritten by John and signed 'Love, John and Yoko' and he ended it by saying, 'So whadya you think of that?' – obviously wanting me to reply. Because it was never passed on to me and then apparently sold I missed out on a dialogue with John Lennon, which would have been a great thing to have.

IAN ANDERSON
Village Thing lasted till '74. We thought it was a great idea when Transatlantic approached us to take over pressing and distribution, like they were doing for Bill. Initially it worked quite well but, later on, some artists' albums weren't selling because they weren't in the shops and as far as the artists, who were our friends, were concerned, we were the interface between them and Transatlantic who weren't putting them in the shops. In the end we just bailed out.

BILL LEADER
Nat Joseph sold Transatlantic to Granada. Then Granada sold it off and when the contract came up for renewal it didn't get renewed. At the time, around 1973, there was the Yom Kippur

War and an oil shortage and apparently oil was an important part of making PVC, which they make vinyl records out of, so we lost our pressing people. I'd moved out of London and was living in Halifax and in some way or other there was a bit of an organisation change that ended up with us being put into liquidation. And that was the end.

11 When folk began to rock

Just as the British folk song revival of the late fifties and early sixties had followed the earlier American revival, so folk rock – a term first coined in the States to describe the Byrds' hit 'Mr Tambourine Man' – emerged in Britain in 1967 with the formation of Fairport Convention.

Fairport founder-members Ashley Hutchings and Richard Thompson were heavily influenced by the Byrds, as well as Bob Dylan and Jefferson Airplane, but in their formative years they had also frequented London folk clubs. When Sandy Denny and Dave Swarbrick joined the band, the emphasis was firmly on fusing British traditional material and rock music.

Hutchings and Denny departed Fairport in 1969, shortly after the band's van crashed while returning home from a gig, killing drummer Martin Lamble and Richard Thompson's girlfriend, Jeannie Franklyn. Hutchings furthered the folk rock cause by forming Steeleye Span with Tim Hart and Maddy Prior, while Denny fronted the short-lived Fotheringay.

Like Fairport, Steeleye Span would go through many changes in line-up. Martin Carthy joined in 1970 and Ashley Hutchings departed to form the Albion Band, which began as a group of musicians recruited to accompany his then wife Shirley Collins on her album No Roses.

In 1978/'79 a re-formed Albion Band supplied the music for the National Theatre production Lark Rise to Candleford, *with Ashley Hutchings and John Tams as joint musical directors. Tams and some of the musicians involved in the production then formed Home Service, which continued for the next seven years, re-forming in 2011.*

Folk rock bands had some success in the charts. A Fairport Convention single, 'Si Tu Dois Partir', almost made the Top

Twenty and brought an unlikely appearance on Top of the Pops. *Steeleye Span's 'All Around My Hat' peaked at number five on the singles chart, while the album of the same title reached the Top Ten, as did Pentangle's* Basket of Light *album. Stealers Wheel, formed by Gerry Rafferty after he parted company with Billy Connolly in the Humblebums, reached the singles Top Ten in both Britain and the USA, selling over a million copies. The highest singles chart position for the folk rock bands was the Strawbs' 'Part of the Union', number two in 1973, with their* Bursting at the Seams *reaching the same position on the album charts.*

Folk rock became an important genre in British popular music. Its electric sound did not belong in the folk clubs, but the clubs were where most of its practitioners had come from. They were driven by a desire to progress traditional music onwards, to experiment with old songs in new contexts. And as they did so, in rock venues and on commercially successful records, they took the music to new, much bigger audiences.

ASHLEY HUTCHINGS

I was on the edge of folk until 1969. When we started with Fairport we were a rock group, that's it. Just before the crash and then after the crash totally, I became obsessed with traditional folk music and I started to go to Cecil Sharp House. I wanted to discover. I listened to loads of stuff. You could go upstairs and listen to recordings. I spent a lot of time there.

ROBIN DRANSFIELD

We were at Bill Leader's one day, and Bill had a phone call from Ashley Hutchings to say that he was putting this band together after the split with Fairport. He said, 'I'm looking for people to be in it.' A meeting was set up and Barry and me went round to see Ashley in his flat and also there were Terry and Gay Woods. Me and Barry were on the up at the time, we'd done *Rout of the Blues* and we didn't really feel right about it so we said, 'No, we're going to continue with the duo.' He subsequently got Tim Hart and Maddy Prior in.

MADDY PRIOR

Tim and I wanted to play with other musicians. We'd done four years together, the two of us, and we'd explored more or less what we could. I'd stopped playing the banjo – Tim had picked it up, played it for two months, and he could play it better than me.

DAVE SWARBRICK

Fairport had Sandy join and Sandy, of course, worked a lot in clubs. She probably wanted to expand and get more into self-searching popular music, but she had a tradition of being in the clubs and singing traditional music. They were doing things like 'A Sailor's Life' and other traditional songs and they wanted to give it an authentic feel, I suppose, so they called me in.

RICHARD THOMPSON

When Swarb joined, between him and Sandy they knew everyone, so when we were on tour there would be a party every night, with the McPeakes or the Dubliners or Chieftains, Cyril Tawney, the Watersons, High Level Ranters, the lot. Meeting and playing with the cream of traditional music was a great education. Walking down the streets of Dublin with the Dubliners was something I'll never forget.

DAVE SWARBRICK

It didn't feel like I'd made a big jump from rooms above pubs to big halls. I was earning less money. When I was with Martin, I used to lose more money out of my back pocket than I earned with Fairport. Not just at the beginning, all the time. I never had much money with Fairport. When I did that record later with Lazarus, I got more money from selling that than I did from *Liege and Lief* in total. And that wasn't a lot. But Fairport helped to promote my name and everybody else's.

ASHLEY HUTCHINGS

Me and Sandy left within a week. Fairport said, 'What are we going to do?' and Swarbrick said, 'Let's get Bert Lloyd to sing with us.' I mean, it was never going to happen. Then they said, 'Let's get Andy Irvine to sing with us.' Andy turned it down. He would have been great.

Bert Lloyd came to the unveiling of *Liege and Lief* at the Royal Festival Hall. We'd had the crash, we'd got together, we'd rehearsed, we'd recorded *Liege and Lief* and then we did the one big gig at the Royal Festival Hall and Bert came backstage. He said he loved it.

DAVE SWARBRICK

A large part of what they had planned was to put in extemporisation, which I liked. And that seemed to open up the possibilities of doing other things. At the time, probably they wanted to make a project album that they didn't see as long-term. I think Joe Boyd would have seen it as a novelty thing. I joined them. We made *Liege and Lief*, but then there was all kind of upheavals. Sandy left because she didn't want to stay stuck in the tradition. Ashley left because he wanted to stay more in the tradition.

RICHARD THOMPSON

I always thought our repertoire would come to include plenty of original songs, influenced by the tradition. I thought it was a great concept that would validate us as a band, give us a unique, indigenous style. Sandy and I never stopped writing. That was a point of divergence with Ashley, who wanted to do more trad, and left to pursue that with Steeleye.

ASHLEY HUTCHINGS

I had a vision. I wanted to get into morris music but to be honest it was partly down to the friends I'd made – Sweeney's Men, Johnny Moynihan and Terry Woods and Andy Irvine. Also, at the same time, Tim and Maddy. That was the first line-up of the band – Tim and Maddy, Terry Woods and Gay Woods, his wife, and myself. Terry became my best friend and we had great social times together, but I have to be honest and also say that I think that I had a delayed reaction to the crash.

I was in a strange place in my head, as indeed Sandy was. We left, and the official line is we both left, within a week, for musical reasons. I think we were both traumatised, definitely. I had dizzy spells and then later had a minor breakdown after I'd left Fairport

I lived at Bob Pegg's. He exposed me to a lot of things. He was a very good friend. Bob and Carole were lovely. They formed Mr Fox after I had left. I was going to be the bass player and when I said I wasn't going to be they resented it – fairly, because we'd made plans.

But then I got the phone call from Tim Hart. This was the re-formation of Steeleye. Winter of '69–'70, we formed Steeleye. We'd made *Hark! The Village Wait*, the first album, and we then immediately broke up. We had ructions in the studio. It wasn't a happy album. It was a wonder we finished it. Gay and Terry left, and that was the end of the band and that's when immediately I went to live with Bob and Carole. I recuperated, then there was a phone call from Tim, 'Let's re-form Steeleye – Martin Carthy would like to be involved.'

MARTIN CARTHY

With Steeleye Span we didn't have that much to do with the rock world. You see, folkies in the sixties actually did do quite big gigs sometimes. We'd played places like the Festival Hall and the Albert Hall, Manchester Free Trade Hall. We used to do gigs for the anti-apartheid movement and for CND, and inevitably they would be in big halls.

ASHLEY HUTCHINGS

We worked very differently from Fairport. Fairport didn't chat, really, but with Steeleye it was just like doing a folk club but with a few electric instruments and in halls rather than in a folk club. We did the Highcliffe in Sheffield, but I don't recall any other clubs.

Shortly before I left Fairport we'd met Shirley and Dolly Collins in Liverpool. They were supporting us. That was the first time I met Shirley and, of course, we were married in just a couple of years.

Hearing Shirley and Dolly Collins' *Anthems of Eden* – that was what brought it out. I just couldn't sleep. I was feeling worse and worse, taking heavy sleeping pills and not sleeping, and one morning I felt so awful I put *Anthems of Eden* on. And the tears started to come and I wept all morning. I remember the doctor came round and he said, 'This is good, this is the beginning of the process.' Was it a turning point, musically? It possibly was, you know.

MARTIN CARTHY

I was in the Albion Country Band. The first version was about forty strong. That was on Shirley's album *No Roses*. They never played after that. Then Ashley put the Albion Country Band together – it was Royston Wood, Sue Draheim the American fiddle player, Ashley, Roger Swallow and Simon Nicol. Then he sacked Royston, Steve and Sue. Half the band was stoned and the other half were pretty straight. Ashley had quite a puritanical streak and he was outraged. He brought John Kirkpatrick, Sue Harris and me in and from January 1973 to August I was in the Albion Country Band. Then the band broke up – couldn't get the gigs.

JOHN TAMS

I bumped into Ashley Hutchings, who was then married to Shirley Collins. He was putting something together. He said, 'I want to do a dance band', like Joe Loss, doing English dances, but the dances are sung over, in the way that Anne Shelton would sing with the Joe Loss band. So for them as didn't want to dance, they could listen and join in, and for them as wanted to dance they could dance and sing the while. That was the Albion Dance Band.

He formed that without me. I was doing other things, and then when the time came he gave me a shout and I joined. After about a year of doing that I wanted to do more songs than dance. Also, you had to work a really big venue to get the dance-floor space. Cecil Sharp House would be an average, or Battersea Town Hall – as big a venue as we could get to get four or five hundred in. I thought, 'If we've got a right big space, we can get a thousand in, not dancing.' So Dance was dropped and it just became the Albion Band.

Ashley was domestically diverted at the time. We got a deal with Harvest to make an album, which Ashley had organised but he didn't particularly want to play. So he just played bass and got Joe Boyd to come and produce it. One night at the National Theatre we played the entire album to Joe. He just sat there in an audience of one and he said, 'That's fine. We'll go in the studio and record it'.

He wanted me as co-producer with him, because I'd got the order. When I make an album, I've got the order. It's through being obsessed with theatre, I think. I know how it starts. It has to have a narrative arc. It has to have a point where you put the kettle on halfway through. Because it was on vinyl, it had to have a beginning, a middle and end on each side. So I knew what order I wanted to put everything in when we recorded it. I still make albums like that, even though they're on CD with a lot more tracks.

DAVE COUSINS
Late 1966 I dropped in the Troubadour and Sandy Denny was on stage singing 'Fhír a Bhata'. It's Gaelic. I was mesmerised by her, and after she had finished I went up and introduced myself and said, 'Do you want to join a group?' She said, 'Who are you?' I said, 'The Strawbs.' She said, 'Yeah, all right.' I phoned Tony

Hooper from a call box and said, 'We've got a girl singer.'

We rehearsed for about six months and then we made some demos at Cecil Sharp House. Trevor Lucas came along – that was where Sandy met him for the first time – and he sort of thumped on a guitar case while we were playing. A friend of mine sent the tapes to someone in Denmark who had a record company, and he wanted us to make a record so we went to Denmark. We had a lot of fun: made the record in the day and in the evenings we played in Tivoli Gardens.

We only ever played twice in England with Sandy – once we dropped in at the Greyhound, Fulham Palace Road, and did a floor spot, from which the front cover of the album *Sandy and the Strawbs* came, and we played at Nottingham University. Sandy came up in the car with us, went back on the train with Trevor, and that was the start of their relationship.

I was disappointed when she left. I thought a couple of songs on that album would become hit singles. Major Minor wanted to sign us. I told Sandy. She said, 'I don't want to be a pop singer.' She got very frightened by the idea. She couldn't cope with the idea of being the equivalent to Dusty Springfield. Never mind, we stayed pals.

Then *Top of the Pops* decided to introduce an album spot and we were the first band booked for it. The *From the Witchwood* album had come out and we did 'The Hangman and the Papist'. So suddenly people saw Rick Wakeman playing the organ and the Strawbs were in the mainstream rather than the obscure folk circuit.

Richard Hudson and John Ford had joined the band and they'd recorded 'Part of the Union' as a demo. They were going to put it out and I thought, 'Hang on, they've only just joined the band, so to keep the band together we'll do it with the Strawbs.' Suddenly, there we were at the top of the charts. It was only about a year since we'd left the folk clubs and we were doing a forty-gig tour of the major halls in the country, selling out every one.

The folk clubs were very important for me. I was particularly struck by people like the Young Tradition. I wrote a song, 'Where Is This Dream of Your Youth', specifically for them, to get them into the pop scene. They were not enthusiastic.

RAB NOAKES

The first Stealers Wheel shows – it was just me and Gerry, two guitars acoustic duo. We came up to Scotland to do a couple of shows in that summer of '71, quite nice shows. We did one at the Lyceum Theatre in Edinburgh with Fairport Convention. We did a couple of clubs but they were more little concerts.

I left before the album and 'Stuck in the Middle'. I was delighted for them. It's still a great record. There was a bit too much waiting going on and I was needing to get out and play, that was my thing. I had a solo deal with A&M, then with Warners. The aim was to get a hit and I went to Nashville to make an album. At that time it was mostly the uni circuit I played. It was healthy, well paid and well organised. Great social aspect, too.

I never fully severed a connection with folk clubs although things became more polarised in terms of repertoires. There was a lot of rule-making going on and it all became a bit factional – the 'What is a folk song' kinda thing. I couldn't see the point of all the stipulations about what was okay and what wasn't. I liked this life I'd got playing the universities because it was conducted without too many daft rules and regulations.

12 I used to get them laughing

The folk scene of the late sixties and early seventies was not short of larger-than-life characters. Alex Campbell, who had long relied on an image as a boisterous, hard-drinking Scotsman, was maybe past his best but still working most nights of the year. Diz Disley invariably turned up late, if he turned up at all, but nobody seemed to mind. Disley was not a folk singer, he was a jazz guitarist of the first order who delivered a few comic songs and monologues, improvised the odd blues standard and delighted club audiences with his wit and eccentricities.

Fred Wedlock played the West Country yokel until a new persona as the 'Oldest Swinger in Town' propelled him into the pop charts. Tony Capstick, greatly admired by his comic peers, was from the long tradition of northern music hall comedians, a cheeky-faced tyke who would not have looked amiss if his pet lurcher had accompanied him to gigs.

Teessider Vin Garbutt has made thousands of folk club audiences laugh over the past forty years, without ever singing a comic song. His act has always been balanced between the drama of topical songs and humorous banter in between. Dave Turner, a quirky, innovative Nottingham man, was years before his time, but he lacked the consistency and ambition that could have taken him to a higher level. From the Home Counties Derek Brimstone was another banter specialist as well as an accomplished guitar and banjo player, while Irishman Noel Murphy had modest musical talent but he could hold any audience, anywhere, through the strength of his personality.

Billy Connolly came to notice with Tam Harvey in the Humblebums, a wild, long-haired duo from Glasgow whose gale-force power cut a swathe through the British folk scene before Connolly went solo, never to look back. At the time his

closest contemporaries were Mike Harding and Jasper Carrott.
All three saw what was required to move onwards and upwards,
and that is what they did. They all had chart hits with comic
songs, took their opportunities and went on to mainstream
success, although Mike Harding did return to the music if not
the clubs and for many years presented the BBC's Folk Show on
Radio 2, until he was replaced by Mark Radcliffe in 2012. Like
Fred Wedlock, Tony Capstick was in demand on the after-dinner
speaking circuit, but he never turned his back on the folk clubs.
Diz Disley and Derek Brimstone gradually retired as they aged
and a changing scene left them behind.

For a few years the 'entertainers', as they were often termed,
enjoyed unrivalled popularity in the folk clubs. Some say they
were responsible for their decline. Others disagree, but no one
can deny that during their heyday they made a lot of folk club
audiences laugh.

DAVE BURLAND

There aren't the characters about today – no nutters, no badly
behaved people. Drink was a big part back then. Today they
know it affects your performance. We believed it enhanced
it! Everybody's so politically correct and looks on it as just a
living.

JASPER CARROTT *founder of the Boggery folk club in Solihull, went on to great fame as a comedian*

I'd never been to Jersey before. I got in on the Sunday night to
do the club on the Monday and we went out drinking. Booze
was very cheap over there and I got off my head. We went for
some fish and chips and I wandered into the middle of the road
in St Helier, offering drivers a chip. The police came along and
said, 'Oi, piss off.' They went away. I carried on and they came
back and locked me up. The club organiser had to come the next
day and bail me out, so I could do his club on the night. The club
was packed 'cos the word had gone round. I went back when the

court case came up and got fined £25. I did the club three or four times after that. It was always packed.

BILLY CONNOLLY

There was a guy at Dundee University. He kept asking for 'Needle of Death', and I'm playing the banjo. Every time I finished a song, he'd shout, 'Needle of Death.' I said, 'Listen, it's not a tune for the banjo.' I said, 'I like it, and I like Bert Jansch, but I just don't know it. You keep asking me for a song I don't know. If I knew it, I'd gladly do it for you.' I did another song and there he was again . . . 'Needle of Death.'

So I put the banjo down. I said, 'Just stay where you are . . .' and I step into the audience. I'm walking through all the people. 'Excuse me please, excuse me.' Straight up to him – and I whacked him.

Then I found out he was the treasurer. That was the end of my whacking days. That's when I stopped it. I was the world's only violent hippie. I used to say, 'Don't let the long hair fool you. I like violence!'

MIKE HARDING

The 'Fourteen and a Half Pound Budgie' came about because I had a job working for this bloke and he was a right bastard. He ran kennels and I used to clean them out on a Saturday morning. He was tight, really tight. He'd just give me a shilling for shovelling all the dog shit up.

He kept budgies as well. He had dozens of them. He let them fly round. I used to hate the little sods – they'd shit on you. But this one was a comical thing, it had long claws. The bloke had coconut matting in the house and it used to walk three paces then fall over and smack its head on the floor. So I saw the comic and the horrific aspect of the budgie world.

DEREK BRIMSTONE

I used to get them all laughing, having a good time. That's the beauty of being an entertainer, if it ain't going very well you could always fall back on the chat and if the chat ain't going very well you could fall back on the music. Fortunately, I never, ever, died in a folk club. The only time I died on me arse was when I was doing a dinner somewhere, a firm's dinner. Some of them you'd go down a storm but others – half of them had got their backs to you. I made a rule: anywhere where there's knives and forks, I ain't gonna play.

BERNARD WRIGLEY
The first tour I did was about 1972 or '73 and the only one that my good lady came on. It was about ten nights. We were somewhere near Dover and we walked in and the bloke said, 'You're here, then. Put your stuff down there.' Then he looked at my good lady and he said, 'Stripping about half nine?' I said, 'You what?' We'd got the wrong venue. It was a relief to do the folk club after that!

NOEL MURPHY
There was a lovely big old barn behind the Village Pump at Trowbridge, and the stage was an old wooden hay wagon. The place was lit by candles stuck in wine bottles. I was singing there and I backed into a candle and my hair caught fire. So I picked somebody else's pint up and poured it all over me head. I wasn't going to waste me own pint.

BILL LEADER
Ewan MacColl said, 'There's this Irishman, Brendan Behan. you should get hold of him.' This was very early on, '55 or '56. *The Quare Fellow* was opening at Stratford East. So Ewan gave Brendan the phone number of the place I was working, the Polish Embassy film library, and he came on, 'Where the fackin' Jeysus are you?' He frightened the life out of the lady on the switchboard.

Dick Swetman and I went to Stratford to record him. He wasn't there but he was due, so we went across to the pub on the corner of Angel Lane, which was a street market then. And we saw a disturbance at the far end – it was sort of rippling down – and this feller with a sky-blue tweed suit was approaching, clapping all the traders on the shoulders and nicking their bananas.

He eventually got to us and we said we'd come to record him – 'Bah, Jaysus, let's have a drink.' So we went in the pub. 'Eyyy, shhh . . . tale o' the old iron pot . . .' Great stories. He'd just been in Paris. 'I've had a fellow over there,' he says. 'We had a drink. Turns out this feller – he's the heir to the throne. He's the Czar of all the Russians. And he's stuck in Paris.' I don't think the guy he drank with was exactly driving a taxi, but something like that. And Brendan left him at the end of the evening, felt very sorry for him. He said, 'He's got family back in Russia, working down the salt mines. I told him "Never mind, never mind. I've got a brother who's the prospective Communist candidate in Dublin. I'll try and use my influence and get your family down a pepper mine for the winter." '

He was all heart. He was a kindly sort of soul, and it turned out he'd mistaken who we were. He didn't realise we'd come down to make a recording for a record of him singing the old songs. He thought we'd come to record him singing 'The Old Triangle' in *The Quare Fellow* – because up till now he'd been off stage singing it and he was due to go back to Paris or to Dublin, so someone was due to come down and record him singing it so they could use that when he'd gone.

We explained that we weren't those people, that we were here to record him singing some of the old Irish songs, so we went back to the Theatre Royal to get on with it. Meanwhile Gerry Raffles, the manager who kept the whole theatre thing going, had got several crates of Guinness, part of Brendan's daily ration, and Brendan had to open a few of those to make sure they were all right.

We tried all sorts of places in the theatre to record him but we'd got terrible hum that we couldn't get rid of. Brendan would start singing, but nothing really worked. He'd start off singing a song in Gaelic, there'd be this hum, and eventually all three of us were knocking the Guinness back. We fell over and that was the end of that session.

DAVE BURLAND

I had a very drunken weekend in Sheffield with Dominic Behan and Nigel Denver. I didn't go home, which was not like me at all. We'd done Malcolm Fox's club and I remember having a row with Dominic. He'd got up and sung 'Master McGrath' but it was the way he introduced it – he was very scathing about English people. I said to him, 'You twat, you're taking our money and calling us names at the same time. That's a bit of a cheek.'

So we got drinking and Nigel appeared from somewhere. The three of us were booked at the Marples Hotel in Sheffield on the Sunday. And on the Monday we'd no money, but Dominic went and put a bet on and won some money on a horse and we went off again.

Back then you took a lot of things on face value. I was there, having a drink with Brendan Behan's brother, which is astonishing. But one of the joys of the early folk scene was that all these 'stars' to us, were so accessible. They'd talk to you.

NOEL MURPHY

One Friday night in 1964 I was with a couple of friends at the Tinkers club in the Three Horseshoes in Hampstead. We were standing at the back of a very crowded room and suddenly Gerry Fox, one of the Tinkers, announces, 'The best of attention for Noel Murphy.' I was standing there having a drink and I thought, 'What a wonderful coincidence this is, a bloke of the same name as me is going to get up and entertain us.'

Then the crowd parted in front of me and my mates, who'd told the organiser that I could make 'em laugh, pushed me on. I started off by singing something very silly, and once I got their attention I sang a couple of songs. Like every folk audience I've ever been in they were easy because they were there to have a good time. You couldn't really go wrong.

I used to go up to Scotland and this particular time, '68 I think it was, I was told that once I got to Fife I would come across a group, the Fife Weavers, with a boy wonder on the banjo. I got to this club, the Elbow Room in Kirkcaldy, I listened to the resident group and the kid just stood out – Davey Johnstone. At half time we had a drink and I asked him will you come up for the second half. 'Yeah, I'd love to.' He just picked it up straight away. He was sixteen.

That was in the May time. Then in September I was living in Shepherd's Bush and I was just leaving the house to do a great folk club, the Hop Poles at Enfield, and Davey arrived on the doorstep. He got in the car and came with us and did the second half with me. And we played together for two and a half years as Murf and Shaggis.

He was backing me with the tenor banjo. When he did a banjo solo the crowd would roar. To see him in full flight playing 'The Mason's Apron' behind his head and not missing a beat was really something.

We were great, great pals and there was a great chemistry between us. I was ideal for him in one respect because he was terribly shy. Then he suddenly announced that he was leaving. I said right, good luck, and he joined a band called Magna Carta. They were organised and did more sort of concerts.

He played on a few tracks for an Elton John album and that eventually turned into him joining Elton John and he's still with him forty years later.

CHRISTY MOORE

Noel Murphy was a revelation. I knew all the songs and chords he had but he parcelled them up in glorious fun and roguery. Then Hamish Imlach took me on the road and introduced me to a host of pleasures previously unimagined.

EWAN McVICAR

Hamish lived round the corner from me and he talked for years about writing a book, it was going to be *Mangoes in the Bathtub*, stories and recipes. The publishers said it had to be called *Cod Liver Oil and the Orange Juice*. He never got around to doing it and eventually I sat him down for a week with a tape recorder, telling his stories, yet I was thinking that, with the amount of drink that had flowed through him, he wouldn't remember all that much. He had an astonishing memory!

One of the key things about it was that he swore that all the stories were true, until it was quite advanced, when I told him, 'You realise that if any of it's not true and it's libellous, you'll get sued as well as the publisher.' He went through the book and took half the names out.

If you look at the book it says on the cover there's an introduction by Christy Moore – but there's no introduction by Christy Moore. The publishers scrambled to get it out because Hamish was going to be interviewed on Irish television, which they thought would be great publicity for the book. When he was interviewed the book didn't get a mention. Then Hamish kind of fell out with the publishers and it went out of print for a long time.

ARCHIE FISHER

I met Hamish in the boys' playground of Hyndland Senior Secondary School in Glasgow. He had never been to a mixed-gender school. He had an Indian and Australian upbringing, and he was staring longingly in the girls' playground.

His appearance also attracted attention. He was wearing a black leather jacket and a red fez which he had bought in Port Said on the Suez Canal on his trip from Down Under. 'Interesting,' I thought. I approached him and said hello and his first reaction was to ask, 'Do you want to buy a lighter?' and he produced one of the novelty-type lighters with a fully clothed pin-up that gravity stripped when you turned the sand-filled casing upside down.

JIM McLEAN

Hamish had a house, like a gatehouse, that his mother had left him. His mother was quite well off and he had parties in this place. He was good at making curries and we all used to go when the pubs shut.

He never had any money, always broke, and, of course, he drank an awful lot. His uncle was a grocer and he used to go down there and kid on he was buying toilet rolls or something, but try and get a bottle of booze at the same time. He sold me a mah-jong set for a fiver, a lovely set. Five pounds was a lot of money. I said to him, 'If you ever want it back you can have it – give me a fiver.'

It must have been thirty years later and Hamish is in hospital. He phones me from the hospital and he says, 'Look, if I send a chap down, have you still got that set?' A young feller turned up, gave me a fiver and I gave him the mah-jong set.

DAVE ARTHUR

My fondest memory of Hamish is of him wandering through our flat at midday, casually wrapped in a sheet with his arse hanging out the back, carrying a box of cold takeaway vindaloo curry which he'd bought the night before, ready for breakfast.

DEREK SARJEANT

He got stuck in the bath at a friend of mine's house. They had a hell of a job getting him out. He was too wide for the bath.

BARBARA DICKSON

He was a lovely guy, probably the most generous of all. He treated younger performers well. He'd show you things. Hamish was part of shall we say your maturing education. He was very intelligent, really well read. I loved him.

I said to him, 'What do you think I should do? How do you think I can get some work?' I wasn't having any success in the folk clubs in Scotland. Either I couldn't get to them because I didn't drive, or they weren't offering enough money to cover my expenses. And Hamish said, 'If you can do a floor spot in a choice couple of clubs, then people will see you because the organisers from the area gather in those big clubs.' That weekend he was playing at the Highcliffe in Sheffield and the Londonderry in Sunderland and the Mica in Liverpool. He said, 'I'll give you a lift.'

Hamish knew everybody and everybody loved him. I knew nobody who had anything to say about him that was in any way derogatory. If it hadn't been for him bringing me to those clubs I probably would never have made a living in the folk scene. Hamish said, 'She's really good, give her a chance', and that was it, I was away.

BILLY CONNOLLY

I went for banjo lessons and then the guys that were giving me lessons kept putting me in bands because they always played something else, mandolin or guitars, and they'd say, 'You're going to have to do a couple of numbers to take me off the banjo.' I did a few with the banjo teacher Ron Duff. They were kind of industrial gigs in factory social clubs.

Then I got another guy, Jimmy Steele, and he said, 'Come to the club.' We did a couple of tunes and I sang 'St Brendan's Isle', the Jimmy Driftwood song. I forgot the words, so I said to the audience, 'Listen, I've forgotten the words but the story is . . .' and they were starting to laugh as I was relating the story. And I thought, 'Oh, I like this . . . I like the sound of that when they're laughing.' And that laid out the route for everything that followed, definitely, without question. After that I just took everything very lightly. It was always dead obvious the route I was to take. I could kid myself on that I was going to be a musician, but it wasn't going to happen.

I would get a wee circuit from Jasper when he had his agency. He used to get me Solihull and Walsall and Bristol. He was very kind to me but he would never get me the Boggery. He put me on to Harvey Andrews. I thought he was amazing. He was very nice to me in Walsall.

HARVEY ANDREWS

When Billy comes up in conversation I always think about that gig in Walsall when there were nine people there. We had a drink at the bar and I remember him being really down. We had a long chat. I remember him saying, 'I'll have to find something else to do.' And he did, didn't he!

IAN McCALMAN

The Humblebums was a bit of a mismatch really, because it was a vehicle for Billy. He was always incredibly funny. In the old days you'd watch Billy on stage and he was absolutely brilliant.

Then he did that Nat Joseph live album, which was one of the worst recorded live albums ever, and that's what made him into a superstar overnight. In the old days we used to go on stage and think these guys are hard to follow. You look back now and think Billy Connolly and Gerry Rafferty – no wonder they were hard to follow – they were stars of our time.

MIKE HARDING

I started doing patter. I'd never done it before but I was always telling jokes and messing around. I was one of them funny lads at school, always had a bit of a story, and when I was playing in rock 'n' roll bands we'd be sitting in the van, driving to a gig, and you'd come out with stuff, making the others laugh. Just being daft really, not jokes, just making stuff up. My granddad was a great storyteller, it came from the Irish side of the family. I've always loved monologues.

The material came all the time. I was always writing, always thinking of things, always listening, always studying, reading books on comedy, looking at other people's material. Jimmy James, the *Goon Show*, radio comedy– that was my background. Conjuring up pictures through voices – it's all in that tradition of music hall, variety.

Something would happen and I'd see the funny side of it and be able to relate it as a story. I was at Leeds University one night and I thought, 'I've only done four songs in that set, the rest of the time I'd been gibbering.'

Without the folk clubs, would I have just been a funny schoolteacher? Absolutely, because I would never have gone into the working men's clubs as a stand-up. I hated them. I used to play rock 'n' roll in them. I played in Bernard Manning's club for eighteen months. I was in the resident band.

It was horrible, all that tawdry attempt at showbusiness. The concert secretary, he was a moulder on a Friday and on a Saturday he was an impresario and he knew nowt about owt. 'He must be costing a lot of money, his name's in coloured chalk.'

I owe the folk clubs everything, particularly the folk clubs of Yorkshire, for the best receptions and the best nights. As a Lancashire man I've had the best nights of my life in Yorkshire!

MAARTIN ALLCOCK

I was in a pub, playing a bit of mandolin, and Mike Harding said, 'What you doing in the autumn?' I said, 'Signing on.' And he said, 'Do you want to come on tour with me?' That was my first tour. The band was called the Brown Ale Cowboys. We did a tour which was recorded by Bill Leader, it came out as an album, *Captain Paralytic*.

One night it was the keyboard player's birthday and we all got a bit out of it. I lost my key and was trying to get in my room and I fell off the hotel roof and broke my jaw. The next night Mike was doing all these new jokes to make me laugh, taking great delight in my agony.

NOEL MURPHY

The Scots Hoose is the only pub that I've ever been barred from. I went in one night and the landlord says, 'I'm sorry, Noel, I'm not serving you. You're barred.' I looked at him and I racked my brains. I said, 'How long am I barred for then?' He said, 'Until the mynah bird loses its Irish accent.'

I said, 'What do you mean?' He said, 'I saw you the other

night and you'd had a few and you were leaning down talking to the mynah bird.' It was an amazing mynah bird, very quick. I said, 'Everybody, when they've had a few, has a word with the mynah bird.' He said, 'Yes, but there's only one nationality in the world that pronounces the word bollix.'

DEREK BRIMSTONE

I was in a little group in Hemel Hempstead with Maddy Prior. She used to rule us, Maddy, she was the guvnor, though she was only sixteen. We went round the folk clubs doing floor spots. Maddy said, 'Somebody's got to do the chat. The chat's as important as the singing. Would you do it, Derek? You're always talking.' So it ended up with me introducing the songs, and I found out I could make people laugh. Really, all my humour was introducing the songs. It was Maddy who was the catalyst there. Then I went solo.

The act was all spontaneous. I didn't do too many funny songs – 'She Loved a Portuguese' . . . 'Sir Quincy De Bas'. I was doing a club at Exeter University and one of the students got up and did three superb funny songs. 'She Loved a Portuguese' was one of them. I got talking to him afterwards and he gave me the words. I said, 'Do you mind if I do it?' He said, 'No, please do.' So I did and I never met him again. People say, 'All them funny songs you did!' but I didn't. I had about four or five, that's all, and I used to do a couple in an evening.

When Les Barker wrote 'Nobody's as Old as Derek Brimstone', I was about sixty-five. I loved it. I thought it was a great compliment. He's a good mate, Les. I was seventy-five or -six when I packed up doing the clubs.

It was me and Noel Murphy that talked Carrott into going pro. He was the compère at the Boggery. He was very, very funny. We said, 'Why don't you do a gig?' He said, 'I can't do a gig.' I said, 'You can, just get a couple of half hours together and go and do it.' And he did. And, of course, he went down a bomb and the old pound signs come up in his eyes. He really went for it. Good luck to him, he's done very well. Me and Noel Murphy were his mainstays at the Boggery. That was a fabulous club.

JASPER CARROTT

There was a rugby club, the Old Moseleians and the guy I was sharing a flat with, Les, he said they'd got this room and they were desperate to use it. 'What about starting up a folk club there and I'll fund it.' He'd got fifty quid. This is February 1969. We called it the Boggery – I don't know why. All our friends came to the opening night, ninety people.

I'd been to folk clubs in Birmingham, been to the Campbells' club at Digbeth Civic Hall. I'd seen Harvey Andrews a few times and Diz Disley and I quite fancied the entertainment side. I could play the guitar a bit. I've never been an accomplished musician but I had that desire to get up and entertain. I used to do Tom Lehrer songs – 'Your Hand in Mine', 'Vatican Rag', 'Poisoning Pigeons in the Park' – and I wrote a couple of silly songs. It was nothing, but I did have that ability to relax an audience, which I found out fairly quickly.

Before then I wasn't a kid who told jokes or anything like that. Tom Lehrer was probably the biggest influence in my career. From Tom I learned that you could talk in between songs and that's how I based my act. I learned from him, eventually, how to talk to an audience and not at them. To involve them.

TOM LANE *organiser of Grantham folk club*

We booked Jasper Carrott for £33. He was far more expensive than we would normally pay out, but he certainly brought people in. We got fifty people most weeks, but for him we probably got eighty or ninety. He came on stage – the MC announced him, 'Jasper Carrott' – and he just stood there for about two minutes and he looked at everybody, almost one by one.

He never said a word, just looked at the audience. The place was in uproar. People were doubled up with laughter and he hadn't done anything. Then he said, 'I'm sorry I'm late. I didn't get a lift until I got to Melton Mowbray.' It's not a funny line, but he brought the house down. From then on, he could do whatever he liked, he'd got 'em.

JASPER CARROTT

I realised that, by telling jokes like I did in the early days, you came a cropper. They'd have had Mike Harding or Tony Capstick the week before and they'd have done the gags. You had to have stuff that was personal. That's why I started raconteuring, then nobody could nick the stuff. You live and learn by hard knocks.

I remember doing a club up in Shropshire and dying on my arse because I was trying to be like Tony, doing jokes that were very risqué. He could get away with it – I couldn't. I think it was because you are a reflection of who you are and it wasn't my personality. I learnt a big lesson, to make sure that I didn't step across the line.

It was all one-nights. Everybody thinks I learned my business in Birmingham but in the first five years of my professional career I worked Birmingham three times. I started the agency Fingimigig because I wasn't getting very much work, and I'd got to know Harvey Andrews quite well. So I said, 'I'll start it and I'll push you and myself.' I didn't do tours because of the agency. I was always up in Liverpool, Hull, Portsmouth, the Black Country, Bristol, Plymouth and Exeter, Poynton, and driving back the same night.

I remember starting it in June and I was working five, six nights a month – and in October I worked thirty nights. It was remarkable. It wasn't just through the agency. I was getting work because it went round like wildfire that here was an entertainer that could fill clubs. Harvey was getting a lot of work, then I got other acts and folk clubs. That's how it all started.

For three years the agency lost money. You couldn't make money on 10 per cent. I was working to support the agency. I used to get home from a gig – one o'clock or two o'clock in a morning. At nine o'clock I was up answering the phone, working all day, then four, five o'clock out in the car off to do a gig, come back. I worked myself to bloody death.

I got to the point, it would be about '74, and I had to decide whether I wanted to go on. I'd left the agency and I was earning £35 a night plus expenses, which was quite a lot at that time. John Starkey, who was running the agency with a new partner, came to me and wanted to sign a management deal. I said, 'If we're going to do this, I'm going to have to take a massive step and start charging what Jake Thackray charges.' At that time he charged £75. He did a lot of folk clubs and universities.

Of course, everybody on the folk club circuit laughed their socks off. They weren't going to pay £75 for Jasper Carrott. I'd got three months' work lined up but after that I didn't have a booking, nothing. I did a club in Liverpool, run by Dave Robinson. He gave me my money, £35 plus expenses, and he said, 'We'll book you in again in six months.'

I said, 'You know the fee?' and he said, 'Oh, we're not paying that, stuff yourself.' Then he said, 'I'll tell you what I'll do, I'll pay you £60 against 90 per cent of the door.' That was a hell of a lot of money but I said to Dave, 'Okay, but you tell everybody that you're paying me £75.' I'd worked it out that on the night I'd just done, 90 per cent of the door would have got me seventy-five, probably ninety quid. And once he paid that, the barriers fell down. Then after about nine months I put it up to £100, resistance again. At £100 you were on the limit and there were very few clubs that could afford it. You were down to playing the universities.

MIKE HARDING
I was driving over to Leeds for a gig and listening to the radio, and as I was going through the Pennines I heard this fellow say there's going to be a meeting of the Wild West something – a re-enactment of cowboys and Indians. I had to draw the car over. I was laughing that much. It was a wintery day, sleet coming down, and I just imagined them running round the Lancashire moors dressed as cowboys and Indians. That same night I got up

and I sang, 'It's hard being a cowboy in Rochdale,/ the spurs don't fit right on me clogs./ It's hard being a cowboy in Rochdale,/ 'cos people laugh when I ride past on our Alsatian dog.'

I did it as a throwaway, a chorus with this long introduction I used to do as a piss-take on 'Deck of Cards'. I did it in Cyprus or Germany on a tour with the McCalmans and Wally Whyton, and Ian McCalman said, 'You should write some more verses', so I sat down and wrote four verses to go with the chorus. I sang it and it went down well. In the folk clubs, in its time, it wasn't cutting edge comedy but it was raw enough and it was funny.

I went with Rubber Records for my second album, *Mrs 'Ardin's Kid*, and I noticed on the contract it said you've got to do two singles a year, so I phoned them up and said, 'I've not done the single yet and I've got this song.' I went up and we recorded it. The McCalmans did the 'Red River Valley' humming and I'm doing, 'Never before in the history of mankind has the story been told . . . one man . . . his name . . .'

It was released in the late spring of '75 and I was doing Whitby Festival when Wogan got hold of it, and Pete Murray. They played it and that was it.

JASPER CARROTT

Someone recommended me to DJM Records. They wanted to release an album and they said they'd release a single to see if they could get the name known a bit before the album came out.

They gave me a thousand pounds to record it. At the time I was touring with Chris Rohman, American guy. We were doing universities as a double act and he'd got a song called 'Little Big Bike' which we used to do. I thought, 'I can change that to "Funky Moped"', so that's what we did. Made it for £750 and I'd got £250 to buy a Martin D12-28 guitar. Then the record company said, 'What you gonna put on the B-side?'

The backing group for 'Funky Moped' was Electric Light Orchestra and the producer was Jeff Lynne. 'Magic Roundabout' was a track I had on a private album I'd been selling round the clubs. It was always the most popular thing I did. So I put that on the B-side.

In three weeks it was done and dusted. It sold about 30,000 in the Birmingham area and it was fading away. Then two DJs from Essex walked into DJM Records and they both wanted a hundred copies each of 'Magic Roundabout'. They sold them in the clubs after they'd played it. So DJM sent a copy to every DJ they had on the books and that's what took it up. It sold 850,000 copies and was number five in the charts. It was in the charts for seventeen weeks. And it's still the only hit single with no musical content!

I had about thirty bookings left to do so I fulfilled all the contracts at the original price and then it was time to move on to the concert circuit.

IAN ANDERSON
Fred Wedlock was a local hero in the West Country. He was a teacher, a very intelligent man, well-educated, although with his Bristol accent he disguised it very well. Until the time of his second Village Thing album he didn't want to turn professional.

He was fantastically popular in the West Country. He was slightly different from some of the other guys in that he did funny songs. He did the spiel in between and sometimes went on from there. He just had the skill that some of those guys like Jasper Carrott had – the timing, the context. If you went to see Jasper you might get two songs in a half-hour set. If you saw Fred, you'd get six or seven.

He could make you laugh like a drain with a throwaway line that you'd heard him throw away ten times before. He was very astute at picking up material from other people and bolting it to his own. There was a very funny man from down Southampton way called Alan White, who really should have made it nationally, and there was a guy called Dave Turner from Nottingham. Fred, as well as writing his own stuff, picked up stuff from people like that but very much changed it.

JOHN TAMS

Dave Turner was an absolute original. He did these stream-of-consciousness songs he'd written. He was a good guitarist, a naturally gifted comedian and he did an oblique, surreal comedy that in the sixties was ahead of its time by a decade and a half, if not two. Harding and Carrott and those characters came and that was a show. Dave was ramshackle and blues and jazz and popular culture.

It was either extraordinary, or a bit ordinary. If he was not feeling funny, he'd still try but on another night he'd just floor you. It wasn't rehearsed. It was high risk. He'd sing 'The Wind Cries Mary' and start it off sounding like Hendrix and he'd end with a line 'Bloody 'ell, i'n't it windy'. He was one of the first people I knew who had a heroin addiction.

ROB SHAW *club organiser*

Dave Turner – he used to do that blues thing: 'Looked out of my window, baby, I saw your face. Didn't know you were a window cleaner, baby' and 'Five foot nine from Palestine, he turns the water into wine, has anybody seen JC?'

TREVOR CHARNOCK *committee member, Bradford Topic club*

I booked Diz Disley for a night at the Bradford Topic and he didn't turn up. There were some club organisers there, it was late and he still wasn't there. I said, 'He hasn't turned up.' And these club organisers said, 'We've only come here tonight to see if he does turn up.' They'd all booked him at their clubs and he hadn't turned up for them. I never actually saw him.

MIKE HARDING

Diz Disley turned up late everywhere. He turned up late at the Manchester Sports Guild and Jenks, who ran the MSG, was having a go at him. Diz just said, 'Well, tara then, Jenks, fuck off.' And he walked out. Jenks was a little martinet, a little Hitler, horrible man in many ways, although his bark was worse than his bite and if you faced up to him he'd back down. He ran the Guild with an iron fist and it was a fantastic folk club, packed every night.

MARTIN CARTHY

Diz comes into a pub, asks what does everybody want. They announce what they're going to have and when they've got the drinks in, he reaches in his pocket and he has no money. He says, 'Oh! I don't suppose you'd mind paying for this . . . I find myself between millions.'

DAVE BURLAND

The Engineer at Chalk Farm was run by a short fat bloke who was known as the Singing Toby Jug. It was a highly respected club and I went in on a night off. Disley was there with two really beautiful women in long frocks, like ball gowns – not the sort of thing you see in a folk club most of the time. They were drinking brandy and Babychams.

'David, dear boy,' he said. 'Come and meet my friends. We're drinking brandy and Babychams.' Which was my cue to get 'em in. All the time people are playing and singing, Diz is talking to me and these women. I got a bit edgy, but he didn't bother.

Then the short fat bloke who ran it introduced a young kid who was getting up to do one of his own songs. The lad says, 'I'm very nervous, because I know there are some very famous singers here and I'm a bit nervous about singing my own stuff.'

So the MC says, 'Don't worry about it, young man. We even let blokes like Dave Burland and Diz Disley in.' And Disley puts his head back and looks down his nose at this short fat bloke and says, 'What? Hold your tongue, dwarf.'

Another night he was up on stage and he did this fantastic guitar solo. They clapped him. He said, 'Thank you very much', picked a pint of beer up and drank it all down in one go. He said, 'I'm going to do one by W. C. Handy, and I sincerely hope there is.'

He had another line: 'I only drink because it is a very good cure for a snake bite . . . and I always carry a snake with me.'

HYLDA SIMS

Diz wasn't really a folk singer but he was a great success because
he was such a good performer and a character and such a brilliant
musician, and very funny with tremendous repartee. He managed
to remain very popular although he was always late for everything.

DAVE BURLAND

He had a purple Rolls-Royce. I think he bought it when he lived
with Swarbrick in London. He'd painted it purple but it wouldn't
start and whenever I was with him I had to push it up the road.

BILLY CONNOLLY

He had a grey jacket and a chauffeur's hat. He said, 'You never
get stopped for drunk driving when you wear the chauffeur's
hat.' And he always had unctions and tonics. He had his own
rhyming slang. He was in the Half Moon at Putney and he says
to the landlord, 'Could you sausage me a Gregory?' The guy says
'What?' He says 'Sausage me a Gregory . . . cash me a cheque.'

RICK NORCROSS

One time I went with Diz in his Rolls over to the BBC headquarters
so he could pick up a cheque. We walked up to the front door and
just at that moment there were two guys in monks' clothing
walking out. Big hoods, rope belts, floor-length robes, the whole
nine yards. One of them took a look at Diz and yelled, 'Hello
Disley!' And they grabbed him and started pumping his hand.
It turned out to be Peter Cook and Dudley Moore. It seemed so
bizarre.

   He told me several times about his get-rich plan. He wanted
to ship a vintage Rolls-Royce packed full of Elizabethan chamber
pots to New York City, where he was sure he could make a killing
selling them to antique shops. He swore he could buy hundreds of
them for pennies apiece. I never heard that he'd pulled that one off.

BILLY CONNOLLY

Tony Capstick was a complete one-off. The Highcliffe in Sheffield, that's where I really got to know him. He did this improvised *Under Milk Wood* routine. Oh, I thought I was gonna die. He was funny, Capstick. What a terrible waste of a huge talent.

DAVE BURLAND

Anything Tony turned his hand to, he could do. He could get by on the guitar, he could get by on the banjo, he could sing, he could hold an audience. And when you hear some of the early stuff, he was so politically incorrect – which thank God he remained until he died. He was wonderful. He could fill all the clubs. If they were having a lean patch, they'd book Tony. Over the years he got me in a lot of trouble.

Tony had a great ear for a song. He did the best version of 'To Ramona' that I've ever heard. I've heard it done in a more pretty way but not as soulfully as Tony. He could take the audience with him on a trip – it was almost as if, halfway through when they were enjoying it so much, he'd have to say something to dash it, so he could build it up again.

In 1968 we both decided to try making a living from folk music, although before this Tony began his long association with Radio Sheffield. He presented the folk show, and soon after that Radio 2 beckoned with *Folkweave*.

I remember doing a night in Wolverhampton with him. Dave Pegg, who was then in the Ian Campbell Folk Group, was there and he asked if he could play bass with us. Tony asked him for his references. Another time I was driving home from Liverpool and giving him a lift and he decided to tell me his life story. As we passed Walton Gaol he was a small child, and by the time we arrived in Sheffield, about two hours later, we had got to the age of twelve.

We used to do the Highcliffe on a Saturday night. One night Tony came and he said, 'I've made a ventriloquist's dummy.' I said, 'Okay, whatever', and he brought it in. It was the most horrendous thing you've ever seen – it was full size, like a Guy Fawkes, with a head and a papier mâché face like Adolf Hitler, with a toothbrush 'tache. Where they usually have a little stick on the back of their heads, so they can move their head inside their body, not Capstick, he had a brush stick on it, so he could harangue the front row.

KEITH FOSTER *teenage friend of Tony Capstick*
I knew his family, his stepfather and his mother and all her sisters. They were all crackers. He admired his uncle John – he jumped off a church spire, he thought he could fly. He broke his back and he was nursed by a nun in some religious hospital. She left the order and married him. His uncle Bob hung himself. His mother was an absolute nervous, twitching wreck. His granddad, who was the supreme patriarch of them all, ruled them with an iron fist. He was a Welsh drunk and Methodist lay preacher, an absolute loony. His stepfather was a miner. He was that drunk one day down Mexborough, he rolled across a road and a car ran straight over the top of him and killed him.

Me and Tony started going to folk clubs in Rotherham and Retford in about 1962. We were eighteen. When he got up to sing, his natural personality just came out. He picked the right songs, the emotive ones, the tear-jerkers and the ones with a story at the back of them. He was always a laugh.

Very early on he got twenty-one days consecutive down in the Black Country, round Birmingham. I had a car, so I went with him, drove him. We were living on people's floors, sleeping on sofas, sleeping in the car. We came back after twenty-one days and I was absolutely exhausted. I said, 'Tony, that's the first and last time for me.' He lived like that for years.

Nobody in the folk clubs had thought about telling a joke in between songs, or giving them a bit of chat. Tony was doing it years before Billy Connolly or Mike Harding or any of them. That came from the working men's clubs. As youths we'd go and see top turns – they'd all got a spiel. Tony wanted to do more than play the guitar, he wanted to entertain.

CAROLE CAPSTICK *Tony's first wife*
He loved traditional music. I think he felt inadequate, quite wrongly in my view, in terms of looking at Martin Carthy and Ewan MacColl or other well-known traditional singers. I think he felt he couldn't live up to his own expectations of what a song should be. So the comedy then started to get more of an importance to him.

Comedy wasn't an effort to him and I think that was one of his problems. Because it wasn't an effort, I don't think he valued it as much as the traditional thing. I think he worried sometimes that traditional musicians didn't respect him.

JOHN TAMS
I first came across him playing with the Wayward Boys and then he went solo. There's always an exception to the rule and the finest singer of Ewan MacColl songs was Tony Capstick. He sang MacColl's songs better than MacColl sang them. It's important that we remember Tony not just as one of the great naturally gifted stand-up comics but as a great singer as well. He had a room-filling voice, his 'Punch and Judy Man' was terrific.

JOHN CONOLLY
When he made his *Punch and Judy Man* LP he did two of my songs on it – that, and 'Charlie in the Meadow'. He did cracking versions of both of them and he gave me a copy of the LP. I always say it's one of my proudest possessions, because in Tony's scrawly handwriting it says, 'Dear John, I'm really sorry what I've done to your songs but if you don't like it fuck off.' You came out of the club with sore sides after a Tony Capstick night, a brilliant bloke.

JOHN LEONARD
We did that hit single 'Capstick Comes Home'. Another song, 'The Sheffield Grinder', had been written for a play *The Stirrings in Sheffield on Saturday Night*. Radio Sheffield had got a brass

band to play it and they used it on the radio as their theme tune. I said to Tony, 'Look, why don't we record the actual song?' and I got Carlton Main Frickley Colliery Band, but on the night we recorded it Tony wasn't available.

Then we needed a B-side and they'd got *New World Symphony*, the Hovis advert. I said we'd record that because Tony had got a routine that he played on the guitar, his bit about 'me and me dad'. We recorded it, and the next day I was driving Tony to the studio and I said, 'I want you to do your Hovis routine for the B-side.'

He said, 'It's only thirty seconds long.' So all that stuff about rickets and 'you spawney-eyed, parrot-faced wassock', all that was created in the car on the way to the studio. He scribbled it on the back of a beer mat and he did it more or less in one take. Then we went to the pub.

We thought it was funny, but we didn't know how funny. We didn't even have the confidence to release it as the A-side. Dave Lee Travis heard it and started playing it on Radio 1, then it just took off. Tony never bothered to learn it – eventually he did *Top of the Pops* and he forgot the words. He had to do it three times and by the third time it wasn't funny any more and everybody was pissed off. I was told by the record company afterwards it's the only record ever where sales slowed down after *Top of the Pops*. Tony was not focused on a showbiz career.

BARBARA DICKSON

After 'Capstick Comes Home' was a hit, John Leonard contacted Bernard Theobald, who was at that time my manager, and John spoke to him about getting Tony out there. I was at the very height of – I call it – my pop powers. So Tony came out on tour with me and he was wonderful. I was very privileged to have him as a warm-up and also he was a very nice person to have on the road. It was an education to sit on the tour bus with him, doing crosswords or quizzes. He was so well-informed, I learned so much from him.

DAVE BURLAND

We made a record – him, me and Dick Gaughan – and we did a live thing down in London. We went down and Tony was unusually sober. He made lots of useful suggestions to do with the concert, then he went out about twenty minutes before it was due to start and he managed to get absolutely wrecked – in twenty minutes. Which is a bloody talent, isn't it? He was like a demented lemming on the stage.

He'd done a song on his own, 'The Big Hewer', and he had a cigarette on the end of a string on his guitar. It was considered very cool in them days. He was wandering about the stage while me and Dick were doing 'Jamie Foyers' and I could see this smoke coming up and I could smell burning. I'm doing backing vocals and I can feel this warm sensation on my leg. He'd set my trousers on fire, on the radio!

He was one of those people who engendered a fierce loyalty in me. I once got up with him when he was absolutely pissed at some festival. He wasn't pissed when he'd asked me, but by the time I got up he was shambling about. Afterwards I was pigged off because it hadn't gone well and this bloke came up and said to me, 'You – I'm surprised at you at letting Capstick get you up and he's as drunk as that . . . You should be ashamed of yourself.' I said, 'Don't you talk about my pal like that, I'll fuckin' deck you!' He just brought that out in me.

JASPER CARROTT

When he died it was a big shock. It was one of those moments in life. It set me back, and I sat down and pondered long and hard. He was a very influential artist for me. I learned how to tell a story from Tony Capstick. I was very fond of him, kept in touch with him all the way through. He was a great guy and a good singer and guitarist. Everyone has got a Tony Capstick story. I must have a dozen.

VICKY CAPSTICK *daughter*

I know I was not going to read the obituaries objectively, but a lot of them described his life as a kind of missed opportunity. I just think they missed the point. The life as a young man that he had mapped out for him was to work as a clerk. He met people that fascinated him and he played music and travelled around and he had a good time. He was a bit of a free spirit. It was like they're dissecting someone and saying these bits about him were good, these bits were bad. People liked him because he took a risk and he was provocative, and he didn't follow a script. He was original – and that's what got him in lots of trouble.

JOHN TAMS

I drove up to the funeral with Mick Peat, from the Ripley Wayfarers. We got to the Rockingham Arms at Wentworth, home of the great club that Rob Shaw ran before corporate nonsense overturned it. And lads in dark blue overcoats and dark suits were gathered, solemnly drinking Scotch in the bar. All standing, nobody sat. Nobody said much.

It's not sombre, it's strong. There's a dignity, a Yorkshire strength and dignity there. Then somebody says, 'He's here.' So all the glasses are on the bar, we go out and a hearse is coming down, very slowly. But about 150 feet above it there's something like sixty or seventy crows, weaving and spinning right above the hearse, following it. So we pile in behind the hearse and stroll down, not particularly solemnly, more gunfighterly. Some had even got big hats on. The roads are empty. It could have looked like were going to kick some ass.

So, we go on down to the church and the wheeling crows are still with us. They follow us all the way there and as the coffin's taken out of the hearse and into the church the crows go and kind of roost in the trees round the church, which is overflowing with people wanting to celebrate this hero's life. So the gunfighters all go in and stand at the back.

The service was terrific. Tony's daughter says, 'I'm sorry if you were expecting a Viking funeral, but we won't be setting fire to him today. 'Cos he probably wouldn't burn. Either that or he'll go up in a blue flash.' It was all good-natured and warm and generous.

I'd arranged with half a dozen people at the back that, when he made his exit, we'd cheer and clap. So I set this round going but some of the people nearest to me were slightly overwhelmed by the moment and couldn't bang their hands together. Then it started to build and this little wave became a massive tsunami of cheering and shouting of 'Encore . . . more . . . more' as they carried him out. I had a feeling that Tony might have liked that.

VIN GARBUTT

To sing serious songs, you can overdo the pathos, and if you can lift the audience between songs it means you don't have to sing funny ones. 'Cos I don't fancy funny songs. I never have done. People think I sing funny songs – it's like a psychological thing. They've had a laugh and they go away and tell people, 'Oh, he sings these funny songs.' I don't. Ninety-nine point nine per cent of my songs are all serious ones.

There are two sides, the humour and the drama. Occasionally, I think I've been too funny on stage and it frustrates me. Humour's the lowest common denominator and if people bring friends along to see a comedian, they can't handle the songs. If they bring them along to hear the songs, the humour's a nice treat. I had some T-shirts that were a caricature of me, sitting on a toadstool playing the tin whistle.

MADDY PRIOR

None of it would work without the other. If it was all too serious, it got really dull. I liked all of it. There were lots of skills going on and they were different skills, they weren't comparative or exclusive. There were a lot of good people around and they were very funny. I have to say that my career generally has been one string of laughter. There were some very funny people. I remember seeing Mike Harding do a gig. He was on for two hours, I thought it was just brilliant.

JIM IRVINE

We lost out through all the comics – Mike Harding, Mike Elliott and all them. It changed from being folk clubs to being entertainment. We lost the opportunity when it went on to be places of entertainment. Which is all right, folk music should be entertaining and it is, but it was over-killing it.

TREVOR CHARNOCK

Mike Harding's last night at the Bradford Topic was in 1975. I was doing the door that night and got down to the club at 6 p.m. to set the room out before the audience turned up. I walked into the pub and there were people there already. When I went upstairs they followed me. I had to block the club room door to stop them coming in before I was ready.

I started taking money and giving out tickets. All I saw were hands and money and before I realised it there were 130 in the room and still there was a long queue down the stairs. I had to explain that there was little room inside the club room but they still wanted to get in. Eventually, I had to put the 'House Full' sign up and turn people, including personal friends, away. I worked out later that there were 178 people in the room. It was a good job the fire inspectors didn't call that night.

PHIL BEER

Some people, wrongly I think, ascribed the demise of folk clubs as being to do with the large numbers of entertainers that came in, and many moved on to much bigger things. I don't subscribe to that view. I'll dig my heels in and say they helped keep the thing on the go by diversifying it. If you went to see someone who was a bit of laugh and they entertained you at a folk club, you might be motivated to come back and hear somebody who was purely musical.

13 A slow decline or a new beginning

By the mid-seventies the folk boom was in the past. Gradually, the number of clubs declined as a new generation came of age. To them folk music was not as relevant as it had been to their parents a decade earlier.

The club network, already split between traditional and contemporary, had become fragmented further. In many clubs this created an oppressive atmosphere that did nothing to encourage newcomers.

Many of the performers who had filled clubs in the late sixties and early seventies had moved on. Connolly, Carrott and Harding were playing concert halls, as was Ralph McTell. Barbara Dickson had been in a hit musical in the West End before embarking on a pop career. Christy Moore formed Planxty, who quickly outgrew the clubs. Bert Jansch and John Renbourn were in Pentangle and on the university circuit. Then America called – as it did for the Incredible String Band and the Strawbs.

Robin and Barry Dransfield split in 1971 just as they were about to sign a lucrative record deal with Warner Brothers. Both went on to work solo and with others but they never recaptured the magic that had delighted club audiences and brought about their astounding debut album, The Rout of the Blues.

One man who was back in the clubs and popular as ever was Martin Carthy. His dalliance with Steeleye Span and folk rock behind him, in 1973 he married Norma Waterson and joined the Watersons, who had recently returned to singing together after a four-year break.

A winter of power cuts in 1974 caused Ashley Hutchings to disband the Albion Band, lay down his electric bass, form the acoustic Etchingham Steam Band and head for the folk clubs. Two years later, with John Tams alongside, he formed a second version of the Albion Band, an ongoing outfit that has seen many changes over the years.

Maddy Prior, following the success of Steeleye Span, was offered the opportunity of a solo project by Chrysalis Records. The result was a collaboration with June Tabor and the critically acclaimed Silly Sisters album in 1976.

Later in the decade June Tabor toured and made three albums with Martin Simpson, whose extraordinary talent as a guitarist was already apparent. He turned professional at the age of seventeen, just a couple of years after Vin Garbutt. Differing in approach, both would become major draws in the clubs.

As newcomers were staking their claims, in early 1982 one of the most popular performers on the scene, Nic Jones, came close to death in a late-night road crash while returning home from a gig. If there was need for a reminder of the precarious nature of the professional folk musician's life, of the hard travelling, of the perils of the road – this was it.

JASPER CARROTT

I think folk clubs started to drop off when the entertainment moved away – Billy Connolly and Mike Harding, when they started to go away from the clubs. That network moved away and I don't think the traditional folk could entertain in such a broad spectrum. What happened was the movement towards entertainment solidified the traditional artists to become much more protective, and that's what survived.

BILLY CONNOLLY

I had always thought that the future was beyond the folk clubs and the Humblebums. We were in Queen Street railway station in Glasgow, we were going up to the east, to Fife and Aberdeen, and I said to Gerry, 'I think we've taken this thing about as far as it will go. I think we should just do another tour for the money and then split. I'll give it three or four months and see if I can exist.' Then he came back to me the following day as if it was his idea. He said, 'Listen, I've got this idea . . .' It was a groundhog day.

CHRIS EUESDEN *singer and club organiser*
The folk clubs began to slip away somewhere around the mid-seventies. The political side of it was taken away so you didn't have that underlying hard core and the hipness of it went, because punk came in and punk did take over that political angle. Young people were going to see punk bands rather than going to folk clubs. Times had changed. The folk clubs that really survived during that period were the real traddie clubs, because they just stayed as they always had done, and they're still there today

IAN ANDERSON
Somewhere in the late seventies, when it all started to go pear-shaped, quite a lot of those people who had been very serious traddies took the corks out of their arses and lightened up. The other warring factions probably didn't. The traditional music people suddenly opened their doors, whereas the people who were interested in entertaining, or were singer-songwriters, didn't.

As well as that, a lot of people had come out of the punk scene and were looking around for something else to be interested in. They weren't interested in what was in the charts and it's interesting how many of them went into either world music or the folk scene.

ROB SHAW
We opened at the Rockingham Arms at Wentworth, near Rotherham, in September 1974. At that time there were clubs that you couldn't take instruments in, clubs that you couldn't sing in, only play instrumental music, and in some clubs you could only play traditional music and only contemporary music in others. We decided to make it as broad a church as possible.

We charged what four pints of beer cost and there were sixty or sixty-five there the first night. We ran fortnightly for three years, then we moved to every week.

ROY BAILEY

People claimed folk clubs went into decline in the seventies. I never experienced that. I don't mean this vainly, but whenever I went to a folk club there were quite a lot of people in, and young people. I was often told by the organiser, 'We don't usually get these people in.' He didn't mean the number. He meant the age. I was attracting youngsters who weren't particularly folkies.

When I moved to Sheffield Polytechnic in 1972, David Blunkett was leader of the Labour Group of Sheffield City Council and he would ask me to sing at events. So, quite unconsciously, I was developing an audience round the country which sustained me through a period when people were saying, 'Everyone's getting older . . . They're going to be dying off . . . There won't be folk clubs in ten years . . .'

MIKE WATERSON

We split up in '68. We'd had enough. Lal moved to Leeds. I stayed in Hull and I wasn't singing so much. I wasn't singing with the family and I started to write. Lal started to write as well and, when she came back to Hull, she said, 'I've written some songs – would you like to hear them?' I said, 'Yeah', and I listened to them and I said, 'I've written some songs, would you like to hear them?' And right out of the blue we'd both started writing songs. I think it was missing the singing that did it.

I had a great difficulty: everybody wanted me to sing Watersons songs, on my own. And they didn't get it. I learned a completely new repertoire of songs I wanted to sing, solo stuff. Then Norma came back. Martin came and did the club. Norma and Martin fell in love 'cos Martin was getting divorced at the time, so things clicked along those lines.

Martin loved the songs that we'd written and said, 'Why don't you make an LP of them?' We said, 'Well, it's not English folk music.' He said, 'It doesn't matter.' So we made *Bright Phoebus* – and the big mistake in our lives was not to put it on stage. We could have done big concerts doing *Bright Phoebus* and we could have still done the folk clubs singing our traditional stuff. We never thought about being two separate entities. People said, 'You're betraying the tradition.' No we weren't, it was just another part of us.

NORMA WATERSON

When we split up I went to live in Montserrat in the West Indies. The night I came home it was a folk night at the Rugby Club. That was the first time the three of us, Michael, Lal and myself, had been together for the four years that I was away. We got to the club and were having a drink and somebody said, 'Come on give us a song', so we stood up and sang a couple of songs, the first time we'd sung together for four years.

Bernie Vickers then came to sing with us but that didn't work out very well and by this time I was courting Martin. It was a very short courtship. We only went out together for about a month and we were married, and it seemed a natural thing for Martin to come into the group because he was part of the family, and that's how that happened.

MARTIN CARTHY

I married Norma in '72, the Albion Country Band finished in August '73 and I did my first gig with the Watersons, having done the odd one when I had a night off. I'd become a fifth Waterson with Norma, Lal and Mike and Bernie Vickers, then Bernie left and I was the fourth member of the Watersons from about September '73.

NORMA WATERSON

We were invited by Jean Oglesby, who was Bob Davenport's wife at that time, to sing at the Shaw Theatre. We did two nights and that was it. The offers came in thick and fast.

MARTIN CARTHY

We did all the clubs. In fact we did mostly clubs. They had changed. They were very much coasting and they were a bit self-satisfied. I can't say that I wasn't self-satisfied, people know I was. When the bubble burst in the second half of the seventies a lot of clubs and a lot of groups went to the wall who probably would not have needed to, had people taken note earlier.

Ultimately, it was a good thing. It did separate the wheat from the chaff, and it did make one look at one's repertoire and say, 'Come on, be really honest about that song.' And you'd say, 'No, it's no good', and toss it aside.

ROY GULLANE

Folk clubs are the lifeblood of traditional music. Everybody should do them. That's where everybody should start. The first time we played in England, it was in Carlisle, the Coach and Horses. We played that when we still had day jobs. We drove back through the night. Then we used to come down to the Lake District quite early on. I always had the feeling that English audiences knew a bit more, were a bit more knowledgeable.

The clubs, for me, teach people not only how to play, they teach you how to perform. There are so many great musicians nowadays, but so few of them are actual performers. I think when you have an apprenticeship in the clubs behind you, you become a better performer.

ROBIN DRANSFIELD

Barry never got on with being on the road, and the constant going round the folk clubs was something that he was beginning to find very tedious, even though he liked the folk clubs themselves. The travelling and all the hassles he didn't like, so we said, 'Why don't we try and get into doing bigger venues? Cut down on the folk clubs a bit and see if we can do more concerts?'

Barry said, 'How are we going to do that?' I said, 'I'm going to ring Jo Lustig.' At that time he had Ralph McTell and Pentangle.

Barry said, 'He'll not be interested in us', so I rang Jo Lustig and three days later we went round and signed a contract.

We were only with him for about six months because my brother then, for reasons best known to himself, decided he didn't want to be in the duo any more. He wanted to pack it in. Jo signed us in the summer of '71. At that point I, on my own, had managed to set up a couple of gigs in North America for me and Barry. One was a concert in Philadelphia and the other was the Toronto Folk Festival.

While were over there doing that, Jo was setting up an autumn tour for Ralph McTell and me and Barry. It was a really good tour. He set up a deal where we were signed direct to Warner Brothers in California, which was quite a coup. We were the first English folkies to be signed directly like that.

We did the tour with Ralph in America and my brother decided during the tour that he didn't want to tour any more, he wanted to get pissed and find a ten-foot blonde, as he put it. So at the end of the tour we split up. Ralph tried his damnedest to not let us do that, but the thing that really finished it was, Jo wanted us to go off and do a tour in America with Mary Hopkin, who'd just had the big hit with 'Those Were the Days'.

I was prepared to do it and Barry wasn't. He said, 'I'm off.' That was about November '71. That actually coloured our entire history afterwards, because when we started putting a band together and trying to get a deal for the album nobody would touch us. We ended up taking it to Transatlantic because nobody else would do it.

I effectively had a nervous breakdown. I'd put the whole of my life and energies into the duo, trying to keep it together with Barry not being very well a lot of the time, and not liking being on the road, and me being the prime organiser and the driver. I was absolutely devastated by it. For about six months I went and lived with Dave and Toni Arthur and roadied for them and mooched about. Then I started singing again the following autumn.

DAVE DEIGHTON

I knew Barry Dransfield from the Barley Mow in Sheffield. I took him home one night after a gig to sleep on my parents' settee, then I shared a bedsit with him in Putney. I was looking for a job and he said what he was doing – making harps. I'd been an apprentice toolmaker in Sheffield, so I went along to where he worked and he got three months' work for me, making threads for Erards – classical harps.

Barry wasn't gigging at the time but the Dransfields' album was out, *Rout of the Blues*. Every time he went into a folk club, everybody knew who he was. He'd get up and do spots but I think he was going through a funny period. He went back home to Harrogate on the train, in his pyjamas.

JOHN LEONARD

In the early seventies I did three or four years as a professional folk singer, working the clubs all over the place with John Squire. We were doing at least twenty gigs a month, all over the country. When we eventually packed in, it was because John wanted to go to teacher training college. I'd got a job at Radio Sheffield, so we cut down to eight gigs a month and for years that's what we did.

We survived the decline in the folk clubs in the seventies, because we were limiting ourselves to eight gigs a month. We were working for £25 to £30 a gig between us. I was paying my mortgage and making a living. I remember John saying, 'If petrol goes up to fifty pence a gallon, we'll have to pack in.'

STEVE TILSTON

There was a period in the seventies when, as a contemporary songwriter-guitar player, you weren't made very welcome. I did become disillusioned. Looking back I can sympathise with it, really. It went all entertainment or very staunch trad.

A lot of my income came from universities and I put a small band together with Matt Irvine on bass and Hamish Stuart on guitar. Hamish became the lead singer with the Average White

Band. We did a tour of the universities. By then the folk scene was starting to polarise – there were some clubs that were definitely traditional, some that liked entertainers, comedians – then the contemporary thing was starting to get short shrift. The grizzled old traddies didn't like young whizz-kid guitar players singing about wearing their heart on their sleeve.

MARTIN SIMPSON

Early seventies, I started to play in the London clubs. I can still remember the hours and hours and hours of being on the phone. I would go through the listings. When I was anywhere, I'd pick up a folk magazine or the folk directory, then I'd just sit and call.

There is nothing quite as heartbreaking as calling up and saying, 'Hello, it's Martin Simpson, would you like to book me?' 'No!' It was that thing of, 'Why should we?' Always on the English folk scene, the rarest of creatures was an agent – and the really rarest of all creatures was a good agent.

CLIVE PALMER

The guy who ran the Half Moon in Putney, Bill Knox, he also ran an agency. He was known as Two Books Billy because he was always getting the gigs wrong. He'd book you at the right gig on the wrong night in the right place, or the right night in the wrong place.

We had a residency at the Half Moon with COB – Clive's Original Band – in the early seventies. We built it up from nothing. There were about ten people there the first night and we built it up to 300. It was just COB – me, Mick Bennett and John Bidwell. We didn't have guests but people used to come down. The last time I saw Sandy Denny she was standing outside the Half Moon with Rod Stewart. They went off together in a white Rolls-Royce.

BERNARD WRIGLEY

I was in the audience at a Fairport gig at Bolton Tech about '73 and a bloke came up. He said, 'Are you Bernard Wrigley?' I said,

'Yes.' He said, 'The group's not turned up to do the support.' I said, 'Oh. I've bought a ticket.' He said, 'We'll give you your money back.' I said, 'I've not got my stuff.' I went home and got my stuff, came back and did the opening spot, thirty or forty minutes. I don't think Fairport turned up until I'd finished.

JASPER CARROTT

Diz Disley phoned me. He said, 'Look, Stéphane Grappelli's in Paris at this bloody posh hotel and playing for sod all. I'm trying to persuade him to come over. Could you get him any work?' So I arranged a tour in the folk clubs. He came over. He did about seven or eight clubs – the Boggery was the first one and it was the first time he'd played with a guitar-based quartet in twenty-five years. This would be about 1973. The interest was enormous. I had people wanting to come from all over the country and he sold out. That's what kicked off Stéphane Grappelli's resurgence.

It was a big night for us. I got there very early to set the chairs out and put the equipment up and there was a kid hanging around. He looked about twelve. I said, 'Can I help you?' He said, 'I want to see 'Stéphane Grappelli.' I said, 'So does the world. Have you got a ticket?' He said, 'No.' I said, 'Well we are sold out.' He said, 'It's all right, can I just hang around until he comes?' 'Yes, all right.'

I went to fetch Stéphane from the hotel and we were walking towards the entrance door and he saw this kid. It was like he was his long-lost son. He grabbed him, he hugged him and he took him into the dressing room. I didn't think anything about it. Then he said, 'Can you find him a seat?'

So Stéphane Grappelli does the first half with Diz Disley, another guitarist and a bass player, has a break, comes back on for the second half and after about two numbers he introduces this kid up on stage. He'd got a violin – where that came from I'll never know. This kid starts playing and he's sensational. He did the whole of the second half – he was sensational, he just blew everybody apart. It was Nigel Kennedy.

That's what the Boggery did, it really led the way. We were responsible for expanding folk clubs into more entertainment clubs. Joe Brown, when he had his band Brown's Home Brew, he came to the Boggery. He got there about four o'clock in the afternoon, he looked round, went, 'Oh, nice dressing room.' I said, 'No, this is where you'll play.' We had 280 in. They were standing on the tables.

CHRIS EUESDEN
Round about '72, we had Bully Wee booked at the Great Longstone club in Derbyshire and they didn't show. We thought, 'What are we going to do now?' The room was full and it just happened that Luke Kelly was in the audience, because the Dubliners were doing a week at the Fiesta in Sheffield and they'd got a night off. He'd come out there with friends but when he saw that we didn't have a guest, he rang up the Dubliners and they came out and did the night.

They were all there apart from Ronnie Drew, and they brought two other guys who were relatives, really good players. So the Dubliners did the night. They weren't bothered about the money. I gave it to the two lads who'd come with them. It was fantastic, at that time they were right at the top of their popularity. That sort of thing embodied the spirit of what it was like then.

SEAN CANNON
When the Dubliners had 'Seven Drunken Nights' I watched it on black-and-white TV. I was quite chuffed that an Irish band had got in the charts. The first time I saw them perform, I went to a show in 1966 at the Gate Theatre, *Finnegan Wakes*.

Then one day in 1980 I got home and my wife said, 'You've had a call from the Dubliners. They want you to give them a ring.' I rang them they said, 'We want you to come up to Edinburgh and sing with us.' They were touring Britain and Ronnie's father had died, so he had to go back to Ireland for the funeral.

I said, 'Well I don't know the keys or anything.' They said,

'Don't worry, it'll be spontaneous.' I caught the fast train but a cow was on the line at Prestonpans and I didn't get to the theatre until ten minutes before the concert started. I went straight on with them. It was very spontaneous. Then I did Blackburn and the Crucible in Sheffield and Ronnie came back.

In '82 I got another call, saying Luke had a problem with a tumour, would I care to go on tour in Germany. I cancelled one or two gigs I had and I've been with them ever since.

JIM McLEAN

Dominic Behan had brought the Dubliners to Phil Solomon at Major Minor. They had 'Seven Drunken Nights' and they suddenly took off. I was working with Major Minor as a songwriter on £20 a week to write pop songs and I'd known Luke Kelly from way back. Then they shot up the charts and they needed a road manager. I said, 'I'll do it' and I got a telegram saying meet them at Stockport, £20 a week but you've got to find your own board.

They got a big advance from the secretary to go back to Ireland for a break. Next thing she got a phone call from Ronnie Drew saying could she send more money to them. She said, 'They've probably not got the fare back from Ireland.' Ronnie said, 'No, we haven't left yet. We're still in Liverpool.' They spent the money before they even got on the boat.

ASHLEY HUTCHINGS

I was in Fairport and Steeleye doing concerts, and then in '74 we formed the Etchingham Steam Band with Shirley Collins, who was my wife, and made the journey back into the folk clubs. That was a real baptism of fire for me, 'cos I'd never been without a mike in my life.

It wasn't a total shock to the system, I'd been to many, many folk clubs, but to actually perform in a club without an amplifier, without a PA, was strange. We had a couple of years with it. It was good. I enjoyed it.

SHIRLEY COLLINS

We did quite a few clubs, mostly in the south-east because of the shortage of petrol. Our first booking was by candlelight – in Southampton, I think – because there was a power cut at the time. That was the main reason the Etchingham Steam Band was formed, there were a lot of power cuts at that time. There was no electricity needed as Ashley played an Earthwood acoustic bass.

We did a short tour of the West Country. That line-up, which included Richard Thompson, Simon Nicol and John Kirkpatrick, was put together at the last minute when my sister, Dolly, had to pull out because of illness. It was more Albion Band than Etchingham Steam Band. We had such a good time. I only wish it had been recorded by someone in the audience.

JULIE MATTHEWS *singer-songwriter, in duo with Chris While since 1997*

I was playing at Stainsby festival in 1990 and Ashley was looking for a keyboard player. He approached me and said, 'Do you fancy joining the Albion Band?' I didn't know who the Albion Band was. I knew Phil Beer, who was in the band, and he gave me a ring and said, 'Look, this could be a really good break for you.'

It's funny, you do get exposure – but you're always a member of the Albion Band. I left and rejoined, and Chris [While] was in the band and we were writing together. It got to the point where we thought, 'Well, actually, we can break away', and that's when everything took off for me and Chris.

MARTIN SIMPSON

In late 1975 I played a gig where I was on the same bill as a comedian. It was one of those gigs where I just thought, 'What the fuck am I doing here?' I was really depressed. People didn't want to hear what I was doing. They just wanted to guffaw. I thought, 'If it's going to be like this, I don't know what I'm going to do.' The next night Bill Leader came to the gig and said,

'Barbara Dickson told me I should come and see you. I'd like to make a record with you.'

The record came out at the beginning of '76 and by the middle of '76 Tony Secunda, who at the time was managing Steeleye Span, he took me on and briefly managed me. I made another record, which never came out, then I opened for Steeleye. So in six months I went from playing the upstairs room at the Frog and Afterbirth to two nights at the Hammersmith Odeon.

In early '77 I was approached by June Tabor's manager. The manager called up and said, 'Look, June Tabor's going out on tour and she'd like you to play the guitar for her.' So I went to Tony Secunda and said, 'June Tabor's asked me to go on tour with her.'

He said, 'You're not fackin' doin' it. You're a star.' I said, 'Sorry?' He said, 'You're a star. You're not fackin' playing guitar for fackin' birds.' I said, 'Okay, Tony' and I left. Shortly after that he tried to get me to assign my publishing over to him – for life. I saw him twice again, he came to a gig in Califonia. Then he died.

Tony Secunda kinda put the mockers on what I could do for a while. I just gigged. I worked with June. I was playing on a bunch of records. I worked at the National Theatre for about a year in *Lark Rise to Candleford*. It was one of those gigs where people came and went. I took over from Martin Carthy in the role. Then June and I made *A Cut Above* in 1980.

TREVOR CHARNOCK

June Tabor – what a voice! I first saw her do a floor spot at Chester Festival in 1975. She was not a booked guest – she was just there as a punter. She swept across the floor in a flowing dress and did two songs. The second time I saw her was the following month at Keele Festival, she finished with 'And the Band Played Waltzing Matilda'. When it ended you could hear a gnat break wind, then the applause came. It was a good job that she was the last act. Nobody could have followed that.

June made me aware of Eric Bogle by singing 'And the Band Played Waltzing Matilda'. I think at that time not many people in England would have heard him. When he toured in 1980 I missed out on booking him at the Topic, but I saw him quite a lot during his tour at clubs and festivals and I said to him that next time he was coming to England to let me know in good time. We finally got him in Bradford in March 1982. It was a packed club and a magic night. Six years on from deciding we should book him, it had happened.

JUNE TABOR

I met Maddy when I was at Oxford and we became friends. We used to see each other occasionally and we were at a festival somewhere. It was the final concert on a Sunday afternoon. We were sitting at the back singing all the choruses and she said to me, 'Why don't we try singing together?' 'Yes, that's a good idea.' So the very next week she came round to my house and it was, 'Right, what shall we do?' We were both quite keen on Bulgarian women's singing, so we thought, 'Let's apply that to an English song.' I said, 'What about "The Four-Loom Weaver"?' So we tried that with the harmonies and what we came up with is what's on the record.

MADDY PRIOR

It was the Bromyard Festival, me and June were somewhat drunk at the back of the tent and started singing harmonies on choruses and we said, 'Oh, we should do some stuff together.' We started off by doing Bulgarian songs, which is why a lot of our harmonies went in the direction that they did. We did gigs but we did a few floor spots as well.

JUNE TABOR

We kept working on it. We did about four songs, and occasionally, if I had a gig and Maddy came along, she'd just appear from the audience and we did the four songs. Archie Fisher said after hearing us, 'The overtones would have deafened a dog.' I quite liked that.

After a couple of years of doing this for fun we had a small repertoire together. Then Steeleye had a couple of hits and Chrysalis said to them, 'If anybody in the band would like to do a project album . . .' and Maddy said she'd like to do hers with me. So we then rehearsed – all of this had to take place in my annual holiday from the library – Andy Irvine, Johnny Moynihan, Danny Thompson and Gabe McKeon, the piper. He'd just won the All-Irish and he'd never been to London before.

I'd never been in a proper recording studio. The record coming out and getting such a reception – it was quite extraordinary. They didn't want us to do a tour. They didn't actually want Maddy to do the album, so we played in some rather strange places which were not commensurate with the fuss that had been made. There were a couple of discos . . . There was one that was like an Alpine village – it was in Liverpool or Newcastle.

Tony Secunda decided that we ought to have an opening act but he didn't want any other music, so we had either a magician or a juggler. It killed the audience. Then Maddy and I had to go out and start with 'Four-Loom Weaver'. We were so nervous.

We did Wakefield Town Hall, where Danny threw his Easter egg at the audience. The audience were leaving at the end and he'd been given an Easter egg with his name on it by the crew, and he threw it at them. There were pieces of chocolate and letters of his name all over the floor and the chairs. He threw it because he wanted to do an encore.

After that it was back to the folk clubs, unaccompanied.

NEIL WAYNE *founder of the Free Reed record label*
Peter Bellamy came to me in the mid-seventies with *The Transports* because Topic and Leader had turned him down, saying it was way too expensive. I knew him through concertinas. He told me who was going to be on it, showed me the libretto, the songs and a few images and tapes. I thought, 'Well, it's got Australian connections. It's got all the big names of the folk scene.' I said I would do it as a double album and he went, 'Really? Two LPs?'

Because of Peter's intensity and vanity about this project, he'd pointed at all the leading lights in the folk scene and said, 'You're in it . . .you're in it . . .you're in it.' I had little to do with the making of the records, though I had to drive to Cropredy and find Dave Swarbrick in his house and bring him back, because the fiddle player they'd got couldn't play. Swarbrick saved the day. 'Four hundred quid, it'll cost you,' he said.

I was told by Peter, 'We'll do it at Nick Kinsey's studio. I don't want you there. I just want you to come at the end of every week with your cheque book.' It cost a fortune. I don't recall how much but it took about eight weeks to record and the bank were summoning me every morning and laying ten cheques on the counter, saying, 'You can choose two today that we'll pay.' It sold about four to five thousand in five years, before I had to close the business in 1981. That was good for a double LP on a small label.

DAVE SWARBRICK

The *Telegraph* printed an obituary of me in 1999, said I'd died. So I had copies made and sold 'em at gigs. I sold them as long as I could. I used to sign 'em 'RIP Dave Swarbrick'. Then Jill, my wife, got the heebie-jeebies. She thought it was tempting fate. It's pretty rare for people to get an autographed obituary.

ROB SHAW

We had Dave Swarbrick and Beryl Marriott at the Rock in 1980 and Dave snapped his fiddle. He was playing it, next to last song in the first set, and the neck just snapped in two, flew over his shoulder and hit the door behind the stage. He'd only brought one fiddle and the club was packed, so he played the last song on his mandolin, and Robin Garside drove home, brought his fiddle back and Dave played it in the second half. Swarbrick, back then, had a permanent cigarette in his mouth and he put a burn on the fiddle. Robin made him sign it 'Swarbrick did this'.

IAN ANDERSON

All through the seventies Fred Woods was running *Folk Review* and it was slowly dying, partly because the club scene was dying. I'd been writing for it, doing record reviews and Fred approached me and said he was looking for somebody to take over, would I be interested? I got a little team together and we were very excited, but then we saw the books and we decided it made more sense to start a new magazine.

At that time, going round the clubs, you could tell that the regions of the country that had the most alive folk scenes also had good regional magazines. There seemed to be a correlation between the two – the better the local magazine, the better folk scene. So we started *Southern Rag* for the central south of England and that was all we intended to be.

But what happened – there wasn't a national magazine and so people started reading it nationally and then internationally and it just grew and grew and in the end it became obvious it had to be a national magazine. So we went monthly and we changed the title to *Folk Roots*, then later *fRoots*.

DAVE BURLAND

The gigs fell off, coming up to the eighties. They were becoming harder to come by and clubs started closing down. It had run its popular course in a way, but it never really died out and now it's reinvented itself. To me, whatever happens now, that first rush when there were few guests and a lot of local performers – that was a golden age.

It was the social thing. It felt like belonging to something that was worthwhile. At one time in the seventies I very naively thought it might change the world. I thought it might make people nicer to each other – which was very naive! People laugh about flower power and there weren't many full-blown hippies in South Yorkshire, but I couldn't see much wrong with what they were espousing, as it were. Some great music came out of it.

JOHNNY HANDLE

There's a Tuesday club at Kiveton Park and I had a little green Citroën, very bright green. I was teaching and doing gigs and I thought, 'I'll get there early.' The last time there'd been traffic and I was late, so I got there at seven o'clock, parked in the car park and I was knackered so I went to sleep. Woke up at quart' to nine.

I staggered up and they said, 'Bloody 'ell, you'll have to do the whole of the second act . . .' I said, 'Hold on – I was parked just next to the entrance, snoring in me Citroën Dyane, with an accordion on the back seat. Didn't nobody see us?' Then odd ones said, 'Ah, we did, but you looked that tired we let you sleep.' I did a good second half though – and they booked me again.

NIC JONES

I came back from Glossop Folk Club in Manchester and I fell asleep. I hit a lorry full of bricks. I'd got a fairly new car, a Volkswagen, and in my other car the heater had never worked. It was a wreck of a car, a Ford Cortina, and I think the heater worked too well in my new car and it sent me to sleep. All my body on the right-hand side was smashed to bits. Everything collapsed. I think the only thing working was my heart.

IAN CAMPBELL

In 1978 our banjo player John Dunkerley, who'd been with us since he was sixteen and was now thirty-four, died of leukaemia. At the same time my sister Lorna and her husband Brian divorced. So suddenly there was no group. Brian had gone off, there was only me and Lorna and she said, 'I've had it really. We've done it all. We don't want to form another group. I fancy going to university.' I said, 'So do I.' I applied and got a place in Warwick University to study theatre studies.

It wasn't that simple, because we had outstanding bookings for at least a year ahead. We'd done some work with two young musicians who were happy to work with us, so we carried on doing one or two things, then we got a trip to Canada in 1981 or '82. An old bass player who'd been with us in the sixties was now established as a teacher in Calgary. We went a storm, so off and on for another four years we took bookings here and there. In '84, Lorna and myself – we were doing benefits in the Miners' Strike.

ROB SHAW

There were times during the Miners' Strike – anybody who'd got a NUM card or a Students' Union card, I was letting in free, just to get numbers in. A lot of the artists, Dick Gaughan and people, they knew the situation and that we had to keep the club going and they helped me out tremendously. I've always thought, if things are going right, never downgrade – get the best people you can afford because then people other than the regulars will come. We did that for quite a while.

JOHNNY HANDLE

I'd decided not to go full time. Because you need to be out and about and not coming home as much as you would. And if you're on the road, you have to rely on close relationships at home, and they have to be strong so you can slip back into them. It's the personal relationships that you have with your family – some things have to go. You lose perspective because you're so into folk music you forget that there's other forms of music and other forms of entertainment. So you can become a weirdo very quickly.

I've never regretted it. In the seventies it was sad to see people scrabble for work. There were more performers coming out of the woodwork and less bums on seats and it's gone on like this until the arty-farty scene took over. Now your future's in the festivals and the arts side, but the arts side is gonna collapse, with the government funding. The hard way is sometimes the best way – doing some gigs, doing some more gigs, building a solid grounding, the way Vin Garbutt used to go everywhere before he started getting gigs.

VIN GARBUTT

Since 1978 I have had a full diary. It's been fantastic. The London folk clubs had packed in during the eighties, most of them, a big folk recession. It never affected me, only in London. I weathered the storm.

For my generation of folk singers, to cross the 'bed barrier' was notable. It came with your fee. About 1980 I got my first hundred quid and from then on I noticed that I always got a bed instead of a settee or a floor. Once you charged £100 it was a case of, 'Oh, we can't put him on the floor, he's got £100.' I can tell you the club where I broke the £100 barrier: it was the Empress of Russia in London. That's where the bed barrier was crossed. I like staying with organisers but I need a break now and again so I stay in hotels.

NOEL MURPHY

Back in '78 I was offered a one-off show on Southern Television, the sort of stuff that goes out at four o'clock in the morning. The producer said, 'It'll be recorded live in Southampton in front of an audience, the usual sort of people who go to everything.' I said, 'Well, do me a favour. Get as many tickets as you can sent out to the local folk clubs. That way we'll have an audience that's on side.' He said, 'Leave it with me.'

So we're backstage, me and a fiddle player and a flute player I'd brought along, and Felix Bowness, who was later the jockey in Hi-de-Hi, was the warm-up man. While he was out there it seemed very flat and as he's coming off and we're going on he says to me, 'Good luck mate, I think most of them are dead.'

I went on and, God, they were. The place was packed and they were all wrapped up in rugs, all slumped and dozing. We got them going a bit with the fiddle and the songs but I found out afterwards that the producer had got a new secretary and instead of sending all the tickets out to folk clubs, she'd sent them to old folks' homes.

ROBIN DRANSFIELD

I moved down to Cornwall in 1986 and decided I didn't want to do it any more. I didn't want to be a part-timer again because you can't give it your proper attention and I wouldn't have been happy doing it on that level.

The folk clubs were at a low point in the mid-eighties. They'd lost a lot of impetus and the audience numbers had gone down and down. Unless you were Martin Carthy or Vin Garbutt or the other star performers who have always pulled a crowd, you were singing to fifteen people sometimes, whereas ten years earlier you'd done the same club and you were singing to 200. It was before the rise of the folk festivals. There were just a few then, while there's three every weekend now, nearly every weekend of the year.

14 Following in footsteps

When children grow up with parents who are professional folk singers or musicians, some of them inevitably take the same route. The music is all around them. They are taken along to gigs and festivals and they often become friendly with the children of other folk people. So in the same way that folk songs and tunes are passed down, one generation of a family can influence the next in their musical taste and direction

From an early age Eliza Carthy's musical destiny seemed apparent. Yet both her parents, Martin Carthy and Norma Waterson, have children from previous marriages who have not gone into folk music. In her mid-teens, Eliza formed a duo with another young fiddler, Nancy Kerr, whose mother Sandra had been a student of Ewan MacColl. For many years Nancy Kerr and James Fagan have been partners; he spent his childhood in Australia, playing with his family band, the Fagans.

The Lakeman brothers' parents, while not professional singers, were very active in folk clubs in north London and later Devon. Sam, Sean and Seth began performing as a family band, as did the five Deighton children, taught from an early age by father Dave, a blues guitarist who turned to fiddle and melodeon.

Tom Paley did not influence his son Ben to take up the fiddle, but the records he made with the New Lost City Ramblers did, and Tom, hitherto a banjo and guitar player, soon afterwards started to play the fiddle himself.

There are more: Derek Sarjeant, stalwart of the early sixties scene, and his son Chris, singer-songwriters Steve Tilston and daughter Martha, Chris While and daughter Kellie who replaced her in the Albion Band. In each case the baton has been passed on.

But just because one generation of a family took up folk

does not mean that the next will. Times change and tastes in music move on. What attracted Eliza Carthy, Nancy Kerr, the Lakemans, the Deightons and all the rest when they were children did not have the same effect on the sons of Ian Campbell or John Foreman, who have had highly successful careers in rock bands.

Blair Dunlop, son of Ashley Hutchings and singer Judy Dunlop, showed no interest in folk music until his teenage years and then not directly through parental influence. But as Hutchings fondly recalls, when he passed on leadership of the Albion Band to his twenty-year-old son in early 2012, it was like the family business was being taken over.

ELIZA CARTHY *singer and fiddler, daughter of Martin Carthy and Norma Waterson, vice-president of the EFDSS*
There were a lot of pubs when I was growing up. I guess some of them were folk clubs and some of the time it was just the pub. My parents were never big on playing in sessions, apart from at Bampton when we went to see the dancing at Whitsun. Then we would sit in the sessions and play.

I remember trips to different places, going to the Edinburgh folk club when I was quite young. My dad was singing there and I remember getting a bottle of Coke and a packet of crisps in the car park. You know, in the summer when they've got a gig and you want to play outside. I remember folk club-style singarounds at the National Folk Festival from being really small, where it would be the same format as a club but part of a festival.

I realised very early on that my family were special in folk music – the way we all used to pile in to the Whitby Festival, so many of us. We'd have our big table in the Spa and everybody would be looking at us. When you're a kid it does make you feel really special. I was kinda very po-faced and reverential about it. I treated it as a kinda duty, a sort of destiny, a continuous line back through the gypsies in our family and the family on my dad's side.

SAM LAKEMAN *brother of Seth and Sean, son of Geoff and Joy Lakeman, residents in the sixties at Herga folk club in London*
My earliest memories of folk clubs are sitting quietly with a glass of lemonade and a packet of crisps with Sean and Seth in a corner of various clubs. I couldn't tell you which ones. I can't have been more than four and it seemed to be the most natural thing to see our mum and dad get up and wander over to the front of the room and sing a song or two. It was always an extremely friendly environment and no one seemed to mind us being there.

I definitely remember having favourite songs that were sung by some of the regulars of our local club, the Who'd Have Thought It, and loving the familiarity of it all. I'm sure there were occasions we complained about going along but it was also an excuse to stay up late and be around adults doing grown-up things, which could often get quite raucous.

I remember watching Mum and Dad in their group Dockyard and Warships performing in Bodmin folk club and feeling quite chuffed at the response they got. That acceptance is a large part of the appeal of the clubs. It really is like a large family, where you all support each other. I was probably very naive and innocent but those early experiences have left a lasting impression on me.

BLAIR DUNLOP *leader of the new Albion Band, son of Ashley Hutchings*
I'd gone to Cropredy every year and gone to my dad's gigs, but he wasn't a pop star and when you're eleven years old there's a world of difference between your dad and somebody who's on TV. Then when I look at old film of him and when I listen to *Liege and Lief* and *Unhalfbricking* and other records, I think they were amazing. But it's hard to admit it to him because he's my dad.

I always knew he had a fan base and supporters but it wasn't until I was about sixteen and listened to the records that I became aware of his great work and that's when I became a fan of Richard Thompson as well. Fairport were like family friends. I saw a lot of musicians, that was the norm.

I've been playing the guitar since I was six but I started to take it seriously when I was about sixteen or seventeen and I discovered alternate tunings and started playing more folk songs, listening to older recordings.

NANCY KERR *fiddler, daughter of Sandra Kerr*
I was part of that second generation of the kids of revival folkies but until I was in my teens I hadn't really met any others who were playing or interested in music. I was really a loner, it was a bit of a rarefied experience.

Mum used to do library concerts all around London and I used to go with her. They were folk concerts for children and they were fabulous. I loved that. I think at some level I knew that I was getting to see other kids getting into the music that I was into. That was very early, I'm talking about when I was five, six, seven.

ELIZA CARTHY
My biggest inspiration was my musical partner, Nancy Kerr, who I met when I was fifteen or sixteen years old. She'd been playing since she was about four, so I really looked up to her, I really admired her. We were the same age but she was so much better than I was. I wanted to up my game so I could play with her.

We got together in '92. We did a small tour for Folkworks supporting Chris Wood and Andy Cutting, our big heroes at the time. Our first gig was at the Black Swan in York. Me and Nancy, we used to do these folk club tours, it was great. I used to drive but at seventeen I was a terrible driver. I landed up in few ditches.

NANCY KERR
We met at Sidmouth when we were about thirteen or fourteen. Liza came to stay with us because she was interested in playing the fiddle. I remember Martin and Norma taking us around at first to a few gigs, but Liza learned to drive very quickly – by seventeen or eighteen she was driving us.

It was quite young to be going round the folk clubs on our own but that's what we did. We lived in Whitby and shared a house at one point, and I still remember the feeling of heading out over the moors to our first gig of a tour and it was that real excitement of being off travelling.

We were young and we were fantastically looked after. I still remember that frisson of excitement at being independent. I loved the responsibility of getting to the gig on time and doing it under our own steam. I don't remember any unpleasant incidents or not feeling right. We were in a community as far as we were concerned.

KELLIE WHILE *daughter of Chris While*
They're only a year or so older than me, Eliza and Nancy, but they were streets ahead of me. They'd been doing gigs for ages. I remember seeing them play together at somewhere like Redcar Folk Festival when I was about sixteen.

My mum and dad were singing together so I remember, when I was quite young, we'd travel about a lot to folk clubs and festivals. I remember seeing Bernard Wrigley when I was five or six at a club in Manchester and thinking it was really loud and his voice was hurting my ears. My first proper memory of a folk club, sitting and listening, was the Bothy club in Southport and seeing Dave Burland. He sang 'If I Had a Boat', the Lyle Lovett song. I was about twelve. I think my mum was doing a floor spot.

When I left school I worked at Andy's Records in Southport, got enough money to buy a car so I could do gigs and then, when I got offered the job in the Albion Band after my mum left, I became a full-time singer because there was enough work there to just about earn a living. I was nineteen when I joined in the mid-nineties and I was with them till 2001.

JAMES FAGAN *bouzouki player, in duo with Nancy Kerr*
When I was growing up in Sydney I don't remember a time

when I wasn't being dragged along with my sister to see touring English artists like Martin Carthy or Vin Garbutt. Lots of people went out to Australia in those days. There was a big awareness in the seventies of what was going on over here and my parents were very much a part of it.

Mum was a singer at school and she got into it probably through my dad who discovered Davy Graham – that changed his life for ever. He learned that classic finger-style and that's been his mainstay ever since. Dad is really the reason why my family are a folk family. My mother very quickly picked up on singers like Joan Baez, Peter, Paul and Mary and Joni Mitchell and then ultimately got interested in the English tradition.

BEN PALEY *fiddler, son of Tom Paley*
My dad's music in the New Lost City Ramblers is some of the earliest music that I ever knew that I ever heard more than once. He has influenced me deeply. I remember realising that he was kind of well known in a very small world when he took me on tour in Sweden when I was about twelve. That was a really great time. My stepdad played a bit. He was in skiffle bands. He was knowledgeable. He wrote a lot about music and I learned a lot from him, so I had a really wide taste.

I was going to folk clubs when I was really young, then I lived in the States for a while. We came back in '79 and I was going to clubs then when I visited my dad. I have really warm memories of that scene.

CHRIS SARJEANT *son of Derek Sarjeant and Hazel King*
My parents ran the Surbiton folk club before I was born. I missed out on the actual club but I certainly haven't missed out on hearing about it, ad nauseam, for thirty years. They performed at clubs and festivals in Germany and Holland so I went there a lot but my memories of being in a folk club are less musical and more about drinking Coke and eating packets of crisps. It wasn't until I left home and felt an element of nostalgia and

homesickness, that led me back to folk music.

Dad tells me that I first saw Martin Carthy when I was two or three. I remember seeing him in Dorset when I would have been about seven, at Graham Moore's club. It was Carthy and Swarbrick and I found it excruciatingly boring. But then not so long ago I did a gig with him in London, we shared a dressing room. It's strange how things happen.

I met Steve Benbow when I was a child, and later on. We used to come up to London and go and see him and sit with him and play blues stuff. He'd show me things. My dad would say that Diz Disley used to push me up and down the High Street in my pram. What I wouldn't give to chew the fat with some of these people now.

MARTHA TILSTON *singer-songwriter, daughter of Steve Tilston*

My dad's been a massive influence on my music, and on my songwriting. Not just Steve, Maggie Boyle (Steve Tilston's ex-partner) as well. I kinda grew up thinking everyone wrote songs and played music, or their dads did. Then my parents split up and I ended up living in London with my mum and stepdad and drama was always around, and art, so being creative seemed to be part of being human. That's how we were brought up.

Me and Sophie, my sister, were in the Moses basket under the cash register at the folk club that Mum and Dad ran, the Louisiana in Bristol. Whenever we went to visit Dad, he'd always have two or three gigs a week, so we'd go off to the folk clubs with him. We'd go to festivals and things, it was great.

For some of my friends it's been a struggle with their parents, trying to convince them that they want to do something creative with their lives rather than doing a steady job. But for us, that was a steady job.

If you grow up thinking it's normal, before you've even decided you want to do what your dad's doing, or you mum or whoever, you just are doing it because writing songs becomes like a diary, though I've always felt slightly outside the folk world because I mostly write my own stuff.

NORMA WATERSON
It's so natural for me to sing with family it just seems normal. Singing together is joyous for us. It always was, from being children. Our Lal used to say as kids, whenever we got nervous, we always used to sing. And we did, we'd get into a situation and it would take the nerves away.

As soon as you were at a festival and there were a couple of families there, you always moved to each other and sat around and chatted about what it was like . . . the Coppers, the McPeakes, all of them. They were lovely times. Musically we were so privileged.

ELIZA CARTHY
Chris Wood used to come and stay at our house when I was a kid. I'd started to show interest in the fiddle when I was about thirteen or fourteen years old. I'd been playing it at school for a couple of years and I really wasn't enjoying it. Dave Swarbrick came to stay, to play with my dad again. He was quite a remote figure was Dave. Chris was much more hands on. I was messing around with the mandolin and the fiddle and he gave me some pointers, like how to sing with the violin, which gave me a bit of a head start. Really, I'm self-taught after that.

NORMA WATERSON
When Liza was about twelve or thirteen she totally dropped the folk music. She saw Prince at one of the big venues and went out with her friends to music that wasn't folk. She was still doing bits and she used to borrow our books – we've got a big room with books and stuff – and one day she'd borrowed the Child Ballads and she went upstairs and started reading them. About two or three hours later she came running downstairs and said, 'Mam, have you read the stories in this book?' I said, 'Yes, I have love.' She said, 'These stories are wonderful! Oh they're fantastic. I'm

going to get my dad to teach me these.' And we knew then that we'd got her!

ELIZA CARTHY

I used to stay at home for the regular touring and then sort of hit the road in the summer. I remember lots of traditional singing when I was a kid in those kind of settings. Seeing people like Sheila Stewart and Walter Pardon, Fred Jordan, people like that. Probably the earliest folk club I remember going to and singing at would be the Robin Hood's Bay club, when it was in the Bay Hotel. It moved up to the Dolphin after that.

When I was about thirteen or fourteen years old and I was starting to think that maybe I would like to have a career in music, I used to go down and practise my singing on them. I remember seeing Peter Bellamy at the Bay folk club. I used to sing 'Froggie Would A-Woo A Mouse' and 'Tom Pearce's Grey Mare – Bill Brewer, Jan Stewar', 'Arry 'Opton . . .Tom Cobley and All'. I used to sing 'Babes in the Wood' and I'd probably get up and sing that South African freedom anthem, something political. I was political at that age. It was all going on.

I told my mum I was leaving school to be a musician when I was thirteen. She said, 'No you're bloody not. You're going to university.' I left my A levels when I was seventeen, about three months before the exams. The music teacher said, 'Have you done any work?' I said, 'No. I'm not going to either. I've done.' I had a tour lined up for that November.

We were on with the Water Daughters at the Vancouver Festival in 1988. That was my first gig – 30,000 people. We did a tour of the folk clubs with Lal and Marry. I came across a photo recently of us at the Spread Eagle in Leicester.

GEOFF LAKEMAN

It happened by osmosis. We never beat them about the head to force them to play instruments or sing, or tied them to the chairs to listen. It was there, in the same way that most households have Radio 1 or the telly blaring in the background. We had Martin Carthy and Chris Newman as close friends. We'd all play together. When the kids were like eight, nine or ten they were already playing their instruments to a very high degree. It's going to rub off.

There was a little club started out in a place called the Who'd Have Thought It pub at Milton Combe. It's the next little village to where we live, and for about ten or twelve years I was one of the residents there. The kids were playing in a family band with Joy and were just about to formulate the Lakeman Brothers.

Though I say it myself, they were bloody prodigious and that was really their stamping ground because we would go down there and they'd play. They had a stage very early on – Seth would have only been about ten, Sam eleven and a half, Sean would have been about fourteen. So not only did they get to play, they also got to witness and hear, very close up and first-hand, people like Chris Wood, Steve Knightley and Phil Beer, people like that.

SAM LAKEMAN

We all chose our instruments without any pressure or suggestion from our parents, although they did encourage us to practise, and as soon as we could play a few notes or chords we were roped into playing a few songs as a family band. It was very innocent at the beginning and more as a novelty at family parties and for busking on holiday in France, to earn a bit of pocket money. But pretty soon we had a proper repertoire and would venture a performance or two at the local folk club.

NANCY KERR

Folk music was what both my parents and their friends played together. The connection with Ewan MacColl was always there. I went along with mum when she was teaching, the early days of workshops. It was very obvious to me that she had a training and I knew that had come from her time with Ewan.

I'd listened to recordings of the Critics Group that my mum was on, like *The Fight Game*, and Peggy Seeger had always been a voice in our house, mostly because she made a children's album which was a massive influence on me. Mum's sources were the traditional singers. So I heard people like Queen Caroline Hughes and Cecilia Costello and some of the Irish singers, the older singers.

I started learning the fiddle at school, aged five. I entered one of the Northumbrian competitions at quite a young age. I think it might have been eight or nine. I entered the novice competition.

Dad was Northumbrian so we were always going up there and they had these rich sessions, performance tradition. There I'd see in village halls people playing. I'd see The Shepherds – Will Taylor and Will Atkinson, Joe Hutton. I'd see Aly Bain come down for gigs.

I saw a lot of music in Northumberland. I had pretty informal and pretty sparse tuition from Will Taylor. I was never a pupil of his but I would go and visit him and watch him play, listen to him talk. Then back home I'd listen to his recordings pretty avidly and pick it up from there. It wasn't quite from the horse's mouth, but it was like he was my guru.

SANDRA KERR

It's the way the music always works, passing it down and by osmosis almost. With Nancy it was a much more organic process than the way Ewan taught me. I didn't ever treat Nancy like a pupil. Music was an organic part of our family life. Her father was a Northumbrian piper, I played several instruments, we all sang. She chose fiddle, which neither her father nor I played. We played a lot together, especially when she was around the age of ten, eleven, twelve.

I used to get rather worried when she was at school and they had to write what they'd done over the weekend. Every Monday it was, 'Mummy and Daddy took me to a pub and played music and I fell asleep.' I was always expecting social services to come round and say, 'What are you doing with this child?'

NANCY KERR

Mum was a massive influence in that she was always there. So
was Dad, and they tried to shape it to be fun, not to be hard work.
At the same time there was a sense of, if you're going to do it,
do it properly, so there were standards. There was a sense of, yes,
this is the music of the people but there's no reason not to do it
to the absolute best. There is a discipline here. I think that came
from Ewan.

They balanced it pretty well. They weren't pushy. I think they
were a bit surprised when I decided to do it professionally and I
think there were a few warnings there.

ASHLEY HUTCHINGS

Blair was musical from an early age and he was encouraged
by his mum. There are some pictures of him from about four,
banging a tambourine on stage and from quite early on he had
guitar lessons. He passively listened at Cropredy and places like
that, came to a few gigs in folk clubs with me, but he didn't show
a real interest until a few years ago.

BLAIR DUNLOP

It wasn't my dad who got me into folk. It was Jim Moray at
Sidmouth in 2009. I'd gone down with my mum and dad. One
night I was playing and Jim invited me to play with him. I didn't
know who he was, but it was one of those moments, and then I
really got into the tradition. Nic Jones is a massive influence on
me, guitar-wise, Martin Carthy as well.

I didn't take to it when I was younger. I think my dad and my
mum both being into folk music – if anything it pushed me away
and it took very much an outside influence like Jim Moray to get
me into it. Music I was always into, but not necessarily folk music.

I started to do a few floor spots at folk clubs in Derbyshire, then
got a few gigs and smaller stages at festivals. I was doing theatre
work and a lot of stuff at school – I was on a drama scholarship
so I had to do a lot of acting. I'd done the odd support for my dad

when I was younger, and for my mum but I only really started doing gigs as I was leaving school.

ELIZA CARTHY

It's not just my mam and dad, it's the whole family, the sound of the family. My parents are very, very passionate about a certain way of doing things when it comes to traditional music. I was very impressed by that and I wanted to do things the same way – learning everything from the traditional singers and learning to sing a certain way, and learning to write material in a certain way, like the way my dad re-writes ballads. I wanted to do that, treating the songs as part of a continuum, rather than trying to make a definitive version.

STEVE TILSTON

When Martha was younger I wasn't aware that she was musical, but she was obviously there watching and listening and soaking it all up. Her mother and I split up, and when she came down to stay when we were in Bristol there were loads of musicians coming in and out and obviously it rubs off. She knew Bert and John Renbourn and people like that, John Lee, who was a flamenco guitarist, he was about a lot. When she was about thirteen she wrote this bunch of songs on the piano, but she always had an interesting take on guitar playing. She was never just a strummer.

MARTHA TILSTON

I thought Bert Jansch was Tom Baker. *Dr Who* was on and I thought he was Dr Who. I used to go and tell my friends at school that I knew someone famous, Dr Who, not realising that Bert was famous in his own right for being the musician he was. He was a friend of Dad's. He just came in and played guitar but it just seemed to me that everyone played guitar, anyway.

GEOFF LAKEMAN

I suppose the point when Joy and I realised that all three of our sons were going to be professional musicians was when it became too uncool to keep playing in the family band. We were doing yacht clubs and steam fairs and village fetes as the Lakeman Family band and at some point in their very early teens the lads got a booking or two as the Lakeman Brothers.

Joy had some health problems and had to stop playing, so she gave her violin, her great-grandmother's violin, to Seth and it's still his primary instrument that he plays on stage. The rest is history, the way the Lakeman Brothers evolved into Equation, and all the various things that have happened since.

SAM LAKEMAN

I can't remember when, but at some point we started playing the odd tune in the set without Mum and Dad and it wasn't long before we all started to want to do things our way and not how they wanted to do things. So we started performing a few low-key gigs here and there as the Lakeman Brothers.

It was strange to see people's reactions to our performances. There was definitely an element of novelty about the shows we did. It was a mix of genuine musical ability and precocious showing off. People weren't used to seeing teenagers performing like that back then and we definitely split our audiences.

We knew most of the young performers around the UK scene at the time, as we'd always be slotted into some kind of New Tradition concert at folk festivals. I suppose it was quite adventurous to finish school and at the weekend get in our car in deepest Dartmoor – Sean was the only one old enough to drive – and head up country to a folk club hundreds of miles away, play a gig or two and stay the night with someone you'd never met before, then head back to Devon for school on Monday.

There was none of the hype and instant media attention you get nowadays. We took everything one gig at a time, and were doing it purely for the love of the music and the enthusiasm other folkies showed toward our arrangements and music. I remember great nights at the Hoy at Anchor folk club in Leigh-on-Sea, the Davy Lamp in Washington and the Black Swan in York. It was great fun to meet up and play with everyone. The last thing on our minds was making a living from playing folk music, so there wasn't even a hint of competition over market share or the like.

People were obviously surprised at the musical ability but they were more impressed or puzzled by our genuine enthusiasm for traditional music. Unlike some of the other younger folkies, we dressed in regular teenage clothes and didn't have the folkie look at all, and it left some people a bit baffled. To be honest, there were times I questioned why we played this type of music when I could also be forming a band with my friends to play something else.

NANCY KERR

I've got friends who don't come from a familial thing with folk music and they're just as involved. I teach people on the Newcastle degree course, and often young students will come into the session and when they introduce themselves they'll say, 'I'm not from a folk music background.' They're saying that as if it's a weird thing, when actually a lot of people aren't.

JON BODEN

It was quite strange coming into it, because most of the other people in my age bracket are all kids of folk revival people. The kids of the famous folkies, who became famous, I think are slightly detached from the core community of folk club kids.

FAY HIELD *singer of traditional songs, formerly in the Witches of Elswick*

My mum's a morris dancer and my dad was a folk club-goer so I'm one of that generation who were put to sleep under the table. This was Keighley, the Bacca Pipes folk club. My dad sang and played guitar. He wasn't a gigger, he did a bit of James Taylor-type stuff.

The people who made an impression on me in those early days were the friends, the regulars. The visiting guests I don't really remember. The regulars from the Bacca Pipes – it was a really strong singers club. They're very enthusiastic and they're also fabulous singers, so that feeling of being surrounded by people singing just for fun and for the love of it and songs that you've heard and that you love – when something familiar comes up, that sensation. That's what they gave me and that's what I got from them, that feeling of joy of singing.

CHRIS WHILE *singer-songwriter, part of duo with Julie Matthews*
When the kids were small we used to take them to festivals and gigs so they were around music. We didn't want to push them into it, but Kellie always used to sing and she was about fifteen or sixteen when she got up at gigs with me and sang harmonies. I joined Albion Band in '93. I was member number 101 and when I left the band in '97, Kellie joined.

KELLIE WHILE
When I was about thirteen, I started doing a couple of songs. If I could persuade someone to give me a lift I'd go to the folk club in Kirkham and the Star in Salford and the White Swan in Stockport. This was round about 1990. You could still turn up and do a floor spot.

If I hadn't had parents that were part of the folk scene I probably wouldn't have even known about a folk club, because none of my other friends listened to any folk music. My parents loved British folk music. My mum obviously loved Fairport and Sandy Denny, people like that. They listened to a lot of Nic Jones, Martin Carthy, June Tabor and Martin Simpson. But they loved American music as well. So I got brought up on a broad range of that stuff.

JAMES FAGAN

The local club where we lived in Sydney was the Hornsby Ku-ring-gai folk club, That was an English-style folk club where residents would sing floor spots and then you'd have the guest on. Most of the clubs at that time were in social halls, scout halls, community centres – you brought your own booze and there was usually a buffet. So me and my sister, we'd go along and hear some singers but we'd also get to eat smoked oysters and try a bit of Coca-Cola.

Me and my sister and the two girls next door formed a folk-singing quartet when we were nine or ten and we used to go and do gigs at the local folk club. We were called the Four Seasons. We sang things like 'Froggy Went a-Courtin'', a lot of songs that we'd heard from the American folk revival and songs that we wrote. We were by far the youngest performers they ever had at the folk club.

CHRIS SARJEANT

Despite having had parents who were folk singers, I still found my own way into it. I think subconsciously I took in an awful lot. I remember seeing Martin Carthy in a documentary about Bob Dylan, and I went and found Carthy's second album and pretty much from the moment I put it on I thought, 'This is brilliant.' It was almost an epiphany moment, like this is what I want to do. I didn't really start performing until I got through the Northern College in 2004. Then I went out from there and Dad was a great help. My first love is with the English traditional stuff. I just think there's so much scope.

I worked up a bit of material and went to Islington folk club in about 2007 and did a floor spot. They came up afterwards and said they'd book me, so I did a shared booking with David Campbell, Ian's son. He's a great singer. I also went to Cecil Sharp House and did a couple of floor spots and got a booking, then I went a bit further afield.

DAVE DEIGHTON

When we were living in Holland, I taught the kids to play. They were very young, I used to give them daily lessons, five minutes each. I started them on tin whistles doing simple tunes, then I started teaching Kath and Arthur mandolin and fiddle and Maya played the flute. We played at family weddings and christenings then when we came back to England we took it a bit further.

Arthur was still at the infant school when we started doing real gigs. I remember him refusing to play cricket with the hard ball, because I'd told him stories about getting your fingers broken. That took a lot of doing for a little kid at school – 'I'm not playing cricket, I play mandolin.' He got ragged about it but he was more interested in playing mandolin than cricket.

ARTHUR DEIGHTON *mandolin player with the Deighton Family*

Dave taught us all music at home from the age of four upwards. By the time we were eight we'd choose our main instrument. I tried fiddle but didn't have the patience to master the bowing. At that age you want an instrument that looks cool, so I ended up on the mandolin, which at age eight or nine is as big as a guitar.

We were brought up quite strictly and we had to practise every day without fail. It was more important than homework. At that age it was twenty minutes a day. By the time I was twelve or thirteen it was an hour. But then it became voluntary. While my friends hung out outside in the cold getting up to no good, I'd practise for hours on end.

DAVE DEIGHTON

The kids were very young but a lot of people who knew music knew that it wasn't a gimmick – they knew it wasn't about the kids. People who didn't know saw it as a novelty act. That really did annoy me. It was nothing to do with novelty. I'm not that sort of person. We played, and we played properly.

I think, too, that if you're not true English, true Anglo-

Saxon, you don't fit in with the English folk scene, not in the old traditional folk clubs. That's what it seemed like in the eighties.

ARTHUR DEIGHTON

My first gig was at nine years old when we still lived in Holland. I knew two chords and was allowed to play with Dave and his band. Can't remember the tune, though it went down a treat. The first gigs with the Deighton Family band were at our primary school. Then we moved on. That's when people saw potential in the family as more than just a family that happens to make music.

Obviously, there was a cute factor. All these little brown kids playing American rock 'n' roll and old-time music. We did our covers of 'Blue Suede Shoes', 'Travelling Light' and a few tunes, usually the American old-timey stuff like 'Magpie' and 'Cotton-Eyed Joe', 'Give the Fiddler a Dram', 'Blackberry Blossom' and such.

DAVE DEIGHTON

The Rockingham at Wentworth was the first real gig. Rob Shaw gave us a few supports until we built up an audience, then we did our own night and then people wrote about us and word got around. We went around with Sean Cannon from the Dubliners, to his gigs. He lived near us back then, in Barnsley. John Leonard got us on the radio so that helped – that's immediate. Then we did *Blue Peter*!

JOHN LEONARD

I did three albums with the Deightons. They could have been massive. They were fantastic. They were all individual characters and great musicians. I remember Dave playing in Rotherham in a duo, Dave and Sharon, in the late sixties. He always was a great guitar player – the Deighton roll, we used to call it, that little ripple he did with his fingers that nobody could learn how to do. Then he taught the kids. He worked really hard with them.

Me and John Squire used to stay with him and Josie in Holland.

Then when they came over here, a mate of mine, Trevor Dann, who was working for BBC Television, was looking for somebody for a programme. I suggested the Deightons and he put them on. I sorted out three record deals for them and I loved working on all of them.

ARTHUR DEIGHTON

When the Deighton Family first LP came out, that was amazing. I was happy as Larry. Hearing ourselves on John Peel's and Andy Kershaw's shows was even more thrilling. At fifteen you're still a bit worried about what friends and peers think and playing with your family wasn't considered cool.

The first really big audience was Dranouter folk festival in Belgium in 1984. We played as special guests of the Dubliners in front of about 8,000 people. They applauded after a mandolin solo. I couldn't believe it.

In '85 and '86 the buzz was starting to grow. That led to Rogue Records putting our first album out. After that we did all the major folk festivals and folk clubs spanning the whole of Great Britain and extending to Belgium, Holland and Denmark.

It all felt normal. We didn't know any different. I think I've inherited my ability to sleep anywhere under all circumstances. We slept on a lot of floors and came back often in the middle of the night.

DAVE DEIGHTON

The first album, *Acoustic Music to Suit Most Occasions*, was Album of the Year on National Public Radio in America. We did five weeks over there, all the major venues and festivals. We played mostly concerts, radio station live concerts. There was so much hype because of the record, that we could fill the places.

We were getting all these media gigs that a lot of people would sell their grandmothers for. I was proud of it all but I never ever got excited. I'd been playing all my life, I knew the reality of it all. It's a hard way to make a living.

ARTHUR DEIGHTON

There was occasional stress and tension, what with our old man being a worryguts and all the deadlines and the 4,000 miles we covered. Understandably, as a father you get worried when your teenage daughters and son are suddenly being approached by all kinds of people at gigs and getting a lot of attention. My sisters and I have always been close but the whole experience of playing together and the US and Canadian tour created an even bigger bond. How many families have this kind of experience?

ROSALIE DEIGHTON *now a solo artist, recently a member of the Storys*

Touring America, the heat and long-distance travelling – we'd just drive down endless highways, roads I thought were never going to end. We played so many radio stations – I was only thirteen but I felt that when we played in America we were 'home' in a way. They greeted us with open arms. We were a band and not a novelty act. We played the Edmonton music festival – that was a highlight – with 50,000 people watching us.

TOM PALEY

Ben started playing the fiddle when he was six years old. He took some lessons and he used to come around with me to folk clubs. He liked the music. Probably, why he took up the fiddle was he wanted to play that kind of music that I didn't play, but then two years later I started playing and luckily it didn't put him off, because he got to be a terrific fiddler. It's great playing in the band with him.

BEN PALEY

A dinner lady at my school asked me if I wanted to learn violin. I was living with my mother and stepfather and I went home and said, 'Do I want to learn violin?' and they said, 'Yes, of course you do.' I wasn't convinced and they played me a record – I can't remember what it was, an old-time band, and I went, 'Oh yes, I like the sound of that, I'll do that.' After I'd started, some months later I realised that what I'd been listening to was the banjo! I was only six years old. By that time it was too late, I'd started.

The dinner lady was an amazing woman. She was called Maisie, she came round to our house and taught me, classical lessons. Then my stepdad gave me a book. I can picture it, a green, old-time fiddle book.

I was in London playing recently, a gig in the afternoon, and I realised that Frankie Armstrong was on in the evening. She was a best mate of my parents and I hadn't her seen her for years, so I went to the club. I was a bit late, and when I went in loads of people turned round and waved and smiled at me. And I thought, 'Dammit, that's like my extended family almost.' Because I didn't have much extended family in England when I was growing up. I have really strong memories of that scene and those people.

WIZZ JONES

When we went to Germany to do festivals, we'd do gigs as the Jones Family – Simeon would play flute and Martin would play dulcimer and Danni guitar and Sandy, my wife, would play banjo. Then I started playing with Simeon when he was a teenager, in London. He played sax and flute and harmonica. Then he was at university and started to get gigs with rock bands and he did all that.

We do a little bit still. People say, 'Would you like to record again?' I've not got the desire or the muse to record but there's stacks of stuff I'd like to do with Simeon.

JOHN FOREMAN

When my two sons were young they both had guitars. Chris, who is in the band Madness, used to come round with me a bit but he was more interested in ska.

IAN CAMPBELL

My son Dave ran a club at the Empress of Russia in Islington for years. It was the club that Bob Davenport ran and where Dylan came in the eighties. He moved up and he's living in Birmingham now. He goes down to London every two or three weeks and does a few clubs. He's well known in London but strangely enough he's hardly known in the Midlands.

My other sons, Ali and Rob, were embarrassed by the Campbell group. Ali was desperately embarrassed. Folk music – he just thought it was so beyond the pale, he didn't want to be associated with it. He was the one who launched UB40. He was attacked in a pub and blinded in one eye – he was glassed. He got criminal compensation which was a few grand and he spent it all on buying the equipment, the instruments and so on, for UB40.

I used to say I've got four sons, two of them are talented and two of them are rich. Robin and Ali were in UB40, Duncan and Dave were the folkies. They're just different.

MARTIN CARTHY

I've noticed when I'm doing solo gigs that I get some young people in my audience and I know that it's because of Liza. When it first happened they used to come sidling up to me and say, 'Are you really Liza's dad?'

TOM PALEY

There's a guy, an American, Cedric Thorose, who plays dobro and guitar. He makes dobros. And he has a daughter, Leanne. She's got to be a very good fiddler. I said to him, 'Cedric, you and I have a problem in common with Martin Carthy. We used to be known for our own music. Now we're getting to be known as the fathers of great fiddlers.'

ASHLEY HUTCHINGS

People had asked me for years, was I going to get the Albion Band back together with the old faces? I resisted that. It didn't really appeal to me, though I've stayed friends with nearly everyone. It didn't seem artistically right.

Then it dawned on me one morning when I woke up. A light bulb went off in my head, that the answer was to ask Blair, would he be interested in taking on the Albion Band? I felt that he could handle it, emotionally as well as practically and technically. Initially, I thought I'd be kind of lurking in the background, pulling a few strings in the shadows, but very early on the band was formed with Blair and friends, and then friends of friends, and suddenly there was a group.

BLAIR DUNLOP

We were on a train and he said, 'Would you take the Albion Band on?' and I said I'd love to. By then I was doing a lot of traditional stuff, mainly acoustic, but I love the sound of folk rock. To be able to bring that to the twenty-first century and to a newer audience – I couldn't pass it up. The fact that the Albion had over 160 members over the years – it was like, well, why not have a new line-up? It's been different all the way through. If we're not the Albion Band which line-up is? We did the first gig at Cheltenham Folk Festival in 2012 on my twentieth birthday, 11 February 2012. I'd crashed the car twice in one day on the drive down.

ASHLEY HUTCHINGS

When he said yes, he'd take it over, it was remarkable, very pleasing to me. There are a lot of youngsters on the folk scene who have taken up the mantle from their parents – Eliza, Nic Jones's son Joe is playing guitar for Nic now, quite a lot, but this is something very different. The family business has been taken over.

15 We've had it easy, to put it bluntly

The nineties brought a new wave of interest in folk music. A host of young singers and musicians were emerging, some from the clubs and sessions, others by way of the degree course in folk music at Newcastle University. Meanwhile club audiences were diminishing and their average age increasing as the next generation of enthusiasts avoided rooms above pubs and headed for arts centres and festivals.

A study funded by the Arts Council in 2003 referred to 350 folk festivals held in the UK the previous year, with a total of 350,000 attendances. Steve Heap of the Association of Festival Organisers, who undertook the study, said, 'Folk music and folk festivals are key to the socio-economic and cultural life of our communities.' Once, the same thing could have been said about folk clubs, whose members comprised most of the audiences at the early festivals.

In July 1965 the Guardian *reported 'the biggest folk festival ever held in Britain', attended by 500 people at Keele University. Later the same month, 1,400 tickets at £1 each were sold for the first Cambridge Folk Festival, with a line-up that included Paul Simon, Peggy Seeger, the Clancy Brothers and the Watersons. At Cambridge 2013, 10,000 tickets were sold at £126 each within hours of going on sale, with the Mavericks, the Waterboys and Bellowhead topping the bill.*

A change in the way folk music was presented on BBC Radio came as a blow to the clubs. In 1999 Smooth Operations won the contract to produce the Folk Show *and brought in Mike Harding as presenter. Both he and producer John Leonard had spent years on the club circuit but the feeling was that it was time to focus on fresher developments in the music and on newer artists who appealed to the younger generation. With weekly figures of up to a million listeners, the format was understandably regarded as a great success. In late 2012 it was refreshed again when Mike Harding was replaced by Mark Radcliffe.*

It could be said that the folk scene has never looked healthier, that radio listening figures along with record sales and festival attendances prove the point. But at grass roots level there is scepticism that the newcomers have not paid their dues, that business has been put before music and that this bubble will burst just as the last one did.

Back then there were still gigs to be had in folk clubs, if not as many as at the peak of the boom. Everyone had come up through the clubs, done floor spots, travelled the country taking bookings wherever they could. Few of today's bill-toppers have done that. Hardly any of the new generation have run their own folk clubs and many festival performers have never played them. If the worst happens, where will they go?

IAN ANDERSON

I wasn't surprised at all when it came back in the nineties. That was exactly what we'd been working for, and pushing and hoping and dreaming about, ever since we began *fRoots*. All of us involved in the magazine had been event runners, club organisers. I'd been a professional musician, so our approach to it has always been grass roots up.

The folk scene lost a generation by being boring and stand-offish. It was only when the next generation came along and they were people who weren't embarrassed about folk music because they'd grown up with it.

LOUIS KILLEN

I hadn't been here for ten years and I came across from America in '91 for a tour that Peter and Jenny Bellamy set up. Three weeks, I think it was. The clubs that booked me hadn't changed much. They were the traditional clubs, but they were becoming fewer and fewer, so it was hard to get a tour put together. The other clubs had apparently changed and the festival scene had begun to grow. People weren't coming to the clubs any more. They'd go to the festivals because it was easier for them. They could hear all the people at the festivals.

JOHNNY HANDLE

I was teaching at a residential school for maladjusted kids and they burned the school down. I was made redundant so I came back to performing in the nineties. There were more singaround clubs, very few clubs booking artists more than perhaps once every six weeks, so the scene had changed, but there was still the same enthusiasm for the music.

JOHN McCUSKER *multi-instrumentalist and composer, formerly in Battlefield Band*

The first group that I formed myself was a band called the Parcel o'Rogues. I was thirteen and we played as guests at just about every single folk club in Scotland over the next three or four years. That was where I learned to play in front of an audience.

Very often we used to go and do floor spots, so we'd be on early and get the bus or the train home. We often couldn't wait to see the main act because we had to be up for school next day. When the oldest member of the band could drive he used to take us in his car. He was seventeen and I was fourteen.

The Star folk club in Glasgow, that was the biggest club, and even to get a floor spot was something. We got a floor spot and we kept on coming back and back, and trying to get better and then we finally got a gig there. The Glasgow Star – run by an amazing man, Arthur Johnstone . . . They sold that out and at the time it felt like that was by far the biggest gig we'd ever done. I've still got the poster that says 'Parcel o' Rogues – Sold Out'. Even though I've gone on to play with lots of people, that's still a milestone. It couldn't have been more exciting.

We made a record, *Parcel o' Rogues*, and that's how I got in Battlefield Band. Their record label and manager saw us in a folk club and they put out the record and then they asked me to join when I was sixteen. The first gig I did was in St George's Square in Glasgow, an open-air concert in front of 10,000 people, New Year's Eve. Only a few weeks before that I'd been playing in folk clubs.

DAVE BURLAND

One thing that has surprised me is that the second generation never took it on themselves to start clubs like we did.

ELIZA CARTHY

We've had it easy, to put it bluntly. We've been very lucky because our parents established those stages for us. We saw an existing network and went straight into promoting ourselves, rather than promoting other people, straight into careers rather than a community. It's been much more about making records and getting on stages and stuff rather than being a community.

I think that is changing in the last few years. There are many more activists on the scene now than there used to be. People who maybe aren't interested in making records but are interested in starting their own clubs. Or, people like Jon Boden and Fay Hield, who want to do both and actually give something back to the community. It's been a long time coming, that kind of thing. I really applaud them.

JON BODEN

I didn't discover folk clubs until I was twenty-three, round about 2001 at the Royal Oak in Lewes. When I was at university in Durham I went very regularly to the Colditz Hotel which was a Thursday night singing session rather than a folk club – a singaround. I loved it there. That was my first live singing experience. Before that I was listening and singing round camp fires and stuff at Forest School camps.

I did some floor spots at Lewes. I think I went two or three times and then Vic Smith, who ran it, said, 'Come and do a gig.'

Shortly before he said that, I'd met John Spiers at a session in Oxford, so I said, 'Can I bring a box player I've just met?' He said, 'Yes.' John was at Cambridge University and went to Cambridge folk club, and he phoned them up and asked them to book us. So our first ever gig was Cambridge, then we did Lewes, then Oxford. We did three folk clubs within probably three months. That's how we started.

Through putting a set together for the gigs we then had the bones of an album which we demoed and sent off to Fellside. Then we got a record deal and we got an agent. So really, quite quickly we were doing, I'm guessing, forty folk clubs a year for the first three or four years. We both had day jobs and we were driving off after work and driving back to go to work next day.

My involvement in Bright Phoebus is – I thought I should be doing my bit for the promotional side of the folk scene. Musicians as a profile are the people for whom it is easiest to set up a successful venue or venture. Then Kit Bailey was also thinking about running some gigs so the two things came together. In the end Kit did 99 per cent of the work.

FAY HIELD
A lot of the early folk clubs were started by professional musicians or semi-professional musicians in groups, so they were the residents. That whole resident culture seems to have dropped off. It's rare around the country for that to happen now. Whereas with Bright Phoebus at the Greystones in Sheffield – it's set up with Martin Simpson, Jon Boden, James Fagan and Nancy Kerr. It's like it used to be.

That's what the draw was in the first place – for audiences to come and see those sorts of people in a different role, actually putting on the gigs. Most of the big clubs were run by professionals. Everybody's very precious about the folk club – that what it is now isn't what it was thirty years ago.

I'm an organiser. I love filling in tax returns, spreadsheets. I like clipboards. I started an arts festival when I was nineteen, in Haworth, which still runs as a community event. I started a co-operative agency when I was twenty. Setting up community organisations is something I've done every couple of years, so starting folk clubs is a similar sort of thing. That's partly fulfilling the organisational need in me as for any good of the world.

Maybe a lot of other people of my generation aren't like that. A lot of the folk club organisers I know aren't necessarily performers. James and Nancy had a club down in Bath and there's Sam Lee's club in London, the Magpie's Nest. Sam Lee was more an activist before a performer.

SAM LEE *club organiser and singer*
I grew up in Kentish Town and knew nothing about folk music. I used to go as a child to summer camps, Forest School camps, a sort of breakaway group from the Woodcraft Folk. It is a very left-field organisation and within it there's a strong campfire singing culture which I later found out was very much influenced by the folk club movement.

I spent the summers absolutely enthralled, singing songs like 'The Larks They Sang Melodious', 'The Nightingale', lots of chorus songs, some Waterson-esque songs, classic folk songs like 'Barley Mow', First World War songs. When we were cutting vegetables in the kitchen, we'd be singing. When we were chopping wood, we'd be singing sea shanties to rhythm. They became very central to the social bond. There was the idea they were our songs and they didn't exist outside.

I started to want to know about the songs and I discovered the Watersons and bought their boxed set. I really liked it, but it was always about trying to tap into the root – where did they get their songs? Then I discovered Phoebe Smith and Jimmy McBeath and the Coppers on record. I started to come to Cecil Sharp House every week to the Tuesday night folk club, which was the most unique place that I'd ever seen – loads of old men get up one by one and sing.

I learned a new song every week off the records and by going to the sound archives. I was lucky – in 2005 I went and worked with Peter Kennedy in Gloucester. This was about six months before he died. I'd read his books and I then had access to a massive archive. Within a year I'd learned a hundred songs.

When we first started the Magpie's Nest in 2006 we wanted to have an open mike. We wanted to put professionals on as well and we wanted a representation of the new folk and the old folk and the no folk – not folk songs, singer-songwriters who are touching upon it.

We had no idea who would turn up, but there were lots of people because there was a great call for it from young people who knew that something like this existed. Cecil Sharp House wasn't what they wanted because it was an alien environment. The Magpie's Nest has been the instigation for a lot of other folk clubs in London, and other events in response to the same reasons why we started.

JON BODEN

I think a lot of people who get into performing by straight away going on to big stages with lights and PA probably would find playing a folk club intimidating. You're so close to the audience and you're not put on a pedestal in quite the same way. There's no having a backstage and walk on. And people tell you what you're doing wrong. You pick up immediately the response from the audience.

One person came up to me after a club gig and said, 'That was really good but I didn't understand the words in a couple of the songs.' It was an acoustic gig. He said, 'You either need to articulate better or play your instruments quieter.' At the time it wasn't necessarily what I wanted to hear but I totally took it on board, then focused on it for the next few gigs.

VIN GARBUTT

A lot of the younger singers – they're not treading the boards. They don't have to tread the boards. They're involved with record companies that have the promotion, who will tell the world that they're really good. I'd hazard a guess most of them won't last. They're brilliant performers and singers and musicians but if they haven't done the clubs they've nowhere to fall down to.

DAVE SWARBRICK

In the early days a lot of people went to clubs for singalongs, chorus songs where everybody joined it. That was their *raison d'être*. That's not so much now. I won't pretend to understand the scene any more. Nowadays you have conservatoires: they're training people to do this music, they're churning out people that to me all sound the same. That's logical, because they're all taught by the same person.

It creates a problem because a lot of kids are very, very good, dynamite players or singers who want work, but there isn't the work there to support them. And unless they get some recognition, i.e. sales on a CD, they're not going to get anywhere. The only way they're going to get sales nowadays is if they're nominated for an award from the BBC. And if they're not nominated for an award, then the record company will drop them. So it's not a scene that I pretend to understand.

JOHN McCUSKER

The folk club is, if you're lucky enough, where you start off. It's where you learn your craft, where you learn how to speak to an audience, how to entertain. The amazing thing about a folk club is it gives you a gig, a platform to play when nobody else will give you a gig. You learn how to hold an audience. People are right there in front of you. They hear every single note.

It's been interesting watching folk clubs change throughout the years, watching the folk scene change but, if you become more successful, then sometimes you have to leave the folk clubs behind because they become too small.

MARTIN CARTHY

What happened with Waterson Carthy was that we started off as a trio, Norma, Eliza and me. That wasn't until 1990. We went to the States for Norma and I to do some workshops at Augusta in Elkins, West Virginia. It's a week-long folk festival and you're doing mostly lectures and at the end of the week the tutors did a concert. This was our first gig and we did about twenty, twenty-five minutes and, I'll say it, we were fabulous. I've got the recording. One song we did, 'Sleep on Beloved', was just astonishing. Norma sang 'Coal Not Dole', I sang a thing called 'Perfumes of Arabia', about the first Gulf War, and Eliza played the fiddle and sang.

Then we did about three gigs in St Louis as a trio, sang around and did the first album. Liza had formed a band, the Kings of Calicutt, with Nancy Kerr. They expanded, bringing in Saul Rose, then they brought in a hammer dulcimer player. It got to be quite a big band at one time. And they all came and played on Waterson Carthy's second album.

JAMES FAGAN

I saw Waterson Carthy in Australia. That's indirectly how Nancy and I came to meet. I met Martin when he was doing a solo tour about 1990 and Eliza about three years later. When I came over here in 1995, when I was twenty-three, Nancy and Eliza were living together and working together. I went to visit Eliza in Whitby and within about a week I was on the road with the Kings of Calicutt, playing bouzouki and singing harmony.

When Nancy and I started doing the folk club circuit in '97, we were definitely one of the youngest acts out there. It was pretty much unchanged from the old days. If you looked at a bill from '97 you'd see Vin Garbutt, Martin Carthy, Maddy Prior, the middle ground of people like Pete Morton, Kevin Dempsey and then our age group – there was a smattering of acts like Ben Paley, Damien Barber, people like that.

We came in as a duo at a really good time, because the folk

club scene was at the peak of wondering what the hell was going to happen next. We were welcomed with open arms and we found that, because we were singing a largely traditional repertoire and we were in our early twenties, and we could play our instruments and we were interested in harmony singing, we got work left, right and centre. Within a year we were well established, through the folk circuit.

PHIL BEER

In the middle of January '92 Steve Knightley and I embarked upon a seventy-eight-date club tour. At that time if there were days off, we'd try and fill them with something, anything. I used to find that a day off – you lose the momentum, so if we could find a little break-even gig on a Monday we'd go and do it.

I was thirty-seven then, Knightley was thirty-six and we realised that that there had to be a plan this time. One of our golden rules was we would always carry our own PA – for absolute consistency, night after night, with a sound engineer who knows our music. So we got a reputation for always sounding good.

Then an Australian guy, Gerard O'Farrell, a sound engineer who lived round the corner from me, came and did fifteen nights for us, and at the end of the gigs we sat in the pub and he said, 'I've got an idea. I've been looking for something to manage and you guys are it – but I've got some radical ideas and here they are.' He outlined this formidable list of ideas – some of it we rejected, some of it made absolute sense. He said, 'You're never going to charge a fee again, from now on we will attempt to drive up ticket prices but we will take 80 per cent of the net. If no one comes, we lose money.'

He said, 'What this will do is empower a whole bunch of people to take a risk on putting on a gig where they wouldn't before.' We looked at him and thought, 'You're right!' – and we work to this model today. Apart from festivals, where you have no choice, Show of Hands doesn't charge fees. We work to a percentage.

FAY HIELD

The Witches of Elswick started off just like my career as a whole. Me, Bryony Griffith, Becky Stockwell and Gillian Tolfrey all lived in this flat together in Newcastle and we got into the habit of going to sessions and inviting people back to our house afterwards and there'd be loads of tunes. They'd sing a song or get me to sing a song and we'd start singing together.

It just sort of developed. We'd sing in the session and then someone asked us to do a floor spot and a festival – it built up. We were just drunken-women-walking-home-from-the-pub-type singers and then people were paying us.

We did quite a lot of festivals and built up a big, loyal following. It was all quite haphazard. We didn't set out with a career plan. We did some great gigs. Then I moved down to Yorkshire and Bryony moved. Between the four of us we had two weddings, two babies, two relocations, two full-time jobs and it was just not practical any more. We did it for fun. We did get fees but they were never going to tip the balance.

After the Witches I took quite a break, did the odd gig with Jon. We did Whitby. The first time we met was at a Yorkshire Dales workshop's young performers' concert, which I was the MC and they were booked at. We met a couple more times that summer and got together at the Sidmouth Festival.

Going solo was more about making an album than gigging. I toyed with the idea of making an album when I was twenty. I even took an advert out in *Tykes News*. It had a picture of the album cover – it was going to be called *Rover* and it said something like 'Available in the Spring'. I took that out to spur me on but I never made the album. That'll confuse people in years to come.

With *Looking Glass*, Jon had been pretty instrumental in kicking me up the backside to do it. It took a long time to get it together. I just wanted a record that I was really proud of, to show the grandchildren, kind of thing. It was going to be self-released then Jon said, 'Why don't we send it to Topic?' They took it on and part of the deal was that I would tour it if they were going to invest in it, so we agreed a level of touring that I could manage with the kids. We started touring in the February 2010 and it came out in September. I'm really pleased because I'm not sure I would have done it. Topic gave it a certain level of profile.

LUCY WARD *winner of the Horizon Award for Best Newcomer at the 2012 Folk Awards*
When I was fourteen my mum and dad bought me a guitar for my birthday. I didn't know that folk music existed beyond Bob Dylan and Joni Mitchell but I've always been into lyrics and stories, and it started to really capture me. One of the first things I heard was June Tabor's *Anthology*. That just captured my imagination and I played it over and over and over again.

From there I started to delve deeper and learn things, and it's grown. A lot of things the tradition perhaps takes for granted, songs they've grown up singing, for me are new revelations. My dad used to drive me to clubs and sessions all over because I wasn't old enough to drive and I enjoyed playing them so much. If it was a school night, I used to have to make my apologies at half time, because I had to be up for school in the morning.

When I finished my A levels I took a gap year to go round playing sessions, and that winter I was in the Young Folk Awards. Mick Peat turned me on to that. He announced on the *Folkwaves* programme on BBC Radio Derby, 'If anyone knows Lucy Ward's number, can you email me.' He told me about it and I managed to get to the final in 2009. I was seventeen – I'd just turned eighteen at the final. It's sort of rolled on from there.

I'd started to get gigs but the Young Folk Award stepped it into another gear. My first ever proper paid gig was supporting Steve Tilston at the Kiln in Swadlincote. I always had part-time jobs and I'd quit them if I couldn't get the weekend off to go and play at festivals. It slowly grew and then after I was nominated for the Folk Awards in 2012 I had enough gigs booked in for the year and that was my progression into being full-time professional.

JOHN TAMS

I'd been out of it during most of the nineties – and strangely enough not out of it. I'd been out of performing but I'd been inserting folk songs into a popular piece of drama that had twelve to fourteen million viewers every week, so I was still perceived to be the folk singer. When I came back, having tried to inhabit this character Daniel Hagman – who is a folk singer as well as a soldier – I was still perceived to be a folk singer, so I hadn't gone away.

I did notice that it had changed. I tend not to listen to that much music, and I tend not to go out on busman's holidays, so I'm very influenced by the select number of people I listen to, and it finds its way into my writing – and my style, if I'm not careful. When I came back I decided to make an album, the first solo album I'd ever made, *Unity*, so I didn't really pay much attention. I just thought I want to get these songs, that I'd been writing in Russia, off my chest – songs about Michael Heseltine shutting the pits down while I'd got my back turned. I just wanted to make a shout.

I'd gone to Lal Waterson's funeral and we had a drink at a pub called the Flask afterwards, a wake. Tony Engle of Topic Records was there and I'd been around Topic for a long, long time. I'd done field recordings in Ireland for Topic and done sessions. I played on Roy Harris's album and Archie Fisher's album and so Tony was known to me and I to him. He said, 'I'll give you a three-album deal.' It meant I could get some good players in, pay them proper money, rent a studio.

JON BODEN

I'd been toying with the *Folk Song a Day* idea on the Internet and, getting the BBC Folk Singer of the Year in 2009, I thought, 'If I'm going to do it, this is the year.' I was concerned that it might come across as a sort of presumptuous thing to do. At the outset I knew about 200 songs, so I had to learn a lot more. I started with 'Pleasant and Delightful' because I started at midsummer, and it's one of those songs that is well known but people don't sing any more. It was one of my favourites on the Forest Camps. It's another example of how the culture of the folk club has evolved in its own kinda time frame.

GRAHAM MOORE *composer of songs influenced by the tradition*
Dick Gaughan heard me sing 'Tom Paine's Bones' in a club at Ringwood in Hampshire, then he contacted me through the organiser and I sent the song to him. Dick took the exact arrangement which he saw me playing. I'd written it one morning round about 1999.

Shirley Collins sent me an email. She said, 'Forgive me for writing but I heard someone sing "Tom Paine's Bones" last night and I didn't think, until I heard it, that there could be a modern song which could be any good by comparison with traditional song.' I emailed back and said, 'Are you *the* Shirley Collins?' She said yes and I thought, 'Well, that's an affirmation.' Then I went and lost the email.

JOHN TAMS
I like to get laughs in between the songs and I like to get tears during the songs. If the audience are laughing then they're listening. And once I can get them to listen to a throwaway line, then I can get them to listen to a line that I don't want to throw away. Also, I love to get them to sing, because singing is good for you.

The funny thing is, having been away and come back, I'm singing to people who were my age when I started. Now they've had their children and come back and are revisiting their former haunts and some of the singers who entertained them forty years ago. But it is an ageing audience in the clubs.

LUCY WARD
Folk clubs are the point, really. That's where people want to hear me and that's where I want to play, but when you go to any

of the folk festivals the mix of ages is opened out, kids right through to grandparents. At clubs, generally, you're looking at audiences who are fifty plus.

A lot of the people running clubs are of that age. These are people running it from passion. They don't have the time or the resources to push their clubs to newer and younger people or, necessarily, the know-how to do that. It's a place that they enjoy to go and share the music. It's sad when you see how many folk clubs over the past couple of years have shut their doors, some for financial reasons, others for health reasons with people getting older and not wanting to put themselves through the stress of putting gigs on any more.

VIN GARBUTT

Folk Roots or *fRoots* never wrote anything about me and about 1996 I sort of realised I was in a media shadow. My diary was full but my new CD of the time, the live one – I thought it was in the shops but when I looked in shops all over the country there was no sign of it. I phoned up Topic and the feller I was talking to had never heard of me. This is the biggest folk music distributor, my distributor, and he doesn't know who I am.

fRoots had had nothing to do with me and in 1999 I did a round-the-world tour. It was called *The Take It Easy after 30 Years on the Road Tour*. Me and my agent, Jim McPhie, decided between us to put a full-page advert in *fRoots*. It might have still been *Folk Roots* then. It cost me £750. It was a lesser tour than I'd done in the past but it was still huge and round the world.

The following year was the first Folk Awards and Mike Harding, after dishing the awards out, said, 'A special mention must go to Vin Garbutt who's just finished his biggest tour ever.' And me and Pat, my wife, were sat there going, 'No, it wasn't! It was *Take It Easy*.' But then we thought, 'They wouldn't know this – there was never anything in print.' There's no way any of them would know I'd ever played in America or Canada or New Zealand or anywhere.

The following year I got the Best Live Act at the Folk Awards, then I got an honorary Master of Arts degree at Teesside University. I put it down to that 750 quid spent on telling the world that I was successful, because nobody else did! I did a lecture at Teesside University with the title *Thirty-seven Years of Successful Anonymity*.

JOHN LEONARD

I was at the BBC twenty years, then I left to join Nick Barraclough at Smooth Operations and we pitched for the *Folk Show* on Radio 2. I thought what was wrong with it at the time – and a lot of people will disagree with me, and have done – was that the folk show on Radio 2 was very much based on the folk clubs. But a lot of the folk scene had moved out of the folk clubs by that time. I thought that some of the more influential artists were not doing folk clubs any more and that was not being reflected in the programme. When we took it over the figures for the *Folk Show* were the lowest they'd ever been, the lowest of any of the specialist music programmes.

Radio 2 were saying that means nobody is interested in folk music, so why are we doing a show? But I said, 'I think they are interested but we need to take it up a league.' At that time, 1995, there were lots of things being recorded on the folk scene that were not very good. I said, 'Let's concentrate on the people who are doing it well.' A lot of things were going off – the degree course in folk music at Newcastle, Folkworks were training kids – a lot was going off and I think we were part of it.

We get between three-quarters of a million and a million listeners every week now. The Arts Council will tell you that, if you take every folk festival in Britain, there are only 350,000 actually go. That's a very significant minority, but more people are listening to folk music on Radio 2 than anywhere else.

I would never ever claim that we were the revolution, but we were part of, at that time, the emerging talent where Kate Rusby, Seth Lakeman, Eliza Carthy, Nancy Kerr and James Fagan –

young people – were coming in and doing it really well.

   With the Folk Awards, once a year you get the chance to stick your head above the parapet and say, 'This is the music that we're proud of this year.' I think about it all the time. We have a team of people. We've had Jack Elliott over, Steve Earle, Joan Baez has been twice. Every year we've tried to get Bob Dylan. We came ever so close in 2009.

16 We were a community

This book has been formed by the memories, anecdotes, insights and opinions of singers, musicians, club organisers and many other people who have been involved to varying degrees in the British folk clubs. Some go back more than half a century, others came in only during the last few years. All have had different stories to tell. Here, some of those interviewed take an overview on what the clubs and the folk scene have meant to them.

They speak of a community, a vibrant network of like-minded people drawn together by their love of the music. They recall how the folk clubs provided opportunities for anyone to sing and play and to hone their performing skills; of the intimacy and immediacy of pub rooms where the performer was only a few feet from the audience.

They remember the atmosphere, the humour, the feeling of being safe in a folk club, of how there was never any trouble and everyone was welcome. They praise the hard work of organisers who have kept clubs going, some of them for decades. They discuss the merits of floor singers and marvel at the common repertoire that existed in many clubs in the early years.

They speak of the joy of meeting people, of making friends throughout the country, of the camaraderie among performers on the road. And they recall the relentless touring, the long hours of driving, of the folk singer's life being a hard life, but one that they chose.

Some bemoan the way folk clubs have changed since the sixties and seventies, others say the clubs declined because they didn't move on. Ashley Hutchings admits he once thought the clubs would eventually disappear. Dave Swarbrick expresses the opinion that they are better now than they ever were. Vin Garbutt believes they are essential. Eliza Carthy thinks the folk

scene would be very different without them. Old hand Mike
Harding and relative newcomer Sam Lee both declare the folk
movement will never die. And who would argue with Richard
Thompson when he says that he hopes the folk clubs that are
still running will be there for ever?

MARTIN CARTHY

It was magic. It was fantastic – very, very exciting. You were part
of this huge community. It was an astonishing moment. We had
this totally anarchic thing, this network of human beings who
managed to co-operate with each other because they all had one
thing in common – the love of this music. And a love of the fact
that they were discovering it for the first time. The audiences and
club organisers for the most part were, say, eighteen to twenty-
five, and the performers were the same. It was our thing.

Those clubs in the sixties – that whole thing never should
have worked. The network couldn't have been any looser. It was
absolutely wonderful – rooms on top of pubs, behind pubs. Some
of the rooms were a nightmare. They could be very shabby. I can
only think of one club that had microphones and that was 1968
time and Manchester Sports Guild.

CHRISTY MOORE

We were very much a community. We provided each other with
contacts, info, a bed, curry houses, directions, warnings about clubs
that were a bit light on fee matters. There were occasionally a few
people involved in rivalry, but they invariably fell by the wayside.

There are many clubs that stick in my memory – the Bay
Horse, Bentley; the Cheshire Cat in Congleton; the Skillet
Pot, Birmingham; the Folk Centre in Glasgow; Mucky Byre
in St Andrews; The Forum, East Kilbride; Muriel Graves in
Cockermouth; the Marsden Inn, Tyneside; the Upper George in
Halifax; the Blue Bell in Hull; the Rugby in Hull; the Barley Mow
in Sheffield; Ted and Ivy Poole's club in Swindon; the Elliotts' in
Birtley; the Robin Hood in Blyth. I could go on all night.

PEGGY SEEGER

I remember that the folk clubs felt very fresh and there was a huge amount of enthusiasm. I think they began to give me the most pleasure when our policy kicked in, singing songs in your own language. All of a sudden everybody was singing English songs and Scottish songs, instead of the American ones. Because I found that every country has its rhythm – it comes from its speech. And speech comes, of course, from its history, its social layout, the whole thing that makes up a nationality. And when the English started singing English songs, it was as if they were settling down and coming home. To hear them singing 'Three score and ten, boys and men, go out from Grimsby town' – this is singing the history and singing the belonging. And when that started to happen, I enjoyed the clubs much more.

BILL LEADER

It was like Victorian music hall in a way, open and easy access and facilitating the people who had some talent. Many people couldn't get up in any other context, but they could do in a folk club even though they'd got nothing at all to do with folk. All those comedians who came through – it gave them an opportunity.

NIC JONES

The great thing about the folk clubs is that you were there with forty-odd people and they could heckle you. It was great, you could converse with the audience. It wasn't like, 'I'm the star and you're the audience', none of that sort of thing at all. And if you were rubbish, they'd tell you. It's good for people to start playing, with a guitar or a fiddle or whatever. They could play in a folk club. It was good fun.

JIMMIE MACGREGOR

It was the first time since the Elizabethan time that young people were actually making their own music. Up until the middle fifties everything you got was packaged – professional people doing it. Suddenly, it was thousands of young people playing guitars, learning songs, entertaining themselves and entertaining other people.

And from that emerged a tiny proportion of people with real talent who were committed and went on to develop it. It was a wonderful period and I'm very grateful to have been involved in it. It was an exciting time to be young and creative.

STEFAN GROSSMAN

There was an incredible folk scene in England . . . it was vibrant. In America you'd have to travel 500 miles to find a club to play in. Here you could travel fifteen miles and there were another two clubs to play in.

There were so many folk clubs, so many places to play, to get an audience, or that had audiences that would come no matter what. You had the whole gamut, people like the Spinners, a folky group, to the real hard-core traditional unaccompanied British trad stuff, to the singer-songwriters and the whole blues revivalist thing.

Back home, a very vibrant scene was happening in Greenwich Village and I was hanging out with all the black bluesmen. Then there was Dave Van Ronk and Phil Ochs and all those people. They were a generation above me but my interest was only in guitar playing. When I got to England it was that type of scene, times ten!

BOB DAVENPORT

When you were coming down the M1 and you met up with people at the Blue Boar, there was that camaraderie. If I haven't seen Martin and Norma for thirty years, when we do meet we pick up where we left off. You don't have to say anything because you know each other so well.

WIZZ JONES

It was fun when you were young. We were on the road a lot in
the summer, with the kids in the VW bus. We'd call it a holiday
but it wouldn't be a holiday at all. In my life I've only ever been
anywhere where there's a gig. It's a psychological thing – even
my wife still thinks of it as not work. We all say, it's not like a
real job, but I'll tell you what – it's fackin' hard sometimes. But
you bring it on yourself. I'm knocked out that I can still work,
do gigs, because so many of my mates have gone. And people are
still clapping. I think that's great.

DAVE ARTHUR

When we were young, we found it very exciting and we
considered ourselves to be supremely lucky to be doing a job
that we loved, and that we could live, travel and work together,
which we did every day. Twenty-four hours a day and seven days
a week, never apart for thirty years.

The travelling was tiring, particularly for Toni, who was the
driver. I didn't learn to drive until it was too late to be much help.
When you're young, sleeping on floors and people's settees is a
novelty. The novelty gradually wore off.

It was a hard life, it bloody was. We didn't do it for the money.
We just loved the music. We wanted to play it. We wanted to be
part of it. It was fun but it was grim at times, especially in the
early days when we hitched all over the country after having
first got our son's babysitting organised.

We'd set off from south London in the early afternoon and hitch
up to Lancashire, Yorkshire, the West Country or wherever for a
£10 fee, do the gig and then at eleven o'clock at night leave the club
and hitch back to be home by morning when Jonathan woke up.

We did this in fog, rain, snow, sun. One time the weather was
so cold that Ralph Smith, the Accrington folk club organiser, felt
so sorry for us that he paid us our fee and then bought us tickets
for the overnight coach back to London. It was a kind gesture
that was greatly appreciated.

DICK GAUGHAN

It can be a tough way of life and a month on the road would probably kill most people who've no idea what it involves. Most people's experience of travelling is limited to holidays and there is literally no point of contact between their experience and my reality which would enable them to even begin to comprehend what living on the road is all about.

The standard comment – 'What, you get paid all that for an hour and a half's work?' – displays an almost total ignorance of what being a travelling musician involves. It also betrays a deep contempt for creative work in general.

By the time I knock off all the costs of doing my job, I probably end up keeping about 15 per cent of what I earn and my taxable income over a year is roughly what I'd earn stocking shelves in Tesco. Being on the road isn't a career – it's a way of life. Anyone who gets that the wrong way round isn't going to hack it for long. After a decade they're going to be completely burned out and bitterly disappointed unless they get lucky and hit commercial success outside the folk world.

I've played many times in places where I've arrived after eight hours' hard driving through foul weather, roadworks and traffic jams, with no time to eat and needing to at least wash my hands before I try to play, then had to wade through puddles of urine in the pub lavatory – the only so-called dressing room available – to get to a filthy, broken wash basin, in the company of the local drunk who grabs me by the shoulder and demands to know, 'Are you t'turn, then?'

It's times like that you think, 'Aye, they're right. I only do this for the glamorous lifestyle.' The only difference between me and a long-distance truck driver is that at the end of the drive the truck driver logs off and goes for a meal and a decent night's sleep – I go to work.

It's just the way of life I chose and it's the price you pay if you decide to do something outside the accepted mainstream. Fame and riches are generally reserved for those prepared to play the

WE WERE A COMMUNITY

game and toe the line. I've never been interested in fame or what other people regard as 'success'. I just do what I do and if people want to listen, I'm honoured. If they don't, that's fine too. I'll keep doing it for those who do want to hear it.

CLIVE PALMER

I liked the folk clubs better than concerts. The audiences listened and there was a good atmosphere. They were usually in quiet places where you could drive home without being bothered by the police.

JUNE TABOR

They were huge in introducing me to traditional music and many of the great contemporary singers. It helped me find the music, love the music, be able to become a performer. If it hadn't been for folk clubs I would never have done that. Folk clubs were an absolutely unique way of giving people the opportunity to perform in front of an audience and to learn how to do it.

BARBARA DICKSON

It was the environment where I could hone my craft. Somebody once said to me, 'It's all because you're very young and when you're that age influences are enormously important, and you remember them for the rest of your life.' I do think we were very privileged. I'm not being a fogey here but there is nothing now that is the equivalent of that.

JASPER CARROTT

Folk clubs were like havens for people of any age. You could go to a folk club and be perfectly safe. There was no violence, no trouble, and they were entertainment. You weren't spoken at, you were spoken to. I think the folk clubs gave everybody an idea of what responsibility was in entertainment. Comedy was more than just one-line jokes about twenty Irishmen and mothers-in-law.

MIKE HARDING

It was a very broad church and they would listen to people and give them a go. Some of the clubs – there'd be fantastic residents and they'd do a tight twenty minutes or they'd do your half an hour. There were others where the residents really were self-indulgent and not all that good.

To an extent, there is the reason for the demise of the folk clubs: to some people it was their club, their way of expressing themselves and not a way of letting other people express themselves. I've often had my set cut down because the residents had over-run. Last time I sang in a folk club for money was in 1975, but I still play in sessions in Manchester and in Ireland.

MADDY PRIOR

They've been very important in that they've given us lots of performers and they were a great training ground for a lot of people. A lot of comics came out of it. Donovan may not have played in folk clubs, but he came out of that culture. He went to the folk clubs. It had an effect on that whole generation.

The great thing about the folk world is that it's very kind. The people are very kind to each other on the whole. It's how music should be. You get some that aren't, but generally speaking people are very thoughtful.

There's not a lot of money to be made. You can make a living out of folk music, just about, but you probably have to do other things. I was lucky in that Steeleye had a hit, but you're not going to make serious bucks unless you get a massive hit. I've enjoyed the folk clubs, always enjoyed the company, and people are very nice and it's served me personally very well.

MIKE WATERSON

They were places where anybody could get up. The first time I met Ian Manuel, he came into the club and at the door he said, 'What's going on?' The woman said, 'It's a folk club', and he says, 'Oh,' and walks in. She says, 'No, you've got to pay, and if you sing you don't have to pay.' 'Right,' he says, 'I'll sing', and he went up on the stage with no introductions, no nothing. There was nobody on the stage at the time. It was the interval, and he sang 'Blue Suede Shoes'. Somebody leaned across and said, 'No, it's a folk club. You've got to sing a folk song', so he sang 'Eppie Morrie', thirty-seven verses of 'Eppie Morrie'.

RICHARD THOMPSON

The clubs were and are a crucial stepping stone for young performers. I always liked the floor singer concept and for the idea to succeed the quality will vary drastically. I also liked the sometimes rather brusque equality of the clubs. As a performer you were nobody special, rather one of the crowd who happened to sing. Encores were sometimes begrudgingly granted, and then only after everyone had promised to return their beer glasses to the bar.

SHIRLEY COLLINS

Folk clubs are the best place to learn your skills as a performer. You're close to the audience, something I always enjoyed. It seems to me a pity that some of the young singers have gone straight to concert performance. They've missed out on a good, heart-warming experience.

But what smoky places they were in the old days – singers sticking a newly lit cigarette on the end of a guitar string and singing through the curl of smoke. I expect they thought it looked cool!

And an extra and important part of the folk clubs was the friendships formed with the organisers – the warm hospitality and talk at the end of a gig.

JOHN LEONARD

There was a system – you went to a club and they had floor singers. You rang up and got a spot and if they liked you, they booked you. That's how it worked. You could build a career from floor singing. That's what I did, I built a living up from it.

When Hamish Imlach first came to the Bay Horse in Doncaster, he brought John Martyn with him. John got up and we booked him straight away. That's how John Martyn got established. He travelled with Hamish, as did the Humblebums and Barbara Dickson.

The folk clubs were safe. It was a really kind of vibrant, underground scene. Nobody knew about it. Your parents didn't like it. It was perfect.

ROBIN WILLIAMSON

They offered an opportunity to people who were just starting out to perform. It's nice to have things which are round the edges and are not controlled by the mighty media, and that's what the folk clubs were. They were about a time.

JOHN TAMS

If you hadn't got anywhere else to go you could go to a folk club and you'd be welcome. They seemed to hold an arms-round sense of belonging, which meant that they were inclusive. We all found ourselves seemingly on the same end of the rope for pulling in the direction, some of which was obviously political. They were all old left-wing. I've never been to a Tory folk club yet.

I think what it taught that generation in the late fifties and early sixties was how to listen. They attached themselves to the information they were being told . . . sung. In folk clubs you weren't dancing, you were having a pint and a Woodbine and listening to turns who were telling you stuff, and you had to re-adjust your head.

So I think we were one of the new generations. Dylan knew that and a lot of the great lyric poets did, Cohen and Simon. It took us a while in the UK to catch up. We hadn't quite grown yet. Also, it was very hard to find the songs. It was all American stuff. So that generation taught us how to find as well as how to listen. I can't believe how lucky I was to be around at that particular time.

MARTIN SIMPSON

It's the intimacy of transmission and the sense that you're involved in something of great value. You're there and the audience is there, generally speaking, because you all really love this music and because you're all really interested in it. That might sound a bit precious, but within that framework I can do whatever I want. If I want to wheel out a banjo and play a version of a Randy Newman song, if I want to do a political diatribe, I can do whatever I want.

But it's like Danny Thompson says – you don't actually get paid for playing. You do that for free. You get paid for sitting in a car on a motorway . . . for flying . . . staying in a crap hotel. I wouldn't complain, though. I think sometimes the hardest part is being away from home. Without a doubt it's difficult for someone who is in a relationship with somebody who makes a living by getting lots of attention.

And for yourself – the whole thing about going away and getting lots of attention and being shot full of adrenalin for weeks on end – then you come home and you feel like shit, because you're coming down from it all. And for a lot of people on any music scene there's always a temptation to try and settle that down a bit. Drinking is the obvious way and the acceptable way, but it's not a very good idea. That can be like hard work sometimes. But I'm not complaining.

NOEL MURPHY

I was offered two gigs at the end of '64 and a pal of mine asked me, how long did I think it was going to last? I said, 'It's going to last until I have to ask for a gig.' I got forty-two years out of it and I never asked for a gig. All the time, I'd be doing a gig somewhere and somebody would come up to me and say, 'We've got a little folk club back in my village in Norfolk or Kent or

Staffordshire or wherever, would you like to come and do a gig?' So every time I did a gig, I knew they wanted me. I hadn't touted for business.

There was a whole band of us. We were the ground force in folk music. We weren't the ones who were going to go on to be Paul Simon or Al Stewart or Ralph McTell, we were the grass roots – Johnny Silvo and Diz Disley, Vin Garbutt, Derek Brimstone and Gerry Lockran, bless him. All that crowd.

I was forced to pack it all in, reluctantly, in 2006, after forty-two years. I just ran out of gas. I was still doing folk clubs. I had very strong feelings about the folk clubs and the folk scene. I know a lot of friends of mine and people I worked with went on to great things. Good luck to them. I never wanted to go down that route.

In 1964 people offered me a fiver to come and do their folk club. I thought, 'That's two weeks' rent – I could have thirteen nights off every fortnight for the rest of my life!' It hasn't quite worked out that way.

GRAHAM MOORE

You could go anywhere in the country and go to a folk club and you knew that you would have an affinity with people. It's almost like going into a church. I think what it's about is – I'll listen to you, if you'll listen to me. And it's that regime of the floor singer which is detested by so many, but it's respected, because that's where so many people have come from. That is the key to it. There are so many great names who began like that.

IAN McCANN

Wherever you went there was a sort of repertoire that all folk club aficionados knew. It wasn't just choruses – 'Mingulay Boat Song', 'Whiskey in the Jar', 'Wild Mountain Thyme', 'Leaving of Liverpool', 'Last Thing on My Mind' – all those songs, it was a like a classic canon.

JIM IRVINE

The folk club in its initial concept, the revival days – it was the best political platform we've ever had, the working class. But they didn't exploit it and they didn't utilise it, they just let it go. Then the middle classes came in and they had the money to buy the instruments, the Martin guitars and the accordions and the fiddles. Now you canna go to a place that's not run by somebody that gets three months' holiday a year.

NIC JONES

The trouble is that people nowadays want to be superstars rather than playing in clubs in rooms in the back of a pub. We used to charge a reasonable fee, ninety quid or something like that. That's nothing these days. They charge a fortune.

JULIA JONES *wife of Nic*

I think it was partly that the folk clubs didn't move on. They should have evolved. All the youngsters now – they don't want to do folk clubs. They left it to somebody else. People like the Unthanks and Kate Rusby – they only want to do the big venues. So if they're not running the clubs that make the circuits, which is what used to happen, when we all peg it there's not going to be any folk clubs.

DEREK BRIMSTONE

It was a joy, an absolute joy. You got to know people so well. Right back from the mid-sixties till I packed up in about 2008, I'd be doing their club every year and I'd stay with them. I watched their children grow up. I was very lucky. I enjoyed every minute of it, a marvellous forty years.

PHIL SMILLIE *the Tannahill Weavers*

You've got to take your hat off to the people who run folk clubs because there's no support from anybody. It's their love and them taking the risks that runs those clubs.

GEOFF LAKEMAN

The organisers are the backbone, the people who put the chairs out and took the tickets and booked the artists. Sometimes they were the floor artists as well, but often they were people who didn't want to sing or play but they were just as passionate about the music. We owe a collective debt to all of them.

ROB SHAW

We had some memorable nights but one that sticks in my mind is when we put Townes Van Zandt on. He was fine when he arrived but somebody got hold of him and he drank a bottle of Pernod before he went on. He talked like he was drunk anyway, so you couldn't really tell. I asked him if there was anything he needed. He said, 'A bottle of Pernod, your car and your money.' Then he said, 'Have you got a wife?'

MARTIN CARTHY

Why do I still play folk clubs? It's what I know. There's an understanding there. I love the way the folk club works. I love the fact that folk clubs over the years have allowed me to wander up blind alleys, fall flat on my face, make terrible mistakes, make laughable mistakes, sound like an idiot, sound okay, struggle, learn my trade – and they've paid me, on the button, to do it. And they've looked after me.

That's a really good reason for going on, but basically I love the freedom. People will allow you to do what you like – and you belong to them. It's that idea, that there's a kind of ownership of you. I don't mind that at all. I relish it. And I love the fact especially that, if you go along to a folk club, you get that whole floor singer ethic.

You'll hear a bunch of floor singers who are anywhere between rotten and very, very good. Once in a while you're going to run into somebody you've never heard of, who is going to blow you clean out of your socks – do something which is absolutely brilliant, utterly sublime. They would not have a chance to air that anywhere else. That's why I like doing the folk clubs.

JASPER CARROTT

I think folk clubs were very undervalued in their effect and their influence.

The range of music, particularly from the singer-songwriters – Harvey Andrews, Ralph McTell, Allan Taylor – they formed a base groundwork for people to listen and go on and use it further. If you trace back the roots of a lot of successful pop artists and groups, you'll find there's a root in folk clubs. The name Electric Light Orchestra came to Roy Wood after he saw the Pigsty Hill Light Orchestra at a club in Birmingham, the Elbow Room.

Folk clubs formed the basis today of comedy clubs. It's the same thing but much more compartmentalised. It was a great grounding for me. Without that I would never have gone on.

JOHN LEONARD

When we started the Folk Awards, I thought there should be an award for folk club organisers. That's the roots of what it's all about. We had one and I realised after a number of years that different people were winning it, but they were the same people – they were in their sixties, they'd been doing it for forty years. They were running a club and the strength of those people had kept that club going.

The clubs had stayed much the same and they were impossible to go to as a newcomer. A newcomer – to go in for the first time to this club that had been running for forty years by the same people – could not grasp the culture. And so new people are not going to folk clubs.

IAN McCALMAN

Television and ease of entertainment – technology – killed off the folk clubs. We like to say they're still going but you can't do a twenty-five-gig tour of Lancashire now.

There was no way you could do a folk club and stay in a hotel. That would have been your money gone. And if they put you up in a hotel you always got the worst bloody room in the place. We did it and that's the reason we're known.

Usually, it was sleeping bags in one room and sometimes we didn't even have that. Some places we were in barns, whatever there was. It really was a hard bloody life – and we were doing well! We were on network radio, doing *Country Meets Folk* and all that.

ROBIN DRANSFIELD

Ian Dury used to say, 'If you can't spit into the back row, the gig's too big.' That was the folk clubs. It was just magical when we started in the sixties. There was nothing else like it and I think that gradually got diluted. You can go to a folk club now and the same people will be there who were there when I first did it in 1969. They're about a hundred years old.

FAY HIELD

They play a massive role for the people who are in them and who have been in them and loved them. For new people that join them and get the bug, I think they're hugely important to their sense of belonging and identity.

An awful lot don't advertise in anything bigger than the regional folk magazines, which you can only buy in folk clubs, so it's an ever-decreasing spiral. But for the people that do it, I think it's vastly important. I don't see much of a distinction between the people who listen and the people who sing. That's why it's a club rather than a concert series.

SAM LEE

Folk clubs as an idea will never die. I think hand-made, self-made music, self-promotion, the cottage industry is going to forever be there and there are loads of music nights popping up that are strong and packed to the rafters with people. It's happened independently and in total isolation to the traditional way, but that will happen. It's happening at festivals.

JAMES FAGAN

I saw an interview recently with Peter Bellamy at Whitby Folk Festival the year that he died, where he was asked how he felt the future of folk was going. This would have been in 1991 and he was very pessimistic about it. He said, 'I think these things go in cycles but it seems to be on the down.'

I think if he were alive today Peter Bellamy would have to acknowledge that not only has it survived but it's flourished in its own way – not in an exact template of the seventies, it's always going to be something new, but there is a club circuit and there are still young people out there who are interested in doing it.

The clubs are getting thinner on the ground but the festivals are getting bigger and bigger. My optimism for the folk club itself is less than my optimism for the folk movement. I'm not so clear about the folk club as we understand it and I wonder where that's going.

ASHLEY HUTCHINGS

If anybody had asked me in 1970, would it carry on all these years, I would have said, 'No, it's going to die out like the folk clubs are going to die out.' But it hasn't. It's gone from strength to strength and the musicianship is just phenomenal now, wonderful, wonderful players.

It would be nice to have a few better singers. In the sixties we had some wonderful singers and they really did their research. They knew all about the songs that they were singing. Sadly, I think a lot of the youngsters just take songs from other recordings, Martin Carthy or whoever, and don't always credit either. We were always very keen to credit the sources, forty to fifty years ago. But it's in pretty safe hands. It's in a healthy state.

LOUISE EATON

The reason why the Bradford Topic has kept going all this time, from 1956 to now, is because it's always been committee-run. Lots of folk clubs were run in the early days because somebody had the brilliant idea, then as soon as it started to lose money it finished.

We were very fortunate that we did finally have premises where we didn't have to pay a rent because the pub made money on the drinks that were sold. Even in the thin times they let us have the room. But the basis was that every year there was an AGM – all stemmed on a political approach and people were elected to be the secretary, to book the singers, etc. There's been involvement throughout.

STEVE TILSTON

Part of me is really drawn to that old idea about one man and his guitar, travelling around. Of course, there were times when you had to stay in a stranger's house but a lot of those people are not strangers any more. I made some good friends. I think the British folk scene is so tenacious. A sentence of death has been pronounced on it so many times, but it still keeps on. But obviously, given the demographic, then the age of a lot of the people . . . The song 'The Road When I Was Young' is about that.

DAVE BURLAND

I think the odd thing about working folk clubs was you never realised how popular you were. You were doing a gig and moving on, doing another and moving on, and you didn't see the people who were there until maybe eighteen months later. The advent of festivals changed all that because then you began to see people in different places. One of the first I did was Whitby. Me and Capstick did Whitby together, that shook a few people.

RICHARD THOMPSON

I still drop in to the clubs when I have the chance. I see little change in the true folk clubs, but now there are arts centres that overlap for a lot of performers, and with the gap closer than it's ever been, it's easier for folk artists to reach a wider audience.

I'm so glad that there are some clubs hanging on, some of them getting long in the tooth. There must be a few that have been around for fifty years. It's comforting to think how that world is consistently serving the community and resisting the superficial trends of music. It's a less politically driven scene now, reflecting the times, and I don't think there are as many clubs as there were in the sixties, but I hope they'll be there for ever and I hope the new interest in folk isn't a flash in the pan.

JOHNNY HANDLE

We had a fiftieth anniversary night at the Bridge in Newcastle. We all came back – Louis Killen, Ray Fisher, Colin Ross, Tommy Gilfellon, Alistair Anderson, John Brennan, Jim Hall; Benny Graham was a singer from the floor. The place was packed. Mike Waterson got up – he did a duet with Louis Killen. There were some people who'd been there at the very first night of the club, when it was at the jazz club.

After everybody had gone away I sat in the room and I could still hear them singing. For about twelve years I was the MC and I could hear all the voices. It sounds a bit romantic but there's so many famous people had sung in the room and so many good nights for a lot of people and we'd had so much enjoyment just out of being there. It's an important room.

DAVE SWARBRICK

I think the clubs are better now than they ever were. Audiences are much more involved, that stands to reason. A lot of people who went to folk clubs in the old days no longer go – it was a passing interest. Nowadays folk club regulars are well informed. Probably all have their own little libraries of material and a good percentage of them are performers. So it's the nicest possible atmosphere on the whole scene to play to, because you're playing to people who appreciate what you're doing.

It wasn't like that in the early days. The atmosphere among the smaller ones, between say forty and seventy people, can't be beaten. I prefer to play those if I can. I like them to save up for a while.

RALPH McTELL

It has never been played better than it is at the moment, in my view, which has largely kind of bled over from the Irish enthusiasm for the traditional. You think of the young upstarts: they're not upstarts any more, they're probably moving towards their forties, but it's wonderful the way they play and the way another kind of community, a fellowship of musicians, has arrived at festivals where they never stop playing.

At one time it was only the banjo players who were playing all night, now you've got the melodeon players and the fiddle players and the tradition is alive and well and flourishing and I've grown to love it.

And folk clubs with their absolute honesty and their total egalitarian view of anyone who gets up on stage – you're equal, you're not protected in the same way you are on the bigger stage. I relish the bigger stage, I must say, but for pleasure I still go to folk clubs.

TOM PAXTON

I have an enormous affection for the folk clubs. I can't do many of them because they're too small and there's a lot of people couldn't get in. Every success that I've had in the UK I owe to the folk clubs, the support they gave me and the network they provided.

I can tell you about the effect it had on me. It was to broaden my ears, to bring new harmonies into my ears, and new lyrics, and the musicianship. When you listen to people like Maddy

Prior and June Tabor, Martin Carthy, Danny Thompson – these are fabulous musicians.

VIN GARBUTT

The English club and concert scene is still essential. It's essentially the sixties teenager getting older. Some of the younger performers have got a younger audience but the audience hasn't found them because they were regulars at a folk club – the media has told them that they're worth going to see. So they get big audiences but they're not folk club supporters. It might just develop into big concerts and festivals at one end and singarounds at the other.

MIKE HARDING

Early on I was down in London. I wasn't gigging and I went to see Tim Hart and Maddy Prior in a club. Tim Hart said, 'I'll get you a floor spot here', so he went to the organiser and said, 'This bloke is really funny', and I got up and did 'Napoleon's Retreat from Wigan' and something like the 'Rochdale Annual Fair'.

Tim knew that there were like eleven bookers in the club that night and I got booked all over the south-east, Chelmsford and all over the south-west, down to Cornwall. Tim Hart didn't need to do that at all – it was Tim's good-heartedness.

This is why the folk music movement will never die and it's also why big business can never take it over because it's a people thing. It relies on people making music for themselves – and they'll always do it. Which is why I love it to death.

ELIZA CARTHY

I see the folk scene and people's professional music career as being two separate entities these days. It's not so much the community that it was. I felt a real painful separation when I realised that – not only that I might feel separate from them, but that they might feel separate from me. I saw the folk scene as my extended family.

As far as the folk clubs are concerned, I think they are absolutely invaluable. They are a place to pass music around, to try new things, to try old things, to remind yourself what the old things are. They are clubs, in a sense a closed network, although there are plenty of far-reaching people out there that have wider visions.

They serve a purpose, for everyone to remind themselves what their favourite songs are and why we're all here. It's a cottage industry, an industry that's supported my family, my dad, for fifty years. I think the folk scene would be very different without the clubs. I'll be interested to see where they're going to go in the next ten or fifteen years, because they're quite unfashionable in a lot of ways, but in other ways that's the way that a lot of people are going. New people are starting up their own clubs. It will be interesting to see how the old club network will react to that.

The Clubs

During the period covered in *Singing from the Floor* an inestimable number of folk clubs has existed, some for only a short time, others for decades. It is unlikely that any comprehensive list of all known folk clubs could ever be compiled; the following is a selection of the clubs that were there in the earliest days of the revival, and the ones that have been referenced by the singers, musicians and others who appear in the book.

London

Black Horse, Rathbone Place Bill Leader and Gill Cook, who worked in Collett's record shop, opened the Broadside Folk Club in the early sixties. It was here that Bert Jansch first sang 'Needle of Death', written as a tribute to his friend Buck Polly, who had recently died.

Bunjie's A cellar folk club below a coffee house in Litchfield Street, Charing Cross, it opened in the mid-fifties and ran through the sixties.

Fox, Islington Green Began in 1964 with residents Bob Davenport and the Rakes. Davenport later ran clubs at the John Snow in Soho, where he gave Peter Bellamy his first floor spot, and the Empress of Russia, St John Street.

King and Queen, Foley Street The first club in Britain, where Bob Dylan sang from the floor in December 1962.

Half Moon, Putney This was more a music venue than a folk club. Gerry Lockran started folk blues sessions in 1963 and most of the leading British and American contemporary folk and blues acts played there, as well as rock bands like the Rolling Stones and the Who.

Herga Folk Club, Wealdstone Began in 1963, later moved to Pinner where it is still in existence. The Lakeman brothers' parents were once residents and John Heydon was club organiser for twenty-three years. The first club to book Robin and Barry Dransfield as a duo.

Les Cousins, Greek Street Opened in 1965 below a Greek restaurant in the same premises that the Skiffle Cellar occupied from 1958 to '60. Les Cousins was the main venue in London for blues and contemporary folk music, with all-nighters on a Saturday.

Roundhouse, Wardour Street Cyril Davies opened a skiffle club in an upstairs room of the pub in 1955. Later became London Blues and Barrelhouse Club, run by Alexis Korner, who brought in visitors like Muddy Waters, Big Bill Broonzy and Champion Jack Dupree.

Singers' Club Ewan MacColl had opened Ballads and Blues in 1957 at the Princess Louise, High Holborn, before starting the Singers' Club with Peggy Seeger in 1961. The club's first location was the Association of Cinematograph Television and Allied Technicians (ACTT) trade union building in Soho Square and later venues included the Princess Louise, Pindar of Wakefield, Merlin's Cave and the Union Tavern. Known for its strict policy regarding traditional repertoire

Scots Hoose, Cambridge Circus A pub in Charing Cross Road, where Bruce Dunnett ran the folk club in an upstairs room, where the Young Tradition were formed and John Renbourn first met Bert Jansch.

Troubadour, Old Brompton Road, Earls Court A cellar room below a coffee house that opened in 1954. The leading folk venue in London until Les Cousins opened, and a stop-off for visiting American folk artists, including Bob Dylan. At different times, Ramblin' Jack Elliott, Martin Carthy and Martin Winsor and Redd Sullivan were resident singers.

White Bear, Hounslow The folk club was opened in 1965 by the

Strawberry Hill Boys, later the Strawbs, led by Dave Cousins. In 1969, with Cousins still involved, it became the Hounslow Arts Lab, where on one occasion David Bowie made an appearance.

Elsewhere

Birmingham, Jug of Punch The Ian Campbell Folk Group opened their first club at the Trees pub in Birmingham in 1959, later moving to Digbeth Civic Hall where the club became known as the Jug of Punch and regularly attracted audiences of up to four hundred.

Bradford Topic Opened in 1956 by schoolteacher Alex Eaton and still running; the Topic is the longest-running folk club in Britain.

Bristol Troubadour A contemporary and blues club, ran from 1966 to '71, with a musical policy similar to that of Les Cousins.

Cambridge St Lawrence Folk Song Society Founded in 1950 by students at the university, although too early to be recognised as a folk 'club'.

Chelmsford Folk Club Where Nic Jones came to notice in the mid-sixties as a member of the Halliard, the resident group.

Cornwall, Folk Cottage An old barn in Mitchell, a hamlet near Newquay and the base for folk and blues in the mid-sixties. Pete Stanley and Wizz Jones were resident and Ralph McTell got his first break there.

Edinburgh University Folk Society Founded in 1958 by medical student Stuart MacGregor and folklorist Hamish Henderson. The following year, resident singers Dolina MacLennan and Robin Gray started a singing night at the Waverley Bar in Edinburgh, where many Scottish performers gained experience. In 1960 a London entrepreneur Roy Guest opened the Howff, a haunt of the teenage Bert Jansch.

Glasgow Folk Song Club Located in a café, the Corner House on Argyll Street, and organised by Norman Buchan and his wife Janey. Archie Fisher, Josh McRae and Hamish Imlach were among the early residents.

Harrogate Folk Club Began in the early sixties, the club where Robin and Barry Dransfield began performing, in a bluegrass group the Crimple Mountain Boys.

Hull, Folk Union One The Folksons, who soon became the Watersons, opened their own club in 1959 in a dance hall. They moved on to Ye Old Blue Bell where in 1965 they and the folk club were featured in the BBC television documentary *Travelling for a Living.*

Liverpool, Spinners Folk Club Opened in 1958 in the basement of a restaurant, Samson and Barlow's. For years, until the demands of their concert and television work took over, the Spinners were the resident group and they made their first record at the club. Later moved to Gregson's Well and the Trident.

Manchester Sports Guild (MSG) An old warehouse in Long Millgate, the MSG opened in 1961 with jazz downstairs and, later, folk upstairs. All the top performers played there and a singer's night on Mondays gave many artists, including Christy Moore, their early opportunities.

Manchester, Wayfarers The first folk club in Britain was started in 1954 by Harry and Lesley Boardman as a 'folk circle' at the Wagon and Horses pub. Two years later this became the Wayfarers folk club at the Thatched House in Spring Gardens

Newcastle Folk Song and Ballad Club Originated with folk nights that Louis Killen and Johnny Handle organised in a jazz club, moving to the Bridge Hotel, where it ran for many years. It inspired other clubs in the Tyneside area, notably Birtley, opened in 1962 by the Elliott family, and Marsden, home of the Marsden Rattlers

Oxford University Heritage Society Founded in 1956, Louis Killen and, later, June Tabor gained valuable experience while students.

Sheffield, Barley Mow Run by Malcolm Fox from 1964 at the Three Cranes. Tony Capstick and Dave Burland were early floor singers and, in 1966, the first club that Martin Carthy and Dave Swarbrick played as a duo.

Sheffield, Highcliffe The Highcliffe folk and blues club that began in 1967 was an early form of today's mini-concert venues. The Humblebums, Barbara Dickson and John Martyn played their first gigs in England there.

Solihull, Boggery Organised and compèred by Jasper Carrott at the Old Moseleians Rubgy Club, it opened in 1969 with a focus on entertainment.

Surbiton Assembly Rooms The biggest folk club in Britain, with two halls, one with 700 capacity. Derek Sarjeant and Gerry Lockran started the club in 1961; by the time it closed it had 23,000 members.

Wentworth, near Rotherham, 'Folk at the Rock' Opened in 1974 at the Rockingham Arms, moving to nearby Maltby in 2007. Soon after founder and organiser Rob Shaw retired in 2012, the club folded.

York, Black Swan The present club, in the upstairs room in one of the oldest pubs in York, has been running since the mid-seventies. It was the venue for Nancy Kerr and Eliza Carthy's first gig together, in 1992.

Who's who

Maartin Allcock Multi-instrumentalist who started out with Mike Harding's backing band during the latter's Rochdale Cowboy days, later a member of the Bully Wee Band and Fairport Convention.

Ian Anderson British exponent of country blues, a resident at Bristol Troubadour in the sixties and co-founder of the Village Thing record label and later *Southern Rag*, which became *Folk Roots* and latterly *fRoots*.

Harvey Andrews Singer-songwriter who worked in folk clubs from 1964 until his retirement in 2012. His song 'Hey Sandy', from the album *Writer of Songs*, was widely popular in clubs in the seventies.

Frankie Armstrong Unaccompanied singer of mostly traditional songs, resident at the Singers' Club and member of the Critics Group.

Dave Arthur Toured the clubs with his wife Toni, singing traditional material and recording *Morning Stands on Tiptoe* and other albums for Transatlantic. Author of *Bert: the Life and Times of A. L. Lloyd*.

Roy Bailey Member of the Three City Four with Martin Carthy and Leon Rosselson, later sang with wife Val and has had a long solo career. Recorded first album in 1971 for the Trailer label.

Jenny Barton Ran the Troubadour in Earls Court from 1958 to 1964.

Phil Beer Multi-instrumentalist, turned pro in duo with Paul Downes in 1975 and later played with the Arizona Smoke Revue and the Albion Band. Formed Show of Hands with Phil Knightley in 1992, still does solo club gigs.

Lesley Boardman With her late husband Harry organised one of the earliest folk clubs, known then a 'folk circle', in Manchester in 1954.

Jon Boden Began in folk clubs in a duo with melodeon and concertina player John Spiers before forming Bellowhead to play festivals.

Joe Boyd Produced records by Incredible String Band, Fairport Convention, Shirley Collins, Fotheringay, Nick Drake and John and Beverley Martyn among others. Published a memoir, *White Bicycles*, in 2006.

Derek Brimstone A leading entertainer on the folk scene in the sixties and seventies. Began at Hemel Hempstead folk club and turned pro after winning the solo artist competition at the 1965 Cambridge Folk Festival.

Dave Burland Barnsley-based singer of traditional and contemporary songs, briefly a member of Hedgehog Pie in the mid-seventies. *A Dalesman's Litany* in 1971 was the first of nine albums.

Graham Campbell Guitarist who in the mid-sixties introduced musicians like Davy Graham and Spider John Koerner to Sheffield at the Sleepy John Club.

Ian Campbell Leader of the Ian Campbell Folk Group, hosted one of the country's largest clubs at Digbeth Town Hall and toured extensively for twenty years from the early sixties. Appeared regularly on radio and television and made more than twenty albums. His song 'The Sun Is Burning' was recorded by Simon and Garfunkel. He died in December 2012, only months after receiving a Good Tradition award at the BBC Folk Awards.

Sean Cannon Formed a group, the Gaels, in Coventry and started a club at nearby Monks Kirby. Worked solo for many years until invited to join the Dubliners in 1982.

Carole Capstick First wife of the late Tony Capstick.

Vicky Capstick Daughter of Tony Capstick.

Jasper Carrott A comedian known universally through television and concert tours. Began in folk clubs and opened the Boggery in Solihull in 1969, one of the earliest folk clubs to focus on entertainment rather than strictly on music.

Eliza Carthy The daughter of Norma Waterson and Martin Carthy, has worked with her parents in Blue Murder, Waterson Carthy and Imagined Village. Turned pro at sixteen in a duo with Nancy Kerr. Nominated for the Mercury Music Prize twice, she has won a number of Folk Awards. Formed the Ratcatchers with Jon Boden and John Spiers and subsequently moved on from the folk clubs to rock venues and festivals. Vice-president of the EFDSS.

Martin Carthy One of the most popular folk singers and most influential figures in English folk music since the early sixties. Paul Simon and Bob Dylan have acknowledged his influence, as have many British singers and guitarists. Teamed up with Dave Swarbrick to play the folk clubs in 1966, was later a member of Steeleye Span and the Albion Country Band. Joined the Watersons in 1973, and a member of Waterson Carthy with his wife Norma and daughter Eliza. Also a member of Brass Monkey and Imagined Village. Made the first of many albums in 1965, still playing the folk clubs both solo and with Swarbrick.

Trevor Charnock Committee member and bookings secretary at Bradford Topic folk club from 1976.

John Cooper Clarke Punk poet who in his early days read his poetry in Manchester folk clubs.

Shirley Collins A major figure in British folk music, her 1964 album with Davy Graham, *Folk Roots, New Routes*, fused folk and jazz and caused a stir among traditional folk followers. Later broke new ground with *No Roses*. Sang and recorded with the Albion Country Band and her sister Dolly until the late seventies. Elected President of the EFDSS in 2008.

Billy Connolly The original Humblebums, Billy Connolly and Tam Harvey, took British folk clubs by storm when they appeared in 1968. Gerry Rafferty soon replaced Harvey and when that duo split up Connolly went solo, concentrating on the stand-up and acting on television and in films.

John Conolly Founder of Cleethorpes folk club where his group the Meggies were resident. His songs 'Fiddler's Green' and 'Punch and Judy Man' have been recorded by many other singers and groups.

Dave Cousins Banjo and guitar player who founded bluegrass group the Strawberry Hill Boys. Changed their name to the Strawbs, had pop chart success with 'Part of the Union' and moved on to the university and rock club circuit. Now back in the folk clubs with the Acoustic Strawbs.

Stan Crowther Formed the first folk club in Rotherham, where he became mayor and later Member of Parliament. He died in 2013.

Karl Dallas *Melody Maker* writer on folk music from 1957 to the seventies, wrote a number of songs, including 'Family of Man', made popular by The Spinners.

Bob Davenport Traditional singer from the north-east, in 1963 he became the first British performer to be invited to the Newport Folk Festival in the USA. For many years resident at the Fox, Islington, and a regular guest in clubs nationwide, he recorded as a solo artist and with the Rakes, Marsden Rattlers and Bolden's Banjos.

Tony Davis Founder member of the Spinners from their days as resident skiffle group at the Cavern Club in Liverpool. Started the Spinners folk club at its first venue, Samson and Barlow's restaurant, along with his wife and the group.

Arthur Deighton Mandolin player in the Deighton Family from an early age, with his parents and four sisters. Now works as a music therapist in Holland.

Dave Deighton Guitarist and melodeon player from Sheffield, with his wife Josie raised five children, who, as the Deighton

Family, made three albums, toured Europe, the USA and Canada.

Rosalie Deighton When the family band folded, made an album *Intuition* with her sister Kathleen, Kate Rusby and Kathryn Roberts. Now works solo.

Nigel Denver Moved to London from Glasgow in 1960, the first British folk singer to be signed to a major label. He made several albums and played folk clubs throughout the country during the sixties, then retired from touring for domestic reasons.

Barbara Dickson Began her career as a singer, musician and actress in the Dunfermline folk club, singing traditional songs. Moved to Edinburgh and was helped in finding gigs in England by Hamish Imlach. A part in Willy Russell's West End play *John, Paul, George, Ringo and Bert* led to acting roles on television and great chart success.

Donovan Hung around the early sixties folk scene but in his own words was 'not allowed to play'. His first single, in 1965, 'Catch the Wind', and a TV appearance on *Ready Steady Go!* launched a career that brought chart success on both sides of the Atlantic.

Robin Dransfield Began in a Harrogate bluegrass group, the Crimple Mountain Boys. Later he and his brother Barry took the folk clubs by storm, recording a seminal folk album *The Rout of the Blues*. Broke up just before they were about to tour the USA. Both went solo but have now retired from the scene.

Blair Dunlop Acted alongside Johnny Depp in *Charlie and the Chocolate Factory* at the age of eleven, emerged on the folk music scene in 2010. The son of Ashley Hutchings and singer Judy Dunlop, took over fronting the Albion Band in 2012.

Louise Eaton With her late husband Alex Eaton, a founder member of the Topic folk club in Bradford, which began in 1956 and has continued without a break.

Chris Euesden Folk club singer and organiser, founder of Circuit Music and Fat Cat Records in York.

James Fagan Grew up in Sydney, Australia, where parents Margaret and Bob were well known in folk circles. Took up the bouzouki and joined the family group, along with his sister. Came to England and teamed up with Nancy Kerr in 1997. An occasional member of Bellowhead.

Archie Fisher Born in Glasgow into a singing family; his sisters Ray and Cilla were professionals on the folk circuit. A stalwart of the early Edinburgh scene, made many appearances at the Edinburgh Festival and presented *Travelling Folk* on BBC Radio Scotland from 1983 to 2010.

John Foreman Popular in the folk clubs where he sang Cockney and music hall songs. As the Broadsheet King he published song collections and for a few years the annual *Folk Almanac*.

Keith Foster Friend of Tony Capstick who accompanied and drove him to gigs early in his career.

Hans Fried Started going to folk clubs at the age of thirteen. Worked in Collett's bookshop in London, a meeting place for folk musicians in the fifties and sixties.

Vin Garbutt For over forty years one of the funniest and most popular acts on the British folk scene; his first album *Valley of Tees* marked him out as a notable songwriter. Has sung all over the world. Changing trends and bouts of ill-health have not slowed him down.

Dick Gaughan Former member of Boys of the Lough and Five Hand Reel, and of the agitprop theatre company 7:84, has made more than twenty solo albums and continues to tour in Britain and abroad.

Brian Golbey Guitarist and fiddler who played in a duo with Pete Stanley in the late sixties, later formed Cajun Moon with Allan Taylor.

Stefan Grossman A pupil of Reverend Gary Davis as a teenager in New York, later a member of the Even Dozen Jug Band, the Fugs and Chicago Loop. Arrived in London in 1967 and quickly established himself, recording early albums for Philips and Transatlantic. Returned to the USA, runs Kicking Mule, issuing records, tutorial books and videos. Still tours occasionally.

Roy Gullane Front man and long-serving member of the Tannahill Weavers.

David Halliday Organiser of the Wheatsheaf folk club in Rotherham in 1966.

Johnny Handle Co-founder of one of the earliest provincial folk clubs, in Newcastle-upon-Tyne in 1958, he guested in clubs all over the country and was a founder member of the High Level Ranters. Famous for his adaptations of folk tales into what he terms 'the Geordie slavver'.

Mike Harding A hit single, 'Rochdale Cowboy', propelled him from the folk clubs, where he blended comedy with traditional song, on to concert stages and television series. Presented the Radio 2 *Folk Show* from 1999 until 2012.

Carolyn Hester A leading light on the Greenwich Village scene in the late fifties and early sixties, she gave Bob Dylan his first recording opportunity when he played on three tracks of her third album. Her producer John Hammond then signed Dylan to Columbia. Married for a short time to Richard Farina, came to London in 1961 for the first of many club and concert tours.

Fay Hield Former member of the all-female group Witches of Elswick; her first solo album *Looking Glass* was released on Topic in 2010. A co-organiser of the Bright Phoebus folk events and Royal Traditions folk clubs.

Ashley Hutchings Founder member of Fairport Convention, Steeleye Span, the Albion Band and Rainbow Chasers. Married to Shirley Collins in the seventies, worked with her in the Etchingham Steam Band and produced the album *Morris On*. Has worked in theatre and toured a one-man show on the life of Cecil Sharp.

Jim Irvine Played fiddle and sang with the Marsden Rattlers, resident at the Marsden folk club on Tyneside.

John James Arrived in London from Wales in 1967, headed for Les Cousins and soon built up a reputation as one of the best finger-picking guitarists around the folk club circuit. His 1972 landmark album for Transatlantic, *Sky in My Pie* featured duets with Pete Berryman.

John the Fish John Langford moved from London to Cornwall in 1960 where he was resident at the Count House in Botallack for many years, as well as touring with Brenda Wootton.

Hughie Jones Joined the Spinners following a visit to their folk club and remained with the group until it folded. Later went solo, known for singing and writing songs about seafaring, ran a club in Liverpool for many years.

Julia Jones Along with her husband Nic, took over the running of the Chelmsford folk club when the Halliard split.

Nic Jones Left the Halliard to go solo in 1969, releasing his first album on Trailer the next year. Cited by many guitarists as an influence, he was very popular in the folk clubs. In 1982 he suffered life-threatening injuries when his car crashed returning from a gig in Glossop and he did not play or sing again in public until 2010 when he joined in a tribute event to his music at Sidmouth Folk Week. Since then has made further appearances with his son, Joe.

Wizz Jones A mainstay of the acoustic folk and blues scene since the mid-fifties, with twenty solo albums and numerous collaborations. Worked in a duo with Pete Stanley, with the band Lazy Farmer and with Clive Palmer. Cited as an early influence by Eric Clapton and Keith Richards; Bert Jansch is reported to have said of him, 'I think he is the most under-rated guitarist ever.'

Nancy Kerr Encouraged to play the fiddle by her parents, met Eliza Carthy when both were in their early teens and they began to play as a duo soon after, later forming the Kings of Calicutt.

Teamed up with James Fagan in 1997; they record for Fellside and tour clubs and festivals.

Sandra Kerr A resident at the Singers' Club from 1964, received intensive tuition in folk music from Ewan MacColl and Peggy Seeger while living with them and acting as nanny to their children. Teaches on the degree course in folk music at Newcastle University

Louis Killen The first British traditional singer to turn professional. *Ballads and Broadsides* in 1964 was the first of more than thirty albums. Moving to America in 1967 he stayed thirty-five years, took part in the Clearwater Project with Pete Seeger and for three years was a member of the Clancy Brothers. He returned to his home town, Gateshead, in 2003 and lived as a transsexual. He died in 2013.

Geoff Lakeman Sang and played concertina from the mid-sixties with his wife Joy. Father of Sam, Sean and Seth.

Sam Lakeman Began in family band with his parents and brothers, now works with his wife Cara Dillon, whom he met when both were members of the group Equation.

Tom Lane Organiser of Grantham folk club in the seventies.

Bill Leader At Topic, Transatlantic and on his own labels, Leader and Trailer, recorded many seminal folk albums, working with Bert Jansch, the Humblebums, the Dubliners, Pentangle, the Dransfields, Christy Moore, the Watersons and Gerry Rafferty, among others.

Sam Lee Began the Magpie's Nest folk club in Islington in 2006 and studied in Aberdeen with the late Scottish ballad singer, Stanley Robertson. His debut album *Ground of Its Own* was nominated for the 2012 Mercury Prize.

John Leonard Played folk clubs solo and with fiddler John Squire, joined the BBC and went on to become Head of Music before starting Smooth Operations with Nick Barraclough and producing the Radio 2 *Folk Show* and the annual Folk Awards.

Gef Lucena Founder of Saydisc records and co-founder of Village Thing in Bristol.

Jimmie Macgregor and **Robin Hall** Became household names during a four-year stint on BBC TV's *Tonight* show and were together responsible for many viewers' first exposure to folk music. They made many records and played concert halls all over the world.

Dolina MacLennan A singer and actress from the Isle of Lewis, present at the beginning of the folk club scene in Edinburgh. Later appeared in films and television plays.

Ian McCalman Gave his name to the McCalmans, the trio he formed at architectural school in 1964. Played thousands of folk club gigs and made records. Retired from the group in 2011.

Ian McCann Multi-instrumentalist, member of Alex Campbell's backing group, the Malcolm Price Trio and Orange Blossom Sound. Led his own trio, the Roan County Boys, and did many solo gigs around the country.

John McCusker Played in folk clubs at twelve, formed Parcel o'Rogues and joined the Battlefield Band in 1989, when he was sixteen, remaining with them for eleven years. A multi-instrumentalist, he has played and recorded with a range of singers and musicians from traditional performers to Mark Knopfler.

Jim McLean Writer of Republican songs in the sixties, including a whole album recorded by Nigel Denver, *Scottish Republican Songs*. Worked as the Dubliners' tour manager for a short time, later founded a record company, Nevis.

Ralph McTell A follower in his teens of Wizz Jones, greatly influenced by the old blues and ragtime guitarists. Resident at the Folk Cottage near Newquay in the mid-sixties, after living in Paris where he wrote 'The Streets of London'.

Ewan McVicar Involved in the first Glasgow folk club; his song 'Talking Army Blues' was a minor hit for fellow Glaswegian Josh

McRae. Author of a biography of Hamish Imlach, *Cod Liver Oil and the Orange Juice*.

Julie Matthews A member of St Agnes Fountain, Blue Tapestry and the Albion Band, wrote eleven songs for the 2006 BBC *Radio Ballads* and since 1997 has worked in a duo with Chris While.

Michael Moorcock In the fifties was editor of an early folk music magazine *The Rambler*. Went on to become a prolific and highly successful sci-fi author.

Christy Moore Arrived in London from Ireland in 1967, moved to Manchester where he visited clubs, doing floor spots and building up his reputation as a singer of traditional material and songs of social commentary. Formed Planxty, a band that played clubs in their early days, and later Moving Hearts.

Graham Moore Dorset singer-songwriter who has written musicals *Tolpuddle Man* and *England Expects*.

Noel Murphy One the folk scene's great characters who arrived in London from Ireland in 1964 and filled clubs throughout the country for forty-two years. In the late sixties he and Davey Johnstone worked in a duo as Murf and Shaggis.

Rab Noakes Emerged in the late sixties as a singer-songwriter. Founder member of Stealers Wheel with Gerry Rafferty but left before their record success. Signed by Warner Bros as a solo act, he moved on to the university circuit, later working as a producer for BBC Scotland before returning to the clubs.

Rick Norcross American singer and guitarist, spent some time in Britain in the sixties and early seventies. Later ran a folk club in Florida and now leads Rick and the Ramblers, a western swing band in Vermont.

Jim O'Connor Member of the Critics Group, wrote 'Have You Seen Bruce Richard Reynolds?', recorded by Nigel Denver and, forty years later, by the Alabama 3.

Ben Paley Son of Tom Paley, lived in America with his mother and stepfather as a child and studied with legendary Nashville fiddler Jim Buchanan. Plays with his father in the New Deal String Band, as well as in several other line-ups.

Tom Paley Banjo/guitarist and later fiddler, as a young man played with Woody Guthrie. A founder member of the New Lost City Ramblers, whose records inspired many British musicians, moved to Britain in 1965, formed the New Deal String Band with Joe Locker. In 2012 at the age of eighty-four he celebrated the release of a new album *Roll On, Roll On* with a series of folk club dates.

Clive Palmer Original member of the Incredible String Band, his laid-back manner probably held him back from the recognition many thought he deserved. Left the ISB after their first album, later led the Famous Jug Band, Clive's Original Band – known as COB – and Temple Creatures.

Tom Paxton Already well known on the New York folk scene, he came to Britain for the first time in 1965. His songs 'Last Thing on My Mind', 'Rambling Boy' and 'Can't Help But Wonder Where I'm Bound' had preceded him and were for a time part of the folk club repertoire. He still plays concert halls and makes records.

Maddy Prior Sang at the St Albans folk club; in 1965 she drove Reverend Gary Davis on his UK tour, soon afterwards joining Tim Hart in a highly successful duo. They were founder members of Steeleye Span with whom she still tours. Recorded and toured with June Tabor as the Silly Sisters.

John Renbourn Eclectic guitarist, best known for his solo albums, duo work with Bert Jansch and as a founder member of Pentangle.

Chris Sarjeant Guitarist and singer of traditional songs; his first album *Heirlooms* was released in 2012.

Derek Sarjeant Sang and played guitar in folk clubs and around Europe for many years with his late wife Hazel King. Organiser of one of the biggest folk clubs in the country at Surbiton Assembly Rooms.

Philip Saville Television director who brought Bob Dylan to London in December 1962 to appear in the play *Madhouse on Castle Street*. Subsequently directed many television plays and series including *Boys from the Blackstuff*, besides movies in Britain and the USA.

Peggy Seeger Banjo, guitar and autoharp player, half-sister of Pete Seeger, came to England in 1956 and met Ewan MacColl whom she later married and sang with until his death in 1989. MacColl and Seeger had a huge influence on the British folk scene, especially through the BBC *Radio Ballads* and the Singers' Club which led to the Critics Group.

Rob Shaw Organiser of Folk at the Rock in Wentworth, South Yorkshire, and later at Wesley Hall, Maltby, until he retired in 2012.

Ethan Signer Mandolin player with Massachusetts-based bluegrass group, the Charles River Valley Boys. Lived in Britain in early sixties. Recorded with Bob Dylan at Dobell's record shop and was part of the latter's impromptu performance at the Troubadour in January 1962.

Martin Simpson Guitar virtuoso from Scunthorpe who began doing paid bookings at the age of fourteen. Recorded his first album for the Trailer label, toured as a member of the Albion Band and worked with June Tabor before emigrating to the USA where he stayed fifteen years. Back in Britain he quickly reclaimed his role as one of the folk scene's leading performers.

Hylda Sims A member of the London Youth Choir in the early fifties and later the City Ramblers skiffle group with her partner Russell Quaye. Opened the Skiffle Cellar in premises that later became Les Cousins.

Phil Smillie Flute, whistle and bodhrán player with the Tannahill Weavers, joined in 1975.

Paul Snow Played the clubs in the early and mid-sixties and for a spell was Alex Campbell's driver.

Geoff Speed Presenter of folk programme on BBC Merseyside from 1967. Paul Simon was staying with him at his home in Widnes around the time he wrote 'Homeward Bound'.

Pete Stanley Pioneered the bluegrass banjo in Britain, initially in a dynamic partnership with Wizz Jones, later with Brian Golbey and Roger Knowles. In recent years has concentrated on teaching the banjo.

Rod Stradling Melodeon player and organiser of the Fighting Cocks club in Kingston and later the King's Head in Islington. Editor of *Musical Traditions* magazine.

Dave Swarbrick Fiddler with the Ian Campbell Folk Group from 1960, when he was eighteen. Teamed up with Martin Carthy in 1966 and was a member of Fairport Convention for ten years from 1969. Later formed Whippersnapper and played on many other artists' records. In 1999, after a prolonged period of ill-health, he read his obituary in the *Daily Telegraph*. He had a successful double lung transplant in 2004 and returned to playing both solo and with Martin Carthy.

June Tabor Singer of traditional songs who began at Leamington Spa folk club. Recorded *Silly Sisters* album with Maddy Prior in 1976. Had a spell away from music to run a restaurant. Has worked with the Mrs Ackroyd Band, Flowers and Frolics and, notably, the Oyster Band.

John Tams Organised a folk club in Alfreton, Derbyshire, in the mid-sixties. A member of Muckram Wakes, joined the Albion Band, was musical director at the National Theatre for eleven years. Formed electric folk rock band Home Service in 1986. Has had a dual career as an actor, playing Daniel Hagman in the TV series *Sharpe*. Musical director of the 2006 *Radio Ballads* and Songmaker for the hit stage musical *Warhorse*. Returned to the folk scene in the early 2000s in a duo with Barry Coope.

Dolly Terfus Folk music enthusiast and regular at the Troubadour in the early sixties.

Richard Thompson Founder member of Fairport Convention, left in 1971 and for a short time went into the folk clubs as an acoustic act with his then wife Linda. Renowned for his guitar technique and songs that have been recorded by many rock and folk artists.

Martha Tilston Singer-songwriter, daughter of Steve Tilston. Began on the alternative festival scene, later part of the duo Mouse.

Steve Tilston Influenced by Bert Jansch and Wizz Jones, left Leicester for London and Les Cousins, then became resident at the Bristol Troubadour. His first album, *An Acoustic Confusion*, was well received. Worked with his former partner, the singer Maggie Boyle, and John Renbourn in Ship of Fools, and with Ballet Rambert, but mostly as a solo artist.

Lucy Ward Won the Horizon Award for Best Newcomer at the 2012 Folk Awards. The previous year her first album, *Adelphi Must Fly*, was released to positive reviews.

Mike Waterson With his sisters Norma and Lal, and their cousin John Harrison, opened one of the early provincial clubs, in Hull. The group changed their name from the Folksons to the Watersons and focused on unaccompanied traditional songs. Recorded *Frost and Fire* in 1965, the first of many albums for Topic. After the Watersons folded in 1968, made an acclaimed album of self-penned songs with Lal, *Bright Phoebus*. Re-formed the Watersons in 1973. Died after a long illness in 2011.

Norma Waterson A member of the Watersons, married Martin Carthy in 1973. Her eponymous solo album of contemporary covers was nominated for the Mercury Prize in 1996. Mother of Eliza Carthy, the pair have sung live on record together and toured in Waterson Carthy and other groups.

Neil Wayne Concertina player and collector, and founder of the Free Reed record label.

Chris While Left the Albion Band to form a duo with Julie

Matthews. At Cropredy in 2007 she took the place of the late Sandy Denny in Fairport Convention's re-creation of the *Liege and Lief* album.

Kellie While At the age of nineteen, replaced her mother, Chris, in the Albion Band. Left in 2001 but continued to play in the Albion Christmas Band. Recorded an album with Chris in 2006; they occasionally work as a duo.

Colin Wilkie An early Troubadour performer, with his wife Shirley Hart played clubs around the country before moving to live in France and then Germany, where they have worked extensively in theatre, television, clubs and at festivals.

Robin Williamson Founder member of the Incredible String Band with Clive Palmer and Mike Heron, went from the folk clubs to the US rock circuit, playing Fillmore East and West and the Woodstock Festival in 1969 before later returning to small acoustic venues.

Jeannie Winsor Formerly Jeannie Steel, sang with her husband Martin Winsor, who was, with Redd Sullivan, a long-standing resident at the Troubadour.

Audrey Winter Wife of the late Eric Winter, left-wing journalist and founder of *Sing* magazine

Heather Wood Along with Peter Bellamy and Royston Wood, both deceased, member of the short-lived Young Tradition, whose art-school look, rock 'n' roll swagger and dynamic a cappella arrangements of traditional songs caused a stir on the late sixties British folk scene.

Pete Wood Traditional singer based for many years in the north-east. Member of the Keelers, has also worked with the New High Level Ranters and the Johnny Handle Band.

Bernard Wrigley Traditional and comic singer, actor, monologuist and concertina player, given the nickname the Bolton Bullfrog by A. L. Lloyd.

Acknowledgements

Without all the people who are listed in the Who's who, *Singing from the Floor* would not have happened. Their kindness in so many ways, not just in giving me their time, is greatly appreciated. There are a number of other people who I must also thank:

Dave Watkins at Faber & Faber, Jarvis Cocker, who took the manuscript there, and Paula Turner at Palindrome.

For permission to use photographs: Lesley Boardman, Laurie Stead and Trevor Charnock, custodians of the archive of the late Brian Horton, Terry Foster, Peter Green, and Jim and Alison Chapman McLean.

For their help and encouragement in a variety of ways over the four years that this project has been underway: Mark Anstey, Stuart Basford, Gerry Bates, Martin Bennett, Alex Broadhead, Pete Civico, Mark Dowding, Jenny Fox, Scott Gardiner, Dick Greener, Raymond Greenoaken, Malcolm Hill, John Hodge, Peter Kay, John Marsh, Sheila Miller, Adam Morawski, Alan Senior, Dave Start, Geoff Travis, Martin Val Baker, Amy and Chris Willsher and, not least, my wife Sheila.

Index

11.3.14